GENDER AND T
IN EURIPIDES' POL1

Gender and the City
in Euripides' Political Plays

Daniel Mendelsohn

OXFORD

UNIVERSITY PRESS

OXFORD

UNIVERSITY PRESS

Great Clarendon Street, Oxford OX2 6DP

Oxford University Press is a department of the University of Oxford.
It furthers the University's objective of excellence in research, scholarship,
and education by publishing worldwide in

Oxford New York

Auckland Cape Town Dar es Salaam Hong Kong Karachi
Kuala Lumpur Madrid Melbourne Mexico City Nairobi
New Delhi Shanghai Taipei Toronto

With offices in

Argentina Austria Brazil Chile Czech Republic France Greece
Guatemala Hungary Italy Japan South Korea Poland Portugal
Singapore Switzerland Thailand Turkey Ukraine Vietnam

Oxford is a registered trade mark of Oxford University Press
in the UK and certain other countries

Published in the United States
by Oxford University Press Inc., New York

© Daniel Mendelsohn 2002

The moral rights of the author have been asserted

Database right of Oxford University Press (maker)

First published 2002
First published in paperback 2005

British Library Cataloguing in Publication Data

Data available

Library of Congress Cataloging-in-Publication Data

Mendelsohn, Daniel Adam, 1960–
Gender and the city in Euripides' political plays/Daniel Mendelsohn.
p. cm.
Includes bibliographical references (p.) and index.
1. Euripides–Political and social views. 2. Political plays, Greek–History and
criticism. 3. Man-woman relationships in literature. 4. Euripides. Children of
Heracles. 5. Politics and literature–Greece. 6. City and town life in literature.
7. Euripides. Supplices. 8. Sex role in literature. I. Title.

PA3978 .M43 2002   82'.01–dc21   2002072558

ISBN 0–19–924956–3
ISBN 0–19–927804–0 (pbk.)

1 3 5 7 9 10 8 6 4 2

Typeset by Regent Typesetting, London
Printed in Great Britain
on acid-free paper by
Biddles Ltd, King's Lynn, Norfolk

For my teachers,
Froma Zeitlin and Jenny Strauss Clay
δισσὼ γάρ ἀστερ᾽ . . .

CONTENTS

PREFACE

It is now nearly half a century since a book-length study has been devoted to the two tragedies commonly referred to as Euripides' 'political plays': *Children of Herakles* and *Suppliant Women*. Although the appearance of Günther Zuntz's still-influential monograph *The Political Plays of Euripides* in 1955 did much to revive serious critical interest in a pair of works that had been, and often continue to be, written off as flat, uninteresting, and anomalous failures within the Euripidean (and indeed within the tragic) canon, the fifty intervening years have witnessed a scholarly and critical ferment that has revolutionized our understanding of Greek tragedy, and indeed of ancient Greek culture and society as a whole. It is the aim of the present study to make use of more recent critical modes in order to re-evaluate Euripides' political plays, and in so doing to allow them at long last to take their proper place within the Euripidean corpus.

Exceedingly influential among the various schools of criticism that have emerged during the crucial past generation of classical scholarship are the feminist and the French. The former has contributed vastly to our understanding of the Greeks' assumptions about sex and gender; the latter—the Paris-based school of historical anthropologists led by Jean-Pierre Vernant, and influenced by the French structural anthropologists in the early part of the twentieth century—has altered our understanding of the dialectical workings of the Greek mind as expressed in legal, religious, and artistic institutions. Although the logical implications of their respective methods could be seen, ultimately, to conflict—the tendency of the former to superimpose contemporary paradigms and assumptions (about psychology, gender, and power) on a culture from the distant past runs counter to the latter's insistence on respecting that culture's historical uniqueness—the two often complement each other. For instance, the patriarchal system that is the subject of the ongoing investigation and critique of the feminists seems to have been both justified by and perpetuated in certain foundational cultural associations,

expressed in law, ritual, and literature, that are the subject of
highly nuanced investigations by the French. (Associations, for
example, between the feminine, dirt, and 'the natural', on the
one hand, and between the masculine, reason, and 'civilization',
on the other.) The insights afforded by these two ways of reading
Greek culture have allowed us, in many cases, to see a cultural
logic at work in texts and practices that had once seemed incoherent.*

Although I make no attempt to hide my indebtedness to
key insights afforded by these schools—along with more traditional philologists, their members are frequently and gratefully
acknowledged in these pages, and those readers who strenuously
resist either school are likely to be unpersuaded by what follows—I am just as eager to avoid critical and interpretative
orthodoxies of any kind; and indeed I use my first chapter to
point out certain excesses that owe more to ideology than they do
to critical sensitivity, and hence tell us more about the critics
than they do about the plays. In attempting to chart an interpretative path somewhere between a reductive Scylla (the tendency
to read works of literature as little more than vehicles for
promoting the ideological agenda of, say, patriarchy, with little
interest paid to the artist's special, subversive role) and a hopelessly naive Charybdis (an interpretative stance that utterly
ignores the possibility of ideological agendas altogether), I like
to think I am heeding the lesson of these two works, which, as
I hope to show, argue in a very complex manner for negotiation
and delicately achieved equilibria, as opposed to monolithic cer-
tainties.

Because the issues I have alluded to here (admittedly in very
circumscribed fashion) are likely to be of interest to a reading
public not necessarily restricted to academic classicists, I have

---

* There is, of course, a vast literature of, and on, these two schools; readers
unfamiliar with them would do well to consult, on the French School, the brief
but very useful overview by Simon Goldhill in 'Modern Critical Approaches to
Greek Tragedy', in P. E. Easterling (ed.), *The Cambridge Companion to Greek
Tragedy* (Cambridge, 1997), 331–4, and Froma Zeitlin's Introduction to her
collection of Vernant's writings, *Mortals and Immortals* (Princeton, 1991), 3–24.
A useful collection of feminist writings on the classics that represents many
methodological and theoretical subdivisions within the general rubric of feminism is Nancy Sorkin Rabinowitz and Amy Richlin (eds.), *Feminist Theory and
the Classics* (London and New York, 1993).

attempted to make the discussion that follows accessible in a number of ways. The first chapter offers a brief overview of the vexed interpretative history of the two plays, and goes on to suggest that critical bafflement about their aesthetic merit has, in fact, been largely due to a failure to incorporate the insights of which I have just spoken—especially insights about the role of women in Greek society. Because it goes on to review some important arguments that have been made about women both in Greek society and on the Athenian stage, part of that introductory discussion will already be familiar to many classicists. But this review is a necessary preliminary both to understanding my own position, which builds upon some pre-existing approaches to the role of women in tragedy, and to appreciating the interpretative schemes that structure my extended discussions of the works themselves.

I have, moreover, loosely structured those main sections as running commentaries on the action of the plays. In part this is because these works are quite often unfamiliar even to classicists, and hence casual references to specific events that transpire in them are bound to have less impact than would references to the events that transpire in (say) *Medea*. But even more, as my readings of the texts are meant to demonstrate, the subtle play of doublings and reversals, of masculine and feminine gestures and intonations, that enables these works to create their specific political meanings is best appreciated in a truly 'dramatic' context: that is, as we encounter them during the course of the play. Although such an approach, as opposed to a more thematic treatment, occasionally yields some repetition, as gestures, words, and themes encountered in earlier scenes are brought once more to the reader's attention for the purposes of comparison, this chronological explication has the advantage of allowing the reader to appreciate the political plays as works for the theatre as well as works for the *polis* and its citizens.

Also for the benefit of the engaged, non-classicist, 'general' reader, extended citations from the texts are given both in Greek and in English translation; translations are mine unless otherwise stated. Since the purpose of such citations is to illuminate specific points as part of an ongoing argument for a specific interpretation, these translations are often more literal than lovely. In paraphrasing or quoting single words or shorter bits of the texts

in the body of my narrative, I have chosen to transliterate the
Greek into Roman characters. Although unsightly to the eyes
of those who read Greek, this transliteration allows Greekless
readers to 'read' repetitions—for example, in words like *phyō*,
pephyken, and *ephyn*, which are related to or derived from *physis*,
'inborn nature', 'generation', or 'birth', an all-important concept in *Children of Herakles*—as a reader of Greek would. These
repetitions forge crucial meanings in the text, and are worth
being able to see for oneself. In transliterating Greek words into
Roman characters, I have rendered *kappa* as 'k', *chi* as 'kh', and
upsilon as 'y' throughout. The only place where Greek appears
untranslated and untransliterated is in those notes devoted to
textual and palaeographical issues likely to be of interest to
classicists only.

The transliteration of Greek proper names presents a problem
that is by now well known; I have chosen an equally well-known
solution. The Romans' own transliterations of Greek names
have tended to stick: hence we generally speak and write of
Aeschylus rather than Aiskhylos, Plato rather than Platōn; tend
to use Latin *-us* endings rather than the Greeks' *-os*; and so forth.
The convention I have followed in rendering Greek names into
English represents (once again) a compromise of sorts. Extremely familiar names retain their Latin forms here: Sophocles rather
than Sophokles, Oedipus rather than Oidipous. If you adopt
'Aiskhylos', after all, you are forced into increasingly pedantic
and, finally, uninhabitable corners: 'Aiskhylaian theatre' is as
terrifying to behold as the Erinyes are. But I have seen no reason
not to transliterate less canonized names more accurately: hence
Iolaos for Iolaus, Alkmene for Alcmena, Erekhtheus for Erech-
theus, and so forth. One of the lessons we have learned from the
French is that the Greeks are, finally, much stranger to us—more
'other' than 'self'—than we would once have thought. It seems
worth while to replicate this notion as often and reasonably as
possible, to have things 'look' Greek, even in orthography. As
for the names of ancient works for the theatre, I have generally
chosen to translate rather than transliterate these, since their
titles are often illustrative: it is pointless to refer to *Hiketides*
when you are speaking about *Suppliant Women*, or to *Herakles
Mainomenos* when the play is about exactly what its title refers to:
The Mad Herakles. (In the case of line references within the text,

however, I have used conventional abbreviations used by classicists for the names of plays, for the sake of space and conveni-
ence: hence *Hkld.* (from *Herakleidai*) for *Children of Herakles*,
Su. for *Suppliant Women*, *Med.* for *Medea*, *Septem* for the *Seven
Against Thebes* (*Septem contra Thebas*), and so on.)

One translation choice that may appear strange to those
already familiar with these texts is in the name of an important
character. Although a late tradition gives to Herakles' daughter
the name 'Makaria', she is never named in the play, and there is
no reason to believe Euripides intended her to be known as
anything other than *parthenos*—a word that means, literally,
a 'virgin'. A long-standing tradition renders the name of this
character as 'the Maiden', a word whose quaint and rather
Victorian connotations have become annoying in general and are
especially inappropriate in the context of this play's unsentimen-
tal and often violent action; and yet to call her 'the Virgin'—
ostensibly the literal translation—risks evoking powerful and, to
a great many readers, distracting Christian overtones. *Parthenos*
in Greek certainly could, and often did, have the technical sense
of a female with an intact hymen, and yet it more generally has
the sense of the English word 'girl', the French *jeune fille*, or the
German *Mädchen*—a term, in other words, whose common
usage assumes, to some extent, the technical meaning 'virgin'
without sounding as clinical. The reason that Herakles' daughter
appears in the play at all is that, as a young unmarried female
child, she fulfils the divine specifications for a sacrificial victim;
yet almost immediately after she gives up her life in (she thinks)
exchange for the undying renown generally awarded to male
heroes, she is swiftly forgotten during the remainder of the play.
And so here she shall be 'the Girl': emphatically young and
female, and just as emphatically anonymous.

Ironically, the dictatorial force of critical habit I alluded to in
speaking of transliteration prevents me from translating accurately the one title I would have liked above all to render
precisely. When Euripides' audience went to the theatre of Dionysos to see a performance of a play called *Herakleidai*, it is
almost certain that they thought they were going to a drama about
the *sons* of Herakles. The Greek -*idēs* (plural -*idai*) patronymic
ending denoted first of all a man's sons and then, more generally,
his descendants; under Athenian law as known to Euripides'

audience, only the most extreme circumstances permitted a man's name, house, or property to be transmitted via his daughter. In a play called *The Sons of Herakles*, the bold actions of the dead hero's virgin daughter on behalf of her kin—a Euripidean innovation in a well-known and beloved patriotic myth—must have been all the more surprising. The fact that scholars invariably refer to this work as *The Children of Herakles* is, in its way, symbolic of the interpretative problems that have always haunted the political plays; the elision of gender-specific meanings, the failure to hear overtones of sex and gender in these ostensibly purely 'political' works, are symptomatic of a long-standing critical state of affairs. That state is one that the following pages attempt to alter.

This book owes a great deal to the support and generosity of a number of people and institutions over the past few years. It began life as a dissertation submitted to the Classics Department at Princeton University, where Andrew Ford and Richard Martin, who sat on my dissertation committee, offered excellent readings and helpful suggestions at the earliest stages of my thinking and writing about Euripides and his political plays. The transformation of that thesis into a book would have been unthinkable without the comments and suggestions offered by a number of people who read the manuscript as it evolved. I am particularly indebted to Judith Mossman and to the other, anonymous reader for the Oxford University Press, both of whom painstakingly critiqued the manuscript, and to Hilary O'Shea for her interest, support, and patience. Above all, I am grateful to Lily Knezevich, who patiently read through the manuscript at every stage of its development, offering countless helpful editorial suggestions and criticisms and, best of all, giving me an idea of what the reaction of the 'intelligent non-specialist reader', that semi-mythical beast, might really be.

The pages that follow examine, among other things, Euripides' penchant for dramatizing the disastrous consequences that result when men fall into the hands of powerful women. I am happy to say that my own experience would not have proved useful fodder for our playwright in this respect. It was my great good fortune to fall into the hands of the dedicatees of this book at an early enough age to have been profoundly moulded by them: Jenny Clay, when I was an undergraduate; Froma Zeitlin, when I was a graduate student. It is true that, like the pairs of female figures in the political plays, they represent, in their ways, quite different modes—of thinking, and teaching, and writing; but in my case, the contrasting and yet complementary examples of these two extraordinary women could not have been more constructive for, or more warmly and gratefully accepted and acknowledged by, the man who encountered them. Their influence on me has been as great as any teacher's, or friend's, can be; for me they have always been, and will continue to be, 'twin stars' like those that miraculously appear at the climax of *Children of Herakles*: the brilliant lights by which I always chart my course. Whatever I have written that is good, is theirs.

D.M.

Princeton, New Jersey
November 2001

ABBREVIATIONS

AJP	*American Journal of Philology*
BICS	*Bulletin of the Institute of Classical Studies* (University of London)
CP	*Classical Philology*
CQ	*Classical Quarterly*
CR	*Classical Review*
CW	*Classical World*
FrGrHist	F. Jacoby (ed.), *Die Fragmente der griechischen Historiker* (Berlin and Leiden, 1923–58)
GR	*Greece and Rome*
GRBS	*Greek, Roman, and Byzantine Studies*
HSCP	*Harvard Studies in Classical Philology*
HTR	*Harvard Theological Review*
JHS	*Journal of Hellenic Studies*
LSJ	H. G. Liddell, R. Scott, and H. S. Jones (eds.), *A Greek–English Lexicon* (Oxford, 1968)
MD	*Materiali e discussioni per l'analisi dei testi classici*
PCPS	*Proceedings of the Cambridge Philological Society*
PP	*La parola del passato*
QUCC	*Quaderni urbinati di cultura classica*
REG	*Revue des études grecques*
SAWW	*Sitzungsberichte der Österreichischen Akademie der Wissenschaft in Wien*
SO	*Symbolae Osloenses*
TAPA	*Transactions of the American Philological Association*
WS	*Wiener Studien*
YCS	*Yale Classical Studies*
ZPE	*Zeitschrift für Papyrologie und Epigraphik*

'The glue of the democracy.'

Demades, a 4th-century Athenian politician, on the Theoric Fund, the state subsidy established in Athens to encourage attendance at dramatic festivals

(Plutarch, Moralia, *10.1011)*

'There are more women in them than men.'

Lucian, on Athenian tragedies

*(*On the Dance, *28)*

I
Introduction
Gender, Politics, Interpretation

> *The drama is a celebration of Athens.*
> Aristophanes of Byzantium,
> in his introduction to
> Euripides' *Suppliant Women*

> *And just how, you creep, do my Stheneboias 'hurt the city'?*
> Euripides, complaining about his reputation
> as a subversive, in the comic poet
> Aristophanes' *Frogs* 1049

Interpretative *Aporia*

How to reconcile these two 'Aristophanic' comments about Euripidean theatre? This question sums up the task confronting contemporary critics eager to re-evaluate the tragedian's least-esteemed and still widely neglected plays: *Children of Herakles*, composed around 430 BC, at the beginning of the first decade of the Peloponnesian War, and *Suppliant Women*, first performed about 423 BC, towards the end of that decade.[1]

---

[1] In the absence of external evidence for production dates of Euripidean plays, certain metrical considerations—specifically, the proportion of resolved iambic feet to the number of iambic trimeters in a given play—have proved to be a fairly reliable indicator of the date of composition, the percentage for an undated play being compared to those of reliably dated works. (For a discussion of this method see first T. Zielinski, *Tragodoumenon Libri Tres*, 3 vols. (Cracow, 1925), ii. 133–240, and E. B. Ceadel, 'Resolved Feet in the Trimeters of Euripides and the Chronology of the Plays', *CQ* 35 (1941), 66–89.) In the case of *Children of Herakles*, this figure (5.7%) seems to place the play somewhere between *Medea* (431; 6.6%) and *Hippolytos* (428; 4.3%). Internal references (e.g. the prophecy that Eurystheus' body will protect Athens from foreign invaders) have persuaded some scholars that the play was produced in 430, before the first large-scale Spartan invasion of Attika; so Günther Zuntz, *The Political Plays of*

The first epigraph, a rather laconic though influential appraisal of *Suppliant Women* as little more than a panegyric of Athens, was provided by the Hellenistic scholar Aristophanes of Byzantium around the turn of the second century BC in his own introduction to this play; it set the precedent for the simplistic evaluation of that work—and of *Children of Herakles*, with which it continues to be paired—that persists to the present day. When the scholar Günther Zuntz referred to the *Suppliant Women* and to *Children of Herakles* as Euripides' 'political plays' in the title of his still-influential 1955 study of these works, he was merely articulating what was already implicit in his predecessor's judgement, made two millennia earlier. For both scholars, the works were patriotic paraphrases of fifth-century Athenian political discourse.[2] Even the generations of Euripidean scholars who

Euripides (Manchester, 1955), 83 ff., followed (albeit somewhat tentatively) by the play's most recent editor, John Wilkins, in *Euripides* Heraclidae: *with Introduction and Commentary* (Oxford, 1993), xxxiii–xxxv, a useful discussion with full bibliography.

The dating of *Suppliant Women* is given a typically thorough discussion in the superb edition of this work by Christopher Collard, *Euripides Supplices, edited with Introduction and Commentary*, 2 vols. (Groningen, 1975), i. 8–14; Collard offers ample bibliography and summary of other scholars' arguments. (All references to Collard are to vol. ii, his Commentary, unless otherwise noted here.) The metrical evidence (14.2% resolutions) points to a date in the mid-420s: cf. *Andromakhe* (almost certainly *c*.425: 12%) and *Hekabe* (425/4: 14.7%). Internal evidence points strongly to a date soon after 424. In November of that year the Boeotians had refused to return the bodies of the Athenian war dead for burial after the battle of Delium (Thuc. 4. 89–101); the desperate attempt to retrieve such bodies is of course the drama's great *Leitmotif*. For a detailed account of the play's allusions to the battle of Delium, see Sophie Mills, *Theseus, Tragedy, and the Athenian Empire* (Oxford, 1997), 91–7, and also the extended analysis by A. M. Bowie, 'Tragic Filters for History: Euripides' *Supplices* and Sophocles' *Philoctetes*', in Christopher Pelling (ed.), *Greek Tragedy and the Historian* (Oxford, 1997), 45–56.

[2] Zuntz, *The Political Plays of Euripides*. In fairness to Zuntz, it should be said that his book was produced as an effort to counter the strict historicism of scholars such as Grégoire, who in his discussion of *Suppliant Women* rather typically sees the play as little more than a vein rich in the ore of contemporary political allusions (L. Parmentier and H. Grégoire (eds.), *Euripide* (Paris, 1923), 92 ff.). Although Zuntz posited a more general connection of the plays' contents to contemporary events (*Political Plays*, 20 ff.), and indeed was among the few who attempted to show an overall coherence in the works' ostensibly disjointed elements, he still sought to present the plays as an unmediated endorsement of Athenian civic ideology.

succeeded Zuntz (i.e. the great majority of critics and classicists for whom Euripides' work is characterized by subversive ambiguities) have tended to accept this evaluation. Still commonly thought of as the playwright's 'patriotic' or even 'frankly ideological plays', *Children of Herakles* and *Suppliant Women* continue today to be dismissed as unambiguous endorsements of Athenian institutions, dramas in which formal rigour and narrative coherence have been sacrificed for the sake of the anachronistic inclusion of chauvinistic, even 'propagandistic' passages in praise of Athens' imperial democracy and in support of its social and political arrangements.[3] Hence despite an interpretative history that runs from Aristophanes to Zuntz, critical appraisal has remained largely unchanged since the time of the plays' first scholarly commentators.[4]

As such, the works in question have always seemed wildly out of place in the canon of a poet who even in antiquity—as the second of our Aristophanic epigraphs suggests—was considered something of a subversive, one whose dramatic representations of female sexual passion (to use the most notorious example), such as that of the wanton Stheneboia in a lost eponymous drama, were so shameful that his plays could somehow 'hurt' the city itself. It is still possible to hear echoes of this most ancient assessment of Euripides in the voices of most contemporary

[3] For a good overview of various approaches to tragedy in its relations to history and, more specifically, the concept of ideology, see Barbara Goff's Introduction to her collection *History, Tragedy, Theory: Dialogues on Athenian Drama* (Austin, Tex., 1995), 11 ff.

[4] The descriptions of *Suppliant Women* quoted here are those of Froma I. Zeitlin in 'Playing the Other: Theater, Theatricality, and the Feminine in Greek Drama', *Representations*, 11 (1985), 83 (where Zeitlin classes such plays with 'military' plays); and in 'Thebes: Theater of Self and Society in Athenian Drama', in John J. Winkler and Froma I. Zeitlin (eds.), *Nothing to Do with Dionysos? Athenian Drama in its Social Context* (Princeton, 1990), 146. Cf. Justina Gregory's description of both plays as 'tragedies that strike an overtly patriotic or democratic note' in *Euripides and the Instruction of the Athenians* (Ann Arbor, 1991), 10, and Mills's characterization of *Suppliant Women* as a play whose 'explicit patriotism makes it a good introduction to plays whose patriotism lies at a deeper level' (*Theseus, Tragedy*, 93). These pronouncements recap the judgements of an earlier scholarly generation: for example, Max Pohlenz's discussion of *Children of Herakles* (in a chapter devoted to 'vaterländische Tragödien') in *Die griechische Tragödie* (Leipzig and Berlin, 1930), 371–9, and G. M. A. Grube on the plays as little more than 'propagandistic' (*The Drama of Euripides* (London, 1941), 240).

critics, who have, either in admiration or condemnation, deemed
Euripides' dramatic oeuvre to be one that almost everywhere
(except in our two plays) is preoccupied with uneasily 'modern'
themes: sexual ambiguity, religious doubt, the status of women.[5]
For many of these critics, such themes are, moreover, underscored by daring formal experimentation and an almost post-
modern tendency to comment self-reflexively on tragedy and its
performative conventions. To these characteristics we may add
Euripides' overall tone—something that nearly all students of
Euripides have seen as deeply sceptical and, above all, mordantly
ironic.[6] With these themes, then, with these structural innovations, with this embittered tone, the political plays, with their

[5] In her *Euripides and the Tragic Tradition* (Ann Arbor, 1987), 68, Ann
Michelini notes that a 'strange familiarity and contemporaneity' is a feeling
Euripidean critics have been experiencing for at least a century; for this point see
e.g. Masqueray's *Euripide et ses idées* (Paris, 1908), 399; Gilbert Murray,
Euripides and his Age (New York, 1913), 1, 14; Grube, *The Drama of Euripides*,
15; and Jacqueline de Romilly, *La modernité d'Euripide* (Paris, 1986). For objec-
tions to this view of Euripides as a 'modernist' see the comments of David
Kovacs in *The Heroic Muse: Studies in the* Hippolytus *and* Hecuba *of Euripides*
(Baltimore, 1987), 9. Gregory (*Instruction of the Athenians, passim*) tends to be
in agreement with Kovacs on this subject. Barbara Goff offers pointed objections to both Kovacs's and Gregory's positions in her Introduction (*History,
Tragedy, Theory*, 23 f.).

[6] For a substantial overview of the long-standing critical debate over Euripides as a formal innovator, see Michelini, *The Tragic Tradition*, 3-51; and cf.
Nancy Sorkin Rabinowitz, *Anxiety Veiled: Euripides and the Traffic in Women*
(Ithaca, NY, 1993), 13. Although our understanding of Euripides as an ironic
rationalist goes back to Verrall's *Euripides the Rationalist* (Cambridge, 1895),
more recent titles such as Philip Vellacott's *Ironic Drama* (Cambridge, 1975),
for example, or Helene Foley's *Ritual Irony: Poetry and Sacrifice in Euripides*
(Ithaca, NY, 1985), give an indication of the extent to which current assess-
ments of this playwright's tone and method remain tied to our sense that an
ironic sensibility is at work here. Although Vellacott offers perhaps the most
trenchantly ironic reading of *Children of Herakles* to date (*Ironic Drama*,
179–92), I cannot follow him in much of his appraisal of Euripides' work, and
especially in the neo-Verrallian notion that the poet intentionally wrote for a
'divided audience', concealing his ironic medicine in an ostensibly sweet pack-
age (pp. 15, 19; cf. Verrall, *Euripides the Rationalist*, 101 ff., and E. M. Blaiklock,
The Male Characters of Euripides (Wellington, New Zealand, 1952), 65). Even
before Verrall, the notion was endorsed by J. P. Mahaffy in his *Euripides*
(London, 1879). As a 'solution' to these 'problem plays', the quasi-Straussian
divided-audience interpretation is firmly and convincingly rejected by J. W.
Fitton, 'The *Suppliant Women* and the *Herakleidai* of Euripides', *Hermes*, 89
(1961), 446 f.

apparently straight-faced endorsement of fifth-century Athenian civic and political values, seem always to have had little in common.

Because they have seemed so anomalous, academic criticism of both dramas in question has continued, with a few welcome exceptions, to lag behind the richly imaginative interpretative activity that has been focused on this poet's better-known and more highly esteemed tragedies. On the infrequent occasions when scholars have turned to these works, their approach, as Peter Burian notes, has been 'to abandon "aesthetic" criticism entirely, in favor of treating the play as a repository of allusions to contemporary history. Whatever inconsistencies are found can then be explained as necessary to Euripides' *real* message, which has little or nothing to do with the action of the drama.' Other commentators have similarly recognized a tendency to see both *Children of Herakles* and *Suppliant Women* as interesting or useful merely inasmuch as they can be mined for concrete references to 'the immediate politicking of the Athenian audience at any one particular time': one need only glance at Édouard Delebecque's confident declarations that the Theseus of *Suppliant Women* 'can only be Alcibiades', or that the play as a whole was written 'as an act of electoral propaganda', to get an idea of the results this approach has yielded.[7]

[7] For the 'abandonment of aesthetic criticism', see Peter Burian, 'Euripides' *Heraclidae*: An Interpretation', *CP* 72 (1977), 1; for the plays as sources for 'the immediate politicking' of 5th-cent. Athens, see Oliver Taplin, 'Fifth-Century Drama: A *Synkrisis*', *JHS* 106 (1986), 167. The Delebecque remarks are from his *Euripide et la guerre du Péloponnèse* (Paris, 1951), 221 (translations mine), still the most important book-length example of the strictly historicist approach to Euripides' work. (His discussions of *Children of Herakles* and *Suppliant Women* can be found on 74–94 and 203–24, respectively.) For similar approaches to the plays, see also R. Goossens, *Euripide et Athènes* (Brussels 1962); less recently, P. Giles, 'Political Allusions in the Suppliants of Euripides', *CR* 4 (1890), 95–8; C. Kuiper, 'de Euripidis Supplicibus', *Mnemosyne*, 51 (1923), 101–28; and J. A. Spranger, 'The Political Element in the *Heracleidae* of Euripides', *CQ* 19 (1925), 117–28.

For a brief but lucid critique of the purely historicist approach, see the Introduction to Goff, *History, Tragedy, Theory*, 20 ff., and cf. the slightly earlier criticisms of this brand of historicism in Christian Meier's *Die politische Kunst der griechischen Tragödie* (Munich, 1988), 242. Meier, it should be said, rejects not only the strict historicism of scholars like Delebecque but, conversely, the considerably broader conceptualization of the political to be found in the work

Critical reluctance to engage with these seemingly un-Euripidean works has long seemed defensible for two further, interrelated reasons not explicitly related to the plays' content. There is, first of all, the unhappy state of the texts themselves. *Children of Herakles* in particular has clearly suffered, though the exact extent of the loss or mutilation of the text has been the subject of some debate.[8] Second, and even more disastrously for fruitful interpretative enterprise, there is the ostensibly disjointed structure of the works themselves, which until quite

of the French school. For more on the strictly historicist school see also Michelini, *The Tragic Tradition*, 28-30 and the remarks of Gregory, *Instruction of the Athenians*, 6.

[8] A brief summary: Hermann (in A. Matthiae (ed.), *Euripidis tragoediae et fragmenta*, 10 vols. (Leipzig, 1813–37), viii. 257) had conjectured the accidental disappearance of an episode after 1052, i.e. following Alkmene's order to kill Eurystheus; Kirchhoff later countered with the suggestion that a lost episode featuring a description of the Girl's sacrifice and a scene of lamentation by her survivors had come after the stasimon ending at 629—i.e. following the Girl's exit (*Euripidis tragoediae* (Berlin, 1855), 496 ad 627ff.). Wilamowitz, in his 'Exkurse zu Euripides Herakliden' (*Hermes*, 17 (1882), 337–64 (=*Kleine Schriften*, (Berlin, 1935), i. 82–109)), argued that the loss of precisely one complete episode was unlikely to have been accidental, and suggested instead that there had been a deliberate revision of the text by a 4th-cent. scenarist. Wilamowitz's view was later vigorously (and, I think, on the whole convincingly) challenged by Zuntz, 'Is the *Heraclidae* Mutilated?', *CQ* 41 (1947), 46–52. However, Zuntz's arguments for the integrity of the play as we currently have it were themselves subsequently critiqued by A. Lesky in 'On the "Heraclidae" of Euripides' (tr. H. von Hofe, *YCS* 25 (1977), 227–38) and by the Italian scholar Roberto Guerrini in several articles that appeared in the early 1970s: 'I "frammenti" degli Eraclidi di Euripide', *Studi classici ed orientali*, 19/20 (1970/71), 15–31; 'La morte di Euristeo e le implicazioni etico-politiche degli Eraclidi di Euripide', *Athenaeum*, 50 (1972), 45–67; and 'La morte di Macaria (Eurip. *Heraclid*. 819–22)', *Studi Italiani di filologia classica*, 45 (1973), 46–59. Some of Lesky's key positions were, in turn, sharply rebutted by Martin Cropp in '*Herakleidai* 603–4, 630ff., and the Question of the Mutilation of the Text' (*AJP* 101 (1980), 283–6); the debate continues as recently as Wilkins's 1993 commentary.

For the purposes of the present study, I am persuaded that there was no extended description of the Girl's sacrifice within the play; if there is a significant lacuna, it is likely to occur at the *end* of the play. Wilkins makes the very attractive suggestion that the play ended with an *ex machina* appearance by either Herakles or Athena giving an *aition*—that is, a description of the establishment of a cult of the Girl (or, perhaps, of Eurystheus: Wilkins, *Euripides Heraclidae*, 193, and 'The Young of Athens: Religion and Society in Euripides' *Herakleidai*', *CQ* 40 (1990), 339 and n. 120).

recently has been the almost exclusive focus of scholarly comment (and dismay), and which has led even those critics eager to rehabilitate these works to decry the 'formal incoherence' of these 'odd and unsatisfactory' plays.[9]

In complaining of this formal incoherence, most critics point an accusing finger at what they see as a lack of uniformity in both tone and construction (a criticism, we should perhaps remember, that has been levelled at most of the Euripidean corpus at one time or another). In her rather tongue-in-cheek catalogue of the 'hopeless hodgepodge of aesthetic mistakes' that have been attributed to Euripides by critics of all eras and ilks, the Euripides scholar Ann Michelini lists the poet's alleged penchant for lumping together in a single play 'whole sets of monstrously contradictory traits': 'We break our hearts over the most harrowing and pathetic of tragedians,' she writes, 'only to find ourself in the next scene repressing the terrible urge to snigger.'[10] This criticism has been aimed at *Children of Herakles* in particular; it is a work in which the poet mixes clichés of both high tragedy and low comedy with apparently insouciant abandon, producing what another critic called its 'abrupt and even shocking changes of mood and tone'.[11] So, for example, the virgin daughter of legendary Herakles offers her own life as a human sacrifice to save the city—only to be followed off stage moments later by her late father's companion-in-arms, the ancient and decrepit Iolaos, who teeters off vowing to join the army, his withered limbs weighed down by his armour, his head filled with dim memories of bygone exploits.[12]

---

[9] Fitton, 'The *Suppliant Women*', 460, 430, prefacing his otherwise insightful reappraisal of *Suppliant Women*.

[10] Michelini, *The Tragic Tradition*, 50. Michelini's introductory chapter (3–50) is a useful guide to the vagaries of the playwright's reputation over the past two centuries.

[11] Thomas M. Falkner, 'The Wrath of Alcmene: Gender, Authority, and Old Age in Euripides' *Children of Heracles*', in Thomas M. Falkner and Judith deLuce (eds.), *Old Age in Greek and Latin Literature* (Albany, NY, 1989), 114.

[12] Of course, examples of comparably grotesque juxtapositions are to be found both in the playwright's earliest and in his latest extant works: in *Alkestis*, a voracious Herakles' inappropriate entrance into a house of mourning is among the elements that have caused most critics to believe that this work substituted for a satyr-play, while in *Bacchae* the ageing Kadmos and Teiresias do their best to kick up their heels in Dionysiac abandon. For aesthetic and generic

Yet even when the plays exhibit consistency of tone—as in the case of *Suppliant Women*, with its unrelenting mood of grief and lamentation—scholars continue to complain that a certain haphazardness in construction diminishes the plays' dramatic coherence. In 1970 a scholar writing about *Suppliant Women* complained that

> Part of the trouble lies in the difficulty of discerning any definite line in the play, running through it all and capable of accounting for the various scenes and details satisfactorily. There is, of course, the obvious surface action holding together the different scenes (or most of them) more or less adequately: they are all in some way related to the return and burial of the Argive dead. But within this outer frame of actual dramatic happenings, a large number of topics are touched upon which seem to bear little or no relation to each other.[13]

A generation later, one of the same play's most recent commentators has echoed that assessment, remarking on the 'inherent contradictions and plurality of moods and forms' in the work and cataloguing the 'baffling' and 'awkward' concatenation of its scenes and registers.[14] Critical judgement of the structure of *Children of Herakles* has been comparable, if not actually worse. Writing (significantly enough) on Aristotle's theory of tragedy— the critical cudgel with which, it sometimes seems, nearly every drama that is not the *Oedipus Tyrannos* has been beaten—John Jones dismissed it quite simply as 'a thoroughly bad play'.[15]

It is interesting that when complaining of the unsatisfying structural incoherences of Euripides' work, scholars keep pointing to one type of 'odd juxtaposition' in particular: those moments when, as Michelini puts it, Euripides 'the specialist in female emotional maladies ('*Leidenschaft*')' suddenly becomes a

'problems' with *Alkestis*, see the discussion of Albin Lesky, 'Alkestis, der Mythos und das Drama', *SAWW* 203 (1925), 80ff., and, more recently, Bernd Seidensticker, *Palintonos Harmonia: Studien zu komischen Elementen in der griechischen Tragödie* (Göttingen, 1982), 129ff.; for the intrusion of low-comic elements in the Kadmos-Teiresias scene and the interpretative issues they raise, see Karl Deichgräber, 'Die Kadmos-Teiresiasszene in Euripides *Bakchen*', *Hermes*, 70 (1935), 322-49; and Seidensticker, 'Comic Elements in Euripides' *Bacchae*', *AJP* 99 (1978), 303-20.

[13] R. B. Gamble, 'Euripides' *Suppliant Women*: Decision and Ambivalence', *Hermes*, 98 (1970), 385.

[14] Mills, *Theseus, Tragedy*, 89.

[15] John Jones, *On Aristotle and Greek Tragedy* (London, 1971), 266.

'cold rhetorician'[16]—or, to put it another way, those moments when the Euripides of our second epigraph collides with the Euripides of our first. Here again, *Children of Herakles* and *Suppliant Women* seem to offer special grounds for complaint. In both works, scenes featuring passionate or pathetic women *in extremis* are juxtaposed with long stretches of abstract political discourse ('cold rhetoric') that read somewhat unfortunately like less-than-memorable excerpts from some minor dialogue in Thucydides. *Children of Herakles*'s naively self-sacrificing Girl and its vindictive and homicidal hag Alkmene, *Suppliant Women*'s maenadic erotomane Evadne: all may be recognizable as the dramatic siblings of Polyxena, Iphigeneia, Hekabe, and Medea, but to many scholars they seem hopelessly out of place as they pick their way among passages in which, say, the comparative advantages of tyranny and democracy are weighed at great length, or, as in *Suppliant Women*, the young Athenian king Theseus takes the defeated Argive general Adrastos to task for his unwise political and military choices (*Su.* 176 ff.). In this matter of the plays' flawed form, as in that of their flatly encomiastic and simplistically political content, the ancients again seem to have had the first word: an Alexandrian commentator on Sophocles' *Oedipus at Colonus* cynically ascribed the Theseus–Adrastos exchange in Euripides' *Suppliant Women* to the playwright's practical need to 'stretch out the drama' at that point.[17]

That it is femininity and politics in particular that make for strange dramatic bedfellows in works that are ostensibly 'political' is evident in Grube's comments on *Suppliants*:

This is not one of the great plays of Euripides. Two whole scenes . . . are quite unworthy and have probably suffered textual tampering; the contemporary reference of the debate on democracy strains the epic framework to an unusual extent; *the Evadne episode is not worked into the play at all adequately*; the topical nature of the whole . . . is unusually obvious; character-drawing is almost non-existent, *with the possible exception of Aithra and Evadne, both of whom are of minor importance* . . . [F]or once the propagandist got the better of the dramatist, the result being both hasty and careless.[18]

---

[16] Michelini, *The Tragic Tradition*, 50.

[17] ἕνεκα τοῦ μηκύνειν τὸ δρᾶμα: Σ on *OC* 220.

[18] Grube, *The Drama of Euripides*, 240, 241; emphases mine. Cf. Desmond Conacher's description of the Evadne episode as 'an extreme, and rather intru-

This particular view of *Children of Herakles* and *Suppliant Women* has resulted in the general assessment of these tragedies as odd hybrids, flukes that were tossed off presumably in a moment of typically Euripidean weakness or, even worse, out of a venal desire to win the esteem of the Athenian public and thereby to win first prize at the dramatic festival.[19]

Hence the current state of interpretative *aporia*. On the one hand, the recalcitrant presence of 'cold rhetoric' and 'topical' political references has made *Children of Herakles* and *Suppliant Women* far less appealing as sites for contemporary critical investigations into, say, sex/gender systems or tragic metatheatricality than are other Euripidean works which are thought to exhibit greater coherence of myth, theme, and/or structure.[20] On the other hand, the apparently incoherent intrusion of 'female passions' into otherwise wholly (if rather dully) political dramas has rendered them unappetizing for pretty much anyone interested in trying to interpret the plays from a rather traditional

sive, dramatization of . . . grief' in 'Religious and Ethical Attitudes in Euripides' *Suppliants*', *TAPA* 87 (1956), 23.

[19] The sense that Euripides was unable to resist including extraneous material goes back at least as far as Masqueray, *Euripide et ses idées* (1908); cf. Michelini, *The Tragic Tradition*, 8 f. The view of Euripides as a venal flatterer of his audience was popular in the last century, when some scholars argued that the tragic poets tried to limit their direct references to contemporary Athenian politics to a 'persistent laudation of Athens [that] often exceeds the limits of a self-respecting patriotism': so C. S. Jerram, *Heracleidae* (Oxford, 1907), 7, following K. O. Müller, *History of the Literature of Ancient Greece*, tr. George Cornwall Lewis (London, 1847), 370. Half a century later, Francesco Guglielmino argued that 'patriotic' passages were designed to curry the audience's favour, *Arte e artifizio nel dramma greco* (Catania 1912); those passages are discussed at length by L. Van Hook, 'The Praise of Athens in Greek Tragedy', *CW* 27 (1934), 185–8. The point of such fawning on the *dēmos*, it was further argued, was to win not only favour, but prizes at the city Dionysia; see R. C. Flickinger, *The Greek Theater and its Drama* (Chicago, 1926), xvii, a position that has been taken as recently as Mary Pittas-Herschbach's *Time and Space in Euripides and Racine* (New York, 1990), where the author argues that references to Athens in *Medea*, *Children of Herakles*, *Suppliant Women*, and *Trojan Women* are unsubtle attempts to 'curry the favor of the audience' (p. 5).

[20] Even less recently, the 'topical' political matter was seen as conflicting with the plays' larger mythic framework; so e.g. Grube, *The Drama of Euripides*, 239 f.; W. J. W. Koster, 'De Euripidis Supplicibus', *Mnemosyne*, NS, 10 (1942), 168 ff.; and A. Rivier, *Essai sur le tragique d'Euripide* (Lausanne, 1944), 173 f.

political perspective—except perhaps for those historians operating in the strictest historicist mode, the ones interested in
hunting for tasty morsels of contemporary political allusion
while leaving all the indigestible *Leidenschaft* untouched. This
last point may help explain why it is that the dramatist's so-called
'political' plays can go unmentioned in some of the reappraisals
of tragedy's role as a vehicle for political theorizing that have
appeared in the last decade.[21]

It should perhaps be pointed out that this last oversight is not
exclusive to male scholars (who might be thought less sensitive
to feminine elements and their symbolic uses). Mention of
Children of Herakles and *Suppliant Women* is absent from
various recent studies by women scholars writing about gender
and its place in Athenian ideology about civic identity—an ideology whose valorization of state over family, the collective over
the individual, the native over the foreign was often expressed
symbolically, in a host of literary, legal, and political texts, as a
valorization of the masculine over the feminine.[22] Nor indeed is
indifference to the plays restricted to scholars who, presumably
because they see Euripides as an ironist and social contrarian,
have ignored these seemingly more 'conservative' political plays.
Going against the grain of critical tradition, both Justina
Gregory and Nancy Sorkin Rabinowitz have offered major
reappraisals of Euripides in which the playwright emerges as
a dramatist whose work conforms to, rather than challenges,
the ideological status quo of the imperial, patriarchal Athenian
democracy. For Gregory, who is concerned with the didactic
nature of tragedy in its social and civic context, Euripides is
'more in tune with . . . his society than has been generally
acknowledged'; for Rabinowitz, operating within a more classi-
cally feminist framework, the poet 'recuperates the female
figures for patriarchy' by writing plays 'that impose a gender
hierarchy consistent with and supportive of the sex/gender

[21] For instance, J. Peter Euben, *The Tragedy of Political Theory: The Road
Not Taken* (Princeton, NJ 1990), or Christian Meier in his study of the 'political art' of Greek tragedy (*Die politische Kunst*).

[22] See, for example, Nicole Loraux, *The Children of Athena*, tr. Caroline
Levine (Princeton, 1993; orig. pub. as *Les Enfants d'Athéna* (Paris, 1974)) and
Arlene W. Saxonhouse, *Fear of Diversity: The Birth of Political Science in
Ancient Greek Thought* (Chicago, 1992).

system of the time'. As usually interpreted, both *Children of Herakles* and *Suppliant Women* would seem to furnish ample evidence for both these views; but in these scholars' studies, Euripides' political plays are discussed either briefly or not at all.[23]

Hence although the dramas in question could be thought of as providing something for everyone, the persistence of a simplistic critical evaluation first articulated in antiquity suggests that they have, in fact, failed to provide enough for anyone—either those whose understanding of the plays as 'conservative' is consonant with the first of our Aristophanic epigraphs, or those whose understanding of Euripides himself as a radical accords with the second.

Politics, Women, Interpretation

This widespread interpretative dismay about the form of our texts seems, on closer inspection, to follow from erroneous assumptions about their content. Grube can declare the Evadne episode to be egregious, for example, and can dismiss both Aithra and Evadne as 'minor' characters, precisely because his own understanding of the drama as a 'political play' assumes that 'political' means references to contemporary politicking and governmental institutions, and hence is incompatible with issues relating to gender—'the feminine'. In this narrow reading of the political, the emotional, feminine incursions that we find in *Children of Herakles* and *Suppliant Women* (Alkmene's rage, Evadne's despair), and that are so typical of Euripidean dramaturgy, are bound to appear intrusive and out of place. But careful re-evaluation of what is known about these plays indicates that the inclusion of ostensibly incongruous feminine passions in them was in fact a special Euripidean innovation—a self-

[23] Citations are from Gregory, *Instruction of the Athenians*, 187 and Rabinowitz, *Anxiety Veiled*, 14. Gregory's study is instead devoted to analyses of the *Alkestis, Hippolytos, Hekabe, Mad Herakles*, and *Trojan Women*; Rabinowitz has a brief discussion of *Children of Herakles* (pp. 62–4, 105); her dual focus on sacrificial heroines and vindictive old women precludes comment on *Suppliants*—although, as I shall argue later, *Suppliant*'s female figures are merely variations on those types. For a critique of Gregory's methods and conclusions, see the review by Charles Segal in *AJP* 114/1 (1993), 163–6. Ann Michelini offers a pungent appraisal of both Gregory and Rabinowitz in 'Euripides: Conformist, Deviant, Neo-Conservative?', in *Arion*, 3/4 (Winter 1997), 208–22.

conscious addition of the feminine to mythic narratives that, until Euripides' treatment of them here, had indeed focused on the masculine, martial, and 'political' (in Grube's narrow sense of that word). An interpretative strategy that aims to integrate fully both the feminine *and* the political in these plays seems, then, not only welcome, but appropriate. Before attempting to outline one such approach, it will be helpful first to review the case for the originality of Euripides' own versions of these myths; and second, to rehearse briefly other critics' efforts to integrate the feminine and the political.

Feminizing Ideology: Euripides and the Myths of Athenian sōtēria

Both *Children of Herakles* and *Suppliant Women* treat myths whose potential for exploitation for political ends seems to have been widely realized already in the fifth century. In the most recent edition of *Children of Herakles*, John Wilkins has summarized the mythic tradition concerning the children of Herakles as it was probably received by Euripides:

> After the death of Herakles, his children were pursued through Greece by their kinsman Eurystheus, king of Argos. They fled from city to city as fugitives, arriving at last in Athens . . . Athens alone was strong enough to resist the power of Eurystheus; she accepted the appeal of the Heraclidae as suppliants, defended them in battle, and defeated Eurystheus. The myth is, in this as in other senses, 'political'. The Heraclidae are suppliants *and* refugees: protection of them leads to war between Athens and Argos. The story was incorporated into Athenian political mythology as an example of her fighting for the helpless, and for justice in the face of oppression. It stood in the canon beside the assistance given by Athens to the mothers of the Seven against Thebes [i.e. the mythic *donnée* for *Suppliant Women*] and the battle of Marathon against the arrogant Persians; and as such the story was suitable for treatment both in drama . . . and in patriotic speeches, notably the funeral speech.[24]

The structure of the myth on which Euripides based *Suppliant Women*, to which Wilkins briefly refers, is remarkably similar. Following the unsuccessful Argos-based campaign of Oedipus' exiled son Polyneikes and his six co-captains to storm his native city (these are the 'seven against Thebes'), the harried mothers

---

[24] Wilkins, *Euripides* Heraclidae, xi; emphases are his.

of the dead Argive captains, together with their defeated king
Adrastos, go as suppliants to Athens where they request Athenian aid in recovering the bodies of the Argive dead for burial.
The Athenians, in the person of their king Theseus, intervene on
behalf of the suppliants: in one version of the myth, adopted by
Herodotus, by making war against a recalcitrant Thebes, and in
another and probably older and more prevalent version, dramatized by Aeschylus in a play called *Eleusinioi* (*Eleusinians*), by
arranging a peace-treaty between the Argives and the Thebans.
Because they emphasized Athenian righteousness, the two
myths were frequently invoked in Athenian political oratory,
and especially in the *epitaphioi logoi*, the orations delivered at
public funerals for the war dead; although most of our evidence
is from the generation after Euripides, there appears to be no
reason to think that this pairing was not common earlier on.[25]

Significantly, there is little evidence for Athens' role in either
story *before* the fifth century. This has suggested to some scholars that the versions of the stories on which *Children of Herakles*
and *Suppliant Women* were based originated as instances of
'political myth-making': reacting to Sparta's use of the myths
of Herakles and his descendants to support its own political
agenda, Athens began encouraging Athenocentric versions of

[25] But by no means only in the funeral orations: see, for instance, Herodotos
9. 26–7, in which the Athenians counter the Tegeans' claim to lead the second
wing at the Battle of Plataea with a pointed reminder of Athens' legendary
military assistance to the Argives in recovering the bodies of the Seven. Nicole
Loraux has suggested, however, that the version Herodotos was following in his
recapitulation of the story of the Herakleidai here was the invention of a 5th-
cent. orator who tailored the myth to meet the requirements of patriotic
rhetoric. (*The Invention of Athens: The Funeral Oration in the Classical City*, tr.
A. Sheridan (Cambridge, Mass., 1986), 64, 374 n. 312). In his *Theseus* 29. 4-5, a
doubtful Plutarch seems to consider the version in which Theseus makes war on
Thebes to retrieve the bodies a specifically Euripidean invention that intentionally departs from the plot of Aeschylus' earlier *Eleusinians*.

For invocations of the two myths in formal political rhetoric see Herodotos
9. 26 (cited above); Lysias 2. 7–10 (retrieval of Argive dead) and 2. 11–16 (assistance to the Heraklids); Isokrates, *Panegyrikos* 54–65 and *Panathenaïkos* 168–
74; cf. Plato, *Menexenos* 239b. For discussion of these passages see Collard,
Supplices, i. 4, Loraux, *The Invention of Athens*, 60–70, and Mills, *Theseus,
Tragedy*, 46 f. and 58–65. 'The defence of the Heraclidae was a topos of fourth-
century panegyric,' writes Wilkins (*Euripides*, Heraclidae, xv), 'and we may
reasonably project it back to the fifth.'

these and other myths in order to promote its own interests. This political project meant not only emphasizing the links between the Peloponnesian Herakles and his descendants and Attika (as in the case of the myth of the reception of Herakles' children in Athens by either Theseus or his children, Demophon and Akamas), but in promoting that truly local hero, Theseus, as 'another Herakles', *allos Hēraklēs*, the proverbial epithet noted much later by Plutarch.[26] The Aeschylean treatments of these stories may indeed have been part of that project of civic myth-making. Although too little of his own *Children of Herakles* survives for any coherent reconstruction, the handful of fragments surviving from *Eleusinians* led Jacoby to hypothesize that the roles of Theseus and Athens in that play were Aeschylean inventions intended to bolster Theseus' newly created identity as a second Herakles.[27] This notion is given considerable support

[26] *Theseus* 29. 3; on the epithet see Felix Jacoby, *Die Fragmente der griechischen Historiker*, 16 vols. (repr. Leiden, 1958), 3. B. 1–148. The fullest and most useful discussion of the rise of Theseus as a culture hero of the 5th-cent. Athenian democracy is now Mills, *Theseus, Tragedy*; her chapters on *Suppliant Women* and *Herakles* are particularly illuminating with respect to the 'Heraclization' of Theseus. For the promotion of Herakles himself as a hero with particular associations to Athens, see the remarks of Wilkins at *Euripides*, Heraclidae, xiv and in 'The Young of Athens', 329–30. Mills (p. 136) suggests that there was some competition between Herakles, the panhellenic hero, and Theseus, the native-born civic hero: 'The Athenians never stopped needing to equate the deeds of their national hero with those of Greece's greatest hero.' See also the discussion of W. Robert Connor, 'Theseus in Classical Athens', in A. G. Ward *et al.* (eds.), *The Quest for Theseus* (London, 1970), 143–74.

[27] *FrGrHist* 3. B. 1. 448 and B. 2. 355 ff., on Aesch. *Eleusinians* frs. 267–70 Mette. For more on *Eleusinians*, see Mette's discussion in *Der verlorene Aischylos* (Berlin, 1963), 40 f., and the remarks of Collard, *Supplices*, 4, and Mills, *Theseus, Tragedy*, 229–34. Aeschylus' *Children of Herakles* = frs. 108–13 Mette (= 73b, 74, 75, 75a, and 77 Radt). Wilkins very sensibly argues that the fragments are too scant to be the basis of any coherent reconstruction (*Euripides*, Heraclidae, xviii–xix). Such attempts have, however, been made by R. Aélion, *Euripide héritier d'Eschyle* (Paris, 1983), i. 169–75; H. Weil, *Études sur le drame antique* (Paris, 1908), 123; and Zielinski, *Tragodoumenon*, 90–112.

The view that Theseus' role in the tragic versions of this tale is an innovation of the 5th-cent. playwrights dovetails nicely with the evidence that at the beginning of the 5th cent. the legendary hero was appropriated as the official hero of the democratic state: for this point see Mills, *Theseus, Tragedy*; the remarks of E. D. Francis, *Image and Idea in Fifth Century Greece: Art and Literature after the Persian Wars* (New York, 1990), 43–66; Christiane Sourvinou-Inwood, 'Theseus Lifting the Rock and a Cup Near the Pithos Painter', *JHS* 91 (1971),

by the fact that in the earliest versions of the story it is Adrastos, not Theseus, who goes to Thebes, where he successfully negotiates for the recovery of the bodies of the Seven and subsequently officiates at their funeral.[28] That Euripides chose to treat the two myths previously dramatized by Aeschylus is not merely further evidence of a well-known literary competition (the best example of which may be the younger dramatist's *Elektra*, with its unmistakable allusions to Aeschylus' *Libation Bearers*), but, more importantly, may reflect the frequency with which the two legends were paired in contemporary fifth-century political discourse—something the ancients themselves remarked on.[29]

'Tragedy is a blessed art in every way', the fourth-century comic playwright Antiphanes wrote (fr. 191 Kock 1–4), 'since its plots are well known to the audience before anyone begins to speak.' But the audiences who, at the premières of our two political plays, entered the theatre of Dionysos expecting to see familiar versions of the two great civic myths may well have been taken by surprise. For despite the fact that they had become clichés of political rhetoric at the time—and, therefore, despite the public's inevitable, increased familiarity with them—both myths appear to have undergone considerable alteration at the hands of Euripides in *Children of Herakles* and *Suppliant Women*. This is undoubtedly true of certain minor details that were altered in ways that serve the playwright's particular dramatic

97 f.; and F. Jacoby, *Atthis: The Local Chronicles of Ancient Athens* (Oxford, 1949), 395.

[28] Pindar, *Ol.* 6 (*c*.468), 15 ff., with which cf. *Nem.* 9. 22 ff., and *Il.* 14. 114 (Tydeus' body buried at Thebes; the tomb is mentioned by Pausanias 9. 18. 2). The ancient commentator Aristarkhos attributed this version of events to Pindar himself (*Σ* on *Ol.* 6. 23); elsewhere in the scholia (ad *Ol.* 6. 26), Adrastos' role is said to derive from the epic *Thebais*. The scholiast on the *Iliad* passage suspected the line because it countered the tragic version of events, but that complaint in itself hardly constitutes sound evidence for the primacy of the tragedians over Homer.

[29] For Euripides' plays as 'consciously working against' the earlier versions of Aeschylus, see Mills, *Theseus, Tragedy*, 90. Theseus' disparaging remarks about the validity of eyewitness reports from the front in *Suppliant Women* (849–52) has been seen as a jab at a messenger speech in the Aeschylean *Eleusinians*, just as Adrastos' funeral oration in the same play (857–908) has been taken as a parody of a similar moment in the earlier play. For the ancients' awareness of the rhetorical usefulness of pairing the two myths, see e.g. Thuc. 2. 35, 2. 36. 1; Dem. 40. 7 and 9; Plato, *Menexenos* 239b.

ends;[30] but it is especially striking with respect to the dramas' female characters.

First of all, it is likely that the voluntary self-sacrifice of Herakles' anonymous virgin daughter is the poet's invention: the play is at any rate the earliest source for the story of the voluntary death of Herakles' daughter (called Makaria in later myth but referred to only as *Parthenos*, 'the Girl', in Euripides' text), and it is worth noting that in other known versions of the Herakles myths the hero is given sons but no daughters (of which, in Euripides' play, there are in fact several).[31] As such, the Girl is not only an early example of the playwright's experimentation with the motif of female (and particularly virgin) self-sacrifice, continued in later works such as *Hekabe* and *Iphigeneia at Aulis*, but also an inventive recapitulation of a strong tradition of Athenian civic myths about young girls who kill themselves and subsequently become tutelary deities—figures such as the Aglauridai/Kekropidai, who were driven to suicide by Athena, and the Erekhtheidai, who voluntarily died for their city.[32]

Even bolder than this apparent invention, perhaps, is the poet's reworking of the tradition of the Argive king Eurystheus' death; in *Children of Herakles* this event becomes the vehicle for the famous, indeed infamous scene of Alkmene's violent

[30] In the case of *Children of Herakles*, for example, the Heraklids are received by Theseus' two sons, Demophon and Akamas, rather than by Theseus himself as in most accounts—a detail that enhances the doubling of roles that is an important motif of the play as a whole. For the reception of the suppliants by Demophon and Akamas, see Pausanias 1. 32. 6, Diod. Sic. 4. 57. 6; for their reception by Theseus, see Pherekydes, *FrGrHist* 3 F 84 (=Ant. Lib. *Met.* 33. 1–2). Wilamowitz argued, however, that the source for Antoninus' account was not Pherekydes, but an unknown mythographer whose own source is likely to have been Euripides himself. See his 'de Euripidis Heraclidis commentatiuncula', *Kleine Schriften* (Berlin, 1935), i. 76 f.

[31] For Herakles' daughters as a Euripidean invention, see Wilkins, *Euripides Heraklidae*, xvi, xix–xx.

[32] For Athenian myths of virgin suicides who become courotrophic figures, see the remarks of John Wilkins in 'The State and the Individual: Euripides' Plays of Voluntary Self-Sacrifice', in A. Powell (ed.), *Euripides, Women, and Sexuality* (London, 1990), 180 ff. and in 'The Young of Athens', 333; see also Loraux, *Children of Athena*, 23–6, 52 f. For virgin self-sacrifice in general, see Johanna Schmitt's classic study *Freiwilliger Opfertod bei Euripides: Ein Beitrag zu seiner dramatischen Technik* (Giessen 1921); and for the development of this motif in Euripides' work in particular, see Foley, *Ritual Irony*.

vengeance at the end of the drama. All other extant sources indicate that the villainous Argive king was beheaded at a place known as the Skironian Rocks, either by Herakles' son Hyllos, or by his henchman Iolaos, during the battle waged by Athens on behalf of Herakles' children. According to these narratives, Eurystheus' severed head was brought to Alkmene, who dug out the eyes with weaving pins; subsequently it was buried at Trikorythos, a site thereafter referred to as *Eurystheōs Kephalos*, 'Eurystheus' Head'. Only in Euripides' play is Eurystheus spared death on the battlefield so that he may survive to be taken prisoner, and subsequently put to death, on the orders of Alkmene herself.[33]

Euripides seems to have been just as inventive, in *Suppliant Women*, in his treatment of the myth of recovery of the bodies of the Seven. Here he seems to have introduced two entirely new roles to a narrative that, in all other respects, varies only slightly from his mythic datum. The pivotal role of Aithra—for in Euripides' play it is she who is supplicated by the Argive mothers, and who becomes the instrument of her son's conversion to their cause—is, as Collard notes, 'Euripides' invention and has a purely dramatic motive'. (Outside of Euripides, Aithra is known only as the guardian of Helen when the latter was abducted by Theseus.) Moreover, the entire Evadne episode, and the subsequent scene of Iphis' despair, appear to be Euripidean innovations.[34]

The above suggests that we should resist the tendency among scholars today to treat the political plays as 'minor' works dashed off by a preoccupied and even careless poet. If anything, the

---

[33] Eurystheus beheaded by Hyllos: Apollod. 2. 8. 1, Diod. Sic. 4. 57. 6; by Iolaos: Pindar, *Pyth*. 9. 81, Strabo 8. 6. 19, Pausanias 1. 44. 10; eyes gouged out by Alkmene: Apollod. 2. 8. 1; head buried at Trikorythos: Strabo 8. 6. 19. For the uniqueness of *Children of Herakles*'s version, on the other hand, see Emily A. McDermott, 'Double Meaning and Mythic Novelty in Euripides' Plays', *TAPA* 121 (1991), 127f. and 127 nn. 14–16.

[34] For Aithra's limited visibility outside of Euripides, see Collard, *Supplices*, 5 n. 11; for her role as Helen's protector see Plutarch, *Theseus* 31 and the discussion of Mills (*Theseus, Tragedy*, 7f.). For Evadne as a Euripidean innovation, see Collard, *Supplices*, 8 and n. 26; among other things, he notes the strange absence of any pictorial representation of Evadne's suicide from surviving 5th-cent. art—a subject, as he rightly remarks, that would have been 'promising to the painter'.

evidence indicates that both *Children of Herakles* and *Suppliant Women* were likely to have been seen by Euripides' contemporaries as serious treatments of important civic myths by a major dramatist at the height of his powers. The playwright's purposeful inclusion of feminine elements in his adaptation of well-known civic myths therefore demands serious re-evaluation.

Although the adaptation of myth for the purposes of the tragic stage was, to be sure, nothing out of the ordinary, it is worth noting here a developing consensus among scholars of tragedy that those adaptations were often made specifically in order to render the tragic versions of the myths more efficient as vehicles for comment on, and critique of, contemporary Athenian civic ideology. As the Athenian democracy grew in power during the fifth century, and indeed as Athens herself grew greater and more powerful as an aggressively imperial state, that ideology increasingly required the subordination of the house, the *oikos*, the realm of the individual and the private, to the *polis*, the city, the realm of the collective citizen body and the public—just as it eventually required the subordination of the non-Athenian *oikoi* and *poleis* to those in Athens. Tragedy, with its rich symbolic and theatrical vocabulary of inside and outside, female and male, individual and group—along with its ability to transmogrify and adapt existing myths in intellectually and emotionally compelling ways—was a genre ideally suited to comment on and re-evaluate the ideological tradition of civic myths.[35]

As it happens, the specific form that Euripides' refashioning of his mythic narratives takes—that is, either the enhancement of the roles of pre-existing female characters, or the interjection of newly invented female roles—serves that critical agenda especially well, because of the special symbolic role played by the feminine in the ancient Greek cultural imagination. Our ever-expanding appreciation of that role—part of which was to symbolize the *oikos*, just as the masculine in many ways came to symbolize the sometimes competing interests of the *polis*,[36] and part of which, as we shall see, was to symbolize darker forces

[35] See the excellent discussion of Dora C. Pozzi, 'The Polis in Crisis', in Dora C. Pozzi and John M. Wickersham (eds.), *Myth and the Polis* (Ithaca, NY, 1991), 134 and *passim*.

[36] See e.g. the discussion of Barry Strauss in *Fathers and Sons: Ideology and Society in the Era of the Peloponnesian War* (Princeton, 1993), 35 ff.

within the psyche, society, and the state—suggests that Euripides' transformations of the myths of the Heraklids and the Recovery of the Seven were especially pointed, and should therefore pique the interest of contemporary critics at least as much as it was likely to have done in the case of the Athenians for whom the plays were created.

Politics and the Feminine: Some Interpretative Approaches

In traditional readings of the political plays, such as that of Grube (who considered Evadne to be 'not worked in'), the female characters, inasmuch as attention has been paid to them at all, have been seen as little more than ventriloquist's dummies, through whom the voice of contemporary political and even moral ideology—that is, the voice of masculine concerns—issues unselfconsciously. For example, the self-sacrifice of Herakles' virgin daughter, 'proud and glad to give her life for Hellas', has been the special focus of enthusiastic praise that deems her 'wonderfully winning and perfectly noble', as Murray wrote; Zuntz, for his part, comments that 'the beauty and sublimity of her act is recognized with emotion and sympathy'. Similarly, *Suppliant Women*'s Aithra is generally accepted as a model mother whose timely advice to her immature son Theseus averts a religious and political disaster. Evadne's suicide in the same play has similarly been the subject of occasionally turgid encomia over the years by critics who have seen in this distraught young widow a model of proper wifely devotion.[37]

Yet recent insights into the ancient Greek understanding of the feminine (the female is unruly, sexually and emotionally excessive, wild; she must be tamed, domesticated, 'yoked') and the symbolic expansion of that understanding (the feminine is associated with the wild and the bestial, whereas the masculine is associated with civilization and culture) allow, even demand, a different interpretation, one in which tragedy's women appear precisely in order to problematize the ideologies that the mythic tradition had presumably been created to reinforce. In this interpretation, girls and women are often the representatives of a disturbing and potentially disruptive otherness within the carefully

[37] Murray, *Euripides and his Age*, 90, and Zuntz, *The Political Plays of Euripides*, 80, on the Girl; for Evadne as a model of devotion, see Vellacott, *Ironic Drama*, 164.

constructed world of dramas in which, as so often is the case, the integrity of a city or family is threatened; such an interpretation necessarily eschews a straight reading of tragedy's females and their actions for a more complex and often ironic one.[38] After all, it is only 'wonderfully winning and perfectly noble' for pubescent females like the Girl in *Children of Herakles* (who may be said to represent the individual interests of the clan or the individual household) to die on behalf of the good name of their male relatives, or to save the cities of their male rescuers, if you accept the premise that women and what they represent are necessarily subordinate to men and what *they* represent; that, in other words, the realm of the private is inevitably subordinate to that of the public; that the lives of individual citizens are necessarily expendable for the continuance of the state; and so forth. And indeed, these are among the premises that have been seen as underlying the ideological apparatus of the Athenian state during Euripides' time—an apparatus, at work in literature, law, medicine, art and architecture, that strove to present patriarchy, democracy, and empire as desirable, natural, and inevitable.[39]

The project of the past generation of feminist scholarship has been to expose what one recent critic of *Children of Herakles* refers to as the 'cultural work' of one such ideology—i.e. patriarchy—in tragedy. This project exposes how the allegedly winning and noble actions of females (and indeed, contemporary critics' characterizations of them as 'winning' and 'noble') may be understood as the expressions of hidden, rather darker forces; it is an approach to tragedy that helps to redefine the political in ways that give the contemporary critic considerably more breadth than was available to earlier scholars, aligning its adherents with scholars in many disciplines who are looking at a broad

[38] For this point, see Goff, *History, Tragedy, Theory*, 14: 'That this ideologically charged zone of literature is one of struggle, however, rather than monolithic certainty, may be indicated by the frequency in Athenian texts of representations of apparently noninferior women within a context of similarly frequent remarks about women's "natural" inferiority.'

[39] These examples dovetail with the crisp definition of 'ideology' provided by Goff (*History, Tragedy, Theory*, 11), which I invoke throughout my discussion: '[I]deology usually works to justify the inequities of a particular social arrangement and often to mystify its actual processes; ideology strives to render "natural" what is a culturally specific distribution that favors some elements of society over other elements.'

range of cultural institutions and products from many epochs.[40]
A classic feminist reading of tragedy, such as Nancy Rabinowitz's study of those Euripidean dramas in which two types of
female are contrasted (self-sacrificing virgins and destructive
hags, the same pairing we find in Euripides' political plays), sees
in such pairings a perfect example of how the representation of
females by male authors on the Greek stage confirms both negative and positive stereotypes of the feminine in order, ultimately,
to justify masculine authority and control in everyday life:

[T]he plays establish two models of womanhood—sacrificial and
vindictive—which speak to both women and men. On the one hand,
they set forth codes of behavior giving women in the audience reason to
participate in the culture; on the other hand, they reinforce men's need
and right to continue to control women . . . Women are represented as
torn from associations with other women which might be supportive;
men are encouraged in their relationships to other men.[41]

In this type of reading, Euripides' 'good girls' are seen in Freudian terms, as fetishes; they console the suppressed anxiety of
a male audience fearful of female power. That female power is
violently personified by the author's 'bad women', who, in
Freudian terms, are representatives of the uncanny.[42] This interpretative position is not unrelated to early Freudian explanations
for the prominence of extreme types of females in Greek tragedy:
the fetish/uncanny types, it was argued, were expressions of
psychological responses—'fear, awe, and contempt'—by adult
men to the powerful female figures who held sway over them
when they were small boys.[43]

[40] Compare, for instance, the comments of the French feminist critic
Catherine Clément on the doomed heroines of 19th-cent. opera, whose creators
did much the same 'cultural work' that Rabinowitz attributes to Euripides:
'[W]hat catches them [the heroines] [is] a social system that is unable to tolerate
their presence for fear of repudiating itself. Always, by some means or other,
they cross over a rigorous, invisible line, the line that makes them unbearable; so
they will have to be punished. They struggle for a long time . . . in the labyrinth
of plots, stories, myths, leading them, although it is already too late, to the
supreme outcome where everyone knew they would have to end up': *Opera, or
the Undoing of Women*, tr. Betsy Wing (Minneapolis, 1988), 59.

[41] Rabinowitz, *Anxiety Veiled*, 14, 21. Rabinowitz's study, to which I allude
throughout this section, is the best and most fully argued recent example of this
approach to Euripidean women.   [42] So Rabinowitz, *Anxiety Veiled*, 23–7.

[43] So Philip Slater, *The Glory of Hera: Greek Mythology and the Greek
Family* (Boston, 1968), 4–10 ('fear, awe, and contempt': 10).

The essentially psychoanalytic assumptions and emphases of this type of feminist approach may be contrasted with the material and historicist emphases to be seen in other fairly recent feminist approaches to tragedy. It is possible, for instance, to argue that *Suppliant Women*—a play that begins with wild maternal lamentation but ends with a more orderly ritual led by the male Athenian ruler—reflects actual historical events and political choices in which women played a prominent role: that is, the Athenian state's ongoing legislative efforts, during the sixth and fifth centuries BC, to curtail public mourning and, particularly, female participation in mourning ritual.[44] In this historicizing evaluation of one tragedy's depiction of women's actions, Theseus' attempts to co-opt feminine mourning ritual (*Su.* 932–49) is not seen as a solicitous effort to spare the dead soldiers' mothers more anguish, as the 'surface' of the text might suggest (*Su.* 944), but a dramatic reflection of a concrete contemporary reality, a particular form of political manoeuvring that itself was the response to specific political tensions and anxieties: public funerals, in which emotionally extravagant female lamentation played a crucial ritual role, had a tendency to metamorphose into political demonstrations, publicly staged vehicles for the expression of certain political tensions during both archaic and democratic times.[45] The most frequently discussed

[44] See Helene Foley, 'The Politics of Tragic Lamentation', in Alan Sommerstein *et al.* (eds.), *Tragedy, Comedy, and the Polis* (Bari, 1993), 101–43. (But cf. Foley's more usual, less historicist position, neatly articulated in '*Anodos* Drama: Euripides' *Alcestis and Helen*', in Ralph Hexter and Daniel Selden (eds.), *Innovations of Antiquity* (New York, 1992), 134: 'The women of Greek tragedy have . . . no precise counterparts among the real women of classical Athens; they are constructed to argue out problems and expose social contradictions central to the lives of their masculine creators and to a largely or exclusively masculine audience.') The argument that Theseus' action represents the *polis*'s interest in curtailing female ritual prerogatives in 5th-cent. Athens also appears in Loraux, *The Invention of Athens*, 48f., and in John E. G. Whitehorne, 'The Dead as Spectacle in Euripides' *Bacchae* and *Supplices*', *Hermes*, 114 (1986), 67–70. It is helpful to compare the discussion of John D. B. Hamilton, 'Antigone: Kinship, Justice, and the Polis', in Pozzi and Wickersham, *Myth and the Polis*, 86–98.

[45] Hamilton conjectures that the emotional impact of an aristocratic funeral in archaic Athens would have been comparable to the 'massively orchestrated' and 'often disruptive' funerals of present-day figures such as John F. Kennedy ('Antigone', 89); as a more recent example of how public grief becomes the

of these tensions was the ongoing and sometimes explosive competition among the old aristocratic clans of pre-democratic Athens, who could make funerals into occasions for magnificent displays of their own wealth and prestige and thus challenge either each other or—later on, after the establishment of the Athenian democracy—challenge the new democratic state.[46]

Yet despite the light they shed on long-repressed cultural and historical (and possibly authorial) anxieties about women and the social and political consequences of female action, the two kinds of feminist interpretations of Euripides' women that I have sketched above have as many limitations, in their different ways, as did those interpretations that completely ignored the plays' patriarchal undertones. In the case of the first group of critics, the problem lies in the emphasis on exposing 'patriarchy at work' in the plays—patriarchy, that is, as an expression of real anxieties about real women; on revealing, as Rabinowitz puts it, how 'the role of tragedy as a public art form was in part to keep the system going', by presenting stereotypical images of bad or good types of women, or by 'set[ing] forth codes of behavior giving women in the audience reason to participate in the culture'. Such critiques, in other words, seek to (and in a sense are satisfied to) present the evidence of patriarchy, to expose the 'ideological component'—i.e. patriarchy—and 'the technologies of gender' in given tragic texts that have as their aim the suppression and control of the 'women's community behind the text'.[47] One objection that could be made to such critiques is that they are often based on retrojections of contemporary assumptions (not least, the psychoanalytical) about men, women, and society that are not necessarily Greek. Moreover, while

vehicle for social and political unrest, we might now consider the events following the death of Diana, Princess of Wales, in 1997. For specifics of archaic funeral rites, see Sally Humphreys, *The Family, Women, and Death* (Ann Arbor, 1983), 85–8.

[46] Foley, 'The Politics of Tragic Lamentation', 103. She herself sees the tensions changing once the democratic *polis* is firmly established (p. 108). Suppression of the aristocracy is stressed by M. Alexiou, *The Ritual Lament in Greek Tradition* (Cambridge, 1974), 14 ff., and Hamilton, who wonders rhetorically whether 'the democratic polis [could] tolerate the disruption of massive *genē* funerals'. The answer for him is clearly 'No': 'Athens had enough difficulty coping with the presence of dynamic aristocrats' ('Antigone', 95).

[47] For these points see Rabinowitz, *Anxiety Veiled*, 14, 21.

'women's communities behind the texts' exist today, to be sure, their existence in fifth-century Athens must remain hypothetical; and even if they did exist, there is no reason to suppose out of hand, as the strict feminist critique tends to, that— while no one doubts the existence of patriarchy in Athenian culture—the aims of such a 'women's community', if it did exist, were always and already opposed to those of the dominant community of men.[48]

Even if we accept the terms of the classical feminist critique, however, this interpretative mode seems limited. It is, indeed, more fruitful to take the feminist conclusion—that there was patriarchy at work in Athens and its cultural institutions—as a premise, as our starting point. There is little doubt that tragedy was indeed a man's game, problematizing issues central to the question of male identity while repressing any substantive consideration of real women and their own lives and identities. This point was forcefully made by Zeitlin, and has become the cornerstone of an interpretative approach to the role of the feminine in Greek tragedy that takes femininity as a symbolic value in a discourse that is, ultimately, about men:

Even when female characters struggle with the conflicts generated by the particularities of their subordinate social position, their demands for identity and self-esteem are nevertheless designed primarily for exploring the male project of selfhood in the larger world as these impinge upon men's claims to knowledge, power, freedom, and self-sufficiency—not for some greater entitlement or privilege, as some have thought, that the female might gain for herself, not even for revising notions of what femininity might be or mean . . . *functionally* women are

[48] Foley offers a salutary alternative to the strict feminist schematization in her discussion of the complementarity of *oikos* and *polis* ('The Conception of Women in Athenian Drama', in *Reflections of Women in Antiquity* (New York, 1981), 151-58). 'Clearly,' she writes, 'both men and women share an interest in the *oikos* and in the values which help it to survive. But each sex performs for the *oikos* a different function, each requiring different virtues, and acts in separate spaces, one inside, one outside. Each sex also shares in interest in the *polis* and performs different public functions which help to perpetuate the state, the male political and military functions, which exclude women, the female religious functions' (153 f.). See the very similar comments of Strauss, *Fathers and Sons*, 33–41, and the remarks—accompanying an excellent brief survey of various feminist approaches to tragedy—in the Introduction to *Women on the Edge: Four Plays by Euripides*, ed. Ruby Blondell, Mary-Kay Gamel, Nancy Sorkin Rabinowitz, and Bella Zweig (New York and London, 1999), 61-2.

never an end to themselves, and nothing changes for them once they
have lived out their drama on stage.[49]

Hence the feminist interpretation that has as its final goal the
exposure of patriarchal strategies in response to anxieties about
—and in order to control—*real* women, is, ultimately, of limited
usefulness. Such interpretations cannot help us understand what
textual strategies for regulating and even repressing female characters' words and actions were meant to signify in the explicitly
civic context of the Athenian dramatic festivals during the fifth
century BC, festivals at which civic identity—the city's, its male
citizens'—were not only celebrated but also scrutinized within
the 'safe' space of the theatre; it cannot account for the symbolic
and performative significance that a feminine other may have
had in dramas into which feminine figures were deliberately
interjected—dramas, let us remember, based on mythic narratives that, prior to those additions, seemed quite able to support
(and indeed were invented and promoted in order to support) the
ideological status quo.

And yet if the first kind of feminist interpretation is, as it were,
too broad, failing to take into account the specificity of Greek
culture, the second, historicist-feminist interpretation seems too
narrow, assuming as it does a kind of one-to-one correspondence
between a given play's actions and the contemporary actualities
of that play's historical moment, and therefore failing to provide
an interpretative framework that can accommodate the more
abstract symbolic potential of the feminine in tragedy.

Tragic Woman and Political Difference

What we want, of course, is a happy medium, a framework that
has room for both ideological breadth and historical depth and
can therefore navigate successfully an interpretative Scylla-and-
Charybdis: on the one hand, as Barbara Goff puts it, the classical
feminist interpretation's 'solipsistic assumption that since only

---

[49] Zeitlin, 'Playing the Other', 67; emphasis hers. For this crucial point about
tragic females as 'constructed' vehicles for the expression of anxieties about
male identity, see also Foley, 'The Conception of Women in Athenian Drama',
127–68; Sue-Ellen Case, *Feminism and the Theatre* (New York, 1988), 7 ff.;
Jeffrey Henderson's Introduction to his *Three Plays by Aristophanes: Staging
Women* (New York and London, 1996); and the comments of Blondell *et al.* at
Women on the Edge, 61.

the act of reading animates the text, the text is constrained to give us back ourselves', and on the other, the historicist-feminists' 'fallacy of a full recovery of the past that would be untainted by the critic's own investments'.[50]

Such an approach does in fact emerge in a specific version of the broader, more symbolic feminist reading of Greek tragedy, one in which we reconfigure our understanding of the Greek conceptualization of the political in terms capacious enough to allow us to perceive its structural similarities to the Greek conceptualization of gender categories; the two are, in fact, remarkably concentric. Arlene Saxonhouse has argued that Greek political theory was the intellectual response to what she calls the 'fear of diversity'—a philosophical project meant to impose intellectual control over the overwhelming evidence of the human senses, a system that necessarily resulted in a preference for 'wholeness' over 'diversity'.[51] Translated into civic terms, that tension was evident in what the historian Victor Ehrenberg called the 'clash of opposing forces': a clash, that is, between the city-state, on the one hand ('the state is and must be one'), and society, 'a plurality', on the other.[52] '[T]he focus on power and its pursuit,' Saxonhouse writes, 'the centrality of rationality and its efficacy, and the drive towards uniformity rather than multiplicity . . . tried to move the city towards an unrealizable unity.'[53]

---

[50] Goff, *History, Tragedy, Theory*, 15. Although the present study was essentially complete prior to the publication of Goff's collection, I am happy to see that Goff has identified the same critical dilemma that interests me here (and indeed speaks of it as the problem that the papers she has collected are meant to address: p. 24), and am glad to note here the many useful insights both she and her contributors have afforded.

[51] Saxonhouse, *Fear of Diversity*, 22.

[52] Victor Ehrenberg, *The Greek State* (New York, 1964), 89 (also cited by Saxonhouse, *Fear of Diversity*, 47).

[53] Saxonhouse, *Fear of Diversity*, 51. Loraux has similarly commented on the *polis*'s ideological implementation of what she calls a 'quasi-Parmenidean' philosophical project: '[The] *polis* absorbs plurality in an abstract singularity; contradictions and diversity in the social body are suppressed in the notion of the city . . . the funeral oration makes the city, as signifier and signified, the political expression of the One and this quasi-Parmenidean aim attests that the conflict between the one and the multiple, a philosophical topos, was also the subject of an ideological struggle in Athens' (*The Invention of Athens*, 279). Cf. Plato, *Parm.* 127e8–10. For the Athenian imperial democracy's efforts to present the *dēmos* as a unified body, see Mills, *Theseus, Tragedy*, 45.

The city expressed that particular ideological drive in the mythic stories that it promoted about itself, and which provided tragedy with its narratives. Thus, for example, the important civic myth of Athenian autochthony does not merely establish territorial claims based on the premise of birth from the land itself, but does so in a way that simultaneously suppresses the potentially subversive force of the bonds connecting the autochthonous male citizens to separate mothers or to separate wives. It is a myth, in other words, that necessarily excludes 'the diversity entailed in heterosexual creation'.[54]

This highlighting of the exclusion of the feminine (as a symbol of centrifugal forces of 'diversity') as an integral part of civic ideology leads Saxonhouse quite naturally to her own particular assessment of the uses of the feminine in tragedy. Following Vernant, Saxonhouse sees the structural tensions within the *polis* as the primary focus of tragic scrutiny, as the political leaders presented on stage (*Bacchae*'s Pentheus, *Antigone*'s Creon) make their bids to maintain the unity of the state, often by repressing elements symbolized by the female (or effeminate) characters who are their opponents (the bacchants, Dionysos; Antigone herself).[55] Vernant had described tragedy as

establish[ing] a distance between itself and the myths of the heroes that inspire it and that it transposes with great freedom. It scrutinizes them. It confronts heroic values and ancient religious representations with the new modes of thought that characterize the advent of law within the city-state. The legends of the heroes are connected with royal lineages, noble *genē* [clans] that in terms of values, social practices, forms of religion, and types of human behavior, represent for the city-state the very things that it has had to condemn and reject and against which it has had to fight in order to establish itself. At the same time, however,

---

[54] Saxonhouse, *Fear of Diversity*, 51 f. For extended treatments of the importance of autochthony as an element of Athenian civic and mythic ideology, see Loraux, *Children of Athena, passim*; Saxonhouse, *Fear of Diversity*, ch. 5, 'Autochthony and Unity in the *Menexenus* and *Statesman*'; Strauss, *Fathers and Sons*, 44 (esp. on autochthony and the concept of paternity); and the remarks of Jean M. Davison, 'Myth and the Periphery', in Pozzi and Wickersham, *Myth and the Polis*, 60 f. In her discussion of Greek myths of wandering, Davidson sees autochthony as a subset or 'further nuance' in the broader ideological discourse in which Hellenes are distinguished from 'barbarians', the former being associated with permanent settlements, and the latter with a nomadic existence.   [55] Saxonhouse, *Fear of Diversity*, 51.

they are what it developed from and it remains integrally linked with them.[56]

The Greek dramatic employment of women and the feminine as the principal tragic symbols for the forces ('diversity') that threaten the civic entity and its ideological structures ('unity') goes back to the earliest dramas; one thinks of Aeschylus' *Seven Against Thebes*, in which the Theban king Eteocles must expend as much effort containing the terror of his female subjects, which threatens to undo the city from within, as he does on vanquishing the attacking armies of the Seven, who threaten destruction from outside.[57]

As mentioned briefly above, this particular symbolic role is one for which the Greek association of woman with Nature well suits her: woman in myth is associated with animals and the wild; she is the undomesticated beast that must be 'tamed' by the husband who 'yokes' her; this connection to nature in turn makes her the symbol of a natural irrationality and lack of emotional and sexual self-control. As such, woman is seen in Greek culture and specifically in Attic drama as the emblem of all that is opposed to civilization, a potentially anarchic element within the rigidly organized, carefully hierarchized, and, finally, masculine world of the *polis*, whose male citizens, like the state itself, were meant to be paragons of self-control—'free, proud, independent to the point of autarchy'.[58] This carefully maintained self-sufficiency, as exemplified by both the male body and the *polis*

[56] 'The Historical Moment of Tragedy in Greece: Some of the Social and Psychological Conditions', in Jean-Pierre Vernant and Pierre Vidal-Naquet, *Myth and Tragedy in Ancient Greece*, tr. Janet Lloyd (New York, 1990), 26; see also 'Tensions and Ambiguities in Greek Tragedy', in the same volume (29–48), as well as the related remarks of Pierre Vidal-Naquet in 'Sophocles' *Philoctetes* and the Ephebeia', in Vernant and Vidal-Naquet, *Myth and Tragedy*, 161–79.

[57] P. E. Easterling sums up the terms of the 'vital fifth-century debate' about politics that are symbolized by tragic women, and the various approaches to understanding tragic women proffered by Shaw, Foley, Zeitlin, *et al.*, in 'Women in Tragic Space', *BICS* 34 (1987), 16.

[58] Strauss, *Fathers and Sons*, 215. For women as emblems of uncivilized anarchy see Foley, 'The Conception of Women', 134, and cf. the comments of John Gould in his important article 'Law, Custom, and Myth: Aspects of the Social Position of Women in Classical Athens', *JHS* 100 (1980), 38–59. 'Like the earth and once-wild animals,' Gould writes, 'they [women] must be tamed and cultivated by men, but their "wildness" will out' (57). Anne Carson explores further this much-discussed association between the feminine and the natural in

that was its analogue, is the frequent object of tragic scrutiny. Hence the nagging question of why women are so prominent in Greek tragedy—an anomaly that continues to excite discussion, given women's presumed invisibility in Greek society itself[59]— is answered by looking to tragedy's symbolic uses of the feminine as the symbol of all 'difference' that the civic ideology of the *polis* attempts to suppress. 'To raise questions about order, unity, power, and rationality', Saxonhouse writes, 'the playwrights often turned to the female, for in her difference from the male she revealed a diversity in nature that threatened the physical order and rational control at which the polis aimed.'[60]

The specific terms of this particular conceptualization of the central tensions within the *polis*, and of tragedy's special ability to explore them, are, to be sure, open to question. For example, the model of the antagonistic dynamic between the individual and the state—what Saxonhouse calls 'the abstract city'—has come under attack as an anachronistic retrojection from modern political theory.[61] And yet even if we eschew her particular formulations of the tensions that lay beneath the *polis*'s smooth

'Putting Her in Her Place: Woman, Dirt, and Desire', in David Halperin *et al.* (eds.), *Before Sexuality: The Construction of Erotic Experience in the Ancient World* (Princeton, 1990), 135–69. For tragedy's special interest in violations of the integrity of the male body and its symbolic referents, see Zeitlin, 'Playing the Other', *passim*.

[59] An interesting contribution to the discussion of this question is Bernd Seidensticker's 'Women on the Tragic Stage', in Goff, *History, Tragedy, Theory*, 151–73. Seidensticker here argues that rather than being an anomaly, tragedy's characterization of women—even 'excessive' women—'confirm[s] essential elements of the traditional image of women' (164): for example, that they are associated with the domestic sphere and punish threats to it. As such, he goes on to conclude, tragic females form one clearly identifiable pole in tragedy's exploration of the tensions between 'the basically different interests of *polis* and *oikos*, public and private, male and female'—an exploration that, the author concludes, invariably results in an advocation of 'a healthy and stable society' characterized by 'well-balanced compromise' (166). Although I do not agree with some of Seidensticker's conclusions, what follows will confirm that he and I are in agreement about this general function of tragedy's use of masculine and feminine characters.

[60] Saxonhouse, *Fear of Diversity*, 52.

[61] A critique of the model of the 'adversarial relationship between individuals and [state] authority' can be found in Philip Brook Manville's 'Toward a New Paradigm of Athenian Citizenship', in Alan Boegehold and Adele C. Scafuro (eds.), *Athenian Identity and Civic Ideology* (Baltimore, 1994), 23; but cf. *contra*

ideological surface, there is still ample evidence for what we might call stress fractures in the edifice of fifth-century Athenian democracy and its ideological apparatus—evidence that supports the usefulness of the unity/diversity model of Greek political thought. As the feminist-historicist reappraisal of *Suppliant Women* reminds us, certainly one of these was that between the democratic *polis* and the archaic and aristocratic system it had replaced, of which the memory, both politically and culturally, remained strong.[62] Moreover, recent reassessments by historians suggest that, throughout the high classical period, the twin issues of citizen identity and civic ideology remained the object of constant re-examination and redefinition. Uncertainties about the nature and geographical composition of the state itself seem to have paralleled an ongoing debate about the proper definition of the citizen body—a question that the Periklean citizenship law of 451/50 apparently attempted to address decisively; and even within that body itself, the constitution of the *individual* citizen's identity was open to still further question, given the competing claims to loyalty from, for instance, clan and state, the *genos* and the *polis*, or from the individual household, the *oikos*, and the *polis*.[63] And indeed, despite criticisms of the individual/state paradigm, the attempt by one historian of ancient politics to define democracy—'autonomous participation in the creation of order and unity under the tutelage of reason' (the terms sharply recall Saxonhouse's)—betrays the almost inevitable clash between individual autonomy and the ordered, unified

this criticism Loraux's extensive discussion of the ideological mandate to lay down the individual life (*psykhē*) on behalf of the city—i.e. the common good (Loraux, *The Invention of Athens*, 102 and *passim*).

[62] Foley, 'The Politics of Tragic Lamentation', 104f.; cf. the interesting article by Ian Morris on the aesthetic expression of this submerged conflict between aristocratic and democratic ideology in the design and construction of funerary monuments ('Everyman's Grave', in Boegehold and Scafuro, *Athenian Identity*, 67–101).

[63] Strauss rightly argues for a 'complementarity and homologous nature' of the *oikos/polis* relationship (*Fathers and Sons*, 36–41); still, the fact (as he points out) that the city regularly used the realm of the family as a 'model and idiom' for the larger community it was trying to forge, 'appropriat[ing] the language of kinship as a legitimizing tool' (37, 11), can itself be read as evidence for an ongoing attempt at appropriation and co-option by the state, and hence for competition between the two institutions.

whole represented by the smoothly running system.[64] Any or indeed all of these can be counted among 'the tension-laden relations between [the *polis*'s] parts', which Saxonhouse, following Vernant and others, sees as the proper object of tragic examination.[65]

The usefulness and allure of the unity/diversity model may perhaps be gauged in the way that its terms have been echoed and amplified in the work of some contemporary political theorists, who have similarly appreciated tragedy's abstract symbolic potential. To mention but one: the political scientist Christopher Rocco has recently reappropriated tragedy as a vehicle

[64] The definition is Cynthia Farrar's, in *The Origins of Democratic Thinking: The Invention of Politics in Classical Athens* (Cambridge, 1988), 267. For a critique of Farrar's overall view that the unified popular whole was, in the case of the Athenians, guided by a distinct elite, see Josiah Ober, *The Athenian Revolution* (Princeton, 1997), 121–39.

[65] For 'regional tensions persistent within Attika even in the high classical period' as one of the 'strong centrifugal forces' that threatened both actual and ideological coherence, see the remarks of W. Robert Connor, 'The Problem of Athenian Civic Identity', in Boegehold and Scafuro, *Athenian Identity*, 38–40 (and cf. Loraux, *The Invention of Athens*, 280).

The meaning of the Periklean citizenship law itself remains open to scholarly debate. Alan Boegehold ('Perikles' Citizenship Law of 451/0 B. C.', in Boegehold and Scafuro, *Athenian Identity*, 57–66) anchors his interpretation in the historical realities that might have pressured Perikles, the foremost of which would have been an increasing number of legal disputes concerning inheritance as a result of exogamous intermarriage by propertied Athenians (65). For Connor, on the other hand, the citizenship debate, as expressed in the Periklean law, 'annexes certain considerations into political discourse': legal challenges to citizen status were not an 'aberration' in the system but, in fact, an expected and desirable part of it, 'rais[ing] the basic questions of civic identity and demand[ing] a defense that would affirm loyalty to the institutions and values of the city' (Connor, 'Problem', 40 f.).

The competition between clan and state is, as we shall see, especially important in *Children of Herakles*. Archaic clan loyalty was itself the object of political intervention as democratic Athens evolved: hence Solon's establishment of *telē*, the four property classes, which has been seen as an attempt to wrest power from the aristocratic old guard (Aristotle, *AP* 7. 3–4; see the discussion of Philip Brook Manville, *The Origins of Citizenship in Ancient Athens* (Princeton, 1990), 144 ff.; Charles Hignett, *A History of the Athenian Constitution to the End of the Fifth Century* (Oxford, 1952), 99 ff.; W. George Forrest, *The Emergence of Greek Democracy* (New York, 1966), 161 ff., cited in Manville, 'New Paradigm', 25 n. 19). On Kleisthenes' 508/7 reorganization of the demes as a strategy to break the power of his political rivals, see David M. Lewis, 'Cleisthenes and Attica', *Historia*, 12 (1963), 22–40.

for political theorizing by identifying the tragic pole of the unitary with entrenched, post-revolutionary, post-Enlightenment democracy, which inevitably seeks to normalize and regulate its constitutive elements and thereby falls short of its original subversive project; conversely, the pole that Saxonhouse sees as representing tragic diversity is what Rocco calls 'critical theory', the activity which aims at securing and maintaining a space for democratic speech and action.[66] In terms reminiscent of those set out by Saxonhouse, Rocco goes on to describe how

[t]he very democratic norms that critical theory champions—in this case, those enabling the free, rational, and responsible agent to arrive at uncoerced consensus—function to delegitimate all that is 'other' in self and society. Those feelings, motives, experiences, and desires that remain inarticulate within the schema prescribed by an ideal discourse subsequently become the objects of disciplinary control and normalization.[67]

This particular tragic model allows Rocco to see the *Oresteia*, for instance (with its organizing obsession with the conventions of language, sexuality, and politics) as 'problematiz[ing] the sedimentations and accretions of cultural practices and norms that constitute the self and order, even as it provides democratic norms and identities against which to struggle'.[68] This last point is especially suggestive: because it is so often structured around confrontations between two hostile yet intimately connected parties, tragedy seems to have a special ability to deconstruct political meanings—to show how political critique is ultimately dependent on and bound to the meanings and assumptions it seeks to question. As we shall see, this dialectical if not indeed deconstructive tendency of tragedy is exploited fully in the political plays, in which ostensibly polar terms of masculinity and femininity, exogamy and endogamy, self and other are seen to derive their meanings only through mutual interaction.[69]

[66] Christopher Rocco, *Tragedy and Enlightenment: Athenian Political Thought and the Dilemmas of Modernity* (Berkeley, 1997), 14.

[67] Rocco, *Tragedy and Enlightenment*, 15.

[68] Ibid. 24.

[69] Although I am not interested in pressing a deconstructive approach here, my subsequent discussions of the way that certain terms depend on each other to generate their proper meanings—'self' and 'other' in *Children of Herakles*, 'endogamy' and 'exogamy' in *Suppliant Women*, 'masculine' and 'feminine' in

So the unity/diversity paradigm yields a marvellously plastic model of fifth-century Athenian drama as the vehicle for an investigation into and demonstration of what may perhaps best be summed up as 'the inadequacies of . . . attempts to over-simplify the political world'.[70] As we have seen, such oversimplifi-cation infects certain of our modern interpretative analyses of the plays: the psychoanalysis-inflected feminist, the historicist-feminist. Saxonhouse's method avoids this trap by seeing tragic representations of women as the instrument for complex analy-sis of, rather than the crude vehicle for, a hegemonic agenda. Unlike the classical feminist interpretation, with its Freudian categories and its aim of exposing patriarchy, she acknowledges the importance of seeing the symbolic use of the feminine in the specific context of contemporary debate over civic—that is, mas-culine—identity, and hence avoids reducing the plays to mere justifications of the particular political arrangements that may have existed in Athens of the fifth century BC. Yet the breadth of her appraisal of the female's role in Greek tragedy allows her to avoid the limited view that makes these dramas little more than 'warnings about the threats that women pose to the male order' —that is, the threats of *real* women to the actual operations of the Athenian political system.[71]

Oversimplification is a potential pitfall even within Saxon-house's own framework. In examining the symbolic role of woman in the context of Attic drama and its civic function, I want to avoid an overly simplistic reading of the feminine as standing for any single term within Athenian political discourse, even one so capacious as 'diversity'. And indeed, it would be a mistake to focus solely on the exploitive traffic in (or the political symbolism of) women in these plays. For to do so would be to fail

---

both—will recall certain aspects of that critical mode to some readers. I by no means discourage this. Barbara Goff offers a succinct account of how the decon-structive literary model ('the two polar opposites depend[ing] on one another in order to generate any meaning at all') has influenced recent re-readings of tragic texts (Goff, *History, Tragedy, Theory*, 4 ff.).

[70] Saxonhouse, *Fear of Diversity*, 54; cf. Pozzi, 'The Polis in Crisis', 126–34. In her discussion of the *Ion* (pp. 135–44), Pozzi sees that play as the vehicle for a remedy to certain mythic and ideological deficiencies, esp. the emphasis on Ion's Apollonian heritage to the potentially harmful exclusion of beneficent Dionysiac elements.

[71] For this important distinction see Saxonhouse, *Fear of Diversity*, 54.

to take into account the way in which Euripides' *men* are transformed, and indeed often feminized, by their interactions with
women; the positive outcomes of these transformations, which
I shall discuss in detail in subsequent chapters, appear, if anything, to validate the feminine as a set of traits, or indeed by
extension as a category. The male, as well as the female, must
therefore be the object of critical attention, as both character and
symbolic category. This must be true in general; but it is particularly appropriate when the males who are so affected are kings
like *Children of Herakles*'s Demophon or *Suppliant Women*'s
Theseus, whose actions have important ramifications for the city
that they rule: Athens.

This dual focus should in turn remind us that the appropriate
object of a study of gender and politics in Euripidean drama is
not either end of the gender spectrum, but rather its dynamic
middle. In tragedy's critique of political ideology, the definition
of proper behaviour for both the city and the citizen is never
exclusively aligned with either the wholly masculine or the
wholly feminine—with, that is to say, either unity or diversity—
but is instead arrived at as the result of complex negotiations
between the two poles. Zeitlin has described this same process at
work in Aeschylean drama, where the interaction between male
and female constitutes 'a system of checks and balances in the
civic domain to guard against masculine aggrandizement and
exclusiveness but also to control and modify the "unnatural"
exercise of feminine power'.[72] Indeed, the action of *Children of
Herakles* and *Suppliant Women* demonstrates how the extremes
of either masculinity or femininity, and the complex range of
political and civic meanings associated with each, are problematic and occasionally destructive. It is, instead, through the
mutually refining interaction of male and female characters that
Euripides, in his political dramas, sketches a system of checks
and balances, and in so doing suggests a healthy middle term in
the ongoing competition between masculine and feminine values
in civic debate.[73]

[72] Froma I. Zeitlin, 'Patterns of Gender in Aeschylean Drama: *Seven Against
Thebes* and the Danaid Trilogy', in M. Griffith and D. J. Mastronarde (eds.),
Cabinet of the Muses (Baltimore, 1990), 104.
[73] See Seidensticker, 'Women on the Tragic Stage', 166 f., and cf. Zeitlin,
'Patterns of Gender', 104.

Gender, Space, and the Critique of Ideology

We may now turn to the question of how the deployment of female characters in *Children of Herakles* and *Suppliant Women* helps make those plays part of the tragic project of ideological critique I have described above. How, that is to say, might we answer those who see in these ostensibly well-behaved (the Girl, Aithra) or victimized (Alkmene, Evadne) females either simplistic affirmation of the political, or ruthless co-option by the patriarchal, systems? And how does the project of re-evaluating the works' female figures, of resituating them closer to the meaning-laden heart of the plays and away from the periphery (where critics like Grube would keep them)—in a word, of finally making gender and politics concentric—illuminate the tension-laden relations between the *polis*'s parts?

Political Places, Ideological Spaces: Exile, Supplication

I could begin to answer those questions by saying that the aim of my spatial metaphors in the preceding paragraph is not merely stylistic. An important consideration in any interpretation of these plays is the prominent role played by place, space, and location—unities that, if their implications are followed through, give the works both structural and thematic coherences that have generally been missed. The present interpretation of *Children of Herakles* and *Suppliant Women* will seek first of all to amplify the resonances of the plays' fictive settings: for *Children of Herakles*, the altar of Zeus Agoraios and, more importantly, the Marathonian Tetrapolis in which it stands; for *Suppliant Women*, the sanctuary of Demeter and Kore at Eleusis. Each locale has a special meaning that can, as it were, be excavated; each affects our reading of the actions that transpire in them. For each was a real place, constituted by boundaries and borders, that played a role in Athenian history and, therefore, Athenian civic ideology.[74]

---

[74] A thoroughgoing investigation of space and setting in Euripidean drama is to be found in Irène Chalkia's *Lieux et espace dans la tragédie d'Euripide: Essai d'analyse socio-culturelle* (Thessalonika, 1986). For an interesting extended discussion of the interpretative significance of historical place in one particular drama, see Lowell Edmunds's *Theatrical Space and Historical Place in Sophocles' Oedipus at Colonus* (London, 1996).

But for every place, we might say, there is a 'dis-place': well-defined boundaries imply (indeed, almost invite) crossings, transgressions. Both *Children of Herakles* and *Suppliant Women* are especially concerned with the political implications of their characters' movements—prior to, during, and after the action of the play itself—through and across such geographical and religious spaces. Another way of putting this, one that situates our spatial concerns in a recognizably Greek context, is to say that both works are preoccupied with exile and supplication. Each poses critical questions about identity. Displacement and dislocation (of Herakles' kin, for example, who have been hounded out of their native city of Argos by an implacable enemy) implicitly problematize both civic and heroic identity—the more so, no doubt, for an audience to whom autochthony is a crucial element of civic ideology. Similarly, the act of supplication, which conforms to its own peculiar spatial conventions (and indeed one potential outcome of which is an impious displacement) confronts the ruler who is supplicated with certain moral, religious, and ethical dilemmas: the resolution of a suppliant crisis inevitably helps clarify the political identity of the city itself.

A full appreciation of these places and displacements—geographical and ritual, real and symbolic—and what they signify is therefore critical for our understanding of these plays as investigations of political identity and ideology. Most important, these comings and goings in turn create a coherent theatrical context for another kind of peregrination: that of the female characters' movements through theatrical space. Inasmuch as they often violate the spatial and hence gendered proprieties of fifth-century Athenian culture, these movements are specially suited to alert us to the presence of the tensions with which Saxonhouse is concerned.[75]

[75] For the way in which gendered and tragic conventions intersect, see the provocative discussion by Zeitlin, 'Playing the Other', and cf. Seidensticker, 'Women on the Tragic Stage', 152 f. In an article on Euripides' *Alkestis*, Charles Segal comments that '[i]n the background of the gender divisions of tragedy lies some form of the antithesis of war, male public realm, action, glory *versus* domestic life, private realm, passivity, grief, and weeping. This division, which also tends to place the women "inside", the men "outside", may correspond to some of the social stereotypes of the time' ('Admetus' Divided House: Spatial Dichotomies and Gender Roles in Euripides' *Alcestis*', *MD* 28 (1992), 10).

Why is this so? Each time a female character in the political
plays enters, some mention is made of the social conventions that
assign women to the interior space of the house and men to the
exterior, public space, which is typically the site of political discourse; if such mention is made, it is no doubt because every such
entrance necessarily violates those conventions.[76] This highlighting of the unconventional, even transgressive nature of feminine presence and action on stage reminds us, in turn, of the
subversive, centrifugal energies symbolized by the feminine;
indeed, the references to gendered and spatial proprieties introduce a discordant note even when those entrances are made in
the service of some ideologically desirable end (e.g. the subordination of the individual to the needs of the state). It further
becomes clear, in each of our political plays, that these feminine
disruptions of gendered space at once build upon and echo the
dislocations, alluded to elsewhere in the dramas, of still other
characters: that is, of the plays' *male* figures (e.g. Iolaos and
Adrastos). Hence displacements of both male and female characters mark crises of political, civic, and personal identity.

There is a further level at which the theme of place and
displacement may fruitfully be considered. The characters who
move into and through the spaces depicted in and alluded to in
our plays often recall still other, remoter characters: those who
figure in crucial myths to which the texts allude, myths that are
set in the very same locales as the plays themselves. Like the
dramas that allude to them, these myths involve radical displacements and peregrinations; this overlapping of mythic and tragic
locales will create further opportunity for ironic comment on the
part of the poet. A brief example: *Suppliant Women*'s Eleusinian
setting, the site of the abduction of Kore and of Demeter's distraught wanderings, enhances the dramatic motif of the Argive
mothers' mourning, reminding us of the harrowing effects of
masculine violence even on the mythic level. The layering
of mythic and dramatic scenes of mourning stands in uneasy
contrast to the glib calls for violent vengeance with which this
allegedly patriotic play concludes—vengeance sought in contravention of the protests of the chorus of mourning mothers, who

---

[76] Zeitlin, 'Playing the Other', 72; cf. Foley, 'The Conception of Women',
154ff.

have, like Demeter, travelled very far in search of their children.

Transgression, therefore, is a motif that is present in these works at various levels, providing both structural and thematic unities. Because what I refer to as feminine transgression will be the special focus of my interpretation, I would like to explore in more detail what I mean by the dichotomies of 'gendered space' and the potential for feminine transgression that they create.

A Woman's Place

It is by now widely accepted that in fifth-century Athenian culture, the difference between the sexes was emphasized and symbolized spatially: while men met in the open, public places associated with the City, such as the Agora, the assembly, the theatre itself, women were confined to the enclosed, interior space of the house, in dark and unseen quarters located in the Greek house's most interior part, the recesses called *mykhoi*.[77] There now seems to be general agreement about the cultural motivation for that separation. In her discussion of 'women in tragic space', Patricia Easterling sums up the conclusions reached by various scholars regarding fifth-century appraisal of the feminine in terms that recall those of Saxonhouse and others:

[W]omen are attractive, useful and pathetic, but there is a balancing set of less favourable images. The power of their sexuality makes them dangerous: they are a motivating force in male conflict, they have destructive wiles and guile, and their biological closeness to untamed nature fits them for dark activities like the use of magic, as well as making them disturbingly unpredictable. Since men cannot dispense with women they try to control their more dangerous aspects by secluding them inside the house, limiting their emergence into the wider public world in carefully defined ways.[78]

Now there remains considerable disagreement about the extent and actual force of any social rules or codes that might have actually regulated women's freedom in ancient Athens in the

---

[77] Sarah Pomeroy, *Goddesses, Whores, Wives, and Slaves: Women in Classical Antiquity* (New York, 1975), 79. Easterling notes that the term *mykhoi* could itself connote 'the dark and destructive power of female sexuality' ('Women in Tragic Space', 19). See also Foley, 'The Conception of Women', 130 and E. R. Flacelière, *Daily Life in Greece in the Time of Pericles* (London, 1965), 55.

[78] Easterling, 'Women in Tragic Space', 15.

carefully defined ways that Easterling describes.[79] Yet while this disagreement is of considerable importance to those whose project is to recreate the lived experienced of men and women in fifth-century Athens, it need not impinge on any attempts to use unwritten social conventions as a framework for interpreting literary works such as these plays. Indeed, since my interest is in the dramatic function and symbolic meaning of those codes and the violations of them, the (admittedly) unwritten laws regulating interaction between men and women need *only* have operated rhetorically, as a number of scholars have argued they did.

One thing that we can be sure of is that the conventional division of the sexes, as marked by the tradition (real or rhetorical) of spatial separation, was reflected in the spatial configuration of Greek drama. Like the ones that structured Athenian society, the conventions of Attic drama situated men on the outside and

[79] The best short introduction to, and analysis of, the hoary debate over the position of women in 5th-cent. Athens is given by Simon Goldhill, *Reading Greek Tragedy* (Cambridge, 1986), 105–15; see also Rabinowitz, *Anxiety Veiled*, 3–9. An important early study of the legal position of women in Athens is H. J. Wolff's 'Marriage, Law and Family Organization in Ancient Athens', *Traditio*, 2 (1944), 43–95; see also the discussions of W. K. Lacey, *The Family in Classical Greece* (Ithaca, NY, 1968); A. R. W. Harrison, *The Law of Athens: The Family and Property* (Oxford, 1968); D. M. McDowell, *The Law in Classical Athens* (Ithaca, NY, 1978); and that of Roger Just, *Women in Athenian Law and Life* (London, 1989), 26–104.

In short: The view that women in the archaic and classical world were *in fact* subject to spatial regulation is based largely on the evidence of non-literary texts such as lawcourt speeches and works such as Xenophon's *Oikonomikos*. The exclusion of women from the social and especially political spheres that is described in these texts—which are commonly presumed to represent the truth of Athenian social arrangements in a less mediated fashion than literary texts such as the tragedies—was expressed above all in terms of a spatial sequestering. This 'literalist' assumption about the forensic speeches has been called into question on various grounds: that it is undercut by still other evidence from ancient texts, especially those meant for performance on the comic or tragic stage; that the social and economic realities of a largely agrarian economy cannot have admitted such an impractical social arrangement; or, finally, that such texts—especially the legal works that seem to be free of the ambiguities characteristic of more overtly literary texts—illustrate, in Just's words, 'only those exceptional moments when the law had need to operate, leaving unrecorded the more normal times when it did not'. See also Josiah Ober, *Mass and Elite in Democratic Athens* (Princeton, 1989), 46, who prefers to read them as he might read the tragedies—'as symbol-systems that must be understood in relation to

women in the inside; the Athenian theatre, like the Athenians' houses, had its own spatial syntax of inside (*skēnē*) and outside (*orkhēstra*), of the locus of dramatic action (the theatre) and unseen faraway places (the side-aisles used for entrances and exits, called *eisodoi* and *exodoi*). Margaret Williamson has elaborated this syntax of gendered space as it applies to another Euripidean play, the *Medea*:

Most of the action in a play takes place in an open, public space, the orchestra which is partially surrounded by the audience; this space is also defined as public by the presence in it of the chorus for most of the play. Behind the orchestra, however, is the skene, the stage-building, and behind that a more remote space which the audience normally cannot see. In this and many other plays this unseen space represents the interior of a house: it is, in a phrase adapted by Gould from Wilamowitz, an 'offstage indoors', and the tragedy takes place at the intersection between inside and outside, private and public . . . [a] gap . . . never to be bridged.[80]

their receptors' (p. xiii); A. W. Gomme, 'The Position of Women in Athens in the Fifth and Fourth Centuries', *CP* 20 (1925), 1–25; Just, *Women in Athenian Law*, 107f.; and John J. Winkler, *The Constraints of Desire* (New York, 1990), 18–20. The nature of the evidence used to support the various positions in this debate about lawcourt speeches is itself suggestive, as Foley observes: 'While the contradictory evidence does not break precisely along the lines of genre, prose texts tend to give us one picture of women's lives and personalities, and poetic texts another' ('The Conception of Women', 127). Foley herself assumes the actual confinement of women; cf. Just's comments, *Women in Athenian Law*, 106f. Just cites Aristophanes' portrayal of women as one of many possibly literary counter-examples to the model of strict seclusion—although Just judiciously avoids the extremes that characterize the position of Gomme and his followers, who were apt to use literary texts as evidence that seclusion did not exist, a position Just rightly calls 'optimistic'. For seclusion dismissed on socioeconomic grounds see Pomeroy, *Goddesses*, 79f.: she points out that 'poor women, lacking slaves, could not be kept in seclusion'; cf. Gould, 'Law, Custom, and Myth', 49 on the impracticality of maintaining strict physical separation of women from men in the households of any but the relatively rich. Interestingly, Gould discusses the various 'symbolic' strategies that allowed for the maintenance of gender propriety even among poor rural societies; for comparisons in this respect between ancient and modern Mediterranean cultures, cf. David Cohen, 'Seclusion, Separation, and the Status of Women in Classical Athens', *GR* 36 (1989), 3–15.

[80] Margaret Williamson, 'A Woman's Place in Euripides' *Medea*', in Powell, *Euripides, Women, and Sexuality*, 17. Williamson's discussion builds upon insights first made by A. M. Dale in 'Seen and Unseen on the Greek Stage: A Study in Scenic Conventions', *WS* 69 (1956), 96–106.

In this play, Medea's entrance into the action of the drama is
marked by her announcement that she has left the interior of her
house ('I have come out of the house', *exēlthon domōn*, *Med.* 214):
but what she leaves, of course, is the *skēnē* building. The congru-
ence of her departures from both house and what we would call
the 'backstage' enclosure calls attention to the way in which, in
order to illustrate the operations and effects of the social codes of
gendered space, the Greek playwright could make convenient
use of the spatial codes of the tragic stage. Hence although the
spatial protocols that are violated by female characters in the
works I am examining could be thought of as no more than purely conventional rules—an ideological talking-point, as it were—
they were pointedly recalled by the structures and conventions
that regulated space in the theatre itself.

Reinterpreting Space: Reading between the Lines

An understanding of the spatial dialectics of Greek society as reflected (to whatever degree) in Greek drama thus gives Medea's
opening lines ominous import: 'I have exited from within the
house', with its special emphasis on the oddness of her presence
outside, signals what will turn out to be larger and more radical
disruptions of all kinds of conventions: marital, familial, political. This heightened interpretative awareness suggests that there
is similarly subversive potential in the actions of female characters who, like Medea, self-consciously announce their presence
on stage. For this reason, any failure to read between the lines
with respect to such pronouncements will weaken an interpretation of the play as a whole, leading us, like earlier critics, to dismiss tragedy's transgressive women as minor figures.[81]

It is noteworthy that what Gould saw as the 'conscious

[81] As Grube did in the case of *Suppliant Women*'s Aithra and Evadne: above,
p. 9. For the idea of a female character's expressing 'conscious abnormality' at
exiting from within, see Gould, 'Law, Custom, and Myth', 40, part of his
critique of A. W. Gomme's early article about the role of women in 5th- and 4th-
cent. Greek society (Gomme, 'Position of Women'). Like many others, Gomme
had argued that, judging from the 'freedom with which they come and go on the
stage', Greek women in everyday life could not have been restricted and segre-
gated in the ways that much non-literary evidence, especially the extant forensic oratory, suggests. To support this claim, Gomme cited examples from the
text I have just discussed, the *Medea*. Medea's unconstrained entrance, Gomme
argued, as well as the apparent boldness of her dealings with the Athenian king,

abnormality' of spatial impropriety in Medea's entrance marks the entrances of all of the female characters in *Children of Herakles* and *Suppliant Women*. The Girl and Alkmene, Aithra and Evadne: each enters to the accompaniment of a pointed reference to the conventional spatial assignment of men and women, even as each violates them by leaving the interior of the sanctuary or palace or house. 'Gentlemen,' says the Girl as she makes her crucial entrance in *Children of Herakles*,

I ask you first of all not to level the charge of unseemly impudence (*thrasos*) against me on account of my exit from within (*exodois emais*). Oh yes, I know the saying: 'What suits a woman best is silence, self-restraint, and to mind her own business within her house.' But when I heard your wailing, Iolaos, I came outside (*exēlthon*) . . . (474–7)

Later in the same play, Iolaos' cries of joy on hearing of Hyllos' imminent arrival will bring Alkmene, Herakles' aged mother, onto the stage from within the sanctuary where she has taken refuge with her granddaughters (646 ff.); in order to hear the messenger's victorious report, she must 'come out', as Iolaos

Aigeus, suggested that Athenian women were able to operate fairly freely with respect both to their movements and to their speech.

Gould rebutted Gomme on several important counts: first, that tragedy is a highly stylized, rather than realistic rendering of everyday life; and second, that for every instance of an ostensibly liberated woman, tragedy furnishes memorable counter-examples that would seem to support, rather than controvert, the ideology of female subjugation. (Gould's example is the Tutor's proprietary fussing about Antigone's whereabouts in *Phoenician Women*, 88 ff. and 193 ff.) But above all Gould criticized Gomme's reading of the *Medea* scenes along the lines I have indicated above, pointing out that whereas Medea does indeed move freely on stage, there are special verbal emphases in the text that suggest a certain self-consciousness on her part about the propriety of those entrances and exits; here he cites Medea's *exēlthon domōn*, 'I have exited the house' as an example. For him, those words betray the character's awareness of the 'conscious abnormality' of her violation of social norms. If there were nothing strange about her presence outside of the house, in other words, why mention it at all?

The disjunction between the rhetoric and reality of women's roles has been much discussed since Gomme; see, e.g., Michael Shaw, 'The Female Intruder: Women in Fifth Century Drama', *CP* 70 (1975), 255–66; Pomeroy, *Goddesses*, ch. 6; Foley, 'The Conception of Women', 133 f.; Easterling, 'Women in Tragic Space', 15–26; and Synnøve Des Bouvrie, *Women in Greek Tragedy* (Oslo, 1990), *passim*, where the disjunction is cited as the motivation for that scholar's lengthy study of women in tragedy. Among the most nuanced of these recent studies is Cohen, 'Seclusion'.

orders her to do (*exelth'*, 643). So too in *Suppliant Women*, in which the queen mother Aithra's detainment at Eleusis by the unexpected supplication of the chorus creates a crisis of gendered space: to Theseus' mind, she has been out of the house too long (*khronian apousan ek domōn*, 91) for any good to come of it. It is noteworthy in this case that Aithra feels compelled to excuse herself for violating the same conventions of women's silence mentioned by *Children of Herakles*'s Girl (*Su.* 297–300; cf. 40f.). Later in the same drama, many references are made to the real and figurative restraints placed on the grief-maddened Evadne's movements by her anxious father Iphis (1038ff.).

Space, Gender, and the 'Political' in the Political Plays

The self-consciousness of these characters with respect to the impropriety of their presence outside is what allows us to emphasize the transgressive nature of their various entrances.[82] And yet on one level, these various entrances—and the reactions to them that follow—seem to confirm rather than disrupt a political

[82] The self-consciousness of the female characters' entrances into public space will, I hope, deflect from my own interpretation the critique levelled at Michael Shaw's early discussion of feminine violations of tragedy's spatial dichotomies. Bearing in mind the social conventions I have described above, Shaw had argued that '[b]y the very act of being in a drama, which always occurs outside the house, they [women] are doing what women should not do' ('The Female Intruder', 256). Rightly, this formulation was considered extreme, and was challenged on several points by several scholars. Following Helene Foley, Patricia Easterling enumerated three principal objections: first, that as Gould had already pointed out in addressing Gomme, we must take into account the highly conventional nature of tragedy, which cannot thereby purport to be an accurate reflection of 'reality'; second, that there are in fact dramas whose settings do not obey any 'hard-and-fast rules' (as, for example, *Ajax*'s scene-shift from the Greeks' tents to the fatal shore); and finally, that real 5th-cent. women operated, in various well-known cases, on the 'outside', in the public world: see Easterling, 'Women in Tragic Space', 17f., and cf. Foley's critique of Shaw in 'The Female Intruder Reconsidered: Women in Aristophanes' *Lysistrata* and *Ecclesiazusae*', *CP* 77 (1982), 1–21. Foley elsewhere reminds us that the important exception to the rule of women's seclusion was their participation in numerous public and private religious and ritual activities ('The Conception of Women', 131). For these reasons, the very fact of a feminine presence on stage does not *per se* invariably signify an impropriety. Yet in the plays under present consideration, the special care with which the violation of spatial conventions is articulated by the women themselves suggests that their actions and movements are to be considered as untoward.

status quo. When, in *Children of Herakles*, the Girl steps out from within the confines of the sanctuary where she and the other female kin of Herakles have taken refuge, in order to offer herself freely as a sacrificial victim, she symbolically enacts the principle of *prohairesis*, of sacrificing family ties for civic continuity, that was of paramount importance in the civic rhetoric of the fifth century.[83] Similarly, although Aithra's prolonged absence from the palace leaves her son worried, her departure itself was a legitimate one, since she had left the palace at Athens in order to officiate at an Eleusinian fertility ritual meant to ensure the continued prosperity of the state. In a very different way, Evadne's escape from her father's house, and her subsequent self-immolation on the tomb of the husband for whom she unabashedly expresses erotic attachment, can be seen as a negative example that implicitly endorses democratic ideology (since it dramatizes the disastrous consequences of inappropriate loyalties).

How, then, does Euripides' use of such literal transgressions serve tragedy's critical and analytical project of laying bare the tensions and fissures in the structure of Athenian imperial ideology, as described by Vernant, Saxonhouse, *et al.*—the critique that is brought to life on stage by means of spatial transgression? First it should be said that, even in the case of the apparently docile female characters that Rabinowitz describes as fetish objects, feminine interventions can be seen as attempts to appropriate aspects of masculine, heroic identity. I shall argue below that in *Children of Herakles*, the Girl sees herself as a warrior who will receive long-lasting heroic renown, *kleos*, for her act; and similarly, that Aithra's vicarious interest in her son Theseus' reputation, in *Suppliant Women*, reflects her own desire to avoid the charges she fears will be levelled against him—unmanliness and cowardice. Each female, that is to say, redefines herself in terms of masculine and heroic values.[84] All of these characters

---

[83] For *prohairesis* in Athenian democratic ideology, see the discussion below, p. 84.

[84] Unmanliness, *anandria*: *Su*. 314; cowardice, *deilia*: *Su*. 319. As Easterling observes ('Women in Tragic Space', 21), Sophocles' Elektra is another whose boundary-crossing (cf. *El*. 328 f. *pros thyrōnos exodois | elthousa*) leads to dreams of the honour of saving the house and of being celebrated for her masculine valour, *andreia* (983).

conform to the types of transgressive women to which Charles
Segal refers in his discussion of the dynamics of gendered space
in Euripides' *Alkestis*:

> [T]ragedy's association of women with the interior space of the house,
> though certainly based in the realities of Athenian life, also functions
> as a complex symbolic construct, part of society's image-representation
> or symbolic world-picture of its mental structures and categories, its
> inner landscape, what the French call 'l'imaginaire'. On the far right,
> one could say, of the dichotomization of gender roles, the 'heroic'
> women . . . pose one kind of problematical situation that tragedy
> explores. These women, in some respects, are like male warriors: they
> come to a swift and violent end once their decision is taken; and they
> conform closely to the model of male heroism . . . On the far left are the
> intense, passionate women who kill men or male children, asserting
> female power over males.[85]

As we have seen, Rabinowitz gives Segal's 'far right' and 'far left'
a Freudian spin; but for her, as for Segal, both the ostensibly
positive as well as the clearly negative models are potentially
threatening to men: 'devices that simultaneously acknowledge
and control—acknowledge *in order* to control—female power'.[86]

I want to argue that in the political plays, the pairings of seemingly opposite feminine types—good/bad, fetishized/uncanny,
constructive/destructive—constitute a coherent structural device with particular implications for political theorizing. The
first, 'heroic' feminine entrance has a disturbing potential—that
is, the attempt to appropriate elements constitutive of masculine identity—that 'prefigure[s] disorder'.[87] That disorder later
explodes in more violent assertions of feminine energy that
quite plainly threaten to undermine masculine ideological con-
structs, recapitulating the language and gestures first used by the
perpetrators of these initial, 'failed' efforts: we can say that the
later and quite violent irruptions into the action of the play are
carefully foreshadowed by those initial, ostensibly minor infrac-
tions of domestic thresholds. *It is, in fact, the carefully linked
progress from containment to explosion that constitutes these
tragedies' mechanism of critique.* For in each work, the first

---

[85] Segal, *Dionysiac Poetics and Euripides' Bacchae* (Princeton, 1982), 11 f.

[86] Rabinowitz, *Anxiety Veiled*, 26.

[87] This is Segal's description of the significance of feminine transgression
(*Dionysiac Poetics*, 13).

feminine transgression is an example of what Zeitlin called the successful 'control' of feminine power. The Girl's self-sacrifice saves both city and clan; Aithra's intervention prevents a disastrous policy choice on the part of her son. In the second, more harrowing instances of feminine transgression—Alkmene's bloodthirsty vengeance in *Children of Herakles*, Evadne's erotic Mad Scene in *Suppliant Women*—the poet dramatizes the loss of that control.

In structuring his explicitly political dramas along these lines, the playwright achieves a delicate balance between two potentially contradictory ends. If the first action dramatizes and authorizes the process by which unity is achieved (through the necessary sacrifice, often literalized, of members of the body politic—these being either individuals or institutions such as the *oikos* or clan), the second, more disruptive action reminds us that this process comes at a high cost to some, and hence that unity is necessarily highly unstable. Yet even as these second actions seem to critique overly glib celebrations of unity, the violent disintegrations they portray suggest that the centrifugal energies represented by the Other can, at their own extremes, threaten both individual and, ultimately, civic integrity. It is in this way that feminine transgression serves as an instrument in tragedy's political laboratory, laying bare the always dynamic, sometimes problematic construction of Athenian civic ideology.

To be sure, the dramatic progression from 'fetishized' to 'uncanny' female characters is to be found in other Euripidean works. In *Hekabe*, Polyxena makes a gesture of self-sacrifice similar in many respects to that of *Children of Herakles*'s Girl; her death helps to precipitate the vengeful rage of Hekabe herself, which recalls that of Alkmene.[88] Or one might see in the contrast between *Andromakhe*'s noble heroine (who volunteers for a death that is consistently described as a sacrifice, *sphagē*: *And.* 260, 315, 412, 429, 547), and its emotionally extravagant villainess Hermione, a variation on the same theme. What makes both *Children of Herakles* and *Suppliant Women* unique, however, and worth considering apart from these other works, is the way that these scenes of contrasting feminine types are grouped around

[88] For the motif of the vengeful old woman in general, and for similarities between Alkmene and Hekabe in particular, see Falkner, 'The Wrath of Alcmene', 123–5.

scenes in which *men* are transformed and feminized. That frame-like structure suggests that, in the dramatic economy of these plays, the focus is on the effect of feminine transgressions on the male characters. Prior to the Girl's act of self-sacrifice, Iolaos' narrow allegiance to a heroic, pre-democratic ethos recalls the terms that define masculinity itself in fifth-century discourse: self-containment, rigidity, closure. Following the Girl's example, however, he turns his improbable heroism 'outwards', and in so doing becomes a model hoplite whose exploits are crowned by the twin gods of the democratic Athenian *ephēbeia* (the two-year military training in which Athenian youths served), Herakles and Hebe. Similarly, Theseus demonstrates a rigid political parochialism until the intervention of his mother, after which his growth as a ruler is marked by an unusual restraint in victory, and his adoption of maternal words and gestures.

The deployment of scenes of feminine transgression thus emphasizes the way in which masculine civic identity is enhanced through interaction with the feminine. To be sure, the female characters benefit from no such enhancement through their interactions with men. In a classical feminist reading, this is the crucial point. But we must consider the content of this dynamic as well as its structure; that the men are enhanced at all is worthy of note. For if we accept that the feminine represented those elements of diversity and otherness that posed problems for the unitary ideology of the *polis*, then it is possible to see in these alternating repressions and expressions of female action, in the women's attempts at heroism and their subsequent feminizing effects on the plays' central male figures, not merely the enactment of patriarchal fantasy or nightmare—i.e. the repression of one extreme by the other—but dramatizations of ideological negotiations, of the tensions and ambiguities between those extremes. In political terms, the characters' experience of 'altered states' with respect to gender is an enactment of the ongoing process of alteration and negotiation among the constituent parts of the state itself.

So while it may well be true that Euripides' political theorizing here necessarily relies on and is ultimately complicit with a patriarchal agenda—especially inasmuch as it ultimately reinstates male power, something Rabinowitz argues must invariably be the case—his particular brand of tragic theorizing is none the less striking in its attempt to inflect patriarchy with the feminine, to suggest that ideology imposes itself at a considerable price. Any attempt to construct a space that is wholly uninflected by the assumptions that underpin one's own cultural discourse—patriarchy, imperialism, even democracy—is, after all, doomed; but it is an attempt surely worthy of note. The foregoing discussion will have sketched some ways in which Euripides may have been attempting to create just such a space in his political plays. The crucial point is not that he failed, but that he tried at all. Indeed what makes these works interesting, and I think admirable, is the degree to which they seem self-consciously to struggle with the discourses that inevitably constitute them.[89]

With these considerations in mind, we may now turn to extended discussion of the dramas themselves. I will first discuss the earlier play, *Children of Herakles*—not out of some kind of chronological propriety but, because it is a somewhat less polished (and almost certainly less complete) work than *Suppliant Women*, it allows us to glimpse better the operations of the theatrical strategies I have discussed here. I shall then turn to *Suppliant Women*. In a sense, this sequence will permit us to explore the individual components of our interpretative schema —that is, space and gender—in order. For *Children of Herakles*'s representation of exile and supplication highlights the complex tragic dynamics of space, while *Suppliant Women*'s hyperfeminine Eleusinian milieu seems to demand a reading that foregrounds issues of gender.

---

[89] For this important point see Ober, *The Athenian Revolution*, 10 and Michelini, 'Euripides: Conformist?', 220.

2

Children of Herakles
Territories of the Other

Dislocation and Identity

Children of Herakles is a drama of displacement. The problematics of place, the priorities and codes that govern religious, political, and social space, are underscored throughout the play. It opens with a shocking violation of the religious space represented by the altar standing at the centre of the *orkhēstra*; it traces the desperate flight of a hero's kin who, deprived by exile of their political status, are forced to wander from *polis* to *polis*; and its high point is the self-sacrifice of a young girl who, in order to perform her heroic deed, must cross the invisible but culturally well-guarded border between male and female spaces. A climactic cross-country battle narrative, with its catalogue of geographical details, pointedly echoes those foregoing peregrinations. Throughout the play we can detect a dramatic symbiosis between those overlapping categories of space—sacred, political, gendered, geographical—with each serving at different moments as a metonymical stand-in for the others, expanding and enriching their dramatic meanings.

The play's elaborately interlocked narratives of actual movement through real space and across real boundaries are the particular reflections of the work's more general thematic of dislocation, displacement, and disorientation. This overarching motif establishes a particularly apt dramatic context for the play's investigation of what we might call the boundaries of civic identity. Indeed, metaphorical dislocations are often triggered by literal ones: the flight that brings Iolaos and his charges to Attika, for example, makes him a citizen of nowhere—an ostensibly shameful, stateless status which the old man cleverly turns to his own advantage in rejecting the Argives' claims for extradition (185–8). Similarly, the boundaries of actual states can represent political and ideological territories as well. We know that Argos (off stage to be sure but always lurking in the person of the Argive Herald and, later, of the Argive king Eurystheus himself) is the site of tyranny and violence, whereas Athens (represented by the Marathonian plain where the play is set) is the locus of, if not democracy, then an anachronistic inclusion of the people in the political process (335). The latter is a 'free city', *eleuthera polis* (62, 244, 287), where the king consults his people in open colloquy, *syllogon* (335), and where the fugitives have fled for their lives before the action of the play begins; a place where Lady Justice, *potnia Dikā* (104) is reverenced, and where even the king bends to custom/law (*nomos*) in suppressing his impulse to lay violent hands on the person of the insolent Argive Herald (268 ff.). By contrast, in Argos the Heraklids have 'masters', *despotai* (99), who 'rule over' them (*kratountes*, 100), just as Argos would make herself a mistress ruling over a subject (*hypēkoön*, 287) Athenian state.[1] In Argos, moreover, justice is no lady: it is, instead, the *leusimos dikē*, or death by stoning (60)— the awful punishment that awaits the enemies of the despot Eurystheus upon their return. It is also the place where violence, *bia* (47, 64, 71, 102, 106, etc.), goes unchecked.[2] Unlike the Athenian king, Demophon, the Argive Herald has no qualms about violating religious law by dragging the Heraklids from the sacrosanct space symbolized by the altar (72).

This tour of *Children of Herakles*'s geography, if brief and somewhat proleptic, will at least help to show how the contrasts between the play's various geographical and political spaces can be seen as belonging to the more general tragic dialectic of self and other. What we might call symbolic geography is a peculiar feature of Athenian tragedy, which prefers to displace its theatrical investigation of the *polis*'s own 'self' onto 'other' cities far

---

[1] *Hypēkoös* is, possibly, a loaded word: in Thucydides it is used to describe Athens' subject-allies (e.g., Thuc. 6. 22, 7. 57, 8. 2), but almost never occurs in the extant, overtly patriotic texts such as the Athenian funeral orations, as Loraux notes (*The Invention of Athens*, 81); the one exception, interestingly, is in Perikles' Funeral Oration (Thuc. 2. 41. 3). Mills (*Theseus, Tragedy*, 97–104) offers a useful discussion of the conflation of monarchic and democratic institutions in both *Children of Herakles* and *Suppliant Women*.

[2] For the theme of Argive *bia*, see Anne Pippin Burnett, 'Tribe and City, Custom and Decree in *Children of Heracles*', *CP* 71 (1976), 23; Burian, 'Euripides' Heracleidae', 6; and Falkner, 'The Wrath of Alcmene', 116.

from Athens; just as tragic woman functions as the negative model for the male self whose identity is the object of dramatic scrutiny, so too the cities of Thebes and Argos provide 'negative models' to Athens' image of itself.[3] And indeed, tragedy's topographical anti-Athenses indeed have much in common with tragedy's women. The self of which both Thebes (or Argos) and Greek drama's female characters are the negative models is Athenian, masculine, properly managed and well-organized, and has control over the structures and boundaries of his own body. Indeed the 'inviolable body of the male citizen' is, like that of the city itself, distinguished by well-ordered boundaries and borders, as opposed to the female's body, which is characterized, like the house in which she must remain, by hidden interior recesses; her body's tendency to perforation and leakage makes it 'accessible to penetration and casual aggression', and thus renders it like that of the male citizen's other radical other, the slave.[4] This conceptualization of the male and the female bodies informed the more general cultural association that naturally located men within the limits of the city, and women in the wild regions without—the geography, that is, that the social assignment of women to interior, private spaces and men to exterior, public spaces sought to correct. Thebes and Argos, those standard tragic locales, thus serve as the dis-places for Athens itself much as tragic woman serves to embody a radical otherness from the point of the Athenian male citizen. Both the geographical and gendered others are inextricably linked.[5]

[3] Zeitlin, 'Thebes: Theater of Self', 144–50. Hourmouziades remarks that '[n]one of Euripides' surviving tragedies . . . has its setting in Athens' (*Production and Imagination in Euripides: Form and Function of the Scenic Space* (Athens, 1965), 109). See his n. 1 on 109 for a discussion of the probability that the playwright's *Aigeus* and *Erekhtheus* were set in Athens; the *Theseus*, he argues however, was probably set in Crete, a supposition confidently taken up by Mills (*Theseus, Tragedy*, 252). Even if we take these lost works into account, what none the less emerges is a singular aversion to representing Athens itself on stage.

[4] Humphreys, *The Family, Women, and Death*, xxv, xx, and xxvi–xxvii; cf. Carson, 'Woman, Dirt, Desire'; David Halperin, *One Hundred Years of Homosexuality* (New York, 1990), 96; Loraux 'Le Lit, la guerre', *L'Homme*, 21 (1981), 36–67; Zeitlin, 'Playing the Other', 69–71; and cf. Loraux's remarks on 'Regions of the Body' in *Tragic Ways of Killing a Woman*, tr. Anthony Forster (Cambridge, Mass., 1987), 49–65.

[5] Just offers a useful and comprehensive account of the male : city :: female : wilds formula in *Women in Athenian Law*, 217–79. For the female as the

We must note, however, that in *Children of Herakles* the displacement from Athens to Argos is somewhat compromised. On the literal, geographical level, the drama's Marathonian setting makes it one of few extant tragedies in which Athens or her territories is represented. The city figures prominently as one of the play's real as well as ideological topographies, and hence is forced to share the stage with one of its 'dis-places': in this case, Argos. Such an explicit juxtaposition of Athens and her topographical 'others' occurs in relatively few other extant plays— Aeschylus' *Eumenides* (Delphi and Athens), Sophocles' *Oedipus at Colonus* (Thebes and the Athenian suburb of Colonus), and Euripides' *Ion* (Delphi and Athens), *Suppliant Women* (Argos and Eleusis, a cult site near Athens), the fragmentary *Erekhtheus* (Euboea and Athens), and, to a considerably lesser degree, the *Medea* (Corinth and Athens).

On the one hand, the dramatic contrapresentation of Athens and Argos in *Children of Herakles* makes the contrast between the political and ideological territories of the two cities more explicit: this is why the myth upon which the play is based was so often exploited for patriotic purposes. But this unusual superabundance of locales—one staged, the other implied but very much a presence as the drama unfolds—also creates a certain locational tension that threatens to undermine their discreteness and, hence, to problematize identity (as defined by opposition). The importation of Argive dramas into the Athenian territory represented on *Children of Herakles*'s stage precipitates a suppliant crisis which, as almost always the case with this favourite Euripidean device, threatens to blur the image that the body politic has of itself. A refusal on Athens' part to help the suppliants would undermine the sense of distinctiveness from the many other cities to which the Heraklids had already unsuccessfully appealed (15 f.): that sense of being different was, in fact, a key element of Athenian civic ideology.[6] Conversely, although

symbolic opposite of all that the *polis* represents, see Pierre Vidal-Naquet's discussion of 'the rule of women' (glossing Aesch. *Ag.* 599 *thēlykratēs*) in his essay 'Slavery and the Rule of Women', in *The Black Hunter: Forms of Thought and Forms of Society in the Greek World*, tr. Andrew Szegedy-Maszak (Baltimore, 1986), 208 ff.

[6] e.g. Perikles' proud assertion that Athens sets an example for other cities rather than mimicking them (Thuc. 2. 37. 1). An excellent short discussion of

Demophon does indeed resist the urge to harm the Argive Herald and thus violate religious law (271), his hot-blooded impulse is a very real if momentary threat to his moral superiority over his violent Argive counterpart, Eurystheus, whose representative the Herald is; the act would, if anything, make Demophon the double rather than the opposite of the Herald, who had earlier moved to lay hands on the suppliant Iolaos, a crime that incurs religious pollution, *miasma* (71). So even as the events that transpire when the off-stage Argos impinges on Attic space heighten our awareness of the conventional distinctions between those two places, they can also show how fragile those geographical distinctions, and all they represent, can be.

Similarly, the literal wanderings of *Children of Herakles*'s characters also take them through the murky territories that exist at the boundaries between masculine and feminine and their respective cultural and theatrical referents. The latter include, but are by no means restricted to, the aggressiveness and sometimes even violence that characterize men's explorations of and encounters with the outside world, with each other, and with women;[7] or, conversely, women's association with the family, with the interior of the house (*dōma, oikos*) that is the seat of family life. To take Iolaos once again: his flight from Argos to Attika not only deprives him of his civic identity, but creates a political crisis that is ultimately resolved by the Girl's offer of self-sacrifice. This act, which requires that she leave the inside space assigned to females, will heroize her 'on the male model'.[8] Yet her gesture also throws into high relief the impotent passivity of the old hero himself, whose own offer to help his kin is rebuffed (453 ff.). Although Iolaos is, to be sure, relegated to this passivity by his great old age, certain details suggest the particularly feminine character of his current state. So, for example, in his despair he withdraws into an artificial 'interior' created by the envelop-

what, to the Athenians, constituted the 'uniqueness' of their civilization can be found in Mills, *Theseus, Tragedy*, 56–78.

[7] As exemplified not only by the extreme example of the violent Argive king Eurystheus, but also by the more problematic instances of Demophon's impulse to abuse the Herald, and by the compressed allusion (743 f.) to Herakles' and Iolaos' slaughter of the sons of Hippokoön; cf. also the reference to Theseus' imprisonment in Hades, which was punishment for his attempted rape of Persephone (218 f.); the latter episode is discussed by Mills, *Theseus, Tragedy*, 7–10.   [8] Rabinowitz, *Anxiety Veiled*, 64.

ing folds of his robes, a gesture that recalls the similar veiling of
a modest young virgin only moments before (604; cf. 561).

Iolaos will, of course, eventually reclaim the manly might of
his heroic youth, as a result of the miraculous rejuvenation that is
one of the play's best-known, if least understood features. But he
does so only after travelling through the territory of the feminine—by 'playing the other', in the terms that Zeitlin has set out
in her study of gender and theatricality. As a result of the special
nature of the Girl's intervention—one that comes about as the
result of a violation of gendered propriety—the rejuvenated
Iolaos' restored heroic strength will not be, as it once was, merely an instrument with which to help his blood-kin and a vehicle
for obtaining personal renown; the note of self-sacrifice and
devotion to the city that she introduces is one that will resound
throughout the second half of the play. In this way her brief
moment of glory suggests some constructive uses to which the
feminine propensity for boundary-violation may be put. And indeed at the end of the play, the rejuvenated Iolaos will reclaim his
youthful prowess not in the guise of a legendary hero but as an
Athenian ephebe who literally follows in the footsteps of Athens'
legendary king, retracing the route of Theseus as he performed
his labours of political unification, and thus becoming an 'other
Theseus' just as Theseus himself was an 'other Herakles'. The
play between Athenian self and Argive other is one that Theseus'
epithet, *allos Hēraklēs*, 'another Herakles', indeed alludes to; and
I shall be appropriating that epithet in my section headings as
a reminder of how that original, mythic self–other mutation is
elaborately reflected and mutated throughout this work.

Children of Herakles's fictive setting thus provides a dynamic
backdrop against which identity is questioned and redefined, as
characters are forced to wander the indeterminate spaces
between the poles of Athens and Argos, inside and outside, self
and other. The emphasis on those in-between spaces constitutes
part of the playwright's critique of a radical polarization that
cannot integrate otherness: in this work, we see that the poles
themselves are highly unstable, threatening always to collapse
into each other. Rigid equations between the two genders and
certain cultural categories ('nature' and 'culture' most famously)
often oversimplify a complex reality, and Euripides' handling of

gender and the ideological terms it can represent seems, in fact, to be deliberately ambiguous, as if to caution against such over-simplifications.[9] We shall see how Iolaos is cast in many ways as a representative of heroic and aristocratic behaviour that, in its emphasis on the performance of spectacular feats of almost Homeric prowess in the service of one's own glory and the glory of one's kin, only seems the opposite of the withdrawn passivity associated with the feminine. Yet the narrow scope of his heroic allegiances causes Iolaos to flee his city, leaving him helpless and passive—a state marked by the verbal and gestural vocabulary of the feminine. The dark and enclosing folds of the robes with which Iolaos covers himself are a visual metaphor for the unen-lightened constraints of his own political vision.

At their extremes, masculinity and femininity are poles that, ironically, coalesce into sameness. This collapse, which blurs the categories of self and other, is related to another of the represen-tational strategies to be found in this play, one which also serves to confuse identity. I am speaking here of the process of redupli-cation—a kind of malignant metastasis of selves. The pairing of Herakles' two aged relatives, his comrade Iolaos and his mother Alkmene, is but one of many instances of doubling in the play.[10] *Children of Herakles* features two Athenian kings ('twofold offspring of Theseus', *dissous Theseōs paīdas*, 35); two groups of Herakles' children, the males led by Hyllos and the girls huddled with Alkmene within the sanctuary of Zeus Agoraios; of those two groups, there are two principles, Hyllos and the Girl;[11] two

[9] See esp. Foley's important critique ('The Conception of Women', 140–8) of the Lévi-Straussian male : culture :: female : nature model often invoked in structural anthropology and, she argues, too radically applied to Greek society, as for example in Sherry Ortner's article 'Is Female to Male as Nature is to Culture?' (in M. Rosaldo and L. Lemphere (eds.), *Woman, Culture, and Society* (Stanford, 1974), 67–88) and, more generally, in some of the writings of the French school of Vernant *et al*. Foley is more receptive to the analogy of female to domestic and male to public, though she argues that that model, too, is not unproblematic; see also her critique of Shaw, 'The Female Intruder' (= Foley, 'The Female Intruder Reconsidered').

[10] Iolaos and Alkmene are described as 'this aged pair', *duoin gerontoin*, 39; both are referred to as 'saviours' at 11 and 43. I owe many of these observations on role-doubling to Falkner, *Old Age*, 127 n. 9; see also Burnett, 'Tribe and City', 5 n. 4.

[11] Hyllos 'presides over', *presbuei*, the boys, 45; the same word is used of the Girl's relation to her sisters at 479.

villainous Argives (the Herald at the play's opening, Eurystheus at its close); and the supernatural team of Herakles and Hebe, who appear at the end of the battle scene as the twin deities of youth ('twin stars', *dissō . . . aster[e]*, 854). To this list one could also add the play's two virgin figures, one mortal and one divine, who are loosely associated with Athens and what it ideally represents (the Girl, Athena); and its two mature or matronly females—again, a woman and a goddess, this time linked with Argos and the cluster of attributes associated with that city (Alkmene, Hera). There are as well certain reduplications that indicate the play's bipartite structure: two references to formal supplication (cf. 225 f., by Iolaos, and 1015, by Eurystheus); two corresponding violations of the Hellenic custom regulating supplication (by the Argive Herald at the play's opening, and by Alkmene at its close); two theatrically conventional lackeys, the Servant and the Messenger, of whom we may say that one precipitates Iolaos' action against Eurystheus, and the other, Alkmene's; and, of course, two *poleis*, Athens and Argos.

Whether those two cities are in fact opposites or doublets of each other is, as we have seen, one of the issues that *Children of Herakles*'s dynamic of dislocation raises. The foregoing review of both the transformations and reduplications of characters and roles will show that a certain tension between radical otherness and a confusing propensity to multiplication of the self may be said to organize the play. Another line of my argument should be evident at this point. For these representational strategies— polarization, multiplication—may be said to correspond to the principles of diversity and unity that Saxonhouse sees as characteristic of the Greeks' political thought. The play's representational modes can thus be seen as a theatrical reflection of the terms of a contemporary political and indeed philosophical debate.[12]

---

[12] Before Saxonhouse, G. E. R. Lloyd famously argued that 'polarity' and 'analogy' were the two organizing modes in the archaic Greeks' argumentational method; see his *Polarity and Analogy: Two Types of Argumentation in Early Greek Thought* (Cambridge, 1971). For an interesting discussion of how the twin modes of 'homology' and 'inversion' structure another Euripidean work, the *Iphigenia in Tauris*, see Loris Belpassi, 'La "follia" del *genos*: Un'analisi del "discorso mitico" nel *Ifigenia Taurica* di Euripide', *QUCC* 34/1 (1990), 53–67, esp. 55 f.

Having briefly set out these organizing principles and
suggested how they will inform my interpretation of the play,
I want now to embark on a more detailed discussion of their
operations in one specific place: that is, in the play's fictive setting, Marathon, and at the altar that seems to stand at the centre
of that place—the 'property', we might say, invoking all of that
term's various connotations, where the Heraklids take refuge. I
say 'seems' because here too, even within the Attic, Marathonian
locale that houses the altar of Zeus Agoraios, the disruptive
dynamics of identity and opposition are at play, appropriately
(and quite literally) setting the stage for the transformations and
reduplications that will follow.

The Altar of Zeus Agoraios: Supplication and the Dynamics of Space

A hero is dead or missing, and his helpless kin are persecuted by
a wicked king; a woman, her children, a feeble old man cling des-
perately to the sanctuary provided by an altar. This is a familiar
Euripidean tableau.[13] Supplication itself, whether in real life or
on the Attic stage, is an act that inevitably evokes the powerful
dichotomy of sacred and profane space. According to the conventions of Greek supplication, the sanctuary (temenos) or the
altar within it confers inviolate status on those who establish
physical contact with it; the protected area defined by sanctuary
and/or altar constitutes what Louis Gernet calls a 'definite locale'
standing in implicit contrast to the unprotected secular space
around it.[14] Children of Herakles immediately establishes the
importance of this convention: as Iolaos sees the Argive Herald
coming once more in pursuit of him and his charges, he orders
Herakles' sons to take hold of his robe in order to establish contact with the altar and thus to come within the zone of protection

[13] As, for example, in Helen, Herakles, and Andromakhe. For a discussion of
this type of tableau as particularly useful for emphasizing the immobility and
passivity of the characters, see Michael R. Halleran, Stagecraft in Euripides
(Totowa, NJ, 1985), 80.

[14] See L. Gernet, The Anthropology of Ancient Greece, tr. John Hamilton and
Blaise Nagy (Baltimore, 1981), 183. For the dichotomies of sacred and profane
space in tragic scenes of supplication, see J. Kopperschmidt, Die Hikesie als
dramatische Form (diss. Tübingen, 1967). A comparative ethnographic discussion of the conventions of Greek supplication may be found in John Gould's
authoritative 'Hiketeia', JHS 93 (1973), 74–103.

(48 ff.). The extraordinary lengths to which we see both tragic and real-life Greek villains going in order to lure their prospective victims away from sanctuary demonstrates just how powerful the notion of this inviolate space was; the life-and-death dynamics of supplication would have been as real for Euripides' audience as they were rich in dramatic potential for the poet himself.[15] Thus the stage-picture with which *Children of Herakles* begins immediately and vividly foregrounds what will be the overarching themes of space and place, dislocation and displacement.

The spatial and moral balancing act of which the altar is the fulcrum is felt throughout the play. To ignore the suppliants would, first of all, invite religious and moral condemnation, as Iolaos' cry for help at 71 f. indicates: 'our sacred wreaths of supplication are defiled!—shame for the city, dishonour for the gods'. The same intertwining of civic and religious obligation is to be found again in the chorus's remark that 'it is an impious ("godless", *atheon*) thing for a *polis* to ignore the suppliant status of *xenoi*' (107 f.). But just as to ignore the suppliants would be to risk religious taboo, so too is it clear that to take up the suppliants' cause would entail considerable political risks. The Argive Herald threatens Demophon with war from without:

[15] The best-known examples from Athenian history of the violations of the norms of supplication are the cases of the would-be tyrant Kylon in the mid-7th cent. (Hdt. 5. 70–1; Thuc. 1. 126. 3–12; Plut. *Solon* 12. 1) and the murder of Pausanias, *c*.470 (Thuc. 1.128 ff.). For historical instances in which deceit played a role in removing suppliants from sanctuary, see Hdt. 6. 78–9 (Kleomenes lures the Argive suppliants by pretending they have been ransomed) and Plut. *Agis* 16, 19 (Leonidas falsely promises the suppliant Agis a safe welcome on leaving the sanctuary of Athena Khalkioikos). History also offers grisly examples of outright violations of sanctuary, with suppliants beaten and dragged from altars. Among the most notorious was the treatment of the Corcyrean oligarchs (Thuc. 3. 70 ff.), of whom those who were not dragged away from and killed in front of the *hiera* were entombed alive within them. Further examples are cited by Gould, 'Hiketeia', 82 f. Herodotos (3. 48. 1–4) offers a charming example of suppliants who outwit their violent oppressors. Euripidean references to sanctuary allude to these familiar dynamics of supplication as actually experienced in the 5th cent. In the *Mad Herakles*, the evil usurper Lykos resorts to threats of brute force, a gross violation of religious conventions similar to those reported by Thucydides. Alternatively, *Andromakhe* stresses the importance of the altar's sacral space by highlighting the ruse Hermione uses to lure Andromakhe from Thetis' altar—a variation on Megakles' false promises to Kylon, or Leonidas' to Agis.

Argos is a formidable enemy whose military might has already cowed many other city-states into giving up the suppliants (275 ff.). Yet the moral dilemma posed later by Kore's demand for human sacrifice threatens Demophon with war from within: a civil war between those Athenians willing to defend the Heraklids and those who would not (415 ff.). This tense interplay between the sacred and the purely political is already present in Euripides' choice of the altar of Zeus *Agoraios*, 'Zeus of the Agora' (70), as the setting for his play. The epithet indicates that the action is set at the sacred heart—that is, the altar itself—of a largely (but not entirely) secular space—the *agora*, the Greek *polis*'s 'center of assembly and commerce'.[16]

Yet if the spatial and ethical dichotomies engendered by tragic supplication remind us of the play's penchant for polarities, the supplicatory altar to which Iolaos (or rather, the actor who plays Iolaos) clings brings us back to the other of *Children of Herakles*'s representational modes: that is, reduplication. For the stage altar that is the focus of the play's opening tableau was one of actually two altars that were most likely present in the theatre of Dionysos and clearly visible to the Athenian audience, the other one being the *thymelē*, the permanent altar at which preliminary sacrifices were made and around which the chorus danced, and which was most probably not used as a stage property in the drama.[17] Iolaos' many references to the altar until his rescue by

---

[16] Padel, 'Making Space Speak', in Winkler and Zeitlin, *Nothing to Do with Dionysos?*, 337; so too Wilkins, who points out that this altar is associated with 'the commercial and legal functions of the Agora' (*Euripides* Heraclidae, 59 ad 70).

[17] So Arthur Pickard-Cambridge, *The Theatre of Dionysus in Athens* (Oxford, 1946), 131, where he asserts that the use of the *thymelē* as a stage property would have been 'unseemly'. Concurring with Pickard-Cambridge are Peter Arnott, *Greek Scenic Conventions in the Fifth Century B.C.* (Oxford, 1962), 42–56; Hourmouziades, *Production and Imagination*, 75; Padel, 'Making Space Speak', 340 n. 17; and Joe Park Poe, 'The Altar in the Fifth-Century Theater', *Classical Antiquity*, 8 (1989), 138f., with his bibliography. Hourmouziades (*Production and Imagination*, 75 n. 4) notes that in Aeschylus fr. 379 Mette (attributed to *Prometheus Fire-Bringer*), the expression *kyklōi peristēte* ('stand round in a circle') makes it 'almost certain that the reference is to an altar at the centre of the orchestra'. (For an argument that there was only one altar in the 5th-cent. theatre, however, see Rush Rehm, 'The Staging of Suppliant Plays', *GRBS* 29 (1988) 264–71.) In *Children of Herakles*, the altar, *bōmos*, is mentioned at 33, 44, 61, 73, 79, 124, 196, 238, 244, 249, 344. All of the

Demophon would thus have had two visual referents, like much else in this complex work: one real, the other symbolic, intended for 'play'.

There is in fact one further instance of 'double vision' created by the stage altar that represented that of Zeus of the Agora. For the *agora* is a place that itself has connections to the history of the Greek theatre. Before theatre was institutionalized, the *agora* functioned as a theatre; the theatre's *orkhēstra* was the part of the *agora* where the dancing-floor had been. Later, the theatre became what Webster called 'a sort of duplicate *agora*', because in both places citizen men came together in large groups, and in both places they listened, as the collective civic entity, to important speeches about the nature of the *polis*. 'Both [i.e. the theatre and the *agora*] qualify for the barbarian's suspicious description, as reported by the Athens-struck Greek historian, of the *agora*, 'a place set apart in the middle of the city, in which men get together and tell one another lies".'[18]

This overdetermination of the connections between the altar, the city, and the theatre helps us to answer a question raised most recently by Wilkins, who has wondered about the strangeness of Zeus Agoraios as the object of the Heraklids' appeal. 'Why is the appeal not to Zeus Hikesios, Aidoios, or Soter?', he asks: that is, to the Zeus of Suppliants, or Zeus who has due Reverence for supplication, or Zeus the Saviour (i.e. of suppliants). The question is especially apt in view of the alternative (though probably late) tradition, reported by Apollodoros and a scholiast on Aristophanes' play *The Knights*, that the famous supplication of the Heraklids took place in the Athenian *agora* at the Altar of Pity (*Eleou Bōmos*).[19] A quick glance at Aeschylus' *Suppliants* pro-

play's references to the altar thus occur during the prologue and first episode— that is, until the successful completion of the play's 'rescue' action, and before the news of Kore's oracle is announced.

[18] Padel, 'Making Space Speak', 337; cf. T. B. L. Webster, *Greek Theatre Production* (London, 1956), 5.

[19] Wilkins, *Euripides* Heraclidae, 60 ad 70. Cf. the similar rhetorical objection put by Vincent J. Rosivach, 'The Altar of Zeus Agoraios', *PP* 33 (1978) 32; Rosivach adds Zeus Xenios to Wilkins's list. For the Altar of Pity, see Apollod. 2. 8. 1, and the scholiast on Arist. *Hipp.* 1151. Wilkins rightly comments that this tradition is probably a *post factum* attempt at regularizing the myth. For Zeus Agoraios, see L. R. Farnell, *Cults of the Greek States* (Chicago, 1951), i. 58f., and cf. the discussion of Rosivach (37f.).

vides a clue. In the Aeschylean drama, the suppliant women first make their appeal at the altar of Zeus Aidoios, in due observance of certain religious conventions (Aesch. *Su.* 192); later on, however, they are advised to go to the altars of local deities in order to win the favour of the people (Aesch. *Su.* 480 ff.)—their motivation at that point being more purely political. Here we might recall that it is Zeus Agoraios—that is, 'Zeus who presides over assemblies and trials'—who presides over Orestes' triumphal acquittal at the end of Aeschylus' *Eumenides* (Aesch. *Eum.* 973). In Euripides' play, then, political considerations are foregrounded by the particular setting the playwright has chosen for the action: the children of Herakles are 'appealing to the *people* of Marathon and Attica . . . to their democratic institutions'.[20] In this way the altar of Zeus Agoraios specifically underscores the political—i.e. 'things having to do with the *polis*'. Its centrality in the work's spatial discourse doubly reflects the centrality of both the theatre and the *agora* in the ideological topography of the democratic *polis* itself.

The Centre Cannot Hold: Athens vs. Attika

Yet the altar, despite its central location, turns out to be as ambiguous as the other spaces and locations in this play are, reminding us that every place in *Children of Herakles* has a 'displace' that, if anything, calls into question the nature of boundaries and space. For the apparently overdetermined centrality of the altar of Zeus Agoraios (which stands, so it would seem, at the centre of a centre, the *agora*) is undercut by the fact that this altar is located not in the heart of Athens, as one is indeed tempted to think, but in the Marathonian Tetrapolis (32), a place to which Iolaos later refers as the outer limits, *termonai* (37), of Athens— not its centre, but rather its edges, the suburbs, a 'neutral' space.[21] The spatial primacy of the altar in religious and civic terms, therefore, is offset by the marginality of its geographical location. This altar, then, may be best described as a centre located at the centre (an *agora*) of a periphery (Athens' outlying territories), and thus symbolizes the delicate equilibrium between centrality and marginality, place and dislocation, that is

[20] Wilkins, *Euripides* Heraclidae, 60.

[21] So Chalkia, *Lieux et espace*, 140: note that this is how she describes *Suppliant Women*'s Eleusis as well.

itself central (if we may safely use that term) to the play's signi-
fying strategy.

Those tensions are, as we have seen, often too great to maintain in equilibrium—with the result that even *within* the Attic
territory that supposedly stands in stark contrast to the geographical and moral 'other', Argos, the boundaries between
seemingly discrete places (on-stage Marathon, off-stage Athens)
become blurred. Indeed, if the play's liminal Attic milieu seems
to exist in uneasy suspension with its more specific and central
setting in an *agora*, any certainty we might have about the play's
Tetrapolitan location is itself subverted, in fact, by contradictory
evidence that we are after all in Athens itself. The immediate
appearance, upon Iolaos' calls for help, of an Athenian chorus
(69)—and indeed, only a bit later, of the Athenian kings
Demophon and Akamas (120); the deictic references by both the
Argive Herald and Iolaos to Athens (157, 198; cf. 461, 491, 511,
1026); and, finally, Demophon's casual invitation to Iolaos *et al.*
to enter the (i.e. his own) palace at 340ff., indicating that the
Athenian royal abode is at no great remove: all these have been
taken as signs that the audience is meant to think of Athens itself
as the play's proper setting.[22]

In fact, this indifference to spatial realities serves a special
dramatic and civic point.[23] First, as we have seen, it contributes
to the overall sense of dislocation—the confusion out of which
the various characters will construct their proper identities. But
even more, the striking indeterminacy of location that characterizes this play allows the poet to invoke the symbolic value of

[22] For the way in which the implied (i.e. Athenian) effaces the actual
(Marathonian) setting, see Antonio Garzya, *Euripide Eraclidi* (Milan, 1958), 50
ad loc.; Zuntz, *The Political Plays of Euripides*, 97–104; Hourmouziades,
Production and Imagination, 126; Chalkia, *Lieux et espace*, 143. For 'the pre-
ponderance of the imaginary area over the actual scenery' in other Euripidean
dramas such as *IT* and *Bacchae*, see Hourmouziades at pp. 123–5, and cf. also
Chalkia, pp. 92 f.

[23] Wilamowitz tried to argue that the references to Athens were meant to con-
jure the state—that is, the 'idea'—of Athens, but not its actual boundaries ('de
Euripidis Heraclidis', 77), but Zuntz argues that the opposite is in fact 'demon-
strably true', and that the doubling is 'a basic feature of the play' (*The Political
Plays of Euripides*, 99). For another argument *contra* Wilamowitz, though along
very different lines from those of Zuntz and myself, see Wilkins, 'The Young of
Athens', 330 n. 24.

Marathon and various other Attic locales while keeping the focus trained on Athens itself. By intentionally blurring the boundaries between Athens and the Tetrapolis, Euripides is able to assimilate Athens to Marathon.

This dramatic gesture is a noteworthy reflection of contemporary rhetorical strategies of Athenian self-representation. In the Athenian civic vocabulary, 'Marathon' had especially rich resonance. The site of Hellenic victory over Persian invasion, Marathon was, more specifically, the locus of Athens' greatest military feat, 'a decisive stage . . . a purely Athenian victory', that was repeatedly recalled as part of the rhetoric of Athenian political and civic supremacy.[24] Allusions to the norms of civic behaviour that were exemplified by that historical event and subsequently enshrined in fifth-century civic rhetoric, are to be found throughout this play, conjoined with and sometimes standing in opposition to the recollections of purely mythical, heroic obligations and exploits, of which Iolaos is the living symbol; just so was the Athenians' legendary assistance to the Heraklids repeatedly invoked as the natural precedent of the real-life heroics of the *Marathonomakhoi* who vanquished the Persians.[25] The play's conflation of Athens and Marathon thus mirrors the strategy of contemporary Athenian civic discourse by which the pre-democratic but still influential ethos of heroic valour, with its emphasis on allegiance to kin (*genos*), had to be subordinated to the democratic imperative that citizens cherish and acquiesce in the values of the city (*polis*). That ideological project of realigning aristocratic, clan-orientated values with democratic, *polis*-orientated ones was expressed in rhetorical guarantees of heroic glory to ordinary citizens, or as Loraux puts it by 'transform[ing] the citizens into epic heroes'[26]—just as

[24] Loraux, *The Invention of Athens*, 30. See e.g. Thuc. 2. 34, marking Marathon as a turning point in the funerary customs for those who died in battle; Lysias 2. 25; Demosthenes, *On Organization* 21; in Plato's *Menexenos* (240e1–6) it is 'the radiant model on which every future event ought to be modeled and of which innumerable imitations were already to be found in the current history of Athens' (Loraux, *Invention*, 120). The Athenian orators' emphasis on the critical importance of Marathon explains why those orators turned the second Persian War into 'a mere epilogue of the Athenian victory at Marathon', as Loraux puts it (133).

[25] See Loraux, *The Invention of Athens*, 61, referring to Hdt. 9. 27; Plato, *Menexenos* 239b–d; Dem. 8–10.   [26] Loraux, *The Invention of Athens*, 154.

Children of Herakles's own endorsement of democratic and co-operative over aristocratic and individualistic virtues is expressed in its literal transformation of an epic hero, Iolaos, into a model hoplite and citizen.

This transformation (or, perhaps better, assimilation) calls to mind another set of boundaries that we find in *Children of Herakles*. I refer here to those that separate the pre-democratic, legendary past from the realities of Euripides' Athens; the action of the play will ultimately move the Heraklids from the former space to the latter. In order to see how this mediation is accomplished, we must first explore the ethical and political terrain inhabited by the Heraklids' spokesman and indeed the play's true protagonist: Iolaos.

Pre-Democratic Paradigms

The central figure in *Children of Herakles*'s opening tableau is Iolaos himself. In order to understand the political implications of his geographical displacement from Argos to Athens (as well as his displacement into the territory of the feminine), it is first necessary to identify the coordinates that originally establish this character's position on the political and ethical map. Inasmuch as he is a male, of course, Iolaos represents the 'self' for Euripides' audience of citizen men. But even more, both the style and the content of his utterances on stage mark him, from the standpoint of that audience *as Athenians*, as 'other'—that is, as the representative of an aristocratic, pre-democratic ethos. Various commentators have noted how the old man's speeches are replete with the echoes of Homer and Pindar. He is the living embodiment of a heroic age when action was motivated both by a fierce and sometimes murderous allegiance to kin, *genos*, and by the knowledge that lives lost in serving honour were compensated by deathless renown, *kleos*. The special theatrical atmosphere created by Iolaos' self-conscious references to this milieu constitute what one critic refers to as *Children of Herakles*'s 'illusion of a heroic world', its 'reversion to a Homeric morality'.[27] In order

---

[27] Fitton, *The Suppliant Women*, 452 and 460. The play's archaic milieu is also conveyed by what some scholars see as its 'Aeschylean style and language' (Fitton, 458 n. 3: he cites esp. *Hkld.* 388/*Persians* 827 and *Hkld.* 349/*Septem* 514); see also W. Breitenbach, *Untersuchungen zur Sprache der Euripideischen*

to underscore Iolaos' antique morality, the play refers more than once to epic and epinician topoi, from the archaizing aphorisms through which Iolaos expresses himself to his near-verbatim quotations from Homer.

Iolaos establishes his heroic credentials at the beginning of the prologue. What has brought him to his present predicament, he asserts (6 ff.), is his reverence for two principles: *syngeneia*, literally 'consanguinity' and here meaning allegiance to those who are members of the same blood-kinship group or *genos*; and *aidōs*, the powerful and proleptic sense of shame that guarded against dishonourable action, and a signal Homeric virtue.[28] Here is Iolaos himself on the powerful motivation of *genos* and *aidōs*:

> ἐγὼ γὰρ αἰδοῖ καὶ τὸ συγγενὲς σέβων,
> ἐξὸν κατ' Ἄργος ἡσύχως ναίειν, πόνων
> πλείστων μετέσχον εἷς ἀνὴρ Ἡρακλέει,
> ὅτ' ἦν μεθ' ἡμῶν· νῦν δ', ἐπεὶ κατ' οὐρανὸν
> ναίει, τὰ κείνου τέκν' ἔχων ὑπὸ πτεροῖς
> σῴζω τάδ' αὐτὸς δεόμενος σωτηρίας.

But I, mindful of shame (*aidōs*) and reverencing kinship (*to syngenes*)—
and even though I could have rested easy back in Argos—
I was the one man who shared with Herakles his many labours
when he was among us. But now, since he's dwelt
in Heaven, I've taken his children under my wings
hoping to save them, though I myself need saving.

(6–11)

Inasmuch as *aidōs*, the sense of honour reinforced by a fear of shame, lay primarily in respecting obligations to kin (*genos*) and comrades (*hetairoi*), however, we may see the two terms as intri-

---

Lyrik (Stuttgart, 1934), 122. For the *genos* as the ideological and moral 'anti-culture' of the democratic Athenian *polis* in Euripides' *Iphigenia in Tauris*, see Belpassi, 'La "follia" del *genos*', 64 ff.

[28] For *genos* and *aidōs* in this sense, see David J. Bradshaw, 'The Ajax Myth and the Polis: Old Values and New', in Pozzi and Wickersham, *Myth and the Polis*, 100. Sophocles' Ajax, like Iolaos, is a legendary hero forced to confront a contemporary, everyday reality. For *aidōs* in Homer, see James Redfield, *Nature and Culture in the Iliad* (Chicago, 1975), 113–19. For *aidōs* and *aiskhynē* in this play as a reflection of the 'traditional ethical code' of the 'noble man', see Rosivach, 'The Altar of Zeus Agoraios', 42.

cately interconnected, as indeed they are throughout this play.[29] Formerly, Iolaos' *aidōs* was evident in his devotion to his kinsman Herakles, which is expressed in the many instances of compound words beginning with *syn-* or *meta-* ('with') and *para-* ('alongside') that are used to describe Iolaos in relation to Herakles, whose labours Iolaos shared (*meteskhon*, 8) and whose trusty comrade-in-arms (*pistos parastatēs*, 125; cf. 88), ally (*symmakhos*), and fellow-voyager (*symplous*, 216) on the Labour among the Amazons he once was.[30] Now that Herakles is dead, Iolaos' sense of *aidōs* similarly dictates his behaviour with respect to his dead comrade's children, thereby allowing him once again to honour both *genos* and *aidōs* in terms that are by now familiar: 'Along with these refugee children I too flee-with (*ego de syn pheugousi sympheugō teknois*), and suffer-along-with them even as they too fare ill (*kai syn kakōs prassousi symprassō kakōs*, 26 f.).

Iolaos' affirmation of his own sense of *aidōs* thus goes hand in hand with his exaltation of the tribe, *genos*, before all other social forms, as Ann Burnett has observed:

> The hero of this play is the *genos*, and this is what the principals—Iolaos, Macaria [i.e. the Girl], the invisible Hyllus, Alcmena, and the two groups of children who are seen but not heard—represent in their exuberant multiplicity. Iolaus spells it all out in his opening speech. The best man is δίκαιος τοῖς πέλας (2); he is so by blood and birth (πέφυκ', 2), and being so he is useful to his city and pleasing to his friends. The inner group that is not quite synonymous with city or friends, the group toward which one's most essential duties are felt, is the tribe (41, 45). Iolaus himself has chosen it over city and property (14), freely joining in the Heraclid exile (7) because of his sense of kinship.[31]

The emphasis on 'blood and birth' is, as we shall see, consistent with Iolaos's world-view; it is this (rather than *nomos* as Zuntz argues) that motivates the old hero. The appeal to *aidōs* is,

[29] 'Honoring such family ties is most characteristic of the type of loyalty implicit in the term *aidôs*', Bradshaw writes of Ajax's devotion to both Tekmessa and Eurysakes, 'and Sophocles gives repeated emphasis to the importance and depth of Ajax's familial relations' ('The Ajax Myth', 118). Euripides similarly stresses the extent of Iolaos' allegiance to his kin in *Children of Herakles*.

[30] I owe this observation to Falkner, 'The Wrath of Alcmene', 119f.

[31] Burnett, 'Tribe and City', 14.

moreover, representative not merely of a heroic or even Homeric milieu but, more critically for the play's political discourse, of a pre-democratic world-view—'the individual imperative of aristocratic society'.[32] In the civic discourse of fifth-century Athens, the *genos* was understood to be the form of social organization representing a birth elite that is associated with particularly noble lineage and hence aristocracy. Moreover, the preoccupation with *genos* in either of its prevalent meanings (that is, as either 'good family' or 'high birth') had connotations for the citizen audience that were other than merely social. Aristotle, for example, identifies high birth, *genos*, as a defining characteristic of oligarchy.[33] It therefore seems likely that in the minds of Euripides' audience, the old man's first utterance would have allied him with a form of both social and political exclusivity that stood in stark contrast with the communal and democratic ideology glorified in the speeches of Athenian orators.

Stylistic, thematic, and linguistic elements drawn from Homeric and Pindaric contexts highlight Iolaos' status as the representative of a pre-democratic world-view. The old hero's characteristic mode of self-expression throughout the play is, to begin with, the *gnōmē*, the sententious aphorism, one of which opens the play (1–5). Iolaos' frequent use of gnomes befits someone of his great age—and 'age' could refer here both to his years and to the era of which he is the representative in the play. The play's first two words, *palai pot[e]*, 'Long ago, back when . . .', indicate that the gnome that follows belongs to a bygone era. Moreover, the sentiments expressed by Iolaos are topoi familiar from epic and epinician contexts. For one thing, he seems as motivated by a fear of being ill spoken of as he is by his desire to

---

[32] Burnett, 'Tribe and City', 8. Zuntz, *The Political Plays of Euripides*, 27 calls Iolaos the 'champion of *nomos* [who] finds himself abandoned in distress'. But Iolaos' helpless predicament is the result of his refusal to acknowledge a social code other than the heroic, or a political code other than that of his own aristocratic *genos*. Only later does he become a 'champion' of a truly *political* system.

[33] *Politics* 1317[b]39–41. See Ober, *Mass and Elite*, 118 and 252; cf. Denis Roussel, *Tribu et cité: Études sur les groupes sociaux dans les cités grecques aux époques archaïque et classique* (Paris, 1976), 74 ff. on the 'real prestige' guaranteed by *genos* associations. The powerful aristocratic *genē*, as Ober notes, may not in *fact* have been archaic realities, but rather retrojected fantasies that served the polemical purposes of democratic politicians (Ober, 56 n. 8 and 252).

help his kin (27 ff.): 'I am loath to betray them, lest some man speak of me thus (*mē tis hōd' eipēi brotōn*): "See how, now that these children no longer have a father, Iolaos wouldn't defend them, although he is their kin."' The rhetorical motif of anonymous derogatory discourse is, to be sure, found in tragedy, as in a famous passage in Sophocles' *Ajax* (500 ff.), in which Ajax's concubine Tekmessa proudly refuses to speak unworthily of him; but the device is much better known from epic.³⁴ Moreover, that Iolaos succeeded in achieving good repute or *kleos* during his youth is made clear in his subsequent exchange with the chorus, who have inquired about his identity: 'This body of mine is not unknown' (literally 'unheralded', *akērykton*), he tells the chorus (89; cf. 203 f., 'I myself was often bowed by a burden of praise'); and they respond that they have indeed heard of him (*eisakousas*), long ago (89). Hence the old hero's quasi-Homeric sensitivity to the possibility of bad repute goes together with self-descriptions that liken him to the victorious athletes at Panhellenic games, whose victories were first announced at the games by heralds, *kērykes*, and were subsequently commemorated in songs like those of Pindar. And the origins of Iolaos' *kleos*, as well as its aural reception by the chorus, are relegated to a historical moment (*prin*, 90) that is contemporaneous with the distant one that generated Iolaos' antiquated opening *sententia* (*palai pot' esti*, etc., 1 ff.).

Iolaos' preoccupation with *genos* and *syngeneia*, articulated in language that thus recalls both epic and epinician odes, not only motivates his flight to Attika, but is the operating assumption underlying his claim to aid by Theseus' sons. He argues that Demophon is obligated to the Heraklids because they are, first of

---

³⁴ Indeed, this device appears to be employed in the Sophoclean passage precisely in order to underscore that play's distinctive Homeric ambience. The Greek in the Euripidean passage is remarkably similar to that in the *Ajax*: cf. *Hkld.* 27 ff. . . . ὀκνῶν προδοῦναι, μή τις ὧδ' **εἴπῃ** βροτῶν· | Ἴδεσθ', ἐπειδὴ παισὶν οὐκ ἔστιν πατήρ, | Ἰόλαος οὐκ ἤμυνε συγγενὴς γεγώς, and *Ajax* 500 ff.: καί τις πικρὸν πρόσφθεγμα δεσποτῶν **ἐρεῖ** | λόγοις ἰάπτων· ἴδετε τὴν ὁμευνέτιν . . . τοιαῦτ' **ἐρεῖ** τις. *Il.* 6. 459, Hektor's speech to Andromakhe, is usually cited as the Homeric referent for the Sophoclean allusion: καί ποτέ τις **εἴπῃσιν** ἰδὼν κατὰ δάκρυ χέουσαν . . . ὥς ποτέ τις **ἐρέει** κτλ. See Jebb's comments in *Sophocles. The Plays and Fragments,* vii: *Ajax. Text with Notes and Commentary* (Cambridge, 1896), 82 ad loc.

all, cousins (205 ff.); he mentions the word *genos* twice in rapid
succession (209, 213).[35] As we might expect, this reference to the
claims of *genos* are followed immediately by another appeal to the
claims imposed by what Bradshaw calls the 'normative image of
aidōs': that is, the duty to assist one's *hetairoi*, one's companions-
in-arms.[36] For in addition to the ancient blood relationship connecting the Theseids to the Heraklids, the old man says, there
was the relationship between Herakles and Theseus as *hetairoi*
who made an expedition together to steal the death-dealing belt
of the Amazon queen (214–17).[37] In the same speech, Iolaos
mentions Herakles' rescue of Theseus from Hades (218 f.: the
twelfth Labour), thereby reminding the Athenian kings that
they owe the children of Herakles not only the obligation entailed by *syngeneia*, but that of the saved to the saviour—a strong
reminder of how easily the saviour-self may become the saved-
other. The old man's reminder at 219 that 'all Hellas was
witness' to the deeds he described is surely intended as a spur to
proper *aidōs* on Demophon's part.

Iolaos' genealogical digression at 205–13 thus not only serves
to recall yet another Homeric topos, thereby strengthening the
sense of his heroic and epic character,[38] but more importantly

[35] Herakles' mother, Alkmene, is a granddaughter of Pelops, as was Theseus'
mother Aithra (207 ff.); the Theseids and Heraklids are thus third cousins to
each other. Burian agrees that this claim 'evokes a world of heroic values', but
only in implied contrast with the Herald's 'political opportunism' ('Euripides'
Heracleidae', 5).   [36] Bradshaw, 'The Ajax Myth', 113.
   [37] The importance of that shared experience is overdetermined in this play by
the fact that Euripides seems here to be following, or perhaps even inventing, a
version of the ninth Labour in which Herakles seeks the Amazon's girdle not for
Admeta, Eurystheus' daughter, but for Theseus himself. For this, see Garzya
ad loc. The state of the text, which almost certainly contains a lacuna after 217,
makes too much certainty in determining which myth Euripides uses here
impossible; see Wilkins's note ad loc., *Euripides* Heraclidae, 79 f. Alternatively
(or additionally), Demophon's indebtedness to the Heraklids may be attributed
to the fact that, as a result of that expedition, Theseus won as a bride the queen
of the Amazons, either Hippolyta or Antiope, who according to Pindar was
Demophon's mother (Pindar fr. 176 Snell). This detail further shows the degree
to which the *aidōs*-related claim that Iolaos makes of Demophon is connected,
in this case quite concretely, with *genos*.
   [38] As noted by Fitton ('The Suppliant Women', 452): 'The γένος [*genos*]
claim imparts a heroic, almost archaic flavour . . . Here the γένος claim together
with the later εὐγένεια [*eugeneia*] theme, emphasises the great name of the ances-
tor, and confirms the dramatic illusion of a heroic world.'

implicates the Athenian king and indeed Athens herself in the complex system of *syngeneia* and *aidōs* associated thus far with Iolaos. Iolaos himself assumes that the Athenians will aid the suppliants, even to the death, because they share an ethical code (200ff.): 'Well do I know the character and nature (*physin*) of these men: they'll die for us. For shame (*aiskhynē*) comes before mere survival in the reckoning of noble men (*esthlois*).' The appeal to the Athenians' sense of shame (*aiskhynē* recapitulates the etymologically related *aidōs*) is by now familiar. The fervent belief that *physis*, 'inborn nature' will inevitably be revealed in action recalls Iolaos' use of that word *pephyke* in his opening gnome (2). Burnett glosses this word in the earlier passage as 'blood and birth'; and we should remember that in the fifth century, *physis* is often meant to convey 'an aristocratic bias', especially as it is paired here with reference to the class of *esthloi*, 'nobles'.[39] Appropriately enough, the whole sentiment is expressed in yet another archaizing gnome.

Demophon's almost immediate acquiescence to Iolaos' appeal is couched in terms that make it clear that he subscribes to the same ethical code as does Iolaos himself. In his attempt to intimidate the Athenian king with the possibility of civil unrest, the Argive Herald cannily appeals to the same anxiety about ill-repute that preoccupied Iolaos, insinuating that any defence of the Heraklids will destroy the Athenian king's reputation among his subjects (165–8). Yet the Athenian agrees to protect the suppliants. The three reasons he gives for doing so dovetail neatly with Iolaos' expectations. Demophon recognizes the strong moral claims of both *aidōs* and *genos*; Iolaos' reference to the necessity, *anankē*, of honouring those claims (205) is answered by Demophon's use of the same word in his response to Iolaos' supplication: 'Three avenues of thought compel me (*m'anankaz-ousi*, 236) not to dismiss your request,' he begins. Demophon first mentions his piety—the religious obligation imposed on the supplicand (238–9). Next, he accepts the validity of the appeal to *syngeneia*, and to his obligation to repay his father's debt— a commitment that reminds us that 'this is the archaic world of Epos and not contemporary Athens'.[40] Lastly and most

[39] See E. R. Dodds, *Plato: Gorgias* (Oxford, 1959), 13. In *Ol.* 2. 86 and 9. 100, Pindar comments on the superiority of aristocratic *physis* to *aretai* that can be taught.   [40] Fitton, 'The Suppliant Women', 452.

important of all, Demophon intends to avoid disgrace, *aiskhron*, at all costs (242). Demophon's angry final words to the Herald demonstrate the extent to which the Athenian's personal status is linked in his mind to his treatment of the suppliants, because of the obligations imposed by both *aidōs* and *syngeneia*: 'Nor will you shame *me* (*aiskhynas eme*) by dragging off these people', he declares (285 f.).[41]

Iolaos' triumphant outcry on hearing Demophon's acquiescence confirms him in his aristocratic outlook while underscoring the extent to which the Athenian king's actions conform to it:

> οὐκ ἔστι τοῦδε παισὶ κάλλιον γέρας,
> ἢ πατρὸς ἐσθλοῦ κἀγαθοῦ πεφυκέναι
> γαμεῖν τ' ἀπ' ἐσθλῶν· ὃς δὲ νικηθεὶς πόθῳ
> κακοῖς ἐκοινώνησεν, οὐκ ἐπαινέσω,
> τέκνοις ὄνειδος οὕνεχ' ἡδονῆς λιπεῖν.
> τὸ δυστυχὲς γὰρ ηὐγένει' ἀμύνεται
> τῆς δυσγενείας μᾶλλον·

For children there is no finer prize of honour (*geras*) than this:
to be born to (*pephykēnai*) a fine and noble (*esthlou*) father
and to marry into a noble (*esthlōn*) house. But he who, vanquished
    by desire,
throws in his lot with base men—he will find no praise from me;
he leaves his children an inheritance of shame, all for the sake of
    his own pleasure.
Nobility of birth (*eugeneia*) is a better defence in adversity
than is lowly birth (*dysgeneias*).

(297–303)

Here, in yet another gnomic context, the use of *geras*, 'prize of honour', and the allusion to the formal language of poetic praise (*epainesō*, 300) introduce further Homeric and Pindaric notes that set the tone for aristocratic and indeed even 'reactionary' sentiments: preoccupation with high birth, *eugeneia*; intermarriage among the *esthloi*—'the quality', to give this word its proper, almost Hesiodic sense; and an emphasis on inborn nature, *physis* (*pephykenai* here recalling the earlier references

---

[41] A. W. H. Adkins argues that the lines are proof that Demophon is acting like a 'Homeric *agathos*' (*Merit and Responsibility* (Oxford, 1960), 157 f.). It is fear of being associated with *aiskhron* (700) that motivates Iolaos' famous arming scene later in the play (700 f.).

to *physis* and *phyō*). The collocation of *eugeneia* and *physis* was a particularly charged one in the civic discourse of democratic Athens, where *eugeneia* represented 'the wellspring of those qualities of mind and spirit that made a nobleman a superior person. Intellectual and moral proclivities are traced back to character, which, in the final analysis, is determined genetically'.[42]

Moments later (324 ff.), a grateful Iolaos is inspired to promise that he will one day bring good word of Demophon to his dead father in Hades. The passage (which again stresses Iolaos' preoccupation with *eugeneia* and with being an *esthlos*) has a distinctly Odyssean and Homeric feel. Demophon is clearly *eugenēs*, the old man declares (324); his act both proves his noble paternity and literally 'saves' his good reputation as his father's own true son (*sōizei patrōian doxan*, 325). What the Athenian king has done demonstrates that he is sprung (*phys*) from noble stock (*ex esthlōn de phys*, 325), and that the son is no worse (*kakiōn*, 326) in spirit and deed than was the legendary father—a distinction that indeed only one man in very many can claim (327 f.). These lines represent the acme of heroic praise, recalling the famous words of the disguised Athena to Telemakhos at *Odyssey* 2. 276–7: 'Few (*pauroi*) are the children who live up to their fathers; most are inferior (*kakious*), few (*pauroi*) are superior to their fathers.' And Iolaos' promise to give word of Demophon to the dead Theseus brings to mind another striking Odyssean moment: the dead Achilles' request for news of his own son from Odysseus, who has arrived, living, in the Underworld (*Od.* 11. 492–540). At the climax of that passage, Achilles rejoices to hear that his son, too, has achieved renown as a warrior.[43]

---

[42] W. Donlan, *The Aristocratic Ideal in Ancient Greece* (Lawrence, Kan., 1980), 139. For the Homeric resonances of *geras*—'no less important than *kleos*'—see Loraux, *The Invention of Athens*, 100. For the collocation of *esthlos* and *eugeneia* in tragedy, cf. Antigone's comment to Ismene at Soph. *Ant.* 37 f., 'You will soon show whether you are noble by birth (*eugenēs pephykas*) or merely a base women of noble stock (*esthlōn kakē*:).' For this passage as 'reactionary'— typically so, in tragic discussions of nature and nurture—see Edith Hall, 'The Sociology of Athenian Tragedy', in P. E. Easterling (ed.), *The Cambridge Companion to Greek Tragedy* (Cambridge, 1997), 99.

[43] Another heroic topos: Iolaos will later lament what he believes to be his imminent death only because it would give pleasure to his enemies—another example of his 'antique morality' (443 f.). It is also possible that Iolaos' desire to

The Politics of Dislocation

Demophon's decision to aid the Heraklids appears to bring the first episode—that is, the first rescue action—to a swift and successful conclusion, one that reasserts the validity of a heroic and even Homeric world-view. Athens has demonstrated her *eugeneia* (302: here as elsewhere, a word linked to *syngeneia*) by nobly passing the 'test' (*peiran*, 309) posed by the Heraklids' supplication; the noble sons of Theseus demonstrate through their noble actions that they are indeed *syngeneis* (305) to their Argive kin.[44] And yet as soon as the chorus has concluded its brief but ecstatic hymn to Athens following Demophon's departure (353–80), another dilemma presents itself, one that *eugeneia* seems to be unable to resolve. This inadequacy implicitly points to the fatal flaw in the world-view characterized by a preoccupation with *eugeneia*, *syngeneia*, *physis*, and *genos* in general.

Thus far, the ethos exemplified by Demophon's willingness to help his kin has been as implicitly identified with aristocracy in fifth-century political discourse as it has been explicitly associated with the heroic milieu to which Herakles and Iolaos belong. I want now to consider how the admirable attributes of the latter are inextricably and problematically linked to the politically suspect character of the former. For as we shall see, the desperate flight from Argos that allows Iolaos to uphold his obligation to *aidōs* and *genos* also makes him quite literally 'apolitical', transporting him from within his native city to the periphery of the Athenian state—a literal movement that parallels the metaphorical one which sets him 'beyond the pale' of acceptable behaviour in terms of the fifth-century Athenian discourse of civic responsibility.

---

hold a lottery (*palos*, 546) to determine which of Herakles' daughters will be the victim in the sacrifice ordained by Kore is an allusion to Homeric practice. *Il*. 3. 316, 7. 171 and 181, and *Od*. 10. 206 all attest the technical use of the related verb *pallō* in this sense.

[44] Burnett points out that the tribe behaves collectively much like an epic hero (*Tribe and City*', 19). For discussion of 5th-cent. attitudes to the concept of aristocratic *eugeneia*, see Ober, *Mass and Elite*, 253 f., 261 f. See also his discussion of the 'democratization' of this term in the political discourse of the democratic state (259 f.).

Fleeing the City: Displacement and the Problem of Civic Identity

In order to save their lives, Iolaos and his young charges have fled from their city (14f.). In keeping with the play's geographical dynamics, Iolaos refers to his present crisis and the Heraklids' plight in terms that are pointedly spatial:

ἐγὼ γὰρ αἰδοῖ καὶ τὸ συγγενὲς σεβῶν,
ἐξὸν κατ' Ἄργος ἡσύχως ναίειν, πόνων
πλείστων μετέσχον εἷς ἀνὴρ Ἡρακλέει,
ὅτ' ἦν μεθ' ἡμῶν· νῦν δ', ἐπεὶ κατ' οὐρανὸν
ναίει, τὰ κείνου τέκν' ἔχων ὑπὸ πτεροῖς
σῴζω τάδ' αὐτὸς δεόμενος σωτηρίας.
ἐπεὶ γὰρ αὐτῶν γῆς ἀπαλλάχθη πατήρ,
πρῶτον μὲν ἡμᾶς ἤθελ' Εὐρυσθεὺς κτανεῖν·
ἀλλ' ἐξέδραμεν, καὶ πόλις μὲν οἴχεται,
ψυχὴ δ' ἐσώθη. φεύγομεν δ' ἀλώμενοι
ἄλλην ἀπ' ἄλλης ἐξορίζοντες πόλιν.

But I, mindful of shame and reverencing kinship—
and even though I could have rested easy back in Argos—
I was the one man who shared with Herakles his many labours,
when he was among us. But **now**, **since** he's dwelt
in Heaven, I've taken his children under my wings,[45]
hoping to save them, though I myself need saving.
For **when** their father was **first** released from this earth,
Eurystheus wanted to kill us;
but we ran away. And so our city was lost
while our lives were saved. Wandering, we flee
from one city to another, putting each in its turn beyond the horizon.
(6–16)

The Argive king's heralds continually bully the rulers of various *poleis* into driving out the fugitives, geographically displacing them from whatever land has offered them temporary refuge (a motif repeated at 20, 25, 192). In consequence, Iolaos and the children of Herakles are forced to flee from city to city, *allēn ap' allēs exhorizontes polin*. The text here has been questioned, since *exhorizontes* makes the Heraklids the subject of a verb that

---

[45] The Greek here, *hypo pterois*, could be intended to invoke the same phrase at *Eumenides* 1001 f. If so, it is the first of several possible allusions to Aeschylus. That allusion could curdle into parody was not, of course, out of the question with Euripides, and indeed seems intended in scenes such as Iolaos' arming—'a vignette that has an irreverent likeness to the most highly charged instant in the Aeschylean *Seven*' (Burnett, 'Tribe and City', 18).

'places beyond the frontier' whole cities; but the word is perhaps intended to suggest the changing landscape from the refugees' point of view. The idea indeed seems not to be merely that Iolaos and the Heraklids are perpetually moving from one city to another, as some critics have argued (let alone that the people of these cities are driving out the fugitives, as another 'correction' would have it), but that the refugees' 'city'—that is, whatever place they have most recently arrived in—is itself constantly shifting from one site to the next. The manuscript reading is, in fact, entirely in keeping with the motifs of dislocation and the destabilization of fixed boundaries.[46]

Only Athens, it would seem, enjoys both spatial and temporal fixity. It is the last place left to which the Heraklids can flee (441); its borders, *termonai*, are the last remaining for the Heraklids to cross, and this they now do (38–9).[47] The place to which they have come, and the people who inhabit that locale, are very different from the Heraklids themselves. Within the well-established and readily recognized borders of Athens, its people have lived for a very long time (*daron khronon*, 69), inhabiting (*oikountes*, 69; cf. *katoikein* used of Theseus' children, 35) a city whose identity is thus as clearly marked chronologically as it is spatially. *Daron oikountes* is an epic locution that calls to mind

---

[46] L's ἐξορίζοντες, *exhorizontes*, is a *difficilis lectio* to be sure. The transitive sense of *exhorizō* is 'to send beyond the frontier', and normally takes an accusative personal object; cf. the Herald's order to Demophon at 257, 'you send them beyond your border (*exhorize*), and we'll lead them from there', and *Ion* 504, *Hipp.* 1381, *Tro.* 1106. A. C. Pearson, *Heracleidae* (Oxford, 1907), ad loc., suggested an intransitive sense, as is sometimes the case in verbs expressing motion, thereby making *polin* a kind of locative accusative, and giving the sense of 'migrate' (so Garzya, *Euripide Eraclidi*, 48 ad loc.). Wilkins follows Diggle (*Euripidis Fabulae* (Oxford, 1984)) in emending L's ἐξορίζοντες, *exhorizontes*, to ἐξοριζόντων, *exhorizontōn*, a genitive absolute referring to the people of the unco-operative cities: 'we wander in exile from city to city as people cast us out beyond their frontiers' (*Euripides* Heraclidae, 50 ad loc.). In support he adduces other examples of genitive absolute with unexpressed subject; none of them, however, is Euripidean. Cf. James Diggle, 'Further Notes on the *Heraclidae* of Euripides', *PCPS* 28 (1982) 57–8, and H. Erbse, *Studien zum Prolog der Euripideischen Tragödie* (Berlin, 1984), 120 n. 2.

[47] The *horos* indicates an actual 'frontier marker' (Garzya, *Euripide Eraclidi*, 51 ad loc.), and specifies the more generic *termonai*. Cf. Demophon at 133, a reminder that travel between *poleis* involves the crossing of boundaries: 'Having left the borders (*horous*) of which land do you come hither?'

the Athenians' autochthonous origins, and thus links the concept of immemorial time to that of geographical fixity.[48] The Athenians' uninterrupted habitation of their homeland through the ages is starkly contrasted with the Heraklids' wanderings not only through space but through time as well; the text's repeated contrast of 'then' and 'now' (*hote, nyn, epei, prōton*) mirrors the implied contrasts between the various 'here's' and 'there's' through which they have wandered. By alluding to this discourse of autochthony as he cries out for help, however, Iolaos not only emphasizes these differences between the Athenians and the suppliant Heraklids, but also calls attention to a civic ideology based on the individual's inextricable relationship to the *polis*— the very relationship he abrogates in fleeing his own city, Argos.

Deprived of their own *polis*, the Heraklids attempt vainly to become well established in both space and time. Indeed their lives can be said to depend on their ability to become settled (*hidrymenous*, 19) for longer than the brief respites they have had between attacks by the Argive Heralds sent by Eurystheus to pursue them (19–25). For this reason, we are told (46 ff.), Hyllos and Herakles' other male children are out scouting for a place where they might build a home-camp (*oikioumetha*, 46) from which to defend themselves. Used to describe the Heraklids' actions, *oikioumetha* here recalls Iolaos' description of the Athenians as *katoikountes* and *oikountes* in the lines discussed just above; understood in the context of the play's discourse of civic identity, however, *oikioumetha* of the Heraklids may be said to be a subtle double entendre. The activities in which Hyllos and his brothers are engaged—seeking out suitable terrain and constructing buildings upon it—here refer to their efforts to set up an armed encampment from which to defend themselves against the Argives. But it is hard not to feel here the primary definition of *oikizō* and *katoikizō*—that is, 'to found as a colony or new settlement'. Iolaos may think he needs a place in which to take refuge, yet this language of establishing and building suggests that what the children of Herakles really need is to inhabit a city, a *polis*. That need is precisely what Iolaos articulates in his wistful forecast of the day when the Heraklids will at last be able

---

[48] For the importance of autochthony to Athenian civic ideology, see Loraux, *Children of Athena*, 37–52; the Athenian rhetoric of autochthony appears in Euripidean tragedy in *Med.* 824 ff., *Ion* 29, and *Erekhth*. fr. 50. 5 Austin.

to dwell within their own homes (*dōmat' oikēsēte*, 311), just as the inhabitants, *oikountes*, of Athens presently do.

Apolitical Iolaos

The crux of Iolaos' dilemma, however, is that what causes him to reject the claims of *polis* is his allegiance to *genos*. 'Reject' may seem strong at first, given that the old man is fleeing certain death; he had to leave his city, but surely did not want to. Yet on closer examination, it becomes clear that Iolaos' movement, however unwilling, is merely the latest of many that have taken him away from the civic and civilized centre of the *polis* to distant and savage extremes both geographical and ethical. His words and actions consistently demonstrate that, although his aims are indeed 'noble' (in all senses of that word), he has yet to be integrated within the civilized framework of the democratic *polis*.

The prologue provides the first reminder of Iolaos' curiously apolitical character. In his youth, he declares, he could have remained in Argos, but chose instead to honour the claims of *aidōs* and *genos* by following Herakles on his legendary travels (7 f.). Like most mythic wanderings, those of Herakles and Iolaos (and indeed those of that 'other Herakles', the Athenian founding hero Theseus) follow a predictable mythic pattern. They are, to begin with, accomplished 'by local heroes from a polis as a center'; and the far peripheries to which those civilizing labours take the hero, with their theriomorphic exotica, represent social and economic anomalies—'others' not merely in relation to a specific *polis*, but, we might say, in relation to the very idea of the *polis*.[49] Moreover, just as the places and peoples that Iolaos and Herakles visited are symbolic anti-*poleis* (Hades, Amazons), the very act of wandering is itself associated with un-Hellenic 'otherness' in both the Greek imagination in general and, more specifically, within the special discourse of Athenian autochthony. In the latter, the distinction between autochthonous inhabitants and immigrants had special ideological significance—an ideological subset, as it were, of the larger cultural

---

[49] See Jean M. Davison, 'Myth and the Periphery', 50: 'Myth uses exotic places and people as representations of what it is like to be "not us" as a way of clarifying by contrast and comparison who and what "we" are.' The Amazons are of course an extreme example of social anomaly; see the discussion of W. B. Tyrell, *Amazons: A Study in Athenian Mythmaking* (Baltimore, 1984).

association between civilization and permanent settlements, on the one hand, and between barbarism and nomadism, on the other.[50] Despite the repeated claims of kinship between the Argive Heraklids and the Athenian Theseids, then, the protagonists of *Children of Herakles* —intruders, wanderers, immigrants —represent, in terms of the Hellenic conceptualization of Greekness and in terms of the Athenian civic ideology that placed such great importance on fixity and centrality, the *ne plus ultra* of otherness.[51] This is the proper context for evaluating the old man's acknowledgement that all of his many peregrinations were the result of his reverence for the values represented by *aidōs* and *syngeneia*—the web of values, that is, that the democratic Athenian *polis* was trying to shred.

In light of all this, it comes as no surprise that Iolaos' allegiances cause him to reject not only Argos, but Athens itself. After agreeing to take up the old man's cause, Demophon twice invites Iolaos to leave the altar and enter into the palace (340, 343). Implicit in that invitation to the Athenian ruler's 'house' (*es domous*) is a move into the space of the Athenian *polis*.[52] Yet Iolaos refuses, preferring instead to remain clinging to the altar, consigning his fate to Athens' tutelary deity. It is from that marginal position that he prefers to wish the city well (344f.). This refusal has itself been seen as further proof of the old man's rejection of the *polis* in favour of the *genos*, whose 'ancestral values' Iolaos once again champions here.[53]

---

[50] For this point see Davison, 'Myth and the Periphery', 60.

[51] For the Athenians' self-image as undisturbed by the immigration and invasions that afflict other states, see Hdt. 1. 56, Thuc. 1. 2. 4, and Loraux's discussion at *Children of Athena*, 51 n. 71.

[52] For Athens as the clear if logically improbable location of the palace to which Demophon gestures, see Hourmouziades, *Production and Imagination*, 127.

[53] So, e.g. Fitton, 'The *Suppliant Women*', 460; Burian, 'Euripides' *Heracleidae*', 15. For Burnett 'it strongly suggests that the city will not, in the end, be the savior of this tribe' ('Tribe and City', 15). Her subsequent comments bear repeating here: 'Their [sc. the Heraklids', esp. Iolaos'] rejection of the city as their haven leaves them, of course, on stage to continue as the drama's principals, but it also leaves the suppliant plot in suspension, and it strongly suggests that the city will not, in the end, be the savior of this tribe. . . . Through Iolaus the *genos*, honoring kin ties . . . and coming from a father who was γενναῖος . . . makes its case on the basis of *genos* and τὸ συγγενές . . . Indeed, Iolaus treats

Sophocles' Philoctetes remarks that being without a *polis* is like being one of the dead (*Phil.* 1018). Iolaos' flight seems, if not to have killed him, then to have demoted him to the bottom rung of the ladder of the democratic *polis*'s civic hierarchy—that is, slavery—and thus makes him the 'natural enemy of the political order'.[54] The verb he uses to describe the Heraklids' flight from Argos is *exedramen*, they 'ran away' (14), one that can connote the illegal flight of runaway slaves; this particular sense of the word seems to be confirmed by the Argive Herald's scornful reference to the Heraklids as 'the runaways', *drapetas* (140), a word often used of slaves.[55] And in this context it is worth remembering that slaves, like women, represent the radical 'other' for the Athenian citizen; and indeed like both slaves and women, the Heraklids have a penchant for erratic wanderings that requires hypervigilance on the part of their own 'masters', who seek to confine them.[56] The old hero's peripatetic existence seems to bear out the recent understanding of tragedy's spatial

the rescue of the suppliants as if it derived more directly from the *eugeneia* of the king than from the sanctity of the sacred refuge.'

The special archaic flavour of Iolaos' refusal of the Athenian king's invitation here is underscored by the rather Homeric tinge of his last words to Demophon: he trusts in the outcome of the battle, he says, because Athena, the tutelary goddess of his saviour's city, is every bit a match for Hera, protectress of Argos (347–52).

[54] For slaves as the 'natural' enemies of the political order, see Ober, *Mass and Elite*, 270, and cf. his comments at pp. 24–7, 62f., 270–9. Aristotle (*Politics* 1253[b]32) refers to a slave as nothing more than an 'animate object', *ktēma ti empsykhon*.

[55] For the derogatory force of *exedramen*, because of its frequent association with slaves, see Garzya, *Euripide Eraclidi*, ad loc., and cf. Hdt. 6. 11. 4, where *drapetēs* is clearly associated with slavery, as opposed to freedom, *eleutheria*.

[56] Slaves as the 'other' of the citizen: see Ober, *Mass and Elite*, 270. Just remarks that '[w]omen were consistently portrayed as undisciplined and emotional; they were therefore by nature "unfree"—that is to say, they lacked the necessary qualities for self determination and autonomy. In the extended sense of the word they were "slavish"—not as members of the legally defined category of slaves but in terms of their innate characteristics' (*Women in Athenian Law*, 191; see further his discussion of woman's 'slavish' nature at pp. 186ff., 191–2, and 196–7). For further discussion of the parallels between the status of slaves and women in 5th-cent. Greek thought, see Vidal-Naquet, *The Black Hunter*, 205–23 (esp. 208ff. for his justification for considering women and slaves together). Aristotle warns against over-indulging both women and serfs because of their inherent lack of control (*Politics* 1269[b]7ff.).

dynamics as a system intended to 'prob[e] the connection between possession of civic identity and being inside the *polis*, and the danger which can issue from those who pass from inside to outside, or vice versa'.[57]

In marked contrast to the characterization of Iolaos and the Heraklids as slaves and wanderers, the Argive Herald's formal, almost legalistic request to Demophon for the extradition of the suppliants (134–43) is bolstered by frequent references to his city's power and indeed to his own status within an organized political framework. Unlike his quarry, the Argive pursuer of the Heraklids has a very clear idea of who he is and where he belongs. He begins by stating that he is an Argive (134); that simple fact justifies his actions, which he characterizes as *dikaia*, 'just' (138). The political crisis precipitated by the Heraklids' escape is cast as one limited to his own city's confines, to be resolved by due process of Argive law:

Ἀργεῖος ὢν γὰρ αὐτὸς Ἀργείους ἄγω
ἐκ τῆς ἐμαυτοῦ τούσδε δραπέτας ἔχων,
νόμοισι τοῖς ἐκεῖθεν ἐψηφισμένους
θανεῖν· δίκαιοι δ' ἐσμὲν οἰκοῦντες πόλιν
αὐτοὶ καθ' αὐτῶν κυρίους κραίνειν δίκας.

It is as an Argive myself that I bring this lot back—
Argives, too, runaways from my city—
since they have been condemned to death according to the laws
of the city. And as the inhabitants of that city (*oikountes polin*)
   we are within our rights
to execute valid judgements against our own citizens.

                        (139–43)

The Argives can claim jurisdiction over their countrymen because they inhabit a city, Argos (*oikountes polin*, 142), according to whose laws the Heraklids, who are Argives, must die. The discreteness of the organized political community to which the Herald belongs entitles him to exercise Argive justice in pursuing the Heraklids (*krainein dikas*, 143), just as indeed the discreteness of the political community inhabited by the Athenians

[57] See N. T. Croally, *Euripidean Polemic:* The Trojan Women *and the Function of Tragedy* (Cambridge, 1994), 178. In his section on tragic space (174–92), Croally emphasizes the way in which 'tragedy was interested in how positions in space determined status or identity' (191).

(*tas Athēnas . . . oikountes*, 69) has made Argive 'justice' a cause for special concern for Athens and her own reputation (*polei t' oneidos*, 72).

True to the Greek construction of Hellenic and civic identity, the nomadic and hence intrinsically apolitical existence of the Heraklids is a threat, in different ways, to the political integrity of both Argos and Athens. Putting aside for the moment the consideration that the 'justice' of the former may be construed as harsh or indeed even unjust, let us examine Iolaos' refutation of the Argive Herald's case for extradition. It is an argument that further betrays his essentially apolitical nature. He has 'nothing to do' with Argos, he says:[58]

ἡμῖν δὲ καὶ τῷδ' οὐδέν ἐστιν ἐν μέσῳ·
ἐπεὶ γὰρ Ἄργους οὐ μέτεσθ' ἡμῖν ἔτι,
ψήφῳ δοκῆσαν, ἀλλὰ φεύγομεν πάτραν,
πῶς ἂν δικαίως ὡς Μυκηναίους ἄγοι
ὅδ' ὄντας ἡμᾶς, οὓς ἀπήλασαν χθονός;

We have nothing to do with this man.
For since we no longer have anything to do with Argos
(once their judgement was voted), but rather have fled our fatherland,
by what right does this man here take us away as if we were
Argives—we whom they drove out of that land?

(184–8)

Iolaos represents himself and the Heraklids as exiles, no longer bound by Argive law. It seems clear, however, that the Heraklids had been sentenced to death legally, as the result of a vote, *psēphos*, duly taken according to the city's laws (*nomois . . . epsēphismenous thanein*, 141). The apparent legal force of that vote enables the Argive to refer to the death sentence against the Heraklids as legal judgement, *dikē*; it is not (as for example is the case in the *Mad Herakles*, where another tyrant threatens Herakles' family) merely the tyrant's vindictive whim (59 f.).[59]

---

[58] Reading Valckenaer's almost certain ἐν μέσῳ for the manuscript L's ἐν μέρει, which seems to be a scribal error influenced by the same phrase two lines earlier, in 182. This correction gives us an idiom whose literal meaning has to do with space: 'there is no middle space between him and us'.

[59] Wilkins (*Euripides* Heraclidae, 69 ad loc.) would deny the more literal sense of this line, i.e. 'that a popular vote had been taken', on the grounds that *psēphos*, 'vote', can be vague in tragedy; he cites Friis Johansen-Whittle on Aesch. *Su.* 7. But it is noteworthy that the vote is mentioned twice here (cf. 186); in this context comparison with the *Mad Herakles* is indeed useful. There, the

Here, however, in his formal response to the Herald before the Athenian king, Iolaos neglects to mention the precise nature of the punishment voted in Argos; the impersonal construction *psēphōi dokēsan*, 'it was resolved by vote', at 186 is rather vague (although it does once again foreground the legality and ostensibly democratic nature of the sentence). In his prologue speech, Iolaos had neglected to mention the vote at all, citing only the murderous intentions of the tyrant Eurystheus as the reason for his flight (13). Indeed, a rhetorical sleight-of-hand here transforms the sentence of death into a sentence of exile: Iolaos refers to himself and his charges as 'those whom [the Argives] have *banished* from the land' (*hous apēlasan khthonos*, 188), and then goes on to claim that in forcing the Heraklids to leave their *polis*, the Argive vote has made them foreigners, *xenoi* (189). The success of his ploy can be judged by the frequency with which modern critics refer to the Heraklids not as fugitives but as exiles, which in fact they are not.[60] So if, like Iolaos, the Argive Herald has 'left behind the border' of Argos (133), it is in order to reassert Argive sovereignty; Iolaos' retort at 189 f., on the other hand, implies that for him, civic identity is a technicality, something that reaches only as far as the geographical borders of the city itself.

But the most striking sign of Iolaos' lack of faith in the institutions of the *polis* is his declaration, in the prologue, that in fleeing, he has given up his *polis* to save his life, *psykhē*: 'we lost our city | but saved our lives' (*polis men oikhetai* | *psykhē d' esōthē*). To make one's life rather than one's city the object of salvific action is a violation—indeed, a direct inversion—of the ideological

villain has no need of votes: he merely wishes (*thelei*) to murder the suppliants (*Her.* 138–40; cf. 166 f.). For the importance of the Herald's claim to 'justice and lawfulness' here, see Michael Lloyd, *The Agon in Euripides* (Oxford, 1992), 74. Lloyd goes on to point out that Demophon does not in fact decide in Iolaos' favour because of these 'technical details of their case' (75).

[60] Burian asserts that Iolaos's argument 'fully meets the case' ('Euripides' *Heracleidae*, 5); see also Burnett: '[T]he Argives themselves have put this tribe outside the reach of Argive law by confiscating their properties and denying their rights . . . in so doing [they] have forced *the exiles* out into the realm of general Hellenic custom where true justice is' ('Tribe and City', 7; emphasis mine). Burnett is right to point out that Iolaos' case is 'based on a quibble of jurisdiction', but in swallowing the 'exile' line she fails to see just how sly his argument actually is.

hierarchy implicit in the fifth-century Athenian term *prohairesis*: that is, the 'choice' (*hairesis*) of putting one's city 'before' (*pro*) one's life. In the funeral orations of the democratic *polis*, this principle was the object of lavish praise. The war dead were publicly honoured for having chosen their city over their lives, and the disgraceful choice of life, *psykhē*, was expressed in the derogative verb *philopsykhein*, 'to be a life-lover'.[61] *Prohairesis* and *philopsykhia* were constantly contrasted in the political rhetoric of fifth-century Athens. Orators who wished to hammer home the importance of the former typically invoked the sterling example of those who fell at Marathon—ironically, the very site to which the *philopsykhos* Iolaos has fled.[62] The effect of this passage, then, is to suggest that Iolaos' reverence for *aidōs* and *genos*, which as we have seen is framed in such a way as to highlight its specifically pre-democratic nature, is subtly yet crucially— almost causally—linked to his *philopsykhia*, a moral and political failure in the eyes of the democratic *polis*.[63]

[61] For *prohairesis* in funeral orations, see Loraux, *The Invention of Athens*, 102, and cf. Thuc. 2. 43 (lives in exchange for deathless renown); Aristotle, *Rhet.* 1396ᵃ (voluntary death in battle as a recapitulation of the example of ancestors at Salamis, Marathon, and the war with Argos on behalf of the Heraklids); and Dem. 60. 28 ('better dead than Red': i.e. Athenians of legendary times chose to die fighting for the democratic principle of *isēgoria* first established by Theseus rather than live as *philopsykhēsantes*—like, he implies, the other Greeks (*para tois Hellēsi*)). For this motif see further Loraux, pp. 102–5, 141, 169, and Wilkins, 'The State and the Individual', 185 ff. Aristophanes parodies the ideology of *prohairesis* by slyly suggesting that *philopsykhein* was a common 'reality' behind the high-minded rhetoric of 'the beautiful death for the city'. In *Akharnai*—which Goossens has described as a comic and pacifist retort to such invocations of patriotic rhetoric in *Children of Herakles* (*Euripide et Athènes*, 219–22)—Dikaiopolis concludes a tirade against violence with the proud assertion that he loves, *philō*, his life, *psykhēn* (*Akh.* 357). Cf. *Frogs* 190, where Kharon alludes to the disaster at Arginousai where every man 'fought for his own skin'—*kreōn*, literally, a word that Loraux here reads as a comic 'debasement' of *psykhē* (p. 457 n. 190).

[62] The canonical expression of Marathon as the symbol of noble *prohairesis* is Lysias, *Epitaphios* 24–5.

[63] It is interesting to contrast Iolaos' willingness to flee the city in order to save his life with the quite different choice of Socrates, as described in Plato's *Crito*. In response to his friends' urgings that he flee Athens after being condemned to death, Socrates insists on a kind of moral *prohairesis*: he argues that his former reluctance to leave his beloved *polis*—to 'cross the borders out of the city', as the text interestingly puts it (*Crito* 52b1)—constitutes an implicit but inviolate agreement between him and the laws of the city, one that he could not

Hence in spite of the Heraklids' claims to be like their Athenian cousins—those theatrical reflections of the collective civic 'self' that was Euripides' audience—they are, if anything, quite 'other' with respect to any number of the spheres within which Athenian identity could be defined: mythic, gendered, political. This unexpected difference makes it difficult to see the play as organized around two distinct ethical and ideological poles: Athens/Heraklids on the one hand, Argos/Eurystheus on the other.[64] Instead, it establishes the Heraklids themselves as an un-Athenian extreme, much as Argos might be expected to be. Before turning to examine how this play's other 'migration'— the transgressive entrance of Herakles' virgin daughter—successfully refashions the Heraklid 'others' in the image of the idealized Athenian selves, we must first consider how far short of that ideal the Athenians themselves fall, when first we meet them in the person of Demophon. For the king's unwillingness to sacrifice one of this own people to satisfy Kore's oracular demand in fact re-enacts Iolaos' failure. Inasmuch as it does, the sons of Theseus at this point resemble only too closely the Argive cousins who are supposed to be their 'others'.

The King's Dilemma: Demophon as allos kēryx?

The Heraklids' successful appeal to Demophon precipitates war between Athens and the much more powerful Argos, whose army, arrayed for battle, appears within the space of a brief choral ode (353–80). The Athenians prepare to arm; the city's altars are thronged with sacrificial victims to be offered on behalf of a victorious outcome (398–400). This is precisely the scenario that the Argive Herald had earlier deemed unlikely and indeed insane: in his first exchange with Iolaos he had scorned the idea

now break simply because the city had turned against him. Of Socrates' refusal to abandon his devotion to the *polis*, Loraux writes: 'Despite original aspects of his teaching that were to weigh heavily in the final judgement of the Athenians, he was on the whole faithful to the principal civic norms' (*The Invention of Athens*, 319).

[64] The 'encomiast' critics tend to argue for the 'Athens = Heraklids' equation: so Zuntz, *The Political Plays of Euripides*, 26–33. Belpassi observes a blurring similar to the kind I am arguing for here in the *Iphigeneia in Tauris*, where the apparently straightforward dichotomy Greek/Taurian (i.e. barbarian) is subverted by the Tantalid family history, which suggests if anything the equation *genos* = barbarian (Belpassi, 'La "follia" del *genos*', 65).

that any *polis* would be so foolish (*kakōs phronōn*, 56) as to champion the 'useless power' of the weak Heraklids in the face of Eurystheus' own vast military might. In the political rhetoric of the democratic *polis*, the Athenians' willingness to take up arms on behalf of the Heraklids in the face of their intimidating Argive enemy was, in fact, frequently invoked as the model for the Greeks' equally improbable real-life defeat of the Persians at Marathon, which so famously pitted 'few against many', *oligoi pros pollous*, as Lysias declares.[65] Given these echoes of Athenian civic rhetoric, it is hardly surprising that during that earlier exchange with Iolaos the Herald had gone on to quote, unwittingly but almost verbatim, that other topos familiar from Athenian political rhetoric, *prohairesis*. 'There is no one who would choose (*paroith' hairesetai*, an almost exact paraphrase of *prohairesis*) your pathetic "power" in the face of Eurystheus'', he witheringly tells Iolaos (57), little suspecting that the Athenians would do just that, choosing to fight as 'few against many'.

That choice, it would seem, is a sufficient demonstration of Demophon's *eugeneia* (324 f.)—the aristocratic quality defined by a resolve to honour both *aidōs* and *genos*. And yet an unexpected catastrophe arises (399 ff.). Demophon reports a terrible oracular pronouncement: Kore, daughter of Demeter, requires the sacrifice of a virgin in order to guarantee an Athenian victory. The sacrifice will both save the city and serve as a monument to the enemy's defeat; the virgin, moreover, must be of noble, *eugenēs*, birth (409).

The last detail is crucial. The insistence on the *eugeneia* of the prospective victim (409's *hētis . . . patros eugenous* recurs at 490, *hētis eugenēs*) reintroduces the subject of 'nobility', yet implies that the *eugeneia* demonstrated thus far by Demophon (whose actions are said to demonstrate his own noble patrimony) is somehow incomplete. It is true, as Burnett claims, that 'Demophon is clearly still meant to be admirable of his kind, as good as a ruler *can* be',[66] but if the point of the play were merely to

---

[65] Lysias, *Ep.* 20, 24; cf. Hdt. 6. 109; Thuc. 1. 74. 1; Plato, *Menex.* 240a6–7.

[66] Burnett, 'Tribe and City', 9. Fitton hits nearer the target, I think, noting that Demophon's behaviour here conforms to 'the prudential morality of contemporary Athenian politics' ('The *Suppliant Women*', 454). For the sacrifice as a means of revealing the limits of Demophon's political vision, cf. Vellacott, *Ironic Drama*, 178 ff.

demonstrate Demophon's admirable qualities, it would surely end at line 380—the point by which a rescue action comparable to that of the whole of Aeschylus' *Suppliant Maidens* is swiftly and successfully concluded. The oracle that Euripides has contrived for this play seems intended to test the strength of the civic virtue that Demophon has so easily shown thus far, just as it reveals the moral and political shortcomings of other rulers in other plays of self-sacrifice.[67] His failure to pass the test posed by the play's unexpected second disaster demonstrates the limits of the ethical code that brings him success in resolving the first. Both shortcomings and successes are remarkably similar to those that characterize Iolaos' political failures.

After reporting the news of Kore's demand to Iolaos, Demophon hastens to assert that he would like to be able to help the Heraklids, but cannot at the cost of civil war:

> ἐγὼ δ' ἔχω μέν, ὡς ὁρᾷς, προθυμίαν
> τοσήνδ' ἐς ὑμᾶς· παῖδα δ' οὔτ' ἐμὴν κτενῶ
> οὔτ' ἄλλων ἀστῶν τῶν ἐμῶν ἀναγκάσω
> ἄκονθ'· ἑκὼν δὲ τίς κακῶς οὕτω φρονεῖ,
> ὅστις τὰ φίλτατ' ἐκ χερῶν δώσει τέκνα;
> καὶ νῦν πυκνὰς ἂν συστάσεις ἂν εἰσίδοις,
> τῶν μὲν λεγόντων ὡς δίκαιος ἦ ξένοις
> ἱκέταις ἀρήγειν, τῶν δὲ μωρίαν ἐμοῦ
> κατηγορούντων· εἰ δὲ δράσω τόδε,
> οἰκεῖος ἤδη πόλεμος ἐξαρτύεται.

As you see, I am quite eager to help
you. But I will not kill a child of mine,
nor will I compel any one of my people to do so
against his will. For who would be so mad
as to hand over willingly his nearest and dearest?
You'd see quarrels coming thick and fast—
some arguing that it is only just
to protect the suppliants, others accusing me
of gross folly. If I were to do as you ask,
it would soon be a matter of civil war.

(410–19)

[67] For seemingly arbitrary demands for human sacrifice as a tragic means of exposing political cowardice, see C. Nancy, '*ΦΑΡΜΑΚΟΝ ΣΩΤΗΡΙΑΣ*: Le Mécanisme du sacrifice humain chez Euripide', in H. Zehnacker (ed.), *Théâtre et spectacle dans l'Antiquité* (Strasbourg, 1983) 17–30. For the 'ease' with which

Here the Athenian, who had previously confounded the Argive Herald's sneering expectations that no one would come to the aid of the Heraklids, now unwittingly but completely fulfils them. Earlier, the Herald had confidently asserted that no city would be so foolish, *kakōs phronōn* (56), as to help the Heraklids, thereby making the foreign fugitives' troubles its own, *idia* (146). To do so, the Herald had added, would be foolishness itself, *mōria* (147). Demophon now parrots these very words. Despite his eagerness, *prothymia*, to help, the Athenian declares himself unwilling to countenance the death of one of his 'own'—family, fellow Athenians—in order to protect the suppliants, regardless of the ancient bonds that connect the Heraklids and Theseids. Such a sacrifice of one's nearest and dearest on behalf of strangers, *xenoi*, he says, would be madness (*kakōs . . . phronei*, 413); he fears that the charge of foolishness, *mōria*, will be levelled at himself for preferring the lives of the suppliants to those of his own people (417).

Indeed, in the end, Demophon is quite emphatic about not wishing to make foreigners' troubles into domestic ones. For him, the affairs of the *polis* are a private, even family affair. He states that the threat to his own and to his people's loved ones would precipitate *stasis* and civil war, to which he here refers as an *oikeios polemos*, 'a domestic war'. The adjective, *oikeios*—from *oikos*, 'house'—has interesting resonances. We will encounter it again when Iolaos, lying literally prostrate with grief following the Girl's exit, identifies the reason for his despair as a 'family concern', *phrontis tis oikeios*; he is mourning the imminent death of his kinswoman (634). Although *oikeios polemos* does, by the fifth century, come to mean 'civil war',[68] the literal meaning of the adjective is 'domestic', 'of the same family or kin, *cognatus*',

Demophon makes his decisions, see Burian, 'Euripides' *Heracleidae*', 6; for the oracle as a test of Demophon's character, see H. D. F. Kitto, *Greek Tragedy*, 3rd edn. (New York, 1961), 253. Michael Lloyd also remarks on the way in which the 'initial clarity' seemingly achieved by Demophon's agreement to take up the suppliants' cause 'becomes gradually more clouded as the play goes on' (*The Agon in Euripides*, 73); cf. the remarks of Edith Hall on 'ambiguities' in the character of the Athenian king—'not quite the exemplar of virtue the audience might have become accustomed to expect in an Athenian ruler in tragedy . . .' ('The Sociology of Athenian Tragedy', 120: she refers specifically to the impious temptation to strike the Theban Herald).

[68] e.g. Thuc. 1. 118. 2 and Eur. fr. 173 N.

'personal, private'.[69] This is richly suggestive. For in the context of the ideology of *prohairesis*, which requires a sacrifice of the personal and domestic for public and political good, Demophon's unwillingness to risk 'domestic' stability, as we might put it, is noteworthy. Like Iolaos, he can only see the ramifications of Kore's demands in terms of its effects on his 'house'. That narrow vision indicates the extent to which the ethical obligations imposed by these characters' *aidōs* are limited to a *genos* whose own boundaries coincide with those of the *oikos*.

Displacement and Transformation I: The Girl

However good his intentions, then, Demophon's world-view seems to be as narrowly circumscribed as that of Iolaos himself. In both cases, the limitations of the *genos* creed and the inherent failure of its own brand of *eugeneia* to subordinate *oikos* to *polis* are underscored. Each of these failures points, in different ways, to a problem to which tragedy almost obsessively returns: the manner in which those qualities that had constituted excellence in the archaic world had become problematical for the democratic *polis*, which necessarily subordinated individual accomplishment to the needs and efforts of the majority.[70] It is, in fact, to a decidedly un-heroic figure that Euripides must turn in order to defuse the potentially explosive tensions and ambiguities between the heroic past and the democratic present. The *eugeneia* that alone can save both the Heraklids—and, now, Athens herself—will be that of a high-born female.

The innovative choice of this anonymous girl as the saviour of both *genos* and *polis* serves two purposes. First, it brings the action of the play into alignment with a crucial civic myth that also foregrounds virgin self-sacrifice: that of the Erekhtheidai, the daughters of Athens' founder Erekhtheus who were sacrificed—to Kore, as it happens, at least in Euripides' lost *Erekhtheus*— in order to guarantee victory in a war against Eumolpos, Poseidon's descendant.[71] And behind the story of the Erekhthei-

---

[69] So LSJ.

[70] For this point see Gregory, *Instruction of the Athenians*, 8; cf. Vernant, 'The Historical Moment', Vidal-Naquet, 'Sophocles' *Philoctetes*'.

[71] The subject of Euripides' *Erekhtheus* as reported by Demaratos (*FrGrHist* 42 F 4). In the *Ion*, Euripides makes Kreousa Erekhtheus' only surviving

dai there lurk the spectres of still other virgins, *parthenoi*, who played important roles in the mythic history of Athens and who indeed died 'for Athens' (or, rather, at Athena's hands): the Kekropidai, or, alternatively, the Aglauridai. 'It can be dangerous', as Loraux dryly comments, 'to be a young girl on the Acropolis.'[72]

There is little doubt that this mythological surfeit of doomed virgins inspired Euripides to make the vehicle for salvation in this play not the *eugenēs* king of Athens, but a *eugenēs* young virgin who chooses danger over life. And yet on another, more profoundly symbolic level, the choice of the Girl serves a crucial dramatic purpose. Claire Nancy has argued that in Euripides' plays of voluntary self-sacrifice, the political salvation that requires the death of a victim fresh out of the women's quarters, or indeed childhood, serves only to highlight 'political *aporia*' and the empty rhetoric of masculine heroism.[73] It is indeed appealing to think that, in the case of our play, Euripides assigns the demand for human sacrifice to Persephone, mythology's most famous victim of abduction, in order to underscore the motif of innocent feminine vulnerability, which stands in considerable contrast to the vigorous and sometimes murderous physical exploits of heroes like Herakles and Iolaos.[74] This is not to say that the insistence on a virgin victim must be read as a flat condemnation of masculine heroism—which, after all, has successfully served the *genos* and indeed the world. But it does point to the incompleteness of that kind of heroism. By making the

daughter (cf. *Ion* 279 f.). For the myth of the Erekhtheidai, see Loraux, *Children of Athena*, 25, 210, 215.

[72] Loraux, *Children of Athena*, 225. For the Kekropidai and Aglauridai, see Loraux, pp. 23, 26, and 225 ff., and Wilkins, 'The Young of Athens', 333 f. (where the similarity between the Girl and the mythic princesses is also noted).

[73] Nancy, 'Sacrifice humain', esp. 23 and 29 ('le sacrifice volontaire sonne le glas de l'héroïsme').

[74] For a discussion of the meaning of Kore's demand, see Wilkins, *Euripides* Heraclidae, xxiv and 'The Young of Athens', 336 n. 93. Critics tend to take Kore's demand as a symbol of the arbitrary whims of Fate that test men's character (*à la* Lyssa in *Herakles*). See e.g. F. Stoessl, 'Die Heracliden des Euripides', *Philologus*, 100 (1956), with which cf. the broader discussion of this type of demand in H. S. Versnel, 'Self-Sacrifice, Compensation, and Anonymous Gods', in *Le Sacrifice dans l'Antiquité* (Geneva, 1981), 135–94.

Girl into the saviour of her kin and the state, the poet can dramatize the necessity of integrating 'otherness' into the definition of
aidōs and the heroic ethos it represents. By virtue of her very
marginality within the society she saves, the Girl can serve as a
symbol for the urgent need for redefining and expanding the
communal ethos of the democratic *polis*. 'Marginality' is (typically in this work) literal as well as figurative here; for like so
much else in this play, that redefinition of values is marked by a
series of spatial dislocations. Those displacements in turn signal
still further redefinitions of the characters' gendered identities.[75]

Spatial Improprieties

In order to understand how the spatial disruptions to which I
have just alluded function as analogues for disorientations in
gender, we must turn back for a moment to those other, literal
borders that define the territory of Attika. In the prologue Iolaos
declares that the town whose borders the Heraklids have crossed
is ruled by two kings (35); the supplicatory act in which Iolaos
takes part, he adds, is shared by two old people (*dyoin gerontoin*,
39)—that is, Iolaos himself and Alkmene, the mother of Herakles and grandmother of the Heraklids. The dual form here may
have come as something of a surprise for the Athenian audience,
for what they actually saw on the 'stage' of the theatre of Dionysos was just one *gerōn*: Iolaos himself. Neither Alkmene nor
her own child's female 'tribe' (*to thēly paidos . . . genos*, 41) would
have been visible to the audience. The dissonance between
Iolaos' words and the tableau presented at the altar calls attention to the social and theatrical convention of feminine invisibility: the female members of the hero's family could not be
exposed to view, but must instead remain within, *esōthe* (42),
merely to be imagined by the audience.[76]

[75] This gender blurring may itself reflect certain ambiguities characteristic of
the mythological maidens (the Erekhtheidai and Aglauridai) on whom the Girl
seems to be modelled. These young girls were associated in Athenian myth and
cult with the care of the young men, the *ephēboi*, who would one day serve the
state. The ephebes took their oath in the sanctuary of Aglauros; they set out on
manoeuvres from that of the Hyakinthides. For the role of these figures as
keepers of the young, *kourotrophoi*, and saviours of the city, *sōteirai*, see Emily
Kearns, *The Heroes of Athens* (London, 1989), ch. 2, and Walter Burkert, *Homo
necans*, tr. Peter Bing (Berkeley, 1983), 65 f.
[76] For this point see Chalkia, *Lieux et espace*, 163.

Iolaos draws further attention to these 'spatial relations', as it were, in terms that remind his listeners of the rigid proprieties of male and female space: 'I am ashamed to have young virgins come in contact with a crowd and stand as suppliants at the altar' (43 f.). The act of bringing young girls into physical proximity with the crowd, *okhlos*—that is, into a public space filled with men—clearly violates propriety, *aidōs*, as it applies to inter-actions between the sexes.[77] It is this sense of *aidōs* that the Girl self-consciously and thus 'surprisingly' violates in stepping forth from within the 'house' (represented here by the sanctuary of Zeus Agoraios) and thereby entering the very heart of public, active, masculine life that is, if anything, the home of the *okhlos*, the *agora*:[78]

> ξένοι, θράσος μοι μηδὲν ἐξόδοις ἐμαῖς
> προσθῆτε· πρῶτον γὰρ τόδ' ἐξαιτήσομαι·
> γυναικὶ γὰρ σιγή τε καὶ τὸ σωφρονεῖν
> κάλλιστον, εἴσω θ' ἥσυχον μένειν δόμων.

Strangers, do not charge me with boldness (*thrasos*) because of my exit from within. This before all else I ask.
For a woman, silence and self-restraint
are the finest thing—that, and keeping quiet within the house.

(474–7)

This short apology for her *exodos* is complex and self-contradictory, and sets in motion the intricate process by which the Girl will soften and redefine key terms of masculine heroism even as she herself seemingly yearns to appropriate aspects of male identity. Her paradoxical relation to traditional gender values is reflected in the ambiguous word she uses to describe her

[77] Euripides describes similarly self-conscious interactions between women and the *okhlos* at *IA* 735 and 1030 (of Klytaimnestra interacting with the army), and at 1338 and 1546 in the same work (implying the shameful inappropriate-ness of Iphigeneia's presence before the soldiers). Both Fitton ('The *Suppliant Women*', 452) and E. A. M. E. O'Connor-Visser (*Aspects of Human Sacrifice in the Tragedies of Euripides* (Amsterdam, 1987), 27) discuss the Girl's 'striking' preoccupation with *aidōs* at length. The word used here for 'crowd', *okhlos*, can connote specifically aristocratic disdain on Iolaos' part; see Ober's discussion of this word as an 'insulting' way to refer to the Athenian citizen-masses during the 5th and 4th cents. (Ober, *Mass and Elite*, 11).

[78] For the 'surprising' character of her entrance, see Halleran, *Stagecraft in Euripides*, 20 and 47 n. 9 ('a great surprise'), *contra* Oliver Taplin, who sees it merely as another example of the entrance as a response to on-stage cries of despair (*The Stagecraft of Aeschylus* (Oxford, 1977), 220).

entrance on stage: *thrasos* clearly means 'unseemly boldness' or 'impudent daring' here, but it also has a positive meaning—'courage', or 'boldness'. The particular sense called for at a given moment depends, in fact, on gender, for what is 'bold' for men is, necessarily, 'impudent' for women. And indeed, on one level these lines, which so accurately echo conventional rhetoric about feminine propriety,[79] remind us once again that the movements that take female characters from inside to outside force them to enter the world of public action that is, properly speaking, the world of men. The Girl's words of apology are, in a way, as transgressive as her movement, since they violate the protocols of feminine silence (*sigē*) to which she paradoxically refers, even as in moving outside of the enclosure in order to speak them she ruptures the seclusion (*eisō menein domōn*) that she also ostensibly recommends.

But although the Girl, like the supremely destructive Medea (to cite the most famous Euripidean example, the one used by Gomme), announces her move into that other sphere with the dramatically resonant word *exēlthon*, 'I have come outside' (*Hkld*. 479; cf. *Med*. 214), there is a difference. The difference, of course, is that the Girl's entry into the world of men results in no catastrophes for Athens, such as those the Colchian sorceress wreaks on Corinth. If Medea's exit from the house is a case study in how women's violations of spatial boundaries disrupt crucial divisions between private and public, domestic and civic, civilized and barbaric, thereby causing disaster for the *polis*, the Girl's exit, by contrast, is a perfect example of the proper regulation of women's transgressive energies. The rupture of the boundary that separates inside from outside, which makes possible her offer of self-sacrifice, will also make possible another rupture: the explosion of the restricted circumference of Iolaos' and Demophon's heroic *aidōs*. In this way, the Girl's voluntary exit from within an *oikos* (both the literal one represented by the sanctuary of Zeus Agoraios, and the figurative one, the 'house' of Herakles) in order to satisfy Kore's requirements for saving the *polis* becomes the perfect vehicle for dramatizing *prohairesis*. As such, her action, however unseemly for a female, paradoxically becomes a model of correct and appropriate civic 'boldness'.

[79] Cf. Thuc. 2. 45, Sophocles, *Ajax* 239, Aristotle, *Politics* 1260[a]30.

Yet this action, which helps redefine heroic and aristocratic values in this way, reorientating them to a communal good, also starts to redefine the Girl herself, along masculine lines; her eager appropriation of masculine traits is equally paradoxical. The diction of her speech consistently bears witness to her attraction to a man's 'world of war'.[80] This masculinized, martial identity will conflate attributes both of the legendary past, as exemplified by the Girl's father Herakles and his comrade Iolaos, and of the modern hoplite in the democratic city, which requires of its warriors the *prohairesis* that she demonstrates and which abhors the *philopsykhia* that she rejects. Vernant remarks in his study of the ideology of Greek warfare that the aim of the democratic city was to replace the hero-warrior with the citizen-warrior, one who 'inherits the prestige' associated with heroism but who 'rejects all the disturbing aspects' of the hero—that is, his potential *hybris*.[81] In assuming a military persona that is at once heroic and hoplitic, the Girl can be said to dissolve still other boundaries—those between aristocratic and democratic values—in a way that echoes this ideological project.[82]

The Female Warrior: Almost Virgin?

Throughout the series of speeches and exchanges that constitute the Girl's offer of self-sacrifice, she leaves no doubt as to the admiration she feels for the values Iolaos represents; indeed she admonishes him to educate her siblings accordingly once she has gone to her death (574–6). She dies out of reverence for her *genos* (*prouthanon genous*, 590), thus echoing Iolaos' articulation of the '*genos* creed' in the prologue (*to syngenes sebōn*, 6). Like a Homeric hero, she is fearful of doing anything that will make her an object of ridicule (*gelōtos axia*, 507), or that would make

---

[80] Loraux, *Tragic Ways of Killing a Woman*, 33.

[81] See J.-P. Vernant, *Problèmes de la guerre en Grèce ancienne* (Paris, 1968), 19.

[82] For the 'democratization' of aristocratic terms and values in the political rhetoric of the democratic state, see Ober, *Mass and Elite*, 259ff. '[D]espite the apparent dissonance between aristocratic emphasis on superiority and demotic principles of equality,' Ober writes, '. . . the concepts of *eugeneia* and *kalokagathia* were democratized and communalized in the course of the fifth and fourth centuries and so made the common property of all citizens.' Ober focuses on the democratization of *khrēstos* (Lysias 19) and *kalokagathos* (Lysias 30, Aiskhines 1, Dinarkhos 3).

her seem unworthy of the father who engendered her (*patros d'ekeinou phyntas hou pephykamen*, 509 f.: her use of *phyo* here echoes Iolaos' frequent resort to the same vocabulary). Like Homer's Telemakhos, she is, moreover, anxious to demonstrate that she is in fact the child of her legendary and noble, *eugenēs*, father (*patros ousan eugenous*, 513). Her voluntary self-sacrifice will be the ultimate 'proof' of her paternity in the eyes of the onlookers (*ex ekeinou sperma tēs theias phrenos | pephykas Herakleos*, 541 f.),[83] just as Demophon's promise of aid to the suppliants 'proved' his noble heritage (325). Like both Iolaos and Demophon, she cannot help imagining what people will say of her if she behaves ignobly (517 ff.). In order to avoid such whisperings, she actively seeks a voluntary death that she describes as 'the finest treasure', *heurēma kalliston* (533 f.)—a far cry from the silence and invisibility that are usually thought of as the finest thing, *kalliston*, for a woman, according to the Girl (477). She chooses death, moreover, because it will be the vehicle for her *kleos* (534)—the renown, we should remember, for which Homeric women must typically depend on their husbands, but which is part of the 'essential structuring' of the male heroic ethos.[84] For this reason she steps out of her own accord, 'before being ordered to do so' (*prin keleusthēnai*, 501; cf. *ou takhtheisa*, 'not having been ordered to do so', 479), as eager to demonstrate her heroism as if she were a Homeric warrior preparing for single combat. Her use of *keleusthēnai* in the specifically military context that is established by a figurative reference to the Argive army as 'the inimical Argive spear' (*ekhthron Argeion dory*, 500), is indeed our first hint that the Girl has begun to think of herself as a warrior.

The Girl's motivations thus seem to dovetail neatly with those of Iolaos and Demophon in their heroic, epic milieu. Yet like the Athenian ephebe, whose training for hoplite warfare, with its special focus on communal interdependency and what one orator called 'orderliness, self-restraint, and obedience', paradoxically

[83] This particular genitive form of Herakles' name is an epicism contrary to Euripidean usage, as Garzya points out ad loc.; the anomalous usage is, perhaps, intended to underscore the heroic nature of the Girl's motives here.

[84] The canonical expression of this dichotomy between masculine and feminine renown is *Od.* 19. 124–8, on which see the relevant comments of Loraux, *Tragic Ways of Killing a Woman*, 2 ff.

emphasized the much older values useful to the individualistic hero or lone hunter, the Girl's self-assertiveness is ultimately integrated into a communal programme.[85] 'With her death,' Burnett observes, 'Macaria can repay the championing city (503 ff.) and serve her family as well (590), and so her sacrifice is both city-oriented, like that of Menoeceus, and made for love, as Alcestis' was.' I would reverse the sequence of Burnett's assertions. Given her education at Iolaos' hands, the Girl's allegiance to, and 'love' of, the *genos* is never in doubt; what is genuinely new here is how she integrates that family feeling to service on behalf of the *polis*. Hence when she thinks of war, she is thinking of is not merely the epic combats about which Iolaos reminisces, which enhance the glory of the individual warrior, but also of hoplite battle—which for Athenians meant the communal effort of a citizen militia in the service of the city.[86]

This quasi-ephebic incorporation of individual into communal values is, perhaps, best embodied in the expression the Girl uses when envisioning her own sacrifice, at which she vows to 'stand by', *paristasthai sphagēi* (502). Although the idea of 'standing by' at a sacrifice is nothing new, the verb is normally used of the onlookers or even the sacrificer, rather than the victims themselves. Scholars have attempted to explain *Children of Herakles*'s odd locution in various ingenious ways.[87] The verb is less problematic, however, when we recall its particular association with warfare, and indeed its etymological connection to

---

[85] Isokrates in his *Panathenaikos* (116) describes hoplite warfare as based on *eutaxia*, *sōphrosynē*, and *peitharkhia*. For the Athenian *ephebeia*'s paradoxical conflation of the values of the hero/hunter with those of the citizen/hoplite, see the important discussion of Vidal-Naquet, 'The Black Hunter and the Origin of the Athenian *Ephebeia*', in *The Black Hunter*, 106–28, and esp. 111 ff.

[86] Burnett 'Tribe and City', 16. For the Athenian equation of hoplite and citizen, see R. T. Ridley, 'The Hoplite as Citizen: Athenian Military Institutions in their Social Context', *L'Antiquité Classique*, 48 (1979), 509–48, and Vidal-Naquet, *The Black Hunter*, 85–105, 'The Tradition of the Athenian Hoplite'. 'It was', as Vidal-Naquet comments, 'as a citizen that the Athenian went to war.'

[87] Herwerden and Palmer go so far as to suggest replacing the manuscript's σφαγῇ ('sacrifice') with σφαγεῖ ('sacrificer'); Wilkins adduces *IA* 1551 as a parallel for this proposal: ἡ δὲ σταθεῖσα τῷ τεκόντι πλησίον. For the more conventional usage of *paristasthai*, see Iolaos' use of the same word at 564, οὐκ ἂν δυναίμην σῷ παρεστάναι μόρῳ: 'I could not bear to be present at your death', and cf. *Alk.* 1011, *IT* 726 and 1314, *Hek.* 224, *Andr.* 547, *Hel.* 1582f.

parastatēs, 'comrade-in-arms'. This is, in fact, the word that Iolaos uses to describe his relationship with Herakles (88), and the Girl's appropriation of *paristasthai* suggests, perhaps, that in this too she is somehow emulating Iolaos, casting herself in a supporting role appropriate to her father's heroic and martial milieu.

Yet *parastatēs* had another meaning that would have had additional and quite compelling overtones for the play's audience. For it is also the term used by fifth-century hoplites to describe their companions-in-arms; standing beside, *parastasis*, 'forms the basis of a phalanx's order of hoplites', because 'standing next to' (*paristasthai*) one's comrade was the lynchpin of hoplite warfare.[88] Intimately bound up with notions of communal interdependency, rather than the lopsided hierarchy of subordinate to superior implied in Iolaos' use of the word, *parastatēs* is in fact used prominently in the oath of fealty to the state taken by Athenian ephebes who had been prepared for hoplite warfare. In the oath, as it comes to us in a fourth-century stele from Akharnai and which is transcribed by both Pollux and Stobaios, this comrade within the ranks was typically referred to as *parastatēs*: 'I shall not shame my sacred arms nor will I abandon my next-in-line (*parastatēs*) wherever I am stationed in the line of battle', the hoplite swore.[89] The Girl's implicit self-identification as a *parastatēs* facing death, then, would have been the same as that of the Athenian hoplite in the same circumstances. As both historians and literary critics have commented, the importance of the oath in the military—and thus civic—lives

[88] Loraux, *Tragic Ways of Killing a Woman*, 86 n. 24.

[89] οὐκ αἰσχυνῶ τὰ ἱερὰ ὅπλα οὐδὲ λείψω τὸν παραστάτην ὅπου ἂν στ⟨ο⟩ιχήσω. The text of the oath is transmitted by Pollux (8. 105 ff.); Stobaios (4. 1. 8); the Akharnai inscription appears as Tod *GHI* II. no. 204, published in L. Robert, *Études épigraphiques et philologiques* (Paris, 1928), 296 ff. A concise and informative overview of the oath, its transmission, and civic meanings is to be found in P. Siewert, 'The Ephebic Oath in Fifth-Century Athens', *JHS* 97 (1977), 102–11. Siewert asserts that the text of the 4th-cent. Akharnian inscription is 'a reliable copy of the archaic Athenian civic oath', in order to justify his use of the inscription in establishing allusions to it in 5th-cent. prose and tragedy, as I do here as well; in emphatic agreement with him is Vidal-Naquet, *The Black Hunter*, 97. Cf. also the discussions by C. Pélékidis' *Histoire de l'éphébie attique* (Paris, 1962), 112 f., 75–8; R. Merkelbach, 'Aglauros (Die Religion der Epheben)', *ZPE* 9 (1972), 277–83; G. Daux, 'Le Serment des éphèbes athéniens', *REG* 84 (1971), 370–83; and Ridley, 'The Hoplite as Citizen', 532 ff.

of the Athenians would have given the use of such key words especial resonance for the fifth-century Athenian audience.[90] Here we should note that the first of the deities called upon as witnesses in the text of the oath was Aglauros, one of the courotrophic and salvific females of Athenian civic myth on whom the Girl may well be modelled.

It is in 'holding the line in the face of sacrifice' that the Girl is most explicitly contrasted with Iolaos, her ostensible model. For the hoplite's solidarity with his comrades, his insistence on 'staying put', *paristasthai*, in the face of death, was in fact intimately linked with the rejection of *philopsykhia*—the very trait that Iolaos has demonstrated.[91] Indeed Herakles' daughter twice shuns *philopsykhia* as an unacceptable option (*philopsykhountes*, 518; cf. *mē philopsykhous' egō*, 533). Her identification with the hoplite thus invokes an important topos of the military ideology of the *polis* even as it allows the Heraklids to make amends for Iolaos's behaviour. Unlike Iolaos, who gave up his city for the sake of his kin, the Girl dies both for her kin *and* for the city, *pro t'adelphōn kai gās* (622, where *gās* clearly refers not to Argos, but to Athens itself).[92] Just as her entrance from within in order to die on behalf of the land exemplifies proper civic priorities (subordination of *oikos* to *polis*), so does her rhetoric reflect—even as her actions resolve—the tensions and ambiguities present in a polity that sought to put pre-democratic values to work in the service of a democratic agenda.

---

[90] Siewert asserts that 'Echoes of, or allusions to, this fundamental document in fifth-century authors would be no surprise' ('The Ephebic Oath', 104), and points out relevant examples at Thuc. 1. 144. 4 and 2. 37. 3, Soph. *Ant.* 663–71, and Aesch. *Persians* 956–62. It is noteworthy, in the context of my discussion of *parastatēs* in particular, that Jebb saw the use of this word at *Ant.* 671 as a self-conscious allusion to the ephebic oath (*Sophocles. The Plays and Fragments*, iii. *Antigone* (London, 1900), 127, ad 671). For additional commentary about the allusion to the oath in the Aeschylus passage, see H. D. Broadhead, *The Persae of Aeschylus* (Cambridge, 1960), 231.

[91] Tyrtaios, for example (10. 15–18), contrasts remaining by the side of one's comrades (*per' allēloisi menontes*) with cowardly life-loving, *philopsykhein*.

[92] For this point see Wilkins, *Euripides* Heraclidae, 131, and Garzya, *Euripide Eraclidi*, 104 ad loc.

Inverting aidōs, *Redefining* khrēstos: *Gender into Politics*

After Herakles' daughter concludes her striking speech, Iolaos overlooks the shame he would normally feel at the impropriety normally associated with the public appearance of a young girl. On the contrary, he expresses a kind of comradely sympathy for her plight: 'I am not ashamed (*aiskhynomai*) | at your words, but am pained (*algunomai*) by your fate', he declares (541 f.). This is a far cry from the old man's initial reference to his great-niece, in the prologue, when he declared himself ashamed (*aidoumetha*) at the thought of exposing his young virgin kin to the eyes of the crowd (43 f.). The reversal indicates not so much that Iolaos has changed his mind about gender proprieties, but, I would suggest, that the context in which *aidōs* is meant to be understood in the later passage has changed radically; now, the Girl's actions are being judged by masculine and heroic rather than by feminine, 'quiet' standards.

It is surely for this reason that she incurs no blame for insisting, as she does, that her action on behalf of her kin be publicly proclaimed (*exangellomai*, 531)—the ultimate violation, we might say, of the prohibition on feminine visibility and speech. Similarly, when she expresses the rather immodest wish to prove that she is *episēmos* (527)—a word that, like *thrasos*, can have a double meaning, in this case either 'renowned' or 'infamous', but whose positive connotation is, as in those other cases, more likely to obtain in the case of a man—the Girl is not censured but praised by her great-uncle:

> ὅδ᾽ αὖ λόγος σοι τοῦ πρὶν εὐγενέστερος,
> κἀκεῖνος ἦν ἄριστος· ἀλλ᾽ ὑπερφέρεις
> τόλμῃ τε τόλμαν καὶ λόγῳ χρηστῷ λόγον.

Indeed this speech of yours is even more worthy of one
    well-born (*eugenesteros*)
than was the earlier one—and that one was itself most
    virtuous. You exceed
each boldness (*tolmē*) with more boldness, each speech
    with a more noble (*khrēstos*) speech.

(553–5)

Tolmē, 'boldness', is yet another ambiguous word like *thrasos* and *episēmos*; its pejorative connotation is something like 'impudence'. Yet here again it is clearly being used to compliment

rather than reprove the Girl. Only assimilation to the world of
men—the beautiful treasure she herself had fervently wished
for—allows a female's impudent gesture to be transformed into
an act of praiseworthy daring, guaranteeing her renown in place
of infamy. Iolaos indeed goes on to celebrate her as *eugenēs*, as he
had once praised Demophon; he then awards her 'the compliment most valued in Greek society', by calling her *aristos*.[93]
Moreover, his reference to her daring (rather than impudent)
and renowned (rather than infamous) offer as a 'noble speech',
khrēstos logos, reminds us of his earlier use of that vocabulary in
his prologue speech. There, he denounced the selfish man as
akhrēstos to the *polis* (4), and indeed implied that his own selfless
protection of his kin had made him *khrēstos*. The Girl, it would
seem, has earned this ancient hero's highest praise—by being
likened to him.

But even as the Girl is being redefined in masculine and heroic
terms by Iolaos, she herself is subtly redefining key political
terms, just as her appropriation of *parastatēs* had earlier suggested a new and more civic-minded definition for that term. In
the political lexicon of the fifth and fourth centuries, *khrēstos* is
used to refer to the social and political elites; the orators often
used this word to describe aristocrats,[94] and for this reason, perhaps, it is no surprise that it so readily comes to old Iolaos' lips.
(Even at this late date, the reason Iolaos gives for not preventing
the Girl from performing her *khrēstos* action is that her death will
save her *genos*: 'in dying, you help your siblings', he tells her at
557. Once again, he seems to be speaking solely as a *gennētēs*,
someone from a good family interested in preserving his good
family.) But the Girl, acutely conscious of the suppliants' obligations to the *polis* that has attempted to save them (503 ff., 586;
cf. 622), dismisses the behaviour that Iolaos has thus far displayed—sitting at the altar after having fled death, and wailing—
as 'worthy of ridicule' (*gelōtos axia*), and unsuitable for men who
call themselves *khrēstoi* (507–10). Her understanding of *khrēstos*
is, therefore, radically different from her great-uncle's. That this
is so is, in fact, made clear by her insistence on an *active* role,

[93] O'Connor-Visser, *Aspects of Human Sacrifice*, 24.

[94] See the remarks of Ober (*Mass and Elite*, 13 f.), who cites as an example
Isokrates' recommendation of monarchy as the system within which the *khrēstos*
need not interact with the masses, *plēthos* (Isokrates 3. 16).

freely seeking death to preserve both family *and* city. Hence when Iolaos rather typically suggests that Kore's victim be selected 'passively', by lot (*lakhousa*, 545), the Girl rejects this option quite emphatically (548). This is consonant with her unbidden exit from the sanctuary (479), before being ordered to do so (501); and with her offer to end her life of her own free will rather than by compulsion (*hekousa k'ouk akousa*, 530f.; cf. 550f.). At her hands, Iolaos' *khrēstos* has been democratized, its definition expanding to include a willingness to choose certain death rather than preserve life: the hallmark, in fact, of the citizen-hoplite ethos that was first exemplified at the historical battle of Marathon itself.[95]

Regulating Feminine Transgression: The Lady Vanishes

Hence the old man's praise of his grand-niece's action serves, ironically, to spotlight his own political shortcomings. Yet her example will radically change Iolaos himself: later on, he will avenge his *genos* during a quasi-Homeric pursuit and confrontation, after having joined in the successful defence of the saving city, Athens—a moment crowned by the appearance of the twin deities who presided over the ephebes of the democratic city. Iolaos' 'political' rehabilitation therefore conforms to the model provided by the Girl, an acting-out of both the heroic and hoplitic elements of the warrior identity that she had claimed for herself.

But the Girl herself gets to play those roles only figuratively; it is in providing the useful model that she serves both her dramatic and, we may say, her cultural purpose. The rewards that she craves—renown, heroic burial—are either abbreviated or awarded to men in the play, because they are, in fact, the cultural property of men.[96] This redistribution enacts the successful containment of the potentially disastrous energies that are released whenever women step out of the literal and figurative spaces reserved for them in Greek culture and Greek drama,

[95] The conscious decision to die is, as Loraux observes, the 'lynchpin' of Lysias' account of Marathon (*Epitaphios* 24–6; Loraux, *The Invention of Athens*, 102). See her discussion of 'the beautiful death' at pp. 98–106.

[96] Nancy sees female self-sacrifice as inherently ironic—a willing embrace of an otherwise impossible means of escaping the obscurity imposed on women, even if at the price of their own destruction ('Sacrifice humain', 28).

carefully ensuring that it is always the positive rather than negative values of terms like *thrasos*, *tolmē*, and *episēmos* that are
exemplified by these women's actions.

We can, in fact, sense the disruptive forces hinted at by the
negative connotations of those words, just beneath the surface of
the Girl's speech; the very elements that make her offer praiseworthy are those that make it potentially dangerous. This is most
apparent not in Iolaos's reaction to her speech, but that of the
chorus, which here as elsewhere serves as a better indicator, perhaps, of conventional mores than does a character implicated in
the drama itself. The chorus reacts with some surprise to the
Girl's offer (500–34): 'What shall I say in response to the great
speech, *megan logon*, | of the Girl, who desires to die instead of,
paros, her brothers?' they exclaim (535). Yet *megas logos* is, as
Wilkins remarks, 'unusual in a sense of approval',[97]; and *paros*,
too, is ambiguous, for its ostensible if somewhat unusual meaning here, 'instead of' (we expect something more like *paroithe*,
as in 57, *paroith' hairesetai*) is undercut by its more usual
meaning,[98] 'beforehand', or even 'too soon'. Hence the chorus's
remark can also, or simultaneously, be read as follows: 'What am
I to make of the presumptuous speech of the Girl, who desires to
die before her brothers [i.e. before her brothers can die on behalf
of the *genos*]?' This double entendre retroactively colours our
understanding of Iolaos' assertion that the Girl's refusal of the
lottery 'exceeds bold daring with even more boldness', *hyper-
phereis tolmēi te tolman*, 554 f. Embedded in the prefix *hyper* is the
sense of 'transgressive' excess;[99] indeed for both Demophon and
Iolaos, the Girl's boldness elevates her to a superlative level
where she surpasses all other females ('most boldly enduring',
tlēmonestatēn, of all women, 570 f.; cf. 'surpassing by far all
women in greatness of soul, *eupsykhia*', 597 f.). It is possible that
these superlatives are meant to remind us that behind the positive values attached to the various descriptions of the Girl's act—
thrasos, *tolmē*, *episēmos*, etc.—there is a negative potentiality that
always threatens to explode onto the surface when the feminine
propensity to transgress goes unchecked.

[97] Wilkins, *Euripides* Heraclidae, 120 ad loc.
[98] For *paros* as 'instead of' here, see Garzya's note, *Euripide Eraclidi*, 97 ad
loc.
[99] So LSJ B. II. 2.

But in the case of the Girl, that typically feminine dissolution is, in fact, kept in check once it has served the constructive purpose of dissolving the too-rigid boundaries of heroic *aidōs*. In the text as it currently stands, the Girl's act is not celebrated in the speech of men beyond the brief song of praise offered by the chorus; the other characters become silent about her act almost as soon as she has exited to be sacrificed to Kore. Even if one insists on the possibility of a 'lost' messenger speech describing her sacrifice,[100] a series of substitutions and reversals in fact denies the Girl the titles and honours to which she aspired. According to Kore's oracle, a virgin sacrifice will be a marker of the enemy's defeat, *tropaia ekhthrōn* (402); according to Demophon, it will be proof of the bravery, *eupsykhia*, of Herakles' daughter (569). The Girl herself hints that her act will mark an 'alleviation of toils', *apallagē ponōn* (586), for her family. Yet it is Herakles' *son*, Hyllos, whose Homeric challenge to Eurystheus to meet in single combat during the play's climactic battle-scene is described as *apallagai ponōn* (811), and proof of the challenger's bravery, *eupsykhia* (812); and it is Hyllos, along with Iolaos himself, who erects the marker, *tropaia*, after defeating the enemy and avenging the *genos* (786 f., 936 f.).

Moreover, despite the repeated assertions that the Heraklids' and Athens' *sōtēria* will result from the sacrifice of a young female, *nea parthenos* (402, 490 ff.), and indeed despite the Girl's identification of herself as the saviour, *sōteira*, of her family (588; cf. 577), it is a *male* Heraklid, Hyllos, whom Iolaos rather startlingly hails as 'saviour', *sōtēr*, just moments after the Girl's exit to her death, as Hyllos' servant appears (640). It is Hyllos, therefore, who in effect resolves the suppliant crisis; and it is he, speaking through the Servant, who utters the 'phrase of the formal champion',[101] in bidding Iolaos to rise, *epaire sauton* (635). A scant thirty lines after her departure, the Girl's role has been co-opted by a character who, in stark contrast to her own striking preoccupation with being present and visible, has invisibly shadowed the action of the play from off stage.[102] Later and even more strikingly, perhaps, both the title of *sōtēr* and hero's burial that the Girl had requested (588) are appropriated not by

---

[100] A possibility that I reject: see ch. 1, n. 8 for a discussion of the textual question.

[101] Burnett, 'Tribe and City', 18.

a friend or even an ally of the Heraklids, but by the play's villain, Eurystheus, whose own tomb will be a saving boon (*sōtērios*) for the Athenians in generations to come (1032f.) Given the Girl's wishes and the nature of the sacrifice she makes, we can surely count it among that play's startling reversals that it is the tomb of the villain Eurystheus, and its future salvific value to the Athenians, that are made much of at the conclusion of the play.

The manner in which the Girl disappears from the text, therefore, seems almost to parody her motivations for entering into the world of men. In every respect, the girl's actions are either erased and reassigned, however unsuitably, to the men in the play. But her self-sacrifice galvanizes Iolaos, who after being reduced to a passive and enclosed femininity will rise up, transformed, to put heroic valour in the service of the state.

Displacement and Transformation II: Iolaos

Iolaos' failure to acknowledge the pre-eminence of the community results, then, in a dilemma that renders him completely passive. His passivity, in turn, associates him with another narrow, private, and enclosed world: the world of women.[103] It is the specifically feminine nature of Iolaos' passivity that I want briefly to consider, since an 'experience of the feminine'—

[102] I. F. de Jong has argued in 'Three Off-Stage Characters in Euripides' (*Mnemosyne*, 43 (1990) 1–21) that certain Euripidean characters who remain off stage, and whose actions are merely narrated in messenger speeches, can none the less have great dramatic impact: she cites the Corinthian princess in *Medea*, Neoptolemos in *Andromakhe*, and Aigisthos in *Elektra* as examples of 'focal' off-stage characters the narration of whose deaths offers the 'emotional filtering' that narrated, as opposed to dramatized, events can provide. In a related vein, Judith Mossman has argued that the character who unifies the action of the *Andromakhe*, a work as notoriously disjointed as our political plays, is the absent Neoptolemos ('Waiting for Neoptolemus: On the Unity of Euripides' *Andromache*', *GR* 43 (1996), 143–56). It is indeed possible to see the off-stage Hyllos' search for a place to settle as unifying the action to some extent; see the discussion below, pp. 115ff.; but it is difficult to see him as a focal character in de Jong's sense since, if anything, the climactic narrative in *Children of Herakles* self-consciously dispenses with Hyllos (whose offer to fight Eurystheus is rejected (802ff.) in favour of Iolaos, whose miraculous rejuvenation is the centrepiece of the speech).

[103] See Burnett, 'Tribe and City', 17 for the suppliants as 'passive receivers of aid', and cf. Segal, 'Admetus' Divided House', 16 on the 'enforced passivity' of men that results from the active interference of women.

expressed gesturally in his assumption of attitudes and language belonging to the theatrical vocabulary of the feminine—is what precedes his miraculous transformation.

Displacement, Passivity, Femininity

The Girl's appropriation of masculine and heroic identity displaces Iolaos, depriving him of the heroic identity that he yearns to assume once again. This displacement begins with the Girl's entrance. After learning of the impasse to which Kore's oracle has brought Demophon, Iolaos lifted his voice in a cry of utter despair. It is in response to this noise that the Girl appears:

> τῶν σῶν δ᾽ ἀκούσασ᾽, Ἰόλεως, στεναγμάτων
> ἐξῆλθον, οὐ ταχθεῖσα πρεσβεύειν γένους,
> ἀλλ᾽, εἰμὶ γάρ πως πρόσφορος, μέλει δέ μοι
> μάλιστ᾽ ἀδελφῶν τῶνδε κἀμαυτῆς πέρι,
> θέλω πυθέσθαι μὴ 'πὶ τοῖς πάλαι κακοῖς
> προσκείμενόν τι πῆμα σὴν δάκνει φρένα.

Having heard your moans, Iolaos,
I have come outside—not that I've been ordered to represent
  my kin (*genos*),
but, because I am suitable to do so and am deeply concerned
on behalf of my siblings here as well as myself,
I wish to inquire whether in addition to our ills of old
some other calamity has been added that is eating away at you.

(478–83)

This is not the first time the old man's noise has attracted notice. In the opening scene his cries for help while being bullied by the Argive Herald had precipitated what Wilkins calls a 'scene of great animation': the chorus—and, by analogy, the Athenian king Demophon himself—appear on stage as *boēdromoi* (*boēdromēsas*, 120), the formal term used of rescuers who respond to cries for help (*iugmōn*, 126).[104] Later, after the announcement of Kore's demand, Iolaos' cries bring not the chorus of old men, nor the Athenian king, but a young girl to play the role of saviour. This unusual feminine appropriation of the role of *boēdromos* heralds the Girl's usurpation of Iolaos' role as protector of the

---

[104] For details about *boēdromia* with respect to the play's opening, see Wilkins, *Euripides* Heraclidae, 59 ad 69ff. For an interesting inversion of this motif, cf. *Orestes* 1529, when Orestes comes out in order to keep the Phrygian from crying out.

genos; it is she now for whom the children of Herakles are 'especially' a concern, as they were for Iolaos in the prologue (*melei de moi malista*, 480; cf. 10f.). Her assertion that she is especially suited to taking charge of her clan (*presbeuein genous*) implies a further competition—that is, with her brother, Hyllos, who is described in the prologue as being the leader of his brothers (*Hyllos d'adelphoi th'oisi presbeuei genos*, 45).[105]

Later, the Girl once again renders Iolaos passive, displacing him from the role of family saviour which indeed even now, in the face of Kore's implacable demand, he tries vainly to appropriate for himself in a last desperate exchange with Demophon:

> ἀλλ' οἶσθ' ὅ μοι σύμπραξον· οὐχ ἅπασα γὰρ
> πέφευγεν ἐλπὶς τῶνδέ μοι σωτηρίας.
> ἔμ' ἔκδος Ἀργείοισιν ἀντὶ τῶνδ', ἄναξ,
> καὶ μήτε κινδύνευε σωθήτω τέ μοι
> τέκν'· οὐ φιλεῖν δεῖ τὴν ἐμὴν ψυχήν·

> But do this for me—for not every
> hope of mine for their rescue has fled:
> Give *me* instead of them to the Argives, King,
> and without danger to yourself let my children
> be saved. I ought not to hang on to life (*philein psykhēn*).

> (451–5)

This offer of his own life may not be too little, but it is surely too late. Iolaos' newfound desire to die as the children's saviour ignores both Eurystheus' intentions and the oracular demand[106] (although his use of *philopsykhein* indicates that he has recognized too late the inappropriateness of his earlier desire to preserve his life, *psykhē*, at the cost of his civic status). And indeed, the oracular demand for a well-born young female makes Iolaos utterly beside the point, while allowing the Girl to appropriate not only his role in the action but, in a way, his epithets as well. Earlier, Iolaos had boasted of his once-famous physical strength,

---

[105] The verbal echo is striking if not perfectly syntactically parallel. For this phrase see Wilkins' note ad loc., *Euripides* Heraclidae, 55.

[106] His offer constitutes what Schmitt calls the 'delaying moment' in Euripides' dramas of self-sacrifice, when some alternative to the inevitable moment is offered in order to build false hopes and, thereby, dramatic suspense (Schmitt, *Freiwilliger Opfertod*, 41 ff.). The dramatic potential of what she calls 'delaying moments' helps explain why characters can so easily forget the precise terms of the oracular demands; cf. Garzya, *Euripide Eraclidi*, 89 ad loc.

referring to the renown his 'not unheralded body', *ouk akērykton sōma* (89), had won him as Herakles' *parastatēs* (88). Now of course it is the Girl who plays the role of *parastatēs*; now it is the use to which she puts her body (*katērktai sōma*, 601) that becomes a vehicle for winning a reputation 'not without renown', (*oud' akleēs doxa*, 623f.; cf. *eukleōs lipein bion*, 533) both far and wide (as *exangellomai*, 'publicly proclaimed', suggests).

Iolaos Plays the Other: allê parthenos, allē mētēr

The Girl's departure on her heroic errand at 602ff. leaves Iolaos as stricken and utterly helpless as her arrival had found him. His limbs are loosened with sorrowful pain (*lyetai melē | lypēi*, 602f.); he can barely walk, and must be assisted to his place on the altar, ordering his young charges to conceal him within his garments (*peploisi toisde krypsantes*, 604). This injunction cites nearly verbatim the Girl's request, made only moments earlier, that at the moment of sacrifice her body be duly concealed by her robes (*peplois de sōm' emon krypson*, 561)—a request that duly conforms to the conventions of feminine propriety. Hence Iolaos' veiled concealment not only recalls the gestural vocabulary of young Athenian virgins (for whom the concealing folds of their robes served the same purpose as the concealing walls of the houses within which they were expected to remain), but strikingly makes him the visual double of the Girl herself. And indeed the old man's confinement to this temporary 'interior' space results in a quite literal obscuring of his identity: on entering, Hyllos' manservant fails to recognize him. Having come in search of the suppliants (630–1), the Servant finds only a prostrate, veiled figure that can bear little resemblance to the dignified old man he no doubt expects to see (633). The Servant, alarmed by the old man's helplessness, urges him to get up (*epaire nyn seauton . . . orthōson kara*, 630–5). After the stranger reveals that he has come as Hyllos's representative, Iolaos identifies him as his saviour, *sōtēr* (640), whose timely appearance is comparable to that of the *boēdromos* Demophon earlier in the action (205–6).

If Iolaos' passive, cloaked, anonymous attitude on stage at this moment indicates how far he has fallen from his former heroic, active identity, it also recalls certain other figures familiar from the tragic stage: the helpless female figures whom we encounter in Euripidean plays of the same period. His physical infirmity, for instance, is comparable to that of the grief-maddened Trojan queen in the *Hekabe*—a play to which *Children of Herakles* has often been compared—whose limbs also buckle as her young female relative is dragged away (*lyetai de moi melē, Hek.* 438). Like Iolaos, Hekabe is so distraught that she must be raised up by her attendants (*orthousai tēn homodoulon, Hek.* 60). She, too, is made unrecognizable by misfortune when a messenger seeks her out, as the chorus's remark to Talthybios indicates: 'She is right here, supine on the ground, Talthybios, lying there completely wrapped up in her robes' (*synkekleimenē peplois, Hek.* 486–7). And when Talthybios addresses Hekabe, he uses the formulae similar to those used by Hyllos' servant when exhorting the prostrate Iolaos (*anistas' . . . epaire kai to palleukon kara, Hek.* 499–500). One thinks here also of another Euripidean female, a suppliant who, like Hekabe and like Iolaos, has been rendered servile by hostile circumstances in another play: Andromakhe.[107] When Andromakhe is finally rescued by her saviour, Peleus (cf. *Hkld.* 640, where Iolaos addresses Hyllos' servant as *sōtēr*), she is addressed similarly: *epaire sauton*, 'raise yourself up', he instructs her (*And.* 714). To be sure, the physical abasement and infirmity of these characters is not feminine *per se*; other old men in Euripides, such as Amphitryon in *Mad Herakles*, with whom Iolaos has much in common, are similarly portrayed. But a remark by Amphitryon himself suggests the degree to which physical passivity, abasement, and infirmity have a gendered inflection here. Like Iolaos, old Amphitryon helplessly awaits death at the hands of another enemy of Herakles' *genos*. He remarks that the physical inability to act that comes with age makes old men 'useless' (*akhreion*) and not worthy to be counted 'among men', *en andrasin* (*Her.* 40f.). Similarly unmanned, Iolaos is forced into a useless posture that will stand in stunning contrast to the results of the transformation that follows.

---

[107] The *Andromakhe*'s title character refers to herself as *syndoulos*, 64–5; cf. *Hek.* 495, when *doulē* is used of the Trojan queen. As an example of the marked physical helplessness of Euripidean heroines, one could also cite the delirious Phaidra at the opening of the *Hippolytos*, who appears veiled and weakened, begging to be lifted up by her maids (*Hipp.* 198–202).

Iolaos(') Arms: The Hoplite Transformation

The arrival of Hyllos' servant at 630 marks the beginning of that transformation—if not the literal metamorphosis that the old man will undergo on the battlefield, then an ethical one of which the latter is merely the mythic symbol. We first notice a change in Iolaos when—rather unexpectedly, given his passive self-absorption of only moments before—he sharply rebukes Alkmene for suggesting that military matters are no concern for aged people such as they (664–6). As if to prove her wrong, he goes on to show a marked interest in the disposition of the troops as described by the Servant (668–79). The exchange between the two men—in which Alkmene, significantly, does not partici-pate—provides details of the strength, position, and battle order of the two armies, and is filled with the technical language appro-priate to fifth-century hoplite battle.[108]

Despite his physical frailty, Iolaos wants to join this battle-line, and calls for arms. The arming-scene, together with the rather hysterical entrance of the old man's female counterpart Alkmene, has been seen as a comic interlude.[109] This would-be champion's references to his prowess (e.g. 685, 687) are, after all, clearly based on a dated assessment of his own abilities; he prays that his withered arm might have the strength it *once* did when he fought by Herakles' side (740 ff.). The Servant greets Iolaos' 'foolish speech', *mōron epos* (682), with the wry comment that the old man is unable to do (*drān . . . oukh' hoios te*), but is able at least to wish (*boulesthai*, 692). None the less, Iolaos insists on adding

---

[108] Hence the references to the lieutenants, *promoi* (670); used in Homer, this word gains wider currency in the 5th cent., referring to actual commanders in the field; cf. Aesch. *Ag.* 200, Soph. *OC* 884, Eur. *Tro.* 31; so too the serried ranks of troops (*taxeis*, 673); the all-important left flank (*laion keras*, 671), and the reference to Eurystheus as general, *stratēgos* (675).

[109] Burian describes the scene as 'perhaps the most overtly comic in extant tragedy', and sees the Servant as reminiscent of comic slaves ('Euripides *Heracleidae*', 11); cf. Falkner, 'The Wrath of Alcmene', 119; Lesky, 'On the "Heraclidae" of Euripides', 237; and Zuntz, *The Political Plays of Euripides*, 36 f. Lesky cites *Alkestis*'s Herakles as a parallel to Alkmene here; Zuntz describes Alkmene as 'a chicken in a thunderstorm', although he sees Iolaos' arming as ultimately more straight than comic (*Political Plays*, 29 f.; so too H. C. Avery, 'Euripides' Heracleidae', *AJP* 92 (1971), 555 f.). In this light, Pearson's suggestion that this ridiculous presentation of Iolaos was meant as a parody of a scene from Aeschylus' lost *Children of Herakles* (*Heracleidae*, xiii n. 2 and xvi) is especially appealing, if of course impossible to substantiate.

his feeble weight to the battle-line (689–90). His fervent commitment to helping his friends (*philoi*, 681, 683) stands here in vivid comic contrast to the presumed uselessness of his actions.

For all its quasi-Aristophanic touches, however, the scene signals a crucial moral turning point. Iolaos' words and actions herald a striking departure from the ethical and political positions earlier espoused by both himself and Demophon, and suggest the extent to which his change of heart is the result of the Girl's action. Earlier, the Athenian king—although extremely willing to help his kin (*prothymian tosēnde ekhō*, 410)—claimed to be unable to save anyone but the *philoi* constituted by his immediate family and *oikos* of Athenian citizens (413 ff.); to do so, he claimed, would have incurred the charge of folly, *mōria* (417). In Demophon's case, willingness (*boulesthai*) yielded to practicality (*hoios t' einai*). The Girl's self-sacrifice emphatically reversed that ethical hierarchy. Like the Athenian king, she referred to herself as 'willing and eager', *prothymos* (550, 577), but unlike Demophon she acted on that desire. Moreover, her willingness to give up her life, *psykhē* (550), 'corrected' Iolaos' own life-loving attitude (15), as we have seen. The Girl's gesture of *prohairesis* now serves as the model for Iolaos' present actions. For it now becomes clear to all, even the wry Servant, that the old man is eager, *prothymos* (731), to aid both his kin and his Athenian hosts, despite the physical impossibility of that desire. What is more, he will act on that desire, even if his physical unsuitability guarantees that his gesture will be tantamount to self-sacrifice: the Servant tells him that he is likely to fall dead before any blow of his sword could strike home (686), and the chorus will later admonish Iolaos to reconsider in terms that stress the practical necessity of understanding one's own weaknesses (706 f.). But Iolaos now understands his obligation to subordinate what is possible to what he wishes to do because he knows it is right—he subordinates *hoios t' einai* to *boulesthai*. The fact that he gladly incurs the epithet of *mōros*, foolish, further confirms the contrast with the Athenian king—even as the foolish conscious choice of death in the face of a great enemy recalls that of the real-life Athenian heroes at Marathon.

As if to signal that he has integrated the cooperative values exemplified by the Girl's choice, Iolaos orders the Servant to bring out a hoplite panoply, *hoplitēn kosmon*, from among the offerings that hang within the shrine of Zeus Agoraios (698f.). These arms are the spoils of some earlier exploit, *tropaia* long since dedicated to Zeus—the 'spear-won armour', *aikhmalōth' hopla*. But the Marathonian locale of the shrine can in fact only mean one thing, however anachronistically: that the hoplite panoply that Iolaos will don to defeat his formidable Argive enemy is, in fact, the 'venerable but antiquated relic of the glorious victory at Marathon when a handful of free Greeks—the *Marathōnomakhoi*—bravely stood off the slavish battalions of Persia'.[110]

Like the Servant, Alkmene is shocked by the spectacle of a fully-armed Iolaos, and expresses no little dismay. She exclaims that Iolaos is (literally) not 'in' his right mind (*sōn phrenōn ouk endon ōn*, 709), a locution that yet again recalls the Argive Herald's condemnation of any attempt to save the suppliants as sheer folly (56), and Demophon's rejection of the political risks of sacrificing an Athenian girl (413). The old woman is as brusque here as she was when she had first entered as yet another *boēdromos* responding to Iolaos' anguished cries (646); threatening the Servant (whom she mistakenly believed to be the Argive Herald) with physical force (653), she was the third person to render Iolaos passive as she seized control of the action. (Little wonder that Iolaos describes her in the prologue as a 'fellow-general', *stratēgos* (39).) But Iolaos' assumption of this new hoplite identity serves as a corrective not only for his earlier passivity, but for what we may call the excessive 'activity' of the play's female characters. When an outraged Alkmene remarks that the battle preparations described by the Servant concern neither her nor Iolaos (665), he responds that feats of daring are, in fact, the proper concern for *men* (*andrōn gar alkē*); women, he adds, should concern themselves with children (*soi de khrēn toutōn melein*, 711). Indeed, whereas Iolaos earlier described himself as the passive caretaker of Herakles' children, in need of rescue himself (*autos deomenos sōtērias*, 10f.), it is now Alkmene

[110] So William Arrowsmith, in his Introduction to *Euripides* Children of Herakles, tr. Henry Taylor and Robert A. Brooks (New York, 1981), x. Iolaos here does recall the old men in the chorus of *Lysistrata*; the scene's much-debated comic aspect is due to the tension between the oldsters' vivid recollections of Marathon (explicit in Aristophanes, implicit here) and their present frailty.

who, left with the children while her agemate totters off to battle,
reverts to a querulous passivity: 'If you die, how will I be saved?'
she asks him (*pōs egō sōthēsomai?*, 712). Similarly, Iolaos' vigorous appropriation of activity on behalf of his young relatives
implicitly corrects the problem posed by the Girl's appropriation of heroic action. Earlier, she had claimed that the rescue of
her siblings was *her* 'special concern' (*melei de moi malista*, 480).
But no more. Iolaos' assimilation of the Girl's example thus
restores 'order' as expressed both in his assumption of a new,
civically appropriate hoplite identity, and in the equally appropriate allotment of gender roles.

Relocation and Re-establishment

The play's climactic narrative of the battle between the Argives
and the Athenians (799–866) incorporates all of the various
elements we have seen thus far: hoplites and heroes; highly
improbable geographies; dislocations and pursuits; transformations both figurative and spectacularly literal. Here, however,
the reiteration of these motifs serves to establish rather than
destabilize identity. Heroic prowess and aristocratic excellences
now serve a hoplite ideal on behalf of the *polis*; a fantastic tour of
Attika leads to glory rather than despair; relentless pursuit
promises rather than prevents a return home; and metamorphosis confirms rather than problematizes the nature of the self.

The Messenger's description begins with the Athenian and
Argive hoplite forces (*hoplitēn straton*, 800) drawn up opposite
one another, *kata stoma*, in a configuration that clearly alludes to
the conventions of hoplite warfare (800ff.).[111] There follows a
modulation into a heroic mode: the imminent clash of phalanxes
is nearly averted by Hyllos's surprise offer to take on Eurystheus
in single combat—a challenge that has strong Homeric resonances, and which of course characterizes heroic, rather than
hoplitic, encounters.[112] After a cowardly Eurystheus refuses

[111] For the technical force of the term *kata stoma* at 801, cf. Eur. fr. 781. 33 N.;
Rhes. 409, 491, 511; and Hdt. 8. 11; for *stoma* as the front line of a hoplite
phalanx, see Xen. *Anab.* 3. 4. 42, and cf. Polybios 10. 12. 7.

[112] Cf. Menelaos' challenge to Paris in the *Iliad*. Paul Cartledge ('Hoplites
and Heroes: Sparta's Contribution to the Technique of Ancient Warfare', *JHS*
100 (1980), 18) has concisely described the historical realities of pre-hoplite
warfare which reflected such Homeric descriptions. Fighting, Cartledge notes,
was 'conducted pre-eminently by individual champions, opulent aristocrats

the offer, thereby displaying a shocking lack of *aidōs* (813), the scenario reverts once again to one familiar to fifth-century Athenian eyes: the Messenger's description can only be that of the seamless hoplite battle-line, which depended for its effectiveness on the solidarity of the *parastatai* standing fast side by side behind their shields (823–4). Demophon addresses his troops as 'fellow citizens'—*O xympolītai*—and reminds his people that they are fighting for Athens, the nourishing mother of its autochthonous offspring (825–6). In sharp contrast to the shameless Eurystheus, the armies are eager to avert *aiskhynē*; here we should note that the soldiers are exhorted to show *aidōs* not for themselves, but for their city (*ouk arēxet' aiskhynēn polei*, 839–40; cf. 828)—another allusion, perhaps, to the diction of the Athenian ephebic oath, in which the candidate swore not to shame (*ouk aiskhynō*) his arms nor to betray the fatherland (*patrida*).[113]

It is only now that Iolaos can step out of the ranks and take the action that finally resolves the drama's originally suppliant crisis. The Athenian army, with its Heraklid contingent, have put the Argives to flight (*phygēn*, 842), thereby reversing the relationship between the Argive pursuer and Heraklid quarry that has obtained throughout the drama. It is at the precise moment of the hoplite army's rout of the Argives that Iolaos makes his bid to pursue the fleeing Eurystheus. The old man requests a chariot in which to chase his enemy, and it is noteworthy that his request takes the form of formal supplication (844 f.)—a gesture he had made once before, in his original appeal to Demophon (226 f.). But now everything has changed. Before, the passive old man had appealed to an Athenian king to save the Heraklids: in so doing he asked Demophon to 'become' (*genou*, 228) all the various figures who might feel obliged to a suppliant: kin, friend, father, brother, master (*syngenēs . . . philos patēr adelphos despotēs*, 228 f.). That request, as we have seen, proved highly problematic. Now, an active and vigorous Iolaos entreats his own kin, Hyllos, to grant him a chariot and prays to the gods that he himself might 'become' something he is most emphatically

who have the means to employ horse-drawn chariots as a form of transportation'. For the prohibition against extravagant displays of individual prowess within the hoplite ranks, see Loraux, *The Invention of Athens*, 99 f.

[113] For the oath, see above, n. 89.

not: that is, young (*genesthai neos*, 852). As the earlier supplication had marked Iolaos' low point, the later supplicatory gesture
marks his rehabilitation as a hero who is, for the first time, both
willing *and* able to take vengeance on his family's enemy (*apo-
teisasthai dikēn ekhthrous*, 852). Iolaos now reclaims his rightful
place as a warrior—but only after the communal army's obligations to Athens have been honourably discharged.

The Pursuit of Eurystheus: Iolaos as allos Theseus

With his newly restored vigour, Iolaos rather improbably pur-
sues Eurystheus from Pallene, the deme on the northern slopes
of Mt. Hymettus, as far as the Skironian Rocks, the cliffs
between Megara and the Isthmus, where he finally captures
the tyrant and brings him back in fetters, a living trophy, the
akrothinion (861) to be displayed to a vengeful Alkmene. This
moment, like so much else in the play, is marked by a preoccupation with geography, albeit a 'vague and uncertain' one;[114] still,
the fanciful route that Iolaos takes, surely recognizable as such
by both the dramatist and his audience, allows the playwright to
make a special political point. For the Skironian Rocks were the
site of a legendary victory by Theseus over the giant Skiron,
who, by hurling unlucky travellers off the cliffs, had made passage to Athens from the west impossible. Skiron was only one of
several such brigands whom Theseus had to do away with before
making his way to Athens to claim his birthright: Korynetes,
Sinis (as well as a beast, the sow of Krommyon), Skiron,
Kerkyon, and Prokroustes were all unappetizing types who
preyed on passers-by and travellers, and all had to be killed as
part of a series of Thesean civilizing labours that in many ways
mimicked those of Herakles himself.[115] There is in fact another
Euripidean reference to this site: in *Hippolytos*, Theseus identifies his triumph at the Skironian Rocks with the defeat of evil,
kakon (*Hipp.* 976–80). According to the principle tradition of

---

[114] Garzya, *Euripide Eraclidi*, 124 ad 860 ff.: Theseus' route is 'absurd, if
taken literally', Garzya dryly comments here. See also the remarks of Wilkins ad
loc., *Euripides* Heraclidae, 164, 166.

[115] Theseus' battle with Skiron: see Plut. *Thes.* 10; Strabo 9. 1. 4; Paus. 1. 44.
7 and 2. 1. 3; Diod. Sic. 4. 59. 4. Theseus' exploits with the various other
brigands: Diod. Sic. 4. 59. 1. For the Athenian ruler's labours as typical of a
hero's civilizing exploits, see the discussion of Mills, *Theseus, Tragedy*, 1–25; for
those labours as imitative of Herakles', ibid. 136–9.

Theseus' labours, the Athenian prince's demonstration that he could vanquish evil men literally and figuratively cleared his way to Athens; for these adventures preceded his arrival at Athens, and made possible the revelation of the tokens, *symbola*, that demonstrated his identity to his father.[116]

In vanquishing Eurystheus in this particular setting, then, Iolaos follows the civilizing example of the Athenian king. His heroic valour, like that of Theseus, serves to help the city and to re-establish his personal identity; his pursuits through Attika of wicked men, like Theseus' pursuits, makes passage to the *polis* possible, helping to restore to his 'people' their own proper civic identity.

Repatriation: Identity Regained

Significantly, this victory is marked by a final locating action. In accordance with custom, Iolaos and Hyllos set up the trophy at the site of their victory over Eurystheus:

> νικῶμεν ἐχθροὺς καὶ τροπαῖ᾽ ἱδρύεται
> παντευχίαν ἔχοντα πολεμίων σέθεν.

We vanquished our enemies and a trophy was set up (*hidryetai*)
bearing the panoply of your antagonists.

(786–7)

And later:

> Ὕλλος μὲν οὖν ὅ τ᾽ ἐσθλὸς Ἰόλεως βρέτας
> Διὸς τροπαίου καλλίνικον ἵστασαν.

Hyllos and the noble Iolaos were setting up (*histasan*)
the triumphant image of Zeus-of-the-Trophies.

(936–7)

The setting-up of the *tropaion* symbolizes an ethical and military victory that both results in, and is an analogue for, the Heraklids' own triumphant re-establishment in both spatial and hence political terms.[117] The permanent fixing (*hidryetai, histasan*) of

---

[116] So Diod. Sic. 4. 59. 1.

[117] In the ephebic oath from the Athenian deme of Akharnai (cf. above, n. 89) the verb *hidryo* is used twice to describe the 'established' laws of the city the ephebes swear to defend: καὶ εὐηκοήσω τῶν ἀεὶ κραινόντων ἐμφρόνως καὶ τῶν θεσμῶν τῶν ἱδρυμένων καὶ οὓς ἂν τὸ λοιπὸν ἱδρύσωνται ἐμφρόνως. It is therefore possible that the word had special civic and political resonance for the Athenian audience. For the Akharnai oath, see Siewert, 'The Ephebic Oath', 103.

the sacred image or *bretas* at the very spot where Eurystheus was
defeated symbolically inverts the Heraklids' continual displacement by the Argive king from whatever temporary seat they
attempted to establish (*hidrymenous*, 19) for themselves. This
inversion in turn makes possible the establishment of the
Heraklids in the Argive territory that is their patrimony; and this
repatriation restores them to a valid political, economic, and
religious status, as Alkmene's triumphant cry makes clear:

> ὦ τέκνα, νῦν δὴ νῦν ἐλεύθεροι πόνων,
> ἐλεύθεροι δὲ τοῦ κακῶς ὀλουμένου
> Εὐρυσθέως ἔσεσθε καὶ πόλιν πατρὸς
> ὄψεσθε, κλήρους δ' ἐμβατεύσετε χθονὸς
> καὶ θεοῖς πατρῴοις θύσεθ', ὧν ἀπειργμένοι
> ξένοι πλανήτην εἴχετ' ἄθλιον βίον.

O children! now, now will you be free of burdens,
and free of that goddam[118]
Eurystheus; your father's city
will you now see, and you will take your rightful share in the land;
you'll sacrifice to the gods of your fathers—without which
you've been foreigners with a wretched nomad existence.

(873–8)

It is through his own actions, then, that Iolaos realizes the dream
that he had once thought would come about only through
Demophon's intervention: for Herakles' kin to have a 'home-
coming back into their fatherland' (*nostos es patran*, 310), to
inhabit once more their ancestral dwellings (*dōmat' oikēsēte*,
311), and to enjoy the honours due them as their father's
children (*timas patros*, 311). Putting an end to their long experience as dislocated persons—an experience, as we have seen, that
mimics those typically heroic wanderings at the peripheries of
civilization—the Heraklids will finally return to a *polis*, there to
enjoy the perquisites of civilized life, after Iolaos' re-enactment
of Theseus' Skironian triumph.[119] Indeed, they will return to the

---

[118] The tone of the Greek here drops precipitously. Though common in
comedy, the vulgar phrase Alkmene uses to refer to Eurystheus, *tou kakōs
oloumenou*, occurs only here in extant tragedy: see Wilkins, *Euripides* Heraclidae, 167 ad loc. for this point.

[119] It is interesting to note with Jacoby that place-names beginning with
Skir- (from *skirón*, 'lime') tend to be given to regions that had once been frontiers. *FrGrHist.* 3 B 2 (Suppl. 200–3); cf. Vidal-Naquet, *The Black Hunter*, 115.

very heart, so to speak, of the civilized centre that is the city. For their *nostos* to Argos now makes the Heraklids the doubles not only of the autochthonous Athenian inhabitants (*oikountes*) of Attika, but the doubles of the Athenian kings themselves. Now Herakles' children will be able to inhabit (*oikēsēte*) their ancestral homes, after laying legal claim to their portions of their father's property (*klērous embateusete khthonos*, 875),[120] just as we know the two kings of Athens inhabit (*katoikein*, 35) their own land, having obtained their right to kingship by lot (*pedia tēsde khthonos klērōi lakhontas*, 36). As Alkmene reminds us, without these *klēroi* one is merely a foreigner, *xenos*, doomed to lead the wretched wandering life, *athlion planētēn bion*, that comes from displacement from the *polis*.

The victorious establishment of the *tropaion* not only serves as a metaphor for the Heraklids' long-awaited relocation to Argos, but marks the resolution of another spatial problematic that affects the question of identity: the whereabouts of the dead hero himself. 'One of [*Children of Herakles*'s] concerns', as Wilkins has observed, 'is to prove the divinity of Herakles.'[121] In setting his Heraklid play at Marathon, Euripides may well have been counting on his audience's expectation that Herakles himself would play an important role, given certain well-established mythical and pseudo-historical connections between the hero and this Attic site.[122] Yet as Wilkins points out, it is to Zeus, rather than his hero-son, that the children of Herakles make their supplicatory appeal on arriving in this especially Heraklean site. Herakles' own supernatural status would thus seem to be as much at issue here as is the political status of his kin. It is noteworthy, therefore, that only after the various transformations and reversals that I have mapped above have taken place, thereby establishing once and for all the proper identities of Iolaos and

---

[120] *embateuō* is the technical verb from Athenian law (see e.g. Demosthenes 33. 6, and 44. 19).

[121] Wilkins, 'The Young of Athens', 330.

[122] Herakles was thought to have been one of the gods who presided over the Battle of Marathon, and was represented as such in a painting in the Stoa Poikilē (Paus. 1. 15. 3; for this point see Wilkins, 'The Young of Athens', 330); the Athenian army encamped at the Herakleion at Marathon before the battle (Hdt. 6. 108. 1, 6. 116. 1); the Herakleia at Marathon and at Kynosarges were Panhellenic meeting places; the people of Marathon were the first Hellenes to recognize Herakles as a god (Paus. 1. 15. 3, 1. 32. 4).

Hyllos, can Iolaos make a successful appeal (in the context of another supplication, as we have seen) to Herakles himself. This act, in turn, confirms the hero's divinity. Indeed Herakles' own mother Alkmene admits she had not believed that her son's immortal abode was on Olympos; Iolaos' victory, however, now gives her certain knowledge that it was (871 f.). And in the stasimon that follows, the chorus celebrates this confirmation of Herakles' divinity, a supernatural status that is defined in spatial terms as well:[123]

> ἔστιν ἐν οὐρανῷ βεβα-
> κὼς ὁ σὸς γόνος, ὦ γεραι-
> ά. φεύγω λόγον ὡς τὸν Ἅι-
> δα δόμον κατέβα, πυρὸς
> δεινᾷ φλογὶ σῶμα δαισθείς.
> Ἥβας τ' ἐρατὸν χροΐ-
> ζει λέχος χρυσέαν κατ' αὐλάν.

He has proceeded into Heaven,
your son has, aged lady.
I flee from the tale that
he went down into Hades, consumed
all over his body by the fearful fire.
He touches Hebe's lovely
bed in her golden chamber.   (910–16)

Herakles has gone to the sky. He thereby gives the lie to the tale that he had gone down to the House of Hades, a version which, in a Pindaric mode, the chorus emphatically rejects—that is, 'flees' (*pheugō*). For it is now clear that the house in which Herakles dwells is that of Hebe, not Hades. The establishment of the trophy by Herakles' male kin thus helps not only to reconfirm the Heraklids in Argos—their proper homeland—but to 'locate' Herakles on Olympos rather than down below. The true identity of both father and children has at last been 'fixed'.

Herakles and Hebe: Iolaos and Ephebic Cult

The most obvious sign of Herakles' divinity is, of course, his epiphany on the battlefield where the Athenians defeat the Argives. But it is Hebe's presence that is especially noteworthy. Iolaos had addressed his prayer to her as well as to Zeus (851);

---

[123] For these passages as confirmation of Herakles' divine status, see also Wilkins, 'The Young of Athens', 330 f.

according to the Messenger, experts agree that the two stars who appear on the chariot-yoke represent Herakles and Hebe, his Olympian consort (857); now Iolaos can display the youthful élan of his rejuvenated arm (*brakhionōn h̲ē̲b̲ē̲tēn typon*, 857; cf. 740 ff. *eith', O brakhiōn, hoion h̲ē̲b̲ē̲santa se* . . . etc.). Especially in the context of the foregoing allusion to Theseus' labours, the presence of Herakles and Hebe—Youth personified—here helps transform the newly civic-conscious Iolaos into an idealized Athenian ephebe. Indeed, the goddess's battlefield epiphany above Iolaos literalizes the word 'ephebe', *ephēbos*, since 'youth' is literally 'upon' him: *epi* + *hēbē*. Herakles, Hebe, and Theseus himself are all associated in Athenian cult with Athens' ephebes and armies.[124]

In more ways than just the obvious one, Iolaos' metamorphosis thus represents a complete reversal of his former status. The Argive hero who once abandoned his city for his life first follows the example set by a young girl who much resembles the courotrophic deities in whose sanctuary the Athenian ephebes took their oath; and in his final moment on stage he indeed becomes quasi-ephebic, a youthful figure attended by the divine figures responsible for the ephebes of the Athenian state. Inasmuch as it allows him to 'play' both the hoplite and, later, the ephebe, Iolaos' transformation alludes to figures crucial to the communal ideology of the democratic Athenian state; but inasmuch as his metamorphosis follows his experience of passive and quasi-feminine suffering—and, even more, is modelled on the Girl's example—it argues for the incorporation of 'otherness' into that ideology.

Peripeteia I: Alkmene and the Hyperboles of the Self

The victory of Athens and the Heraklids marks the conclusion of the legendary narrative known to Euripides and treated by Aeschylus; the episode that follows, in which Alkmene erupts

---

[124] For Herakles and Theseus as divine protectors of the ephebes, see Wilkins, 'The Young of Athens', 332–5, and 'The State and the Individual', 188. Although he is not so much interested in how Iolaos serves as a civic model, Wilkins's provocative articles have informed much of this part of my discussion. For Hebe, Herakles, and ephebic cult in this play, see also the Introduction to his commentary in *Euripides* Heraclidae, xxvi.

into the action in order to exact a violent and impious revenge on Eurystheus, appears to be a Euripidean invention. Not surprisingly, this scene has been the object of especially harsh critical puzzlement and outrage, and commentators have long tended to regard the scene as a disturbing intrusion into an action that otherwise seems to be organically whole.[125]

Some critics, like Grube, have tried to get round the 'problem' of Alkmene's outrageous actions by positing a gradual disintegration of the old woman, *à la* Hekabe; but no such progression need be imagined, since the stage for her violent outburst has in fact already been set—by the Girl. A series of structural parallels between the scenes in which the two kinswomen appear makes it clear that the dark but always submerged implications of the young girl's problematic entrance into public space are now fully realized in Alkmene's 'mad scene'.[126] The final episode can indeed be thought of as a recapitulation of the entire dramatic action thus far, a kind of drama-within-a-drama that replicates the structure of the Girl's salvific action while inverting its themes and moral lessons. Like the preceding action, this 'coda' is set in motion by a female's entrance; like that earlier entrance, moreover, the later one results first in the feminization and indeed the domestication of a formidable male character, who subsequently undergoes an improbable transformation into a most unlikely hero. But these similarities only make clearer some crucial differences. Alkmene's transgressive energies are not

[125] For the probable shape of the myth in tradition and as treated by Aeschylus, see Wilkins, *Euripides* Heraclidae, xviii–xix and the discussion above, Ch. 1. On the Alkmene episode as intrusive, see e.g. Grube: 'Alcmene appears so late that there is no possibility of depicting a gradual deterioration . . . The result is that her scene with Eurystheus, which could have made a magnificent climax to a tragedy called Alcmene, is too abrupt and merely horrible' (*The Drama of Euripides*, 175 f.). Other critics have attempted to establish a relationship based on the principle of inversion; hence Zuntz's argument that the encounter between Eurystheus and Alkmene is a *per negationem* affirmation of Iolaos' values (*The Political Plays of Euripides*, 51), and Burian's assertion that 'the relation of the final scene to the rest of the drama is one of tension rather than of harmonious fulfillment, but that does not mean that the relation is necessarily defective' ('Euripides' *Heracleidae*', 4).

[126] Burian also sees Alkmene's revenge as well prepared by what has preceded, although he is less interested than I in the parallels with the Girl's actions. His discussion of the Alkmene scene at 'Euripides' *Heracleidae*', 15 ff. is excellent.

contained; she becomes a murderess rather than a victim; and most strikingly, her vengeance is motivated by an extreme version of the *genos*-creed—the creed that had precipitated the very crises that the Girl's action ultimately resolved. Alkmene's impious act, which dramatizes the dangers of an excessively narrow concern with the individual self, betrays the *kharis* shown the Heraklids by the community of the Athenians. In a final and stunning reversal, her betrayal of Athens will itself be avenged by the intervention of the clan's former arch-enemy, the Argive king Eurystheus.

Enter Alkmene

The most striking parallel between the play's second part and its first, with respect both to its structure and its effect on the other characters, is the one that links Alkmene's entrance on stage to that of her granddaughter, the Girl. Like the Girl, who came in response to the old man's cries of despair (479f.), Alkmene is drawn into the action as a result of Iolaos' shout, *aütē*:

> τί χρῆμ᾽ αὐτῆς πᾶν τόδ᾽ ἐπλήσθη στέγος,
> Ἰόλαε; μῶν τίς σ᾽ αὖ βιάζεται παρὼν
> κῆρυξ ἀπ᾽ Ἄργους; ἀσθενὴς μὲν ἡ γ᾽ ἐμὴ
> ῥώμη, τοσόνδε δ᾽ εἰδέναι σε χρή, ξένε·
> οὐκ ἔστ᾽ ἄγειν σε τούσδ᾽ ἐμοῦ ζώσης ποτέ.

Whyever has the whole house been filled with wailing,
Iolaos? Could it be that once again the Argive herald has come
and done you violence? Feeble is my
strength, yet this much you should know, Stranger:
There is no way that you will ever take these children away while
    I live.

(646–50)

And just as the Girl's entrance seemed in its turn to mimic that of a *boēdromos* who had already appeared on stage—Demophon (121)—Alkmene's response here appears to echo that of the male character who precedes *her*: the Servant. Her astonished interrogative upon entering (*ti khrēma* etc.) picks up the Servant's similar exclamation upon seeing the veiled and downcast Iolaos (*ti khrēma keisai*, 633). Like the Girl, too, it appears that Alkmene appropriates roles that Iolaos himself hopes to play: that of victorious hoplite warrior (as her use of *heilomen*, 'we took in battle', at 962 perhaps suggests)[127] and, more concretely, that of the saviour of her kin. Her defiant final threat to the Servant at 650—'There is no way that you will ever take these children away while I live'—repeats almost verbatim Iolaos' equally heated declaration at 63 ff.: 'You will not take them from me by force . . . not while I live,' he cries. The miniaturized *agon* between Alkmene and Eurystheus that follows has, moreover, been described as a purposeful echo of the one between Iolaos and Eurystheus' Herald.[128]

But Alkmene's high-flown rhetoric here, as she attempts to play the *boēdromos* in yet another rescue action, is somewhat deflated by the fact that the man whom she believes to be the inimical Argive Herald is, of course, a friend—her own grandson's servant come to announce the preparations for what will be a defeat of their enemies. This case of mistaken identity introduces a comic note that stands in vivid contrast to the sober topoi of the Girl's speech, and signals at the level of genre some more serious and substantive reversals to follow: unlike that of the Girl, Alkmene's rescue will not be a constructive one; and unlike that other aged relation of Herakles, who at first was similarly denied a chance to save the *genos* (453 ff.), Alkmene will not enjoy a dramatic metamorphosis that will ultimately permit her to save her kin. If the Girl's entrance marks the extreme of Iolaos' helpless passivity, Alkmene's appearance comes at the moment of his revirilization, as he resumes the active stance of a *Marathōnomakhos* (711 ff.); and whereas the comic tone of Iolaos' arming scene is ultimately redeemed by the high-tragic conventions of the Messenger's speech, in which his unexpected heroics are reported, the comic brio of Alkmene's entrance almost immediately fizzles, as she becomes first a straight man to Iolaos (708–19), and then a silent and sullen figure, invisible and forgotten.

---

[127] I follow Diggle and Wilkins in attributing this line to Alkmene, a welcome change first suggested by Barnes. L gives ll. 962–3, 965, 967, 969, and 971 to the Messenger, and 961, 964, 966, 968, and 970 to the chorus—a disposition that makes little sense given the furious speech by Alkmene that immediately precedes. See Wilkins's note ad loc., 'Euripides' *Heracleidae*', 180, and the remarks of Zuntz, *The Political Plays of Euripides*, 125–8.

[128] Michael Lloyd makes this interesting point (*The* Agon *in Euripides*, 76), noting further that both Iolaos and Alkmene address their Argive interlocutors with *Ō mīsos!*, 'O hateful thing!' (cf. 52 and 941).

Murder : *Self-Sacrifice* :: genos : polis

Even as Alkmene apparently fades out of sight, Iolaos goes on to assume his new hoplite identity, playing out a heroic fantasy of revenge on behalf of his *genos*—a fantasy, as it happens, in which he recaptures the same physical prowess he once had when he and Herakles sacked Sparta in revenge for the death of a kinsman (741 f.).[129] But as we have seen, his duty to his kin is fulfilled only *after* he has put his prowess at the service of the state. In Alkmene's case, however, the 'tribal principle' that insists on avenging the *genos* blinds her to the obligations imposed by the customs, *nomoi*, of the *polis*, which proscribe the torture and execution of prisoners taken in battle (963), as well as the customs of all Hellas, which proscribe the murder of suppliants (1010).[130] The *polis* itself shows reverence for this Panhellenic religious custom, placing respect for the gods above any individual's desire for vengeance (1012–14). The restraint the city displays in doing so (*sōphronousa*, 1012) stands in symbolic counterpoint to the bloody excess required by the *genos*. It is difficult to resist the notion that an innovative Euripides spared Eurystheus (who in other versions of this myth is killed on the battlefield by either Iolaos or Hyllos) precisely in order to highlight this conflict between the aims of the individual within the *genos* and those of the communities of both the *polis* and of Greece itself.[131]

A tart exchange between Alkmene and the Servant (963–73)

---

[129] The allusion is to Herakles' expedition against the usurper Hippokoön, who had deposed Herakles' kinsman Tyndareus from the Spartan throne. In revenge, Herakles killed Hippokoön and all his sons. Garzya (*Euripide Eraclidi*, ad loc.) notes a variant in which the hero takes murderous revenge against the twenty sons of Hippokoön for killing his cousin, the son of Alkmene's brother. The legend is treated by Alkman, and described by Apollodoros, Pausanias, Strabo, and Diodoros; full discussion can be found in Denys Page, *Alcman: The Partheneion* (Oxford, 1951), 26–33.

[130] 'Tribal principle' of blood-vengeance: Burnett, 'Tribe and City', 21. For the Athenian aversion to killing prisoners see Thuc. 3. 58. 3 (Plataea, 427 BC), 3. 59. 1, and 3. 63. 3. See also the discussion of Pierre Ducrey, *Le Traitement des prisonniers de guerre dans la Grèce antique* (Paris 1968), esp. 201–28 ('Mise à mort et captivité'). Although not unknown at Athens—especially in the case of slaves—torture of prisoners of war such as that promised by Alkmene at 958–60 was unusual (Ducrey, pp. 206f.).

[131] It is possible that Alkmene's use of *neikos*, a word with epic overtones, to describe her feud with Eurystheus at 982 is meant to suggest that she imagines herself to be a kind of epic hero.

shows how the aims of the *polis* come into sharp conflict with
those of the *genos*:

> Αλ. εἴργει δὲ δὴ τίς τόνδε μὴ θνῄσκειν νόμος;
> Θε. τοῖς τῆσδε χώρας προστάταισιν οὐ δοκεῖ.
> Αλ. τί δὴ τόδ'; ἐχθροὺς τοισίδ' οὐ καλὸν κτανεῖν;
> Θε. οὐχ ὅντιν' ἄν γε ζῶνθ' ἕλωσιν ἐν μάχῃ.
> Αλ. καὶ ταῦτα δόξανθ' Ὕλλος ἐξηνέσχετο;
> Θε. χρῆν αὐτόν, οἶμαι, τῇδ' ἀπιστῆσαι χθονί.
> Αλ. χρῆν τόνδε μὴ ζῆν μηδ' †ὁρᾶν φάος ἔτι†.
> Θε. τότ' ἠδικήθη πρῶτον οὐ θανὼν ὅδε.
> Αλ. οὔκουν ἔτ' ἐστὶν ἐν καλῷ δοῦναι δίκην;
> Θε. οὐκ ἔστι τοῦτον ὅστις ἂν κατακτάνοι.
> Αλ. ἔγωγε· καίτοι φημὶ κἄμ' εἶναί τινα.

> *Alk.* What custom, then, prevents him from dying?
> *Ser.* It is not the decree of the rulers of this land.
> *Alk.* Why not? Don't they think it a fine thing to kill your enemies?
> *Ser.* Not one who has been taken alive in battle.
> *Alk.* And Hyllos will go along with these regulations?
> *Ser.* He should have disobeyed [the laws of] this land, I suppose.
> *Alk.* *He* [i.e. Eurystheus] should not be alive, nor looking still
> upon the light.
> *Ser.* He was wronged to begin with, when he was not killed.
> *Alk.* So punishment then is not a fine thing?
> *Ser.* There is no way that someone may kill him.
> *Alk.* *I* will. For I say that even I am 'someone', too.   (963–73)

Significantly, the Servant invokes the formal language of the
Athenian state's political decrees (*dokei tois prostataisin*, 964) to
describe the *nomoi* or laws of the *polis*.[132] Alkmene's retort at 967,
however, indicates that for her such laws, *doxanta*, are something that the leader of the Heraklid clan can overstep if he
sees fit. The *nomos* that she honours is the '"heroic" one of fierce
and protracted enmities' that requires the death of the *genos*'s
foe.[133] As the old woman's reiteration of the Servant's sardonic
'he should have . . .' (*khrēn*, 969, cf. 968) indicates, that *genos*
requirement stands in necessary contravention of the *nomoi* of
the *polis*. Reverting to what may well be the diction of aristocratic
snobbery or *kalokagathia*, Alkmene expresses disbelief that the
Athenians do not consider it a 'fine thing', *kalon*, to kill their

---

[132] For this political sense of *dokei* in tragedy, cf. Soph. *Elektra* 29; in later
oratory, see e.g. Dem. 3. 14.   [133] Burian, 'Euripides' *Heracleidae*', 20.

enemies (965, 971).[134] Or, more precisely, *her* enemies, for her speech makes it quite clear that her act will be one of revenge for the indignities and impieties visited on her son, her grand-children, and herself (946–56). This sentiment is entirely in keeping with the marked egocentrism of Alkmene's speeches, which are replete with 'singular references to I/me/mine':[135] Eurystheus has fallen into *my* hands, she asserts (976); the murderous deed will be accomplished by *me*, and his death will be justice for *me* (*emoi*, 980, 1025); never again will anyone be able to expel *me* from my homeland (*eme*, 1052). This insistence on the aims of the self above those of the community culminates in her justification for killing Eurystheus herself after the Servant informs her that 'no one' else will do it: 'for even *I* am "someone",' she declares. Alkmene's demand for personal satis-faction on behalf of the *genos* thus inverts both the structure and meaning of the Girl's act, in which a suppliant sacrifices her-self—that is, a 'self'—in order to satisfy the demands that would save not only the *genos* but the community of others constituted by the inhabitants of the Athenian *polis*.

Alkmene's words and deeds thus realize the potential to subvert the *polis* that is always implicit in women's ungoverned action—and movement. We remember that the Girl had worried that her entrance would be seen as unseemly impudence, *thrasos*, and thereby invite the disapproval of her audience(s), because it contravened the convention that required women to be *sōphrōn* (473). Alkmene, however, displays utter 'disregard for the canons of womanly deference',[136] and virtually invites the charge of *thrasos*:

> Θε. πολλὴν ἄρ' ἕξεις μέμψιν, εἰ δράσεις τόδε.
> Αλ. φιλῶ πόλιν τήνδ'· οὐδὲν ἀντιλεκτέον.
> τοῦτον δ', ἐπείπερ χεῖρας ἦλθεν εἰς ἐμάς,
> οὐκ ἔστι θνητῶν ὅστις ἐξαιρήσεται.
> πρὸς ταῦτα τὴν θρασεῖαν ὅστις ἂν θέλῃ
> καὶ τὴν φρονοῦσαν μεῖζον ἢ γυναῖκα χρὴ
> λέξει· τὸ δ' ἔργον τοῦτ' ἐμοὶ πεπράξεται.

---

[134] See Ober, *Mass and Elite*, 252–5 and 258–61 on attitudes towards *kalokagathia* in the democratic *polis*. In Isokrates (7. 37), *kalōs gegonosi* can mean 'well-born' in the class sense.

[135] See Falkner, 'The Wrath of Alcmene', 120 for Alkmene's 'striking capac-ity for self-assertion' here. [136] Falkner, 'The Wrath of Alcmene', 117.

Ser: Great will be the blame you acquire if you do these things.
Alk: I love this city; there's no denying that.
    But since this man has now fallen into my hands,
    there's no way any mortal man will take him from me.
    Let anyone who wants to call me 'that bold woman'
      (*tēn thraseian*) on account of my actions do so—
    that, and 'a woman who thinks above her station'
      (*phronousan meizon*)
    But this deed will in fact be done by me.

                                       (974–80)

Alkmene welcomes the charge of *thrasos* that will bring blame, *mempsin*, if it allows her to satisfy her desire for vengeance. Rather than remaining *sōphron* within the house, she gladly admits that she 'thinks bigger, *phronousan meizon*, than a woman ought'. The Girl, as we have seen, made a gesture that could be applauded as a 'great speech', *megas logos* (535) so long as it served the city, and as long as the rewards of the heroic status to which she seemed to aspire were distributed 'properly'—that is, among her male relatives. Here, however, *megas* feminine action is not thus regulated; as a result, *megas* expands, as it were, into its comparative form *meizon*—reflecting, we might say, the way in which Alkmene's action has exaggerated and brought to the surface the dangerous potential merely implicit in the Girl's bold and unexpected entry into the action.

Peripeteia II: Eurystheus Plays the Other

As many critics have noted, in pursuing her terrible revenge Alkmene becomes the double of her arch-enemy.[137] Like Eurystheus, she is intent on hounding her enemies to death; like him, she is prepared to violate the Panhellenic *nomos* pertaining to supplication in order to do so.[138] Yet Alkmene's vengeance

---

[137] So Zuntz, *The Political Plays of Euripides*, 36 f.; Fitton, 'The *Suppliant Women*', 457; Avery, 'Euripides' Heracleidae', 560; Burian, 'Euripides' *Heracleidae*', 17; Falkner, 'The Wrath of Alcmene', 121 f.

[138] A further possible similarity: like the Argive king, whose ingenuity in hatching various plots to kill the Heraklids made him a skilled specialist or 'sophist' (*sophistēs*, 993), Alkmene becomes a skilled and facile teacher herself (*egō didaxō*, 1022 ff.), instructing the chorus in the hair-splitting justifications that will allow her to commit an impious murder while at least technically obeying the city's refusal to give up the prisoner. Burian refers to the 'cunning

triggers not only her own assimilation to the model of her 'other', but sets in motion a further and perhaps even stranger series of reversals, in which Eurystheus himself becomes the opposite of the various 'selves' that have defined him throughout the play. In concluding my discussion of *Children of Herakles*, I would like to inventory these permutations of Eurystheus' identity. For these ornate repetitions and inversions make a fitting finale for a drama that has in so many and in such complex ways investigated the volatile relationships between the self and other.

Eurystheus prostropaios*:* allē Parthenos, allē Alkmēnē?

Let us examine first of all Eurystheus' transformation from an implacable pursuer of suppliants into a suppliant implacably pursued. Having been taken prisoner despite his own fervent wish that he might be killed in battle (cf. 969 and 1010), the defeated king whose captured armour served as a *tropaion* now becomes a *prostropaios* (1015), a killer who has turned as a suppliant for purification.[139] Let me suggest here that the etymological recapitulation of *tropaion* within *prostropaios* be considered as a kind of symbol for the dense interactions between space, dislocation, and identity that we find in this drama. As we have seen, the establishment of the *tropaion* at the spot where Eurystheus was captured symbolized the final resolution of the Heraklids' highly problematic series of displacements that the Argive ruler had set in motion. Now, the reference to Eurystheus' status as *prostropaios* brings the supplication motif once again to the fore—and with it the moral and ethical problems associated with violating religious space. In laying hands on the inviolate person of a *prostropaios*, Alkmene will replicate the crime of Eurystheus against herself and her kin, thereby precipitating at the play's conclusion the same religious, political, and spatial crisis with which it began.

According to the Messenger's report (813 ff.), Eurystheus had

---

sophistry' of her 'punning solution' in getting around Athenian *nomos* ('Euripides' *Heracleidae*', 17).

[139] For these terms, cf. Aesch. *Eum.* 41, 234 and see Wilkins, *Euripides Heraclidae*, 187 f. Burian argues further that elements of Alkmene's speech are similar to that of the Argive Herald at 134 ff. Eurystheus' gesture here is in fact the drama's third formal supplication, after the opening tableau and Iolaos' supplicatory gesture on the battlefield (844).

displayed remarkable cowardice when confronted by Hyllos' challenge to engage in single combat: the Argive king had shown himself to be ignoble, *kakistos* (816). In not even bothering to conceal his fear of his enemy from the massed troops, the Heraklids' mortal enemy had shown no *aidōs* (*ouk aidestheis*, 813), nor any sense of shame for his own cowardice, *deilia* (815). Yet when faced with Alkmene's violent threats, Eurystheus shows himself to be a model of valour, echoing, if anything, the Girl's high-minded sentiments. He will not incur the charge of cowardice, *deilia*, for the sake of his life, *psykhē* (983 ff.), just as the Girl had rejected the shameful and unworthy behaviour likely to evoke ridicule, in favour of death (525 f.). Like the Girl, Eurystheus is a suppliant pursued by a vengeful enemy; like her, he describes himself as eager (*prothymos*, 1010; cf. 577) to die— that is, to 'leave life behind', (*lipein bion*, 1017; cf. 534)—rather than disgrace himself; both are thus transformed from unwilling victims of single-minded pursuit to willing victims mindful of their personal honour.[140] The Girl admonished Iolaos to give her due burial (588); similarly, Eurystheus gives specific orders to the Athenians with respect to his own tomb (1030). Both, moreover, are rendered *sōterios*, saviours of the city, by their voluntary submission to death (1032, 1045, 1049 of Eurystheus; cf. 497, 498, 577, 588 of the Girl). To be sure, the sharp contrast between Eurystheus' behaviour as reported in the Messenger speech, on the one hand, and as subsequently dramatized in his confrontation with Alkmene, on the other, highlights the artificiality of his transformation—as artificial, in fact, as the one that turned Iolaos into a vigorous young hero. But that artificiality seems intended to foreground the unlikely parallels I have described here. Like Iolaos' metamorphosis, Eurystheus' is triggered by the anomalous intrusion of a female character; in both cases, moreover, the male figure is displaced into the postures of the female. As surprisingly noble as it may be, Eursytheus' speech suggests, indeed, that he has become a double of the Girl herself.

The text also provides some slight but intriguing suggestions that Eurystheus has appropriated a peculiarly feminine trait

[140] See Burnett, 'Tribe and City', 12–13, and Wilkins, 'The Young of Athens', 332, on similarities between Eurystheus and the Girl. Wilkins observes that both begin as victims and end up as saviours.

from the play's other female character: Alkmene. Upon hearing the Servant's good news at 630ff., Iolaos calls Alkmene out of the sanctuary (*exelth'*, 643). Her worry on behalf of her male kin has reduced her to a state of physical depredation: she has, we learn, been 'experiencing pains as one who is in labour' (*ōdinousa*, 644) and 'wasting away in her soul' (*psykhēn etēkou*). Eurystheus too is someone whose anxiety about the children of Herakles has made him physically sick: he characterizes his desire for vengeance as a disease, *nosos* (990), visited upon him by Hera, whose animosity towards Alkmene's son is well documented. But if Alkmene was in labour with worry, it is Eurystheus, oddly enough, who 'gives birth'. He relates how, maddened by the goddess, he would sit up at night and give birth to, *etikton* (994), various stratagems to kill Herakles in order to alleviate the terror with which he 'cohabited' as if with a spouse (*synoikoiēn phobōi*, 996).[141] The figurative import of the second verb—not uncommon, to be sure—here serves to reinforce that of the first metaphor, much more unusual when used of male subjects.[142] The accumulation of these small details of diction signals a more radical reordering of the identities of Eurystheus and of Herakles' kin.

Eurystheus sōtēr: *The Integration of the Other*

The most striking of all of Eurystheus' assumptions of foreign identities, however, is his transformation into an Attic hero. Here again, location and identity are inextricably linked within the framework of the dialectic of self and other. As we have seen, the final and permanent relocation of the victorious Heraklids from Athens/Marathon back to Argos, predicted by a triumphant Alkmene, is balanced by a corresponding displacement of the defeated Eurystheus from Argos to Attika, where, as the defeated king predicts, he will lie buried before the sanctuary of Athena at Pallene (1031). That larger spatial and geographical

---

[141] For *synoikein* as the 'fact' of legal marriage, see J.-P. Vernant, 'Marriage', in *Myth and Society in Ancient Greece*, tr. Janet Lloyd (New York, 1990), 57.

[142] For these metaphors in both poetry and prose, see Wilkins, *Euripides Heraclidae*, 184 ad locos. *tiktein* appears at *Andr.* 476, Plato, *Sym.* 210d, and, most strikingly, Arkhilokhos fr. 203 KA. Used to describe brooding, *synoikein* seems to have been less vivid, as witness the parallels cited by Wilkins ad loc. from Semonides, Euripides, and Xenophon.

dynamic seems now to be marked at the level of language, in the Servant's report to Alkmene. Eurystheus' reversal of fortune is expressed in terms of space and placement:

> οὐ γάρ ποτ' ηὔχει χεῖρας ἵξεσθαι σέθεν,
> ὅτ' ἐκ Μυκηνῶν πολυπόνῳ σὺν ἀσπίδι
> ἔστειχε μείζω τῆς δίκης φρονῶν πολύ,
> πέρσων Ἀθήνας. ἀλλὰ τὴν ἐναντίαν
> δαίμων ἔθηκε, καὶ μετέστησεν τύχην.

He never dreamed he'd walk right into your hands
when, armed with his veteran shield,
he set forth from Mykenai, setting himself far above justice,
intent on sacking Athens. The opposite is what
the god ordained; and indeed his lot has changed.

(931–5)

Contrary to expectation, Eurystheus' fortunes have not been reversed so much as 'relocated'. Instead of laying waste to Athens after he had left Argos/Mykenai, he finds that the gods have ordained the opposite (*enantian*, 934): he has (literally) entered Alkmene's dangerous orbit, 'coming into her hands' (*kheiras hixesthai sethen*; cf. *es son elthein omma*, 'come into your sight', 887, and *kheiras elthein es emas*, 'come into my hands', 976). This is a moment that Alkmene anticipates with understandable relish (882). The Argive tyrant's abasement once under Alkmene's control is just as literal. He stands with face averted, and Alkmene forces him to turn his head (*epistrepson kara*, 942) and look her directly in the face from where he is located 'opposite' her (*enantion*), in order that she may be sure it is he (942–4). The gestural language of the scene implies a comparison with a stage-picture that marked the nadir of another Argive. Before, a dispirited Iolaos had hung his head down and gone unrecognized by Hyllos' messenger, who had to implore the old man to hold his head up (635). The parallel suggests the extent of the reversal of the Heraklids' and Eurystheus' fortunes, which indeed have now become the opposites of what they had once been.

Eurystheus' *peripeteia* is thus very much a literal one, as he exchanges Argos for Attika, power for imprisonment, pride for abasement—all these transactions and reversals expressed with great syntactical economy and elegance in Alkmene's succinct 'for now you are ruled, nor do you any longer rule' (*kratēi gar nyn ge k'ou kratēis eti*, 944). But just as Alkmene's *enantion* (934) may be said to mark her own perception of extreme difference between her status and that of her debased enemy, who is here quite literally her 'opposite number', the sharp or sudden turning of Eurystheus' head (*epistrepson*) may be said to signal an unexpected turnaround in the ostensibly opposed roles of friend and enemy, self and other. For the 'face' that Eurystheus will prophetically 'reveal' in his closing address to the chorus of Marathonian elders is, in fact, that of a friend to Athens:

> καὶ σοὶ μὲν εὔνους καὶ πόλει σωτήριος
> μέτοικος αἰεὶ κείσομαι κατὰ χθονός,
> τοῖς τῶνδε δ' ἐκγόνοισι πολεμιώτατος,
> ὅταν μόλωσι δεῦρο σὺν πολλῇ χερὶ
> χάριν προδόντες τήνδε.

And it is as one who is well disposed to you, saviour of your city,
that I shall always lie beneath the earth, a metic,
utterly inimical to the descendants of these people [sc. the Heraklids]
when they come hither with a great force
betraying this favour.

(1032–6)

His peculiar status as a protector of Athenian interests after his death is expressed once again in terms that indicate political status as the result of geographical categories. Forever displaced from his realm by the Heraklids' return to it, Eurystheus is forced to undergo the experience of the 'other', his Heraklid enemies; he will be an outsider sharing in (*metoikos*, 1033) a homeland not his own. Unlike the Heraklids, however, who eventually find their way home, Eurystheus will forever remain in this strange land (*aiei keisomai kata khthonos*). As such, he is— like the resident aliens who were known in fifth-century Athens as 'metics', *metoikoi*—an other absorbed within, but never completely assimilated into, the Athenian self.

It is striking that this delicately negotiated integration is described as one that will 'save' the Athenian state, the *polis*. For as Eurystheus prophesies, the tomb of this enemy of both Heraklids and Athenians will ultimately prove to be a supernatural boon to Athens (*eunous kai polei sōtērios*) when, after another and even more shocking metamorphosis of self into other, the Spartan descendants of the Heraklids, forgetting their debt to the Athenians who had proved themselves to be friends, *philoi* (308), return to Athens as enemies. In leaving the Peloponnese and crossing once again into Athenian territory (*molōsi deuro*, 1035), these real-life Heraklids will violate the same *kharis*, the obligation of the saved to the saviour, that Athens had acknowledged in first taking up their cause (220).[143] The play's concluding series of transfigurations of self into other therefore highlights the importance of maintaining equilibrium between those categories, even as it points to a final and most unexpected reversal.

The Alkmene–Eurystheus scene is the culmination of *Children of Herakles*'s interlocked sequences of reversals and reduplications, each of which sheds light on issues of personal and political identity. Each, moreover, is distinguished by the presence of an important female figure, either virgin or matron, mortal or goddess. A conflict between real and symbolic Athens and Argos is represented not only by the unseen, supernatural *agōn* between the virgin Athena and the divine matron par excellence, Hera, to which Iolaos alludes, but is enacted on the mortal plane in the sharply contrasted, staged appearances first of the Girl and, later on, of her grandmother Alkmene. Whereas the Girl's literal self-destruction seemed to have saved both her kin and the city, the extreme and literal 'self'-interest demonstrated by Alkmene will ultimately lead to internecine warfare between her descendants and the Athenians. Inasmuch as it is true that Alkmene's inversion of the structures and consequences of her granddaughter's self-sacrifice ultimately destroys the benefits conferred by the Girl's act, it would appear that the play's final scene is intended to warn against an excessive and unregulated 'otherness' that makes individual claims incompatible with those of the state. And yet it is also possible, perhaps, to see Alkmene as a female figure whose actions, like those of the Girl, are ultimately 'exploited' in order to benefit the city of Athens: her greedy self-interest is, after all, what transforms Eurystheus into an ally and future protector of the state. In either case, 'ideology'—whether political or patriarchal or (more likely) both—

[143] For the ongoing theme of *kharis* in this work, see D. J. Conacher, *Euripidean Drama: Myth, Theme and Structure* (Toronto, 1967), 111–20.

seems to triumph in the poet's treatment of what Rabinowitz calls this 'uncanny' figure of the 'terrible' mother.[144]

But a reading of this episode as a flat expression of patriarchal anxiety about female action and power is, in the end, too simplistic, and fails to take into account the complexity of Euripides' presentation. To be sure, many of the claims made by Alkmene are monstrous, given *Children of Herakles*'s treatment of heroic individuality; but the play's intricately modulated validation of the feminine, as expressed in the Girl's instructive civic example, seems simultaneously to argue for a more complex and nuanced reading of its final scene. Alkmene may indeed be 'terrible', as Rabinowitz argues, but she is also a mother, and in view of this work's slight but crucial invocation of the myth of Demeter and Kore, the claims of the Mother ought not to be dismissed too lightly. It is in this light, perhaps, that we should read Alkmene's stark climactic articulation of individuality and 'selfhood': 'I am "someone", too.' For even as it dramatizes the political dangers of giving too free a rein to the diverse elements that constitute the body politic and its 'members', the play presents scenes of feminine passion that offer an emotionally engaging and dramatically gripping demonstration of the terrible costs exacted in order to maintain the equilibrium conferred by men's laws, customs, *nomoi*.

Hence, like the interpretation of this work as a whole, with which it is inextricably entwined—and indeed, like the play's own representation of its themes and characters—our interpretation of *Children of Herakles*'s female characters must admit of mediation, complexity, even ambiguity. If the depiction of conflicts between opposite types, especially feminine types, constitutes the theatrical vehicle for working out a balanced political and civic identity, it is perhaps no accident that *Children of Herakles*'s moment of dramatic and indeed political 'truth'— Iolaos' enlightened transformation into a model Athenian—is graced, rather unexpectedly, by the presence of a surprisingly complex female figure: that is, Hebe. Like the other Olympians who 'appear', so to speak, in this text, Hebe is a divinity, yet unlike those others she is a god who intervenes quite actively and visibly in the affairs of mortals, as a patroness of Athens'

[144] Rabinowitz, *Anxiety Veiled*, 105.

ephebes; she is (famously) 'youthful', and indeed famously a virgin, but a virgin who ends up as married and indeed as nurturing as Hera herself; by virtue of that marriage, she is associated with Argos but, like her Argive husband Herakles, she is an Argive who ends up as a protector of Athens and its future.

The 'middle ground' of which Hebe may well be the play's representative among its many and varied female figures is, of course, elusive, and was to prove so for Athens herself. Indeed, the terrible and poignant ramifications of the failures against which this play seems to warn—the failure to recognize the integrity of the other, on the one hand, and (remembering Athens' own ultimate susceptibility to the allure of extremism, in contravention of Perikles' warning) the failure to rein in excess, on the other—would become apparent when, in the very distant future, Herakles' Spartan children would return once more to breach the boundaries of Attika.

3

Suppliant Women
Regulations of the Feminine

Eleusinian Paradigms

Suppliant Women is an Eleusinian play; and at Eleusis, as in the play, the feminine is omnipresent. Like the Eleusinian myth that provided the narrative armature for the rituals that accompanied the Mysteries as well as other Demetrian rites, Euripides' drama recapitulates the experience of all mortal women. Like the myth, which is most fully and famously transmitted through the 'Homeric' hymn to Demeter, this play presents young women and old; women who are fertile as well as those past childbearing; girls who, through their fathers' trickery, are given away in marriage; brides who go down to Hades to meet their husbands; and, of course, grieving mothers who leave their proper places in helpless search of their lost children.[1]

Because the mythic narrative is always allusively present in this play, some discussion of the meaning of the work's Eleusinian setting is in order, for to appreciate the subtleties of *Suppliant Women*'s mythic intertext and its distinctly feminine themes is to appreciate the subtle coherences of this oft-maligned work.[2] In this Eleusinian setting, all of *Suppliant Women*'s characters and actions—its nouns and verbs, so to speak—are declined or inflected according to a Demetrian paradigm, allowing us to see

---

[1] For the Hymn and its relation to Demetrian cult, see Helene Foley, *The Homeric Hymn to Demeter: Translation, Commentary, and Interpretive Essays* (Princeton, 1994), and the edition of N. Richardson, *The Homeric Hymn to Demeter* (Oxford, 1974).

[2] The other text to which *Suppliant Women* apparently refers is Aeschylus' *Eleusinians*, the title of which, unlike that of Euripides' play, advertised the drama's connection to Demeter's cult-place. A concise summary of the important Eleusinian cultic allusions that occur in our text can be found in Bruno Lavagnini's 'Echi del Rito Eleusino in Euripides', *AJP* 68 (1947), 82–6.

Demetrian or Eleusinian paraphrases that are more than merely generic; among the latter we can surely count the drama's almost metronomically reiterated tableaux of grief, such as that of Adrastos for his city, or of Evadne for her husband, or of Iphis for his children. Each of these, to be sure, recalls Demeter as vividly as do the newly childless mothers in the chorus. Yet if we keep Eleusis and its narratives firmly in mind, other, more subtle parallels appear: we shall see how Adrastos' veiled lamentation, and Iphis' terrible grief for his daughter, appear to quote (sometimes verbatim) the well-known narrative of the goddess's mourning. So too does Demetrian myth help us to contextualize the words and actions of Evadne, who like Persephone is a bride of Hades whose descent to the underworld leaves a grief-stricken parent behind; or the speeches and deeds of Theseus who, at the play's turning point, will imagine himself as the parent of a girl who has been cruelly abducted, and who will himself undertake a feminine role in ritual mourning—all this after a climactic battle scene in which the Athenian's defeat of an impious enemy is cast as a quasi-agricultural reaping. Euripides constantly exploits the Eleusinian cultic narrative by having his characters 'play' Demeter, or Kore, or even Hades at various moments in order to underscore a given dramatic point. The Eleusinian myth is the other drama that lurks behind Euripides' play, shadowing its action and, like a theatrical palimpsest, making its presence subtly felt just beneath the surface of the action that transpires before the eyes of the audience.[3]

To be sure, the play's Eleusinian intertext helps to clarify the role and function of its female characters—not only Evadne, who provokes a 'Demetrian' crisis of grief and reconciliation, but Aithra, too. The Athenian queen's prologue speech has, I think, received insufficient critical attention; and yet it strikingly recalls the play's Demetrian milieu, not merely because it announces Aithra's fertility sacrifice within the goddess's sanctuary, but,

---

[3] For this point see also Rush Rehm, *Marriage to Death: The Conflation of Wedding and Funeral Rituals in Greek Tragedy* (Princeton, 1994), 110f., and Barbara Goff, 'Aithra at Eleusis', *Helios*, 22/1 (1995), 67–9. Both see the work's hitherto largely neglected Eleusinian setting as the key to its coherences; see also Bowie, 'Tragic Filters'. For a discussion of a similarly 'palimpsestic' use of the Demeter/Kore myth in other Euripidean dramas, see Helene Foley, '*Anodos* Drama', 133–60 (esp. 137).

even more importantly, because it alludes to the curious myth of the Athenian queen's marriage, which, like Kore's, combined elements of both rape and legal matrimony, and which, in taking her from her father's house at Troizen to her husband's palace at Athens, resulted in a typically feminine journey from virginity to motherhood. But the most striking of *Suppliant Women*'s Eleusinian performances—the ones that have the greatest impact, I shall argue, and that most effectively convey the poet's usually ironic message—are those in which Adrastos, Theseus, and Iphis play the feminine role of Demeter. This gendered role-playing, taken from an Eleusinian 'script', thus places *Suppliant Women* securely within the interpretative territory that I have already mapped out in my discussion of *Children of Herakles*, which, in the cases of Iolaos and Eurystheus, validated the experience of the feminine through a less explicit kind of role-playing. Critical sensitivity to these Demetrian performances will, finally, shed light on certain ostensibly inexplicable elements in the text, allowing us, for example, to read Athena's injunction that the sacrificial knives used by Theseus be cast into the dark recesses of the earth as a dark parody of a Demetrian ritual, the Thesmophoria. Long criticized for its ostensibly disjointed structure and unrelated incidents, *Suppliant Women* derives its coherence from a powerful sense of place: that is, its Demetrian setting at Eleusis.

The feminine associations that Eleusis calls to mind are present at several levels, one of which is symbolic and allegorical. The Eleusinian myth was long understood as 'a piece of transparent nature allegory'; the broad outlines of its narrative clearly refer to the dynamics of vegetable fertility, the immutable rhythms of germination, growth, decay, and ultimate regeneration.[4] When Persephone is abducted, the grief of her mother the corn-goddess threatens the world's agricultural productivity; the daughter's return, on the other hand, guarantees a renewal (if only seasonal) of growth. Virgin and mother, marriage and mourning: these are the outlines of woman's life, and they are retraced in Euripides' drama.

---

[4] Walter Burkert, *Greek Religion*, tr. John Raffan (Cambridge, Mass., 1985), 160; cf. Foley, *Homeric Hymn to Demeter*, 71–5.

It is to the details of the mythic narrative, geographically fixed in the drama's setting of Eleusis, that the arcane and idiosyncratic array of Demetrian ritual activities, both at Eleusis and elsewhere, may be said to correspond.[5] Hence, for example, the use of torches at the Thesmophoria and Mysteries, recalling those brandished by Demeter in her search for her lost daughter; so too the prominence of piglets, sacrificed by each initiand during the Mysteries and as part of the Skira festival, and thought to be a reference to the pigs that fell into the cleft that opened up when Hades abducted Persephone.[6] (During the Skirophoria, the tiny sacrificial victims were inhumed in dark crevices in the earth, to be recovered three months later by the exclusively female celebrants of the Thesmophoria.) Likewise, the sitting on the ground, the ritual abuse exchanged by women at the Thesmophoria, the ritual fasting followed by the eating of special foods—all were practised during both the Thesmophoria and the Mysteries, in imitation of the actions of the goddess in the mythic narrative. I recall these particulars of Demetrian ritual because, as we shall see, they are recalled in our text, too, deriving a special interpretative significance from their role in Eleusinian cult, just as, within that cult, they derive their ritual significance from some element of Eleusis' fertility myth, the myth of Demeter the bereaved mother, whose mourning for the fruit of her own womb sympathetically threatens the world's fertility.[7]

---

[5] For Demetrian rites at Eleusis and elsewhere, see G. Méautis, *Les Dieux de la Grèce et les Mystères d'Eleusis* (Paris, 1959); George Mylonas, *Eleusis and the Eleusinian Mysteries* (Princeton, 1961); Carl Kerényi, *Eleusis: Archetypal Image of Mother and Daughter*, tr. R. Manheim (Princeton, 1967); H. W. Parke, *Festivals of the Athenians* (Ithaca, NY, 1977), 82–8, and 55–72; and Burkert, *Greek Religion*, 242–6 and 285–90.

[6] On the significance of the piglets, which are generally associated with Demeter as symbols of fecundity, see Burkert, *Greek Religion*, 243 (Thesmophoria) and 286 (the Mysteries).

[7] See Burkert, *Greek Religion*, 289. For sitting on the ground and ritual abuse, cf. the Hymn, in which Demeter refuses the comfortable chair offered her, preferring in her distress to sit on some kind of low stool (*H. h. Cer.* 196). The ritual *aiskhrologia*, recalling the ribaldry with which Iambē in the hymn coaxes Demeter into laughter, was a feature of the Eleusinian mysteries as well; on the fifth day of the festival, as part of the procession from Athens to Eleusis, masked men mocked the passing initiates with obscene taunts and gestures (Burkert, *Greek Religion*, 287). For fasting in imitation of Demeter, and sub-

But it will be remembered that in the Greek imagination, the agricultural activities in whose use Demeter instructs the Eleusinian hero Triptolemos upon Kore's return—ploughing, sowing, reaping—frequently occur not only in literary but also social and political contexts as metaphors to describe the operations of the female body.[8] Hence the myth of Demeter and Kore is about fertility at another, human level, the level at which the female body and its functions become the object of social transactions. At this level we may also 'read' the ritual acts and performances associated with Demeter, rites that allude to the topography, as it were, of the female body itself, which, like the ploughed furrow, bears the imprint of men's sowing, and brings forth the fruits by which the race of men perpetuates itself. It is in fact this fertile potential of woman's body that guarantees that she will live her life according to the broad narrative outline of the Eleusinian drama.[9] Taken first from the realm of her father, she will be transported to the faraway home of a new husband, there to bear children; later on, in what could be called a terrible parody of that first departure (which was required by the marriage-rite known as the *ekdosis*, 'giving out'), she will briefly leave the house, her proper place, in order to bury a relative—perhaps a dead child—as part of the funerary ritual called the *ekphorā*, 'bearing out'. *Suppliant Women*'s Eleusinian setting, the

sequent enjoyment of ritual meats at the Thesmophoria, see Parke, *Festivals*, 85 f., and Burkert, *Greek Religion*, 244 f.; for fasting at the Mysteries, Parke, *Festivals*, 69, Burkert, *Greek Religion*, 286. Jenny Strauss Clay has argued that there is in fact an 'absence of corroborating evidence' that 'link[s] the goddess's nine-day abstention from food and washing to Eleusinian practice'; instead, Clay sees the fasting as a typically epic motif, meant to denote a 'period of transition' (*The Politics of Olympus: Form and Meaning in the Major Homeric Hymns* (Princeton, 1990), 217 and 217 n. 60).

[8] For the agricultural metaphor as used of women, see e.g. *Timaeus* 91 d. Menander, *Dyskolos*, 842 f., seems to quote nearly verbatim the legal language of betrothal, *engyē*. For a full discussion of the female body and the agricultural metaphors used of it in classical Greek culture, see Page DuBois, *Sowing the Body: Psychoanalysis and Ancient Representations of Women* (Chicago, 1988), 39–85.

[9] The importance of the 'imprint' as the characteristic common to both the womb and the sown field is discussed by Nicole Loraux, *Les Mères en deuil* (Paris, 1990), 109–11. For Demetrian myth as a reflection of the anthropological realities of Rubin's 'traffic in women', see Foley, *Homeric Hymn to Demeter*, 82 f.

mythic site of divine marriage and mourning, reminds us that the structure of woman's life, like the narrative structure of the Demeter myth, is organized around a series of departures and arrivals to and from men's houses.

It is to the first of those movements of women through space, as important a theme in this play as it is in *Children of Herakles*, that I now turn: that is, to Aithra's departure from Athens to Eleusis, where she makes the first-fruits sacrifice on behalf of her city's fertility—and where she makes significant reference to a still earlier departure, from Troizen to Athens, as the fertile young bride of Athens' king.

First-Fruits on Behalf of the City: Femininity, Fertility, Exogamy

The opening tableau that Euripides presents in *Suppliant Women* embraces the extremes of Demetrian and hence of feminine experience. At the stage altar representing that of Eleusis stands Aithra, happy mother of Athens' young king, officiating at the Proerosia, the yearly sacrifice to Demeter of first-fruits meant to ensure the fertility of the Athenian land, *khthōn* (28f.).[10] Aithra herself officiates at this particular sacrifice precisely because the 'fruit' of her own fertile womb is Athens' king; she is the personification of the human fertility of which chthonic and agricultural fertility is the conventional religious and literary analogue. As if to underscore this connection, the epithet she uses of Demeter—*hestioukhos*, 'keeper of the hearth in the Eleusinian land' (1)—reminds us that fertility, which makes Demeter the metaphorical mistress of her own cultic household centred at Eleusis, also places mortal woman at the centre of the house and, in the case of Aithra, of the palace; it is because she is both mother and queen that she makes sacrifice on behalf of the entire city.

---

[10] The practice seems to date at least from the early 6th-cent. An inscription dating to the 420s (*IG* I (2) 76 = *SIG* 83 = *LSCG* 5) suggests that in the late 5th cent., Athens was attempting to revive and reorganize the collection of the first-fruits, which may well have ceased due to the outbreak of hostilities with Sparta. Since it is unlikely, as Parke argues, that the Proerosia was ordinarily a popular festival on the order of the Panathenaia or the Mysteries themselves, its prominence in the prologue of *Suppliant Women*, written at roughly the same time as the inscription, could be an indicator of renewed Athenian interest in the rite. For the Proerosia in general, see Deubner, *Attische Feste* (Berlin, 1932), 68 ff.

But Aithra's opening invocation of Demeter to bless her, and her family, and her city (4–7) does not, as we might expect, segue into a clarification of her ritual mission to Eleusis; this is in fact postponed until the final third of her prologue speech (*hyper khthonos . . . prothyous'*, 28 ff.). Instead, it leads first and quite seamlessly into a description of the mourning Argive women who have left their homes in Argos' land in order to seek their dead children (*lipousai dōmat' Argeias khthonos*, 9), and who now stand around her 'guarding her' in a confining 'circle' (*phrourousi m' en kyklōi*, 103). The juxtaposition of Aithra, sacrificing for her city's fertility, and the Argive mothers, whose desolate grief recapitulates that of Eleusis' tutelary deity, powerfully conveys the range of maternal experiences that are, we might say, typically Eleusinian. Indeed the frequent repetition of the word *khthōn*, 'earth', throughout Aithra's speech (six times—1, 4, 9, 17, 28, 38—in forty-one lines) insistently calls attention to the twofold nature of the women's experience: the land is both the site of fertility (28) and the eventual site of the burial of the Seven (17). It should be said that in critical evaluations of this work, the motif of Demetrian grief has tended to overshadow that of Demetrian fertility, with all of its social and cultural implications; the encroachment on the festal figure of Aithra by the mourning mothers of the chorus could serve as a metaphor for this critical state of affairs.[11] In the theatre of Dionysos, however, the fertility motif, dramatized by the figure of a woman making sacrifice on behalf of her city's agricultural success, would have been as impossible to overlook as was the motif of grief, brought to dramatic life by that circle of keening mothers. Both fertility and mourning, the two main themes of Eleusinian myth, are thus invoked at both the verbal and visual levels in *Suppliant Women*'s opening tableau.

Saturated as it is with references to both human and vegetable fertility—what we may call the primary concern of Demetrian myth—*Suppliant Women*'s opening scene provides an ideal context for Aithra's compressed but prominently placed allusion to her marriage: that is, the social enactment of the 'secondary' level of the Eleusinian myth, at which woman's fertile body becomes

---

[11] A rare exception is Rehm's discussion of the ironies of the juxtaposition of the fertility and mourning motifs (*Marriage to Death*, 115).

the object of transactions between men. The nature of those
transactions is highlighted in Aithra's benediction:

> εὐδαιμονεῖν με Θησέα τε παῖδ' ἐμὸν
> πόλιν τ' Ἀθηνῶν τήν τε Πιτθέως χθόνα,
> ἐν ᾗ με θρέψας ὀλβίοις ἐν δώμασιν
> Αἴθραν πατὴρ δίδωσι τῷ Πανδίονος
> Αἰγεῖ δάμαρτα Λοξίου μαντεύμασιν.

Bless me and Theseus my child
and the Athenians' city and Pittheus' land
where, after he had raised me in his blessed halls,
my father gave me, Aithra, to Pandion's
son Aigeus as a wife, in accordance with Loxias' oracles.

(3–7)

Aithra is here the object (*me . . . damarta*) of an exchange organized by her father (*patēr*, the subject) that awards her to Aigeus
(*Aigei*, the indirect object): her speech reproduces the dynamics
of exogamy grammatically, as it were, as well as descriptively.
Her brief recollection outlines a familiar bit of Athenian mythic
history. The Athenian king Aigeus had gone to Delphi in order
to inquire about his future progeny; the oracular response to
which Aithra here alludes is probably the one he reports in
Euripides' *Medea*, 679–81: not to loose the wineskin's jutting
foot until he arrived at the paternal hearth and home.[12] According to that myth, the Athenian king did not in fact reach his own
hearth straight away: Instead, he stopped first in Troizen, where
King Pittheus got him drunk and thereby contrived the seduction of his own daughter.

This introductory reminiscence of a long-ago union, though
slight and rarely commented upon by critics, is in fact important
for two reasons. First, inasmuch as it recalls some terms of Kore's
mythic marriage as it is described in the Hymn to Demeter, the
Athenian queen's reference to her own union strengthens the
ongoing parallelism between the events described in the play and
those narrated in the Eleusinian myth. Second, it draws attention to the mechanics of exogamy itself, highlighting the crucial
role that marriage (and women, in marriages transacted by men)

---

[12] The reply is listed in H. W. Parke and D. E. W. Wormell, *The Delphic
Oracle* (Oxford, 1956), ii. 48, no. 110. The story of Aigeus' inquiry at Delphi can
be found in Plutarch, *Theseus* 3.

plays in the life of the state. Various marriages will reappear throughout the play—Aithra's, Oedipus', Evadne's—with endogamy and exogamy functioning as competing models for the different ways in which cities may comport themselves.

That Euripides wanted to draw attention to marriage as an institution with considerable symbolic significance for his play is suggested by the fact that this is, in fact, the only version of the myth in which Aithra is the lawful wife of Aigeus.[13] As described in the prologue, Pittheus formally gives away his daughter to the Athenian king: *didōsi*, 'gave me', in l. 6 has the sense of the related word *ekdidonai*, the term whose exact juridical meaning was 'to give in marriage'.[14] Now in the myth familiar from the *Medea*, the 'marriage' that Pittheus so ingeniously contrived consisted of little more than a sexual encounter between a young virgin and a drunken man—if anything, the elements of a rape. At any event, that union, consummated in the house of the bride's father, hardly conforms to what Seaford calls the 'elaborately symbolic ritual' that took the Athenian bride out of her father's house and transported her literally to the house of her husband—the movement described by *ekdosis*.[15] In *Suppliant Women*, however, it is the conventionality and legality of Aithra's marriage that are highlighted, as the use of *didonai* and of *damar*, 'wedded wife', indicate. The story of drunken seduction to which the *Medea* oracle alludes is all but repressed here— or, perhaps better, compressed, since there is the slightest,

---

[13] For this point see Mills, *Theseus, Tragedy*, 105: 'The version of Theseus' birth assumed here is strikingly at variance with older (less flattering) forms of the story.' It is interesting to speculate that the emphasis on the legitimacy of Aithra's union, and indeed Theseus' preoccupation with the purity of the Athenian gene pool (discussed below, pp. 157–60), is a reaction to Perikles' strict citizenship legislation of 451/50.

[14] For *didōsi* conveying the sense of the more formal *ekdidonai*, see Collard, *Euripides Supplices*, 106. For the legal meaning of the latter word, see Wolff, 'Marriage Law and Family Organization', 48; cf. LSJ II. 2 for this usage; and see also Vernant's discussion of *ekdosis* as only one of the formal actions necessary, if not sufficient, to legal marriage in 5th-cent. Athens (*Myth and Society*, 56 f., in his ch. 3, 'Marriage').

[15] Richard Seaford, 'The Structural Problem of Marriage in Euripides', in Powell, *Euripides, Women, and Sexuality*, 152. Seaford cites Plutarch's description of how, in Boiotia, the axle of the cart that took the bride from the house of her father to the house of her husband was burned, thereby destroying symbolically any possibility that the bride would return (*Moralia* 271d).

though perhaps misleading, allusion to it in the closing phrase *Loxiou manteumasin*, 'according to Loxias' oracles'.[16]

In the Hymn, the spectre of rape becomes explicit in the story of Kore's forcible abduction at the hands of Hades. Yet in this narrative (as in Aithra's 'sanitized' version of her own marriage) the violent sexual encounter exists in uneasy suspension with references to the legal forms of marriage; in the Hymn, too, *didonai* is used to indicate 'paternal prerogative' concerning marriage.[17] Foley argues in her commentary on the Hymn that the poem describes the introduction to Olympos of a form of marriage previously unknown there, but which was, to be sure, the norm among the archaic aristocrats for whom the poem was composed—that is, patriarchal, virilocal exogamy.[18] Or, as Jenny Strauss Clay puts it, the aim of Zeus' recourse to a form of 'trickery' resulting in his own daughter's abduction was indistinguishable from the aims of the seventh- and sixth-century tyrants who regularly practised exogamy: to create a 'bridge and alliance' between two hitherto discrete spheres or, in other words, to engineer a 'dynastic marriage' linking the upperworld of Olympos and the underworld of Hades. In this light, what she calls the Hymn's 'shocking and paradoxical collocation' of the legal forms of marriage and the elements of abduction can be seen not as an anomaly, but rather as conforming to the conventional paradigm of Greek marriage itself, in which forced

[16] 'Ae.'s statement that her father gave her to Aegeus "at the command of Loxias" is inexact, but would recall a story well-known to E.'s audience': Collard, *Euripides Supplices*, 106 ad loc. The story to which the *Medea* line alludes is given in full in Apollodoros 3. 207 f.

[17] Clay, *The Politics of Olympus*, 209: 'The collocation of *hêrpaxen* ['abducted'] and *dôken* ['gave in marriage'] in the third line [of the Hymn] is both shocking and paradoxical. If Zeus gives his daughter in marriage in accordance with his paternal prerogatives, why must Hades carry her off?' Cf. her discussion of Kore as an *epiklēros* (213; see also her nn. 39 and 40 at 213).

[18] I am persuaded by Foley's arguments against interpreting the union of Persephone and Hades as endogamous (*Homeric Hymn to Demeter*, 107, *contra* P. Scarpi in his *Letture sulla religione classica: l'inno omerico a Demeter* (Florence, 1976)). Foley points out that although it is endogamous inasmuch as it weds her to a blood relative (an inevitability on Olympos, of course), Persephone's union, unlike other Olympian alliances, makes her physically inaccessible to her mother by relocating her to the home of her husband. Cf. the comments of Jean Rudhardt, 'Concerning the Homeric *Hymn* to Demeter', in Foley, *Homeric Hymn*, 203 ff.

abduction was enacted symbolically and what Foley refers to as 'mock-seduction motifs' recalled, perhaps, a time when abduction did in fact constitute marriage.[19]

Hence Euripides' prologue to *Suppliant Women*, like the Homeric Hymn to Demeter that in so many ways shadows the drama, emphasizes woman's 'abstract importance and crucial role' in exogamy as the vehicles for the continuance of 'patriarchal' continuity.[20] In her invocation of Demeter, the hierarchy of beneficiaries whom Aithra names is indeed symbolic of her own crucial role in the 'traffic in women' that feminist scholars like Rabinowitz see as central to Euripidean dramaturgy and that is so aptly described by the term *ekdosis*, 'giving out'. Aithra names herself first—*eudaimonein me*, she says (3 f.)—and indeed it is she who, by producing a son who is heir to both kingdoms, links the 'city of Athens' (*polin te Athēnōn*) to the 'land of Pittheus' (*tēn te Pittheōs khthona*). In this context, we should note that the 'traffic' of which Rubin, Rabinowitz, *et al.* speak is, therefore, more than mere metaphor in the case of Aithra. For, like Kore, she must move quite literally from within the house of her father in Troizen (*olbiois en dōmasin*, 5) to that of her husband in Athens (cf. 29) in order to realize her father's aims. Indeed we may see her exit from her husband's and son's 'house' to an Eleusinian 'hearth' in order to guarantee the fertility of the land as structurally parallel to her long-ago departure from her father's wealthy homestead in order to guarantee the continuity of the *oikos*. Both exits are meant to ensure fertility that will in turn guarantee the survival of men's houses and of their *poleis*. Her departure from home as a result of the connivance of her father is thus a paradigmatic instance of how men's dynastic and

[19] For Zeus' trickery and his interest in arranging a 'dynastic' marriage, see Clay, *The Politics of Olympus*, 213; for exogamous marriage as a political tool among aristocrats in archaic times, see Vernant, 'Marriage', 67–70. Foley calls Persephone's marriage 'a deceptive and cruel trick foisted by violence on an idyllic mother/daughter relationship' (*Homeric Hymn to Demeter*, 107). For Greek marriage in general, see James Redfield, 'Notes on the Greek Wedding', *Arethusa*, 15 (1982), 181–201; for the Persephone/Kore myth as the symbol in art and literature for marriage as a rite of initiation, see Foley, p. 104.

[20] See Des Bouvries, *Women in Greek Tragedy*, 58 for woman as the 'central element in the continuity of the polis'.

political agendas are served quite specifically by regulating women's movements through the spaces that belong to men.

The terms of this description of exogamy remind us that the Greeks conceived of the female as what Anne Carson calls a 'mobile unit' that could mediate between the fixed positions occupied by men, who were identified with boundary, structure, and civilization. Carson has provided the cultural and anthropological context in which we may situate the connections between women, sexuality, movement, and marriage, all of which come together in the well-known tale of Aithra's marriage:

> Woman is a mobile unit in a society that practices patrilocal marriage . . . and man is not. From birth the male citizen has a fixed place in the *oikos* ('household') and *polis* ('city'), but the female moves. At marriage a wife is taken not just (and perhaps not at all) into her husband's heart but into his house. This transgression is necessary (to legitimate continuation of the *oikos*), dangerous (insofar as the *oikos* incorporates a serious and permanent crisis of contact), and creates the context for illicit varieties of female mobility . . . To isolate and insulate female *erôs*, from society and from itself, was demonstrably the strategy informing many of the notions, conventions, and rituals that surrounded female life in the ancient world.[21]

This description will help explain my use of the word 'regulating' in the previous paragraph and indeed 'Regulations' in the title of this chapter. Woman's ability to dissolve the boundaries between men's houses and cities can be seen as a carefully controlled use of her naturally transgressive nature (as we have seen in our discussion of the effect of the Girl's problematic entrance in *Children of Herakles*). It is, of course, that penchant for excess and boundary-crossing that necessitates woman's confinement to the interior of the house, where the dangerous potential for illicit movement (i.e. adultery) can be contained. Properly regulated, woman's mobility allows for the realization of a constructive and civilized medium between two equally untenable extremes: that of a hypermasculine self-sufficiency that renders men incapable of 'making contact', on the one hand, and hyperfeminine incontinence, on the other, symbolized by women's

---

[21] Carson, 'Women, Dirt, and Desire', 136. The fullest treatment of gender and space in Greek thought is that of J.-P. Vernant, 'Hestia-Hermes: The Religious Expression of Space and Movement in Ancient Greece', in *Myth and Thought among the Greeks*, tr. Janet Lloyd (London, 1983), 127–75.

affinity for Dionysiac principles of liquidity and libido, which are given vent in the untamed and uncivilized wilds that are the antitheses of civilization itself. As man uses agriculture and viticulture to 'impose civilized order on the chaos of nature', just so does he use marriage to tame and exploit the women's elemental, fertile nature.[22] In this context it is no accident that the aim of exogamous marriage in Greek society—that is, to ensure the continuance of the husband's house by means of legitimate offspring—was referred to in the official language of the marriage ceremony as 'the ploughing of legitimate children'.

In his discussion of the representation of marriage in Euripidean drama, Richard Seaford enumerates various ways in which tragic marriages can deviate from this culturally endorsed model of 'transferral, monogamy, and continuity'.[23] The bride's marriage could threaten her family of origin (hence Ariadne's aid to Theseus in the *Theseus*, or Medea's to Jason as recalled in the *Medea*); the bride could set her husband above her family of origin, as in the *Protesilaos*, in which Laodameia commits suicide after her father orders the destruction of a statue of her dead husband, to which she is inordinately devoted (a model for *Suppliant Women*'s Evadne); or, conversely, the bride's residual loyalty to her family of origin could threaten the family of her husband, as in *Andromakhe*, in which Hermione's continued allegiance to her father disrupts her marriage to Neoptolemos.[24] In stark contrast to these transgressive models, Aithra's marriage to Aigeus, to judge from her compressed description of it, was exemplary. Unlike that of Medea or Ariadne, her union clearly fulfilled rather than violated her father's wishes; unlike Laodameia, she bore an heir and thereby became the vehicle for incorporation of her father's domain into that of her husband (as the syntactically parallel 'land of Troizen' and 'city of Athens'

---

[22] Carson, 'Women, Dirt, and Desire', 143. For the significance of the agricultural metaphor within the larger context of gender and ritual considerations, see the discussion of J.-P. Vernant, 'Between the Beast and the Gods', in Vernant, *Myth and Society in Ancient Greece*, 152–4. For women as 'naturally' susceptible to the Dionysiac pleasures of both sex and drink, and hence their symbolic role as 'the representatives or associates of disorder, emotion, passion, irrationality', see Just, *Women in Athenian Law*, 186 f.

[23] Seaford, 'Problem of Marriage', 152.

[24] See Seaford, 'Problem of Marriage', 152–68 for a full treatment of these issues.

in l. 4 suggest); unlike Hermione, she identifies herself fully as a member of her husband's family, as her description of the Athenian palace as 'my house', *emōn domōn* (29) demonstrates (cf. *olbiois en dōmasin*, 5 'in his blessed halls', referring to her father's house from which she dutifully came as a bride).

But the most important comparandum for Aithra's marriage to Athens' king is that of the Theban king, Oedipus, whom Aithra will invoke a few lines after her opening benediction (14), and whose story will indeed shadow this play's action up until its final scene, when he is again mentioned (1078). As so often in tragedy, the situation in Athens stands in stark contrast to that in Thebes. While Aithra's marriage, like that of Oedipus, may be said to have 'fulfilled the oracles of Apollo' (7), the resemblance is merely a superficial one. For the marriage of the Theban royal couple, unlike that of their Athenian neighbours, was, if anything, the extremest form of endogamy; its offspring, moreover, were forced, unlike Aithra's son, to fight to the death in a vain attempt to secure their paternal inheritance (*Oidipou panklērias meros kataskhein*, 14f.). That battle, we should also note, ruined Argos as well as Thebes, because its king Adrastos involved himself and his city in the disastrous expedition against Thebes on behalf of his exiled son-in-law Polyneikes (15f.). Polyneikes, as we later learn, was a total stranger when he was incorporated into the Argive ruling house—an in-law, that is to say, by virtue of an extreme form of *exogamy*.

Standing in implicit contrast to the disastrous marriages that took place in Thebes and Argos, each of which represents, as it were, an extreme pole (endogamy, exogamy) in relation to the institution of marriage—and indeed described in a setting that necessarily focuses attention on the issues of fertility and procreation—Aithra's marriage thus stands as a model for the way in which women may be used to further the constructive relations between dynasties and *poleis*. It is to the symbolic uses to which that model will be put as part of *Suppliant Women*'s political critique that we may now turn.

Engendering the State: Argos, Athens

I have described at length the implications of Aithra's marriage in particular and of exogamy in general not merely because they seem to me to be so prominently featured at the beginning of this text, but also because exogamy and endogamy figure importantly in the debate between Adrastos and Theseus that follows Aithra's prologue. In this scene, the different forms of marriage are used to represent the competing political alternatives of what we might call 'isolationism' and 'interventionism'—alternatives that have quite concrete implications for the action, given the nature of the play's suppliant crisis. Adrastos' own political disaster is described as having been the result of another kind of error, one emblematized by his decision to give his daughters away in marriage (*exedokas*, 133) to total strangers, *xenoi*. This error may itself be thought of as corresponding to one end of the gender spectrum: the undisciplined and uncontrollable one— that is, the 'feminine' one—that Carson refers to in the account of exogamy I have quoted above. For I shall argue that the youthful Athenian king's interrogation of the Argive leader reveals that Adrastos' fatal error in selecting his daughters' husbands was characterized by a typically feminine lack of self-control, a tendency to incontinence, and indeed a willingness to be manipulated by hitherto unknown bridegrooms. Conversely, we shall see that Theseus tends to a just as typically masculine super-continence, a desire to 'maintain form' that expresses itself as an unwillingness to acknowledge obligations to anything that does not lie within the strict confines of his own *polis*—which is here identified with the *genos*, much as it was in the case of Demophon in *Children of Herakles*. The application of these matrimonial models to describe political positions seems justified by the fact that the terms of Theseus' and Adrastos' debate about right action among *poleis* are culled from the conventional vocabulary used of marriage and of the sexual operations of the human body, operations that marriage seeks both to exploit and to regulate.

Feminized Adrastos

Before turning to the actual 'contest of words' (195) between Theseus and Adrastos, however, it is worth pausing to consider once again the stage picture that Euripides presents here, and to draw out its implications for the scene as a whole. For the appearance of the characters on stage betrays their gendered identities as powerfully as do their words.

Aithra's description of herself as being guarded within a circle formed by the chorus (103) indicates that the chorus has created an 'inside' within the exterior, public space of the stage's fictive Eleusinian setting. If we imagine Aithra standing at the stage altar encircled by the chorus members, it becomes clear that Adrastos, the Argive king, remains rather ostentatiously excluded from that circle. When he is first brought to Theseus' (and thus the audience's) attention, he is quite literally liminal, lying prostrate at the gate (*en pylais*, 104) of the sanctuary.[25] This relegation to the margin can be said to reflect his dislocation from the fixed centre of the political cosmos. Adrastos' 'fall' is, indeed, more than mere metaphor. Once a king like Theseus himself (whom the Argive leader abjectly addresses as 'strongest', *alkmimōtaton kara*, at 163), Adrastos, by contrast, is now literally abased, having 'fallen to the floor', *pitnōn pros oudas* (165). His own head reaches no higher at this point than Theseus' knee, which he must embrace in the suppliant's traditional gesture (163–6).

Humbled and marginalized, Adrastos is reduced to disgrace (*en aiskhynais*, 164). Yet more than his political identity has become blurred. Like the displaced Iolaos in *Children of Herakles*, this play's Adrastos cuts an anonymous and vaguely womanish figure on stage when we first see him, wholly absorbed in what has aptly been described as this scene's 'epic' and 'female' world of lamentation. Visually, he is indeed pathetic, 'a weeping lump on the ground, covered by a cloak'.[26] His body and head

---

[25] 'Huddled in misery at the back of the stage' is how Peter Burian describes Adrastos in '*Logos* and *Pathos*: The Politics of the *Suppliant Women*', in Burian (ed.), *Directions in Euripidean Criticism* (Durham, NC, 1985), 131. For a persuasive account of how this scene might be effectively blocked on stage, see Rehm, 'The Staging of Suppliant Plays', 285–7.

[26] Loraux (*The Invention of Athens*, 48) describes the world of the mourning mothers' laments as both epic and female. For Adrastos as a 'weeping lump', see Wesley D. Smith, 'Expressive Form in Euripides' *Suppliants*', *HSCP* 71 (1966), 153. The word used to describe Adrastos' costume here, *khlanidioi*, appears only once more in Euripides, at *Orestes* 42, a passage that similarly describes a feminized male figure who is completely 'hidden' within the garment: *khlanidiōn d' esō kryphtheis*. A further link between Adrastos and the mothers is that the language of his supplication is nearly identical to that used by the chorus a bit later: cf. 165 and 278. Euripides takes advantage of the conventions of supplicatory language in order to underscore the similarities between the Argive king and the chorus that accompanies him; for this point see also

are covered: the body with a *khlanidion* (110), his head with some kind of veil that conceals his identity (*enkalypsas krata*, 112). Moreover, this self-imposed exile into an interior that he has fashioned for himself inevitably consigns him to the silence that is, as Aithra will later remind us (297–300), also the proper state of women: Theseus' brusque command to the anonymous 'covered one' indeed betrays his impatience at being offered wordless cries like those in which the mourning mothers take their self-indulgent pleasure (*kharis goōn*, 79) rather than the speech, *glōssē*, that is the fitting medium for communication between men (112 f.). As one who now prefers the darkness of a hidden interior to the light of day, and who has eschewed intelligible speech for incoherent lamentation, Adrastos would surely have resembled the Argive women around him, to whose grey old age he indeed compares his own (cf. *polias mēteras*, 35, and *gēras polion*, 170, both used of the mothers; and *polios anēr*, 166, of Adrastos himself).

Yet there is perhaps a stronger, even more suggestive visual reference in this stage-picture. Maurice Olender describes the Demeter of the Hymn as follows:

> Changed in the course of her wanderings (*Dem.* 133) into an old woman (101, 113), veiled from head to foot in a dark *peplos* (182–83), and unrecognizable (94–95, 111), Demeter arrives at Eleusis in mourning for her daughter (97). At first, she refuses to accept anything, neither the 'radiant seat'—offered by Metaneira, the wife of Keleos and mistress of the place—nor food and drink (192–201). The goddess likewise gives expression to her grief by abstaining from any word or gesture (199)...[27]

Spatially apart, veiled, uncommunicative: Adrastos not only withdraws into a silent, interior state that is typical of women in general, but more specifically acts out the role of Demeter herself, in the very spot where the goddess 'created' that role. This feminized appearance will serve all the better to underscore the feminine character of the position he argues against Theseus, who, by contrast, has so confidently occupied centre stage.

Burian '*Logos* and *Pathos*', 131. Luigi Battezzato argues that the chorus's excessive grief here is competitive with Adrastos' (*Il Monologo nel Teatro di Euripide* (Pisa, 1995), 145 and esp. 147).

[27] Maurice Olender, 'Aspects of Baubo', in Halperin *et al.*, *Before Sexuality*, 85.

The Ill-Kept Boundaries of Argos

The focal point of the long stichomythic exchange between
Theseus and Adrastos concerning the motivations for the disastrous expedition of the Seven (110–262) is the young Athenian's
interest in the marriage Adrastos made between his two daughters and Polyneikes and Tydeus:

> Θη. ἐκ τοῦ δ' ἐλαύνεις ἑπτὰ πρὸς Θήβας λόχους;
> Αδ. δισσοῖσι γάμβροις τήνδε πορσύνων χάριν.
> Θη. τῷ δ' ἐξέδωκας παῖδας Ἀργείων σέθεν;
> Αδ. οὐκ ἐγγενῆ συνῆψα κηδείαν δόμοις.
> Θη. ἀλλὰ ξένοις ἔδωκας Ἀργείας κόρας;

> Th. Why did you lead the seven companies against Thebes?
> Ad. To please my two sons-in-law.
> Th. To which of the Argives did you give (*exedōkas*) your
>   children in marriage?
> Ad. The marriage-bond by which I united my house was
>   not among kin (*engenē*).
> Th. *What?* You gave away Argive girls to *foreigners?*
>
>   (131–5)

It is clear that Theseus had not considered the possibility that
the Argive king would marry off his daughters to anyone but
Argives; *alla* at 135 is a strong marker of the Athenian king's
'indignant or reproachful surprise'.[28] Instead, Adrastos has married his daughters to complete strangers, *xenoi* (135). That his
attempt at matchmaking represents an abuse of the proper forms
of marriage (as exemplified by Aithra's union) becomes clear
when we consider that its immediate result was another form of
'sending out' from his house, a parody, almost, of the festal marriage rite—that is, the ill-fated expedition against Thebes that
he sent forth *ek domōn* (23) and which reduces him to unseemly
weeping in the prologue (22 f.). As if to compound the sense that
Adrastos' *ekdosis* (cf. *exedōkas*, 133) was transgressive, his sons-
in-law are described as being not merely *xenoi*, non-Argive, but
xenoi who were themselves the objects of a sinister 'sending out'
from their fathers' houses. Before reaching Argos they had been

---

[28] Ann Michelini dismisses Theseus' retorts to Adrastos as little more than
'faint tones of surprise' in 'The Maze of the Logos: Euripides, Suppliants
163–249', (*Ramus*, 20/1 (1991), 24); but for the forcefulness of Theseus' *alla* see
Collard, *Euripides Supplices*, 144, whose description I have quoted here.

forced to leave their homelands (*patridos ekliponth' horous*, 147) for ill-omened reasons: the shedding of kin-blood, *syngenes haima*, in the case of Tydeus; a father's curse, *arais patrōiais*, in the case of Polyneikes (148–50).

Theseus' shocked question at 145—'so *those* were the "beasts" (*thersin hōs*) to whom you married off (*edōkas*) your own daughters?'—is a further indicator of the extent to which the unions to which the Argive king consented fail to fulfil the proper aim of marriage. The reference to beasts is apparently nothing more than a compressed paraphrase of the Delphic oracle that had instructed Adrastos to marry his girls to a lion and boar (140).[29] Yet the motif of bestiality has in fact been set up by Theseus' sarcastically disapproving use of a cognate at 115: 'Just what is it that you're hunting for (*thērōn*) [sc. in supplicating me]?' Beasts, hunts: all this suggests that Adrastos has committed his house to a union that belongs to the world of the hunter, a 'raw', nocturnal, pre-civilized world in which men become as feral and dangerous as their prey. Indeed the nocturnal arrival (*elthonte nyktos*, 142) of these 'beasts' who will become Adrastos' sons-in-law recalls the suspect milieu of the *Iliad*'s Doloneia, which represents a night-time reversion to pre-civilized and primitive tactics that is an anomaly within the epic's daylit world. This is a milieu in which men are not tamers and cultivators, the roles to which the metaphors of the marriage ritual symbolically commit them, but rather the untamed and savage beasts who threaten civilization—or, perhaps, the solitary hunters who alone, at night, dressed in skins, haunt the peripheries of the *polis* in order to ensnare their dangerous prey. In acquiescing to these matches, Adrastos mimics an archetype that is dangerous, hypermasculine, and uncivilized—one, moreover, that is associated with those pre-eminent political 'others', the barbarian and the tyrant.[30]

---

[29] This oracle is the subject of more extended discussion in *Phoenician Women* (409ff.), where we learn that Adrastos, on seeing his house guests Polyneikes and Tydeus ferociously fighting over a bed, realized that they must be the wild animals Delphi was referring to. The meaning of the oracle itself remains mysterious, despite attempts both ancient and modern to see a deeper meaning in the choice of a lion and a boar: see the discussion of Donald Mastronarde in *Euripides Phoenissae* (Cambridge, 1994) 265 ad 411 ff.

[30] 'Hunting is firmly on the side of the wild, the "raw" of night': Vidal-

And yet while men's bestiality is predicated on the assumption of either real (as with Dolon) or figurative (as with Adrastos' sons-in-law) animal attributes, it is of course women who are normally conceived of as being generically liable to slip over the line that separates the realms of the human and the bestial. In Athenian thought, the tendency to conflate the two realms was considered merely an exaggeration of what Vernant calls woman's 'wild character', the distinctly feminine incontinence that always threatens the 'civilized order' that men seek to impose on nature; because her essentially liquid nature (as opposed to the hardness and denseness of male bodies) places her squarely within the world of the elements, of 'plants, animals, and female wantonness', woman is thought of as inimical to civilization itself. (Hence, to return to a more overtly political discourse, the common association between femininity and Eastern, 'barbarian' culture.)[31] As Xenophon indicates (*Oik.* 3. 7–10), the fifth-century Athenian bridegroom would indeed have spoken of his wife as a 'wild animal' who only after time would become 'submissive' to his hand; Menander in the fourth century calls womankind 'one great beast', *megiston thērion gynē* (fr. 488 Kock). But within the Argive royal house, *ekdosis* is perverted, making bridegrooms into wild beasts, *thēres*—in other words, the doubles not only of the violent predators to which hunters likened themselves, but, as the Menander quotation

Naquet, *The Black Hunter*, 117. The equation of heroes and hunters in Greek thought goes back to F. Orth, 'Jagd', in *RE* 9 (1914), 558–684. For hunting as an activity that takes place at the edge of civilized areas, see Vidal-Naquet in his discussion of the *ephēbeia* (*Black Hunter*, 117ff.), and cf. P. Chantraine, *Études sur le vocabulaire grec* (Paris, 1956), 40–65. The tragic representation of the barbarian as bestial, savage, and wild is discussed by Edith Hall, *Inventing the Barbarian* (Oxford, 1989), 125ff. For these same attributes associated with the tyrant, see Hall, p. 126 and cf. Plato, *Rep.* 9. 571c–d, where the tyrant's soul is distinguished by the prominence of its bestial and wild aspect (*to de thēriōdes te kai agrion*).

[31] Carson ('Women, Dirt, and Desire', 143–4) provides an ample discussion of the female's liquidity and latent bestiality; for female liquidity as opposed to male hardness, see also Anne Ellis Hanson, 'The Medical Writers' Woman', in Halperin *et al.*, *Before Sexuality*, 317f. Women as inherently bestial and inimical to civilization: Vernant, *Myth and Society in Ancient Greece*, 153; Carson, 'Women, Dirt, and Desire', 143; Foley, 'The Conception of Women', 134. For the connection between femininity and Eastern-ness see Hall, *Inventing the Barbarian*, 127 and 209–10.

suggests, of the undomesticated 'animals' that the male bride-grooms were supposed to 'tame': the brides themselves.

Theseus again invokes the vocabulary of the bestial, *thēriōdes*, in the subsequent elaboration on matters cosmic (185–217) that prefaces his brusque denunciation of Adrastos' political and religious blunders. He declares himself grateful that the gods themselves have demarcated the human from the bestial (*thēri-ōdous*, 202). The latter is linked in his speech to the primal chaos (*pephyrmenou*) in which all things were indistinguishable—a common collocation in fifth-century Greek thought.[32] It is not difficult to see why the Athenian king is so insistent on these points: primal chaos and the bestial (whether at its hypermasculine or hyperfeminine extremes) were the antitheses of everything that the civilized structure of the *polis*, with its zealously maintained borders, stood for. In the Greek cultural imagination, of course, the female is also characterized both by indistinct boundaries and by a tendency to 'mix' indiscriminately because of her unbridled, bestial wantonness;[33] the disintegration of well-maintained categories—the indiscriminate mixing to which Theseus will disgustedly refer as *symmeixis* (222)—is therefore itself 'feminine'. And indeed, the verb Theseus derisively uses to characterize those who reject the precious distinction between human civilization and bestial, incoherent chaos is *tryphaō*, 'to live in languorous delicacy' (214); here, it cements the complex associations in this passage between bestiality, indiscriminate mixing, femininity and (as it were) a fifth-century Athenian version of political incorrectness, connoting as it does effeminacy, indulgence, servility, Easternness, and a decadent, undemocratic attitude.[34]

[32] Cf. Kritias 43 F 19, 1f Snell, where *ataktos*, standing in for *pephyrmenos*, is also connected with *thēriōdē*. For archaic Greek notions about the primal, 'limitless' chaos in which opposites become conflated, see W. K. C. Guthrie, *A History of Greek Philosophy* (Cambridge, 1962) i. 76–104, and esp. 89 ff. for the 'separating out' of the various elements.

[33] For women's excessive susceptibility to the pleasures of sex and drink, see Just, *Women in Athenian Law*, 186 f.; Carson, 'Women, Dirt, and Desire', 137–45.

[34] For *tryphān* elsewhere in Euripides, cf. *Ion* 1375 f. (a mama's boy); *Ba.* 150 (the maenads' hair); and *Ba.* 969 (Pentheus' transvestitism); in Attic prose cf. e.g. Dem. 42. 24 (trading in a war-horse for a chariot so as not to have to walk), 19. 314 (traipsing through the Agora with an ankle-length himation). E. R.

For Theseus, as well as for twentieth-century Hellenists of the French school, boundary violation and bestiality are both connected to sexuality in general, for which the Athenian, at least, evinces considerable distaste. In Theseus' final chastisement of Adrastos, intercourse itself becomes a metaphor for the evil inherent in Adrastos' extra-national marriage-making:

> ἧς καὶ σὺ φαίνῃ δεκάδος, οὐ σοφὸς γεγώς,
> ὅστις κόρας μὲν θεσφάτοις Φοίβου ζυγεὶς
> ξένοισιν ὧδ' ἔδωκας ὡς δόντων³⁵ θεῶν,
> λαμπρὸν δὲ θολερῷ δῶμα συμμείξας τὸ σὸν
> ἤλκωσας οἴκους· χρὴ γὰρ οὔτε σώματα
> ἄδικα δικαίοις τὸν σοφὸν συμμειγνύναι
> εὐδαιμονοῦντάς τ' ἐς δόμους κτᾶσθαι φίλους.

In which company you yourself seem to be, showing
    yourself unwise,
you who, though yoked by the oracles of Phoibos, gave
your daughters in marriage in this fashion, as though
    the gods had granted it,
forcing your splendid house into intercourse (*symmeixas*)
    with a foul one,
and in so doing wounding your house. The wise man
should not mingle unjust bodies in intercourse
    (*symmeignynai*) with just ones
and should acquire well-favoured friends for his house.

                                                    (219–25)

Dodds, *Euripides Bacchae*, 2nd edn. (Oxford, 1960), 197, associates *tryphao* with *habrotēs*, 'softness', in the previous line: together, the two convey 'the quality of an effeminate or over-fastidious person'. For the feminine and Eastern connotations of *habrosynē*, *tryphē*, *khlidē*, and *malthakia* in 5th-cent. Athenian thought, see Hall, *Inventing the Barbarian*, 126 ff., Just, *Women in Athenian Law*, 187 f., and the discussion of Leslie Kurke in 'The Politics of ἁβροσύνη in Archaic Greece' (*Classical Antiquity*, 11/1 (1992), 91–120), to which I owe the Demosthenes citations and the observation about the specifically political resonances of these words. It is significant, as Kurke points out, that *habros*- words did not take on their negative, 'decadent' connotations until the 5th-cent., when the Persian Wars made the Greeks antipathetic to Eastern ways formerly prized by the cultural elite (Kurke, pp. 101 ff.). Xenophanes (fr. 3 D–K) denounces *habrosynai* as 'useless', *anōphelea*, and therefore comparable to Perikles' silent man—and to the speech of women, according to Aithra here.

³⁵ Given ἔδωκας that preceded it, Scaliger's δόντων here is clearly preferable to L's ζόντων (strongly supported by Conacher, 'Religious and Ethical Attitudes', 18; cf. his comments in *Euripidean Drama*, 101 f., nn. 14 and 15), the inappropriateness of which Porson's ἐόντων merely replicates. Collard 'reluc-

The repetition of *symmeignynai*, 'to mingle together in intercourse', as well as the use here of other language that suggests the
human body and its concerns (*hēlkōsas*, 'wounding'; cf. *nosounta,
nosountos*, 'sickening', 227–8) makes it difficult to pronounce
these metaphors completely dead, and thus underscores the connections between real and abstract—that is to say, corporeal and
political—boundary violation, the transgressive and feminine
propensity of which Theseus is so suspicious.

Engenē kēdeian: *Keeping Athens Pure*

For Theseus, then, Adrastos' bad judgement is characterized by
a failure to recognize crucial distinctions at the level of the
natural, the domestic, the political, and, finally, the cosmic; this
failure is, in turn, symbolized by the 'bestial' marriages arranged
by Adrastos between his daughters and two border-crossing
strangers. The impropriety of Adrastos' impetuous action com-
promises the integrity of his city: Argos is destroyed (*polin apōle-
sas*, 231) because it has become rashly involved in the affairs of
other states. 'Theseus', as one critic has observed, 'rejects *sym-
machia* (246) because it involves *symmixis* (222).'[36] Hence the
internationalist actions to which Adrastos is committed by his
daughters' marriages are themselves defined, by opposition, as
improper and excessive—a parody, as it were, of the uses of exogamy. The fact that Theseus expresses his disdain for political
involvement with other *poleis* as contempt for Adrastos' choice
of sons-in-law, reflects how the structure of extra-domestic
politics reflects that of exogamous *ekdosis*. At the heart of each
lies an act of intercourse.

The exchange between the two kings at 134f., on the other
hand, reveals Theseus' assumptions about the correct manage-
ment of both marriage and foreign policy. Adrastos says that the
marriages he made were not *engenēs*, 'within the *genos*', and
Theseus replies that they must therefore have been unions with

tantly' accepts δόντων, arguing that what Theseus is accusing Adrastos of is 'the
selfish presumption of the gods' favor' (*Euripides Supplices*, 168 ad loc.).

[36] Smith, 'Expressive Form', 158. Even with respect to intra-political
affairs Theseus betrays a preoccupation with what we might call 'boundary-
maintenance': as scrupulously as the gods themselves made distinct species out
of the primal cosmic soup, so Theseus divides up the citizens of the entire *polis*
into three distinct sub-groups (238).

xenoi, 'foreigners'; for the Athenian, *genos* and *polis* apparently amount to the same thing. His dismayed tone in 135 indicates just what he thinks of *xenoi*. For him, the best kind of union is clearly an *engenēs kēdeia*.

It is worth pausing here to note that *engenē*, the word used to describe what Theseus apparently believes is an ideal marriage, seems to belong to the lexicon of Athenian discourse about autochthony, a civic myth whose importance to fifth-century civic ideology has been much commented upon.[37] The language of this scene is closely paralleled by that in other Euripidean works that deal with Athenian autochthony; taken together, these passages suggest a well-established vocabulary that was used to describe the Athenians' autochthonous origins, and upon which the poet drew in his 'Athenian' plays. We can begin with *Ion*, a drama that is especially concerned with the implications of autochthony for Athenian identity.[38] There is in fact an extra-ordinary likeness between the interrogation of Adrastos by the incredulous young Theseus in *Suppliant Women* and an inter-view in the *Ion* between the Athenian prince Ion and Kreousa, the strange visitor to Delphi who, it will turn out, is his own mother. In that early yet oddly intimate exchange, Ion quizzes the Athenian woman about her own marriage:

> *Ἴων. πόσις δὲ τίς σ' ἔγημ' Ἀθηναίων, γύναι;*
> *Κρ. οὐκ ἀστὸς ἀλλ' ἐπακτὸς ἐξ ἄλλης χθονός.*
> *Ἴων. τίς; εὐγενῆ νιν δεῖ πεφυκέναι τινά.*
> *Κρ. Ξοῦθος, πεφυκὼς Αἰόλου Διός τ' ἄπο.*
> *Ἴων. καὶ πῶς ξένος σ' ὢν ἔσχεν οὖσαν ἐγγενῆ;*

Ion. Which of the Athenians was the husband who married you, ma'am?

Kr. No citizen he, but imported (*epaktos*) from another land.

---

[37] Especially by Loraux, *Children of Athena*. In the context of my discussion of the interrelation between the social construction of gender and contemporary civic discourse, it is worth recalling that the 'central position' held by the myth of autochthony in the schema of Athenian ideology has been seen as owing to the fact that it allows the Athenian 'city of men' to 'exclude women from its origins', as Froma I. Zeitlin writes in her preface to Loraux's work (Loraux, *Children of Athena*, xiv); cf. Saxonhouse, *Fear of Diversity*, 111–31 ('Autochthony and Diversity').

[38] See the discussion of George B. Walsh, 'The Rhetoric of Birthright and Race in Euripides' Ion', *Hermes*, 106 (1978), 301–15, and Loraux's chapter 'Autochthonous Kreousa', *Children of Athena*, 184–236.

Ion. Who? He must have been someone noble (*eugenē*) by
          birth (*pephykenai*).
Kr.   Xouthos, by birth descended from Aiolos and Zeus.
Ion. And how was it that he, a foreigner (*xenos*), should have
          got you, when you were of the city-clan (*engenē*)?

                                                    (289–93)

Here Ion draws attention to the sharp divide between *engenēs*
and *epaktos* (and cf. Hermes' earlier description of Xouthos
as *ouk engenēs ōn*, *Ion* 63). Later, a further contrast is drawn
between *epaktos* and autochthony itself: 'I have heard', Ion declares, 'that renowned Athens is autochthonous (*autokhthonas*),
not a race imported from without' (*ouk <u>epeisakton</u> genos*, 590).
Autochthony and foreignness are similarly contrasted in the
Erekhtheus (fr. 360.7 ff.), where the Athenian queen Praxithea
proudly cites autochthony as justification for her decision to
offer her daughter as a sacrifice on behalf of the city. The
Athenians, she says, are not a race imported from elsewhere (*leōs
ouk <u>epaktos</u> allothen*, 7)—that is to say, citizens in name only but
not in fact (13)—but are, instead, sprung from the Athenian soil
itself, *autokhthones* (fr. 360.7 ff.). Within the discourse of autochthony, *epaktos*, 'imported', is suspect because it is inherently
opposed to *engeneia* and hence autochthony itself. This is most
explicitly conveyed in a striking metaphor in *Phoenician Women*,
where the violent assault on Thebes is likened to the deadly
importation of a foreign bride, *gamōn <u>epakton</u> atan* (*Phoen.* 343;
cf. 349).[39]

All this might suggest that the horror Theseus evinces at
Adrastos's marriage-brokering amounts to little more than a
proper Athenian chauvinism, just as his appeal to a well-ordered
universe can be seen as nothing more than a proper piety.[40] Yet
if this reference to a basic element of fifth-century Athenian
civic ideology at first seems appropriate (if anachronistic) in
the mouth of the Athenian hero par excellence, it is not, however, unambiguous. We already know that Theseus' refusal to
acknowledge obligations outside of his own *genos*-as-*polis* puts
him in danger of violating what is never doubted to be a divine
law that requires both burial of the dead and obligation to

---

[39] I owe many of these parallels to Seaford ('Problem of Marriage', 156 ff.).
[40] So Zuntz, *The Political Plays of Euripides*, 54.

suppliants (39 f., 526, etc.).[41] More important, however, is the fact that the exchange between the young king and Adrastos goes on to include pointed references to the saga of Oedipus (149 f.), whose every trouble, we might say, stemmed from a failure to leave the city, and indeed who stayed, in too many ways, within the boundaries of his own *genos*. If we bear in mind what Lévi-Strauss called the 'positive aspect' of the incest prohibition, that is, 'to initiate organization',[42] then the implied comparison between Theseus' rejection of exogamous marriage and a famous case of incest suggests that the Athenian king's rigid insistence on endogamy is as potentially destructive of the *polis* and its civilized institutions as Adrastos' careless exogamies in fact were.

In this way, 'marriage within the clan', that central principle of identity in democratic Athens, with its all-important rhetoric of autochthony, becomes as much an object of critique as was Adrastos' penchant for indiscriminate exogamy, the dynastic tool of aristocrats and tyrants.[43] If Adrastos' position is one that could be described as an excessive promiscuity (in all of the senses of that word) that ultimately threatened the *polis*, then Theseus' stance—characterized, let us remember, by an aversion to 'intercourse'—commits him to what one scholar, in a discussion of the ideology of autochthony in the *Ion*, calls 'a violent pursuit of purity'.[44]

---

[41] Perhaps in order to underscore the dangers of remaining *engenēs*, the poet refers to the reason for Tydeus' flight as family blood-guilt, *haima syngenes* (148), incurred (as we learn from the scholiast on *Phoen.* 417) when Tydeus murdered his uncles Alkathoös and Lykopeus.

[42] *Elementary Structures of Kinship*, tr. James Bell, John Sturmer, and Rodney Needham (Boston, 1966), 43. The exogamy that Theseus rejects is, in this view, crucial to the establishment of human culture itself. For the implications of this equation for the dynamics of Euripidean theatre, see Rabinowitz, *Anxiety Veiled*, 15 f.

[43] For the association of exogamy with aristocracy, see the discussions of Vernant, 'Marriage', 67 ff. and C. Leduc, 'Marriage in Ancient Greece', in P. Schmitt-Pantel (ed.), *The History of Women* (Cambridge, Mass., 1992), 233–94. For the presentation of rape and exogamy in the Hymn to Demeter as possibly a reflection of the developing tensions between archaic exogamy and democratic endogamy, see Foley, *Homeric Hymn to Demeter*, 142–50. I do not think, however, that Euripides' focus here is a critique of aristocracy *per se*.

[44] Walsh, 'Rhetoric of Birthright', 306. In his championing of what Burian calls 'the *kosmos* of the intellect', Theseus here bears a slight resemblance to another young 'sex-negative' Euripidean ruler, the Theban Pentheus (Burian,

Here it is worth pausing to consider the ramifications of the debate between Theseus and Adrastos in terms of Saxonhouse's conceptualization of Greek political theorizing as an expression of 'fear of diversity'. For if autochthony can be described as an ideological attempt to suppress the feminine—which Saxonhouse takes to be a symbol for diversity—then we may say here that Theseus' extreme position represents the dangers that inhere in a system in which difference (here represented by the exogamous incorporation of others) is utterly repressed—just as Adrastos' extreme position points to the centrifugal instabilities that can destroy a system in which such difference fails to be contained within the framework of a unified, organizing whole. The *agōn* between the Athenian and the Argive king thus demonstrates how marriage, ideally the proper form of mediation between masculine and feminine, can serve as a model for those other negotiations upon which the survival of the *polis* depends: those between citizen and foreigner, individual and state, unity and diversity. Both Argos and Athens, as represented by their rulers, have failed thus far to master this most constructive form of self–other integration. If Adrastos heedlessly 'gives out' his two daughters and in so doing parodies the structures and aims of proper marriage, Theseus for his part fails to understand the constructive uses to which the feminine is most optimally put in the transaction called *ekdosis*, of which his own mother's marriage was a 'model' example.

It is only appropriate, then, that the deadlock in which the confrontation between the two kings ends will be resolved by a woman. Not surprisingly, that woman is Aithra herself.

Feminine Interventions

The Theseus-Aithra scene at once replicates and inverts the terms of the Theseus-Adrastos scene that precedes it. Both scenes begin with the same stage-picture, that of Theseus

---

'*Logos* and *Pathos*', 132); for Theseus' uncompromising and 'intellectual' manner cf. also Michael Lloyd, *The Agon in Euripides*, 77 f. Burian's discussion of the tensions between Theseus' hyperrational preference for *logos*, as opposed to the human suffering or *pathos* exemplified by the chorus, is excellent; in seeing the play as being essentially structured around these two poles, he is joined by Umberto Albini, 'Euripide e le pretese della retorica', *PP* 40 (1985), 354–60.

coaxing a veiled and grieving figure to speak. Moved to tears by the sound of the women's lamentation, Aithra adopts the very same posture in which we had previously seen Adrastos: she has completely hidden her face with a veil (286f.; cf. 110) and lowered her head (289; cf. 111 of Adrastos' bowed head). As with Adrastos, she appears at first incapable of articulate utterance, merely crying out *aiai*, and must be coaxed into speech (291f.; cf. 111f.).[45]

Yet unlike the hapless Adrastos, Aithra successfully challenges her son's recalcitrant attitude. Her re-entry into the action of the play has been rightly seen as the turning point of the drama—or even 'the starting point of the action proper'.[46] The queen's speech to her son brings about a radical shift in Theseus' attitude that resolves the play's suppliant crisis: he makes war on Thebes, recovers the bodies of the Seven, and gives them due burial. All this is the result of his mother's persuasion. But just as striking as Aithra's rhetorical success is Theseus' immediate response to it: noting the inappropriateness of being instructed by a woman (343ff.), he hastens to return her to her dead husband's house (360). Apparently, Aithra's intervention into the action, however effective and indeed transformative, is somehow inappropriate, and must be corrected.

Outside the House: The Feminine Threat Defined

Aithra's opening, with its initial emphasis on Demeter's special honorific 'hearth-holder', as well as her reference to her own happy childhood home, confirms the conventional identification of the house, *dōmata*, as a safe centre inhabited by females.

[45] If anything, these parallels further suggest the loss of masculine status associated with Adrastos' suppliant posture. Rehm ('The Staging of Suppliant Plays', 287) also observes that there would have been a 'striking visual echo' between the veiled, weeping figure of Adrastos earlier on and that of Aithra here. Mills (*Theseus, Tragedy*, 109) observes that Aithra's appeals to her son clearly echo those of Adrastos earlier on.

[46] Fitton, 'The Suppliant Women', 431. Aithra 'puts the plot back on track' according to Jeffrey Henderson, 'Myth into *muthos*: The Shaping of Tragic Plot', in Easterling, *Cambridge Companion to Greek Tragedy*, 190. Henderson characterizes Theseus' unwillingness to take up the suppliants' cause until this point as an aberration—one of the 'surprising and unsettling effects' that could result from a dramatist's deliberate 'deflection of expectations' built into traditional story patterns (the story pattern, in this case, being the 'suppliant pattern' in which the king protects the suppliants).

Hence although the queen calls attention to the fact that she has left the palace that was once her husband's and is now her son's, her exit is intended to serve that house, and the city for which it stands, since it brings her to another, symbolic 'hearth' where she will make sacrifice on behalf of fertility. The outside world and its crises, as she later suggests, is clearly the domain of men: 'For in the eyes of wise women it is merely fitting that everything be done by males' (40 f.).

As if to underscore the propriety that places women within the house and men without, the language used throughout the prologue repeatedly associates being outside the house, *ek domōn*, with disaster. Being outside of the house symbolizes the ill-fated expedition, *dystykhestatēn strateian*, of the Seven themselves and the doomed army that Adrastos foolishly sent forth from their homes, *ek domōn* (22 f.). Similarly, the chorus's 'terrible suffering', *pathos pathousai deinon*, and their departure from the house, *lipousai dōmat'*, are closely, almost causally linked (9–11). And indeed, that exit, pitiable as it is, is described in terms that recall the dangerous potential of women who have left their homes. Keening for their dead and tearing their own flesh (71–8), heedless of religious propriety in violating the legal ban on supplication at Eleusis (97),[47] the women of the chorus exhibit precisely the kind of unruly and emotionally self-indulgent behaviour (cf. 79) associated with women who have gone 'out of bounds'—the most extreme example of which is the maenad.

The threat posed by women who exit the house is a spectre that seems to haunt Theseus, and his entrance thrusts the theme of spatial constraints on women into the spotlight. Because Aithra herself is powerless to help the suppliants who surround her, she sends for her son, making due reference to gendered propriety. (Her weak periphrasis at 36 f.—*oikhetai de moi | kēryx pros asty deuro Thēsea kalōn*, 'a herald has gone on my account to the city in order to call Theseus hither'—may be said to reflect her own conventional passivity up to this point in the action.) When Theseus arrives, however, he mentions neither the messenger nor the message, and declares instead that he is 'ruffled with fear', *phoboi m' anapteroi* (89), on account of his mother,

---

[47] The chorus's mourning is unsuited to a delegation to Eleusis, as Collard notes ad loc.; cf. *Hipp.* 806 f. for the notion of an inappropriate, *dystykhēs*, suppliant.

whose prolonged absence from the house, *khronian apousan ek domōn* (90), compels him to come after her (*metasteikhō*, 90). This unusually lengthy absence from the house is what causes him to fear that something untoward (*neon*, repeated at 99) has befallen her. Behind a proper filial concern for his mother's safety, we sense here the larger cultural anxiety that a woman's absence from the house evoked.

Further details of this episode highlight the theme of woman's spatial containment. Aithra's potentially threatening 'misadventure' in leaving the house in fact places her at the centre of another kind of enclosure, the circle of chorus members by which she is enclosed and 'guarded' (102), thereby reminding us of the constraints that Theseus would reimpose upon her. This spatial constraint is, in turn, analogous to the religious obligation that metaphorically binds her. The branches that the chorus hold as tokens of their suppliant status (10) are recalled later; though not literal 'bonds', the 'bond that is no bond', *desmon d'adesmon*, represented by the suppliants' branches none the less binds her metaphorically with the obligation owed to any suppliant. Paradoxically, the adjective *adesmos* connotes a spatial restraint, coming as it may from the vocabulary of the law, where it suggests something akin to our concept of 'parole'—that is, movement that, while ostensibly free (i.e. *adesmos*), is none the less subject to surveillance.[48] Aithra's departure from the house, which in formal terms assimilates her to a pattern of being disastrously *ek domōn*, thus re-centres her within a living wall that reconstitutes those other enclosures, both literal and figurative, that restrain woman's movement.

Public Speaking

But if the literally 'feminine' constraints by which Aithra finds herself immobilized provide an appropriate setting for her declaration of emotional, maternal fellow-feeling with the Argive mothers (56f.), Aithra's conversation with Theseus shows her to be a canny manipulator of 'masculine' speech and logic.[49] We

[48] For *en phylakēi adesmōi* used this way, see Thuc. 3. 34. 3.
[49] As noted by Albini, 'Le pretese della retorica', 357. Mills argues that Theseus is the play's representative of Athenian 'intellect' and Aithra, the symbol of 'the Athenian ability to feel pity' (*Theseus, Tragedy*, 107); but this, I think, is to underestimate the old queen's rhetorical shrewdness.

have seen how, in the case of the Girl in *Children of Herakles*, unexpected movement from an interior to an exterior anticipates a comparably unconventional progression from feminine silence to public, and therefore masculine, speech. Like the Girl, Aithra herself alludes here to the gendered conventions that forbid such speech to women, even as she sets about violating them. She begins cautiously by testing her son's receptiveness to her speaking at all (295), but as soon as she is liberated to speak shows none of the tentativeness she displayed only a few lines earlier. Indeed, her repeated allusion to the convention of feminine silence, *sigē*, even as she steps forth to speak constitutes a concentrated bit of *praeteritio* indeed:

> οὔτοι σιωπῶσ' εἶτα μέμψομαί ποτε
> τὴν νῦν σιωπὴν ὡς ἐσιγήθη κακῶς,
> οὐδ' ὡς ἀχρεῖον τὰς γυναῖκας εὖ λέγειν
> δείσασ' ἀφήσω τῷ φόβῳ τοὐμὸν καλόν.

No: I will not <u>silently</u> (*siōpōs'*) allow myself to incur blame later
on the grounds I kept <u>silent</u> (*esigēthē*) a bad/cowardly
   <u>silence</u> (*siōpēn*) now;
nor as one who fears '<u>For women to speak well is a useless</u>
   <u>thing</u>' (*akhreion*)
will I throw away my own good on account of fear.

(297–300)

The queen's shrewd, two-pronged appeal to formal rhetorical self-justification (her speech, she implies, will be *utile*) and to traditionally reticent feminine propriety bears fruit: Theseus implies that any shame inherent in Aithra's speaking in public would be outweighed by the potential shame of her failure to disclose information that could help her *philoi*: 'It's a shameful thing you've said (*aiskhron g'elexas*), hiding useful/noble words (*khrēst' epē*) from your friends' (296). This formula allows Aithra to exchange feminine values (*aiskhron* would normally apply to women who *do* speak in public) for masculine (bold public speech on behalf of one's *philoi*). Women's speech is literally transformed here from something *akhreion*, 'useless', into the opposite, the etymologically related *khrēst' epē*, 'useful words'.

In fact, Aithra's equation of feminine silence not with the proper demeanour that normally wins approval for women, but with censure and blame (*mempsomai*) belongs quite specifically to the masculine world of fifth-century democratic politics. Her repudiation of *sigē* is consonant with contemporary endorsements of democratic freedom as expressed in *isēgoria*, 'equally free speech for all'.[50] That connection is later articulated by Theseus himself, following his mother's example, in an exchange with the Theban Herald in which the Athenian proudly, if rather anachronistically, praises the protocols of free speech practised in the fifth-century Athenian assembly:

> τοὐλεύθερον δ' ἐκεῖνο· Τίς θέλει πόλει
> χρηστόν τι βούλευμ' ἐς μέσον φέρειν ἔχων;
> καὶ ταῦθ' ὁ χρῄζων λαμπρός ἐσθ', ὁ μὴ θέλων
> <u>σιγᾷ</u>.

This is freedom: 'Who has some
noble/useful (*khrēston*) suggestion he wishes to offer
publicly (*es meson*) to the city?'
He who avails himself of that formula gains glory,
he who does not wish to
<u>keeps silent (*sigāi*)</u>.

(438–41)

Like its historical model, this self-conscious echo of the formal proclamation made in the assembly ('Who wishes to speak out?', *tis agoreuein bouletai*), underscores the importance of vocal participation that literally places one 'in the middle' (as *es meson* implies) of civic life as opposed to keeping silent. This freedom of public and political speech was 'the central freedom that the Athenians cherished', and constitutive of citizen identity: *isēgoria* was 'the right of the citizen to address the sovereign Assembly of the people'.[51] But such participation in the life of the *polis* was seen not just as a right but indeed as a duty: for Perikles in the

---

[50] *Isēgoria* is praised by Euripides more than once: see *Hipp.* 421–5; *Ion* 672–5; *Phoen.* 390–2; and fr. 737. The playwright's penchant for endorsing free speech was well known enough to be cited offhandedly by Aristotle at *Pol.* 1310ᵃ30ff.

[51] Ober, *Mass and Elite*, 296; cf. Burian's comment on this scene that '*Logos*, as the fundamental tool of political life is at the heart of the debate on government' ('*Logos* and *Pathos*', 141). For *isēgoria* as an element of democratic ideology, see Ober, pp. 296–8; G. T. Griffith, 'Isegoria in the Assembly at Athens', *Ancient Society: Studies Presented to Victor Ehrenberg* (Oxford, 1966), 115–38; A. G. Woodhead, '*Isegoria* and the Council of the Five Hundred', *Historia*, 16 (1967), 129–40; and cf. Aiskhines 1. 27 and Dem. 21. 124 and 60. 26. For Theseus as the mythic inventor of *isēgoria*, see Mills, *Theseus, Tragedy*, 99.

Funeral Oration, the man who does not take part in politics was not so much inactive as useless, *akhreion*. The fact that this is the same word that Aithra uses in quoting received opinion about the uselessness of women's speech, and that Amphitryon in another Euripidean drama uses to describe men who have been 'unmanned' by old age, suggests that *akhreion* links gender and politics in a complex way.[52] Public speech and action were as much an obligation for men as enforced silence, *sigē*, and inaction were for women. Hence Aithra's insistence on speaking out conforms to specifically political (and hence masculine) rather than domestic and feminine values.

Bound for Glory

By refusing to remain silent, the queen in fact violates the terms of the aphorisms she had uttered earlier as she waited passively for her son's arrival (40f.), about the uselessness of women's words and the wise woman's recognition that all things are better done by men. Or rather, she assumes a male citizen's role, rejecting the constraints on speech that render women impotent in public life. Like a man, Aithra knows that her 'own good [name]', *toumon kalon* (300), will be preserved not in spite of, but *because* of, bold public speech.

The reason that Aithra is now willing to reject her earlier attitude is, in fact, that it is her own reputation that is at stake. Indeed, 'my good', *toumon kalon*, finds an echo at 320: 'By no means do these things, child, since you are *my* son' (*emos g' ōn*): she is concerned about his actions because they reflect on her. The repeated reference to the effects of Theseus' actions on Aithra herself eclipses her ostensible concern for the good, *kalon*, of both her son and her city (293), which now seems like little

---

[52] *akhreion* in the Funeral Oration: Thuc. 2. 40. 2; cf. Aithra's *akhreion* at 299, and Euripides, *Her.* 40f. For the excellence of public speech on behalf of the polity, see Hdt. 3. 80. 6 and Thuc. 2. 37. 1. In Euripides it is expressed at considerable length at *Phoen.* 390ff., where Polyneikes identifies the inability to engage in *parrhēsia*, free speech, as the most odious aspect of exile; cf. Menoikeus' praise of action on behalf of the *polis* at 1015ff. in the same play, and *Ion* 595–601. Ober (*Mass and Elite*, 296) points out that by the 4th cent., this freedom of speech also implied the freedom *not* to speak out if one had no advice to offer; so e.g. Aiskhines 3. 220 and Dem. 22. 30; but this was a development that would have been repugnant to Euripides' audience a hundred years earlier.

more than a rhetorical ploy.[53] I want to argue that, in the context of reiterated references to unsuitably bold public speech by a woman, this self-assertive concern with her own good name suggests that, like *Children of Herakles*'s Girl, Aithra is gradually appropriating masculine traits.[54]

Indeed, the queen's justification for speaking out takes the form of an endorsement of the bold daring, *tolmē*, which here, as well as in *Children of Herakles*, appears as a marker of feminine transgression. 'If one (*tina*) did not have to be daring (*tolmēron*) on behalf of those who were wronged, I would indeed have remained quiet (*hēsykhōs*)', she declares (304f.). The line suggests several things at once. First, the conditional suggests that *hēsykhia*, 'quiet/stillness', is in fact the proper attitude for a woman: only because of the extraordinary circumstances in which she finds herself, she implies, does she feel compelled to speak (and move) with unwonted boldness. Second, this 'proper' *hēsykhia* is what Aithra will associate so derisively just a few lines later with the underhanded and shadowy dealings of certain cities, and with unmanliness and unheroic cowardice (324ff.). In despising *hēsykhia*, she puts herself at odds with her own 'natural' state. There can be little doubt, in fact, that *tolmē*, implicitly contrasted here with feminine *hēsykhia*, is an attribute that Aithra herself claims to display in speaking out on behalf of the suppliants: *tolmēron tina*, 'someone bold', is clearly meant to refer to herself.[55] Here Aithra is no longer content to bask passively in her son's reflected glory, seeking instead a more outright identification with the heroic man who confidently displays *tolmē*. And indeed like the Girl, Aithra is sensitive to what others might say (314), and to the importance of heroic glory, *eukleia* (315).

[53] 'She begins her speech with ethical hauteur, but after quietly introducing the idea of "honour" (306) quickly builds up a subtle appeal to her son's pride' (Fitton, 'The *Suppliant Women*', 431). Collard (*Euripides Supplices*, 192 ad 320) comments that 'for Th[eseus] to fail her [Aithra] would cause his mother to disown him from shame'.

[54] Goff ('Aithra at Eleusis', 71) makes less of Aithra's violation of norms regarding women's speech, attributing the queen mother's verbal freedom to 'the respect and relative freedom that may reward older women who have successfully, in patriarchal terms, negotiated marriage and motherhood'.

[55] See Collard, *Euripides Supplices*, 189 ad loc. for this point.

Returning to Aigeus' House: The Threat Contained

Theseus' reaction to his mother's bold speech once again demonstrates the uneasy dynamics of gender that operate in this scene. Softening, he agrees to aid the suppliants. Yet what is most striking about this concession is that, at the very moment that Theseus yields to Aithra, the inappropriateness of being instructed by a woman is uppermost in his mind:

> τί γάρ μ' ἐροῦσιν οἵ γε δυσμενεῖς βροτῶν,
> ὅθ' ἡ τεκοῦσα χὐπερορρωδοῦσ' ἐμοῦ
> πρώτη κελεύεις τόνδ' ὑποστῆναι πόνον;

> What will ill-disposed men say of me then,
> when you, the woman who bore me, and who is
>   now so terrified for me,
> are the first to enjoin this task upon me?   (343–5)

'What will men say . . .', *ti gar m' erousin*, is, as I have discussed in the previous chapter, a topos that often imparts an epic flavour; and here it echoes the very words Aithra used earlier to taunt her son into right action: 'Indeed someone will say of you (*erei de dē tis . . .*) that it was through unmanliness (*anandria*) of your hands that you took fright and so refused' (314). The parallelism implies that Aithra's intervention, though ultimately beneficial to Theseus and his city, is potentially as shameful to Theseus as is *anandria*. And indeed, in a somewhat revisionist version of his recent interaction with his mother, Aithra's son highlights his mother's 'terror' on his behalf, thereby erasing her interest, twice articulated, in how any failure on his part would detract from her own reputation. Here Theseus rewrites Aithra into a less subversive and more traditional role: that of a mother filled with excessive concern for her child. Once Aithra's transgressive movement and illicit speech have served her son and his city—once she has played her vital role in the action—gender proprieties are swiftly reasserted.

Accordingly, the climax of his brief response here, at the close of the play's first part, takes the form of Theseus' relocation of his mother to the margins of the action, that is to the interior where she belongs (359 ff.): 'But remove your holy wreaths from my mother, women, so that clasping her dear hand (*philēn prosapsas kheira*) I may lead her back to Aigeus' house (*pros oikous Aigeōs agō*).' Led by her son back to her dead husband's house,

Aithra will now exchange the enclosure constituted by the chorus at Eleusis for that other, safer enclosure, the palace at Athens. Her moment on stage ends, as it began, with a movement towards the house of Aigeus. In this way, her dislocation and eventual relocation during the prologue and first episode recall the spatial dynamics alluded to in her introductory reference to *ekdosis*. Aithra's 'transgressive' appearance dissolves the ideological boundaries between Theseus and Adrastos just as an earlier exit, from her father's house, had once dissolved the geographical, political, and dynastic boundaries between Pittheus and Aigeus.

An 'Other' Theseus: The Hero between Masculine and Feminine

In *Children of Herakles*, the Girl's bold entrance, daring speech, and quasi-heroic action precipitated Iolaos' rejuvenation on the field of battle. In *Suppliant Women*, Aithra's entry, speech, and action also precipitate a battle, with its concomitant *aristeia* for Theseus. But the transformation that takes place at the end of Theseus' battle is, perhaps, even more startling than the one that realized Iolaos' dreams of renewed youth. For even as it shames Theseus, Aithra's intervention none the less successfully softens—I use the term advisedly—her son's outlook; he literally broadens his horizons, leaving the boundaries of Athens and crossing those of Thebes, putting his heroic prowess in the service of an extra-personal, extra-mural and even Panhellenic cause. Yet unlike an epic hero, he seeks not to sack Thebes after he conquers it; and indeed goes on to perform the extraordinary act of burying the bodies of the Seven himself. This playing of a woman's role should not be dismissed as an arbitrary bit of theatre or cynical political ploy, as some critics have argued, but instead as part of the dramatic strategy of Euripides' political dramas in which archaic heroes are transformed—or destroyed—by playing the feminine other.[56]

[56] Greenwood was suspicious of Theseus ('on the whole, he is a good fellow enough . . . But we may discern some odd touches in the portrait'), and takes the Athenian king to task for insensitivity to Adrastos, self-importance, 'priggish sententiousness', and incoherence in the views he expresses (*Aspects of Euripidean Tragedy* (Cambridge, 1953) 108). More serious is that scholar's critique of the political implications of Theseus' speeches. He points to the tension be-

Defining the Terms: Aithra's Advice

Immediately before Aithra challenges her son, Theseus exemplifies a tendency to rigidity of thought and expression, as
expressed in his refusal to aid the suppliants. Even despite his
sympathy for his mother's tears, and indeed his admission that
he, too, is sensible of the piteous effect of the chorus's mourning,
which has 'pierced him through' (288), he none the less displays
the same preoccupation with propriety as he did in the earlier
scene. As before, he is concerned with maintaining religious
decorum, and bids his mother not to desecrate the sanctuary
with her tears (289 f.), thereby recalling his similar disapproval
of the chorus's inappropriate appearance and behaviour (95 ff.).
Perhaps even more significantly, the Athenian ruler's rationale
for suggesting that Aithra should not be moved to lamentation
by the troubles of these other women (291) is that she is not one
of them by virtue of her birth/nature: 'you were not born/are not
by nature (*ephys*) one of them' (292). I have already discussed
how the language of *physis* betrays an aristocratic bias in the
political plays; in the context of the us/them distinction that he
makes in using this word, Theseus' use of *phyo* seems to confirm
his allegiance with the pre-democratic ethos. Such an allegiance
was, in any event, hinted at even earlier, during his exchange
with Adrastos, when he identified the interests of the *polis* with
those of a *genos*, thereby confining both his actions and his city
within rigid ideological boundaries.

It is this view that Aithra successfully explodes in her speech
at 306–33. Like Herakles' daughter, Theseus' mother does so by
simultaneously exploiting and subverting the archaic and heroic
value system to which her son evidently subscribes; she will use

tween Theseus' endorsement of democratic rule and the autocratic tenor of his
own pronouncements (esp. 349 f.); and he also catches the double entendre of
Theseus' ostensibly pro-democracy boosterism at 352–3. The line could either
mean 'I enthroned the *demos* as sole sovereign when I set this land free and made
its people equal' or 'I reduced the *demos* to subjection to one man's rule when I
(nominally) set this land free and made its people equal' (tr. Greenwood). Fitton,
completely discarding the 'encomiast blinkers' that allowed Kitto to conclude
that Theseus 'yielded only to Aithra's plea of religion and honour', later took
Greenwood's points still further, arguing that the ambiguity of the Athenian
king's pronouncements betrays a sinister, self-aggrandizing nature—'more like
a politician than a hero'—whose change of mind following Aithra's speech is
merely the result of 'quite personal motives' ('The *Suppliant Women*', 432).

the appeal of heroic renown—and the potential ignominy associated with shirking heroic exploits—to tempt Theseus into using
his celebrated prowess to benefit not merely his own good name,
but the city and, even more strikingly, a larger, Panhellenic
good. First, she presents the suppliant crisis in a light that could
not help but intrigue her hero son, as a gross crime that his hand
alone (*sē kheiri*) can punish (310ff.). In his previous exploits
Theseus had done just that: he thinks of himself as having always
been a punisher of evil men (341), a claim that is borne out by his
triumph at the Skironian Rocks. Aithra underscores the heroic
nature of the task by referring to it as the 'crown of good *kleos*',
stephanon eukleias (315). Equally effective is her appeal to *aidōs*:
Aithra states that Theseus' refusal to accept what she describes
as a heroic labour, *ponos* (317, 323; cf. *ekponēsai*, 319), would
be attributed to unmanly cowardice, *anandria* (314), and con-
sequently Theseus would be 'caught out'[57] as being *deilos* (319)
—the term that denotes precisely the opposite of what heroes
strive to be. Like the Girl, Aithra is sensitive to the dynamics of
masculine honour within the heroic code.

Yet Aithra innovates, too. She goes on to contrast the kind of
heroic behaviour she has just been advocating with the actions
of cities that are *hēsykhoi* (324f.): 'Cities that are quiet (*hēsykhoi*)
act in a shady manner and have shady expressions, while timidly
looking out for themselves (*eulaboumenai*).' By having Aithra
denigrate this kind of behaviour by using the word *hēsykhos*,
Euripides introduces into his play once more the diction of
contemporary political discourse. In Athens at the time of the
Peloponnesian War, *hēsykhos* had become a political term, like
apragmōn ('uninvolved with affairs')—and *apragmosynē*, like
eulabeia, ('looking out for oneself'), comes from the political
vocabulary of fifth-century Athens, where both are considered
suspect.[58] A vital element of Athenian civic self-identification
was pride in *polypragmosynē*, the 'busybodiness' that character-

---

[57] *ephēurethēs* at 319 is, as usual, distinctly pejorative here: see Collard's note,
Euripides Supplices, 192 ad loc.

[58] As noted also by Burian, '*Logos* and *Pathos*', 136. For these terms in 5th-
cent. political discourse see Victor Ehrenberg, 'Polypragmosyne: A Study in
Greek Politics', *JHS* 67 (1947), 46–67; Knut Kleve, '*ΑΠΡΑΓΜΟΣΥΝΗ* and
ΠΟΛΥΠΡΑΓΜΟΣΥΝΗ: Two Slogans in Athenian Politics', *SO*, 39 (1964),
83–8; and Mills, *Theseus, Tragedy*, 66–9 and 115–23.

ized the Athenian. But *polypragmosynē,* as Victor Ehrenberg long ago noted, was 'above all the characterisation of a dynamic policy' of Athens herself—one that stood, moreover, 'in complete contrast to the static conservatism of Sparta'.[59] This contrast between Athens and Sparta, internationalism and isolationism, interventionism and conservatism, was made most famously clear in the second speech of the Corinthians at Thucydides 1. 70, where the Athenians are described as preferring stressful activity (*askholia epiponos*) to leisured inactivity (*hēsykhia apragmōn*). It should be said here that the positive and negative connotations of (respectively) *polypragmosynē,* on the one hand, and *hēsykhia* or *apragmosynē,* on the other, during Athens' imperial phase represented a considerable change from an earlier time. Indeed the deprecatory connotation of *polla prassein* and *polypragmonein* was quite clear in Herodotos (3. 15. 2, 5. 33. 4), where those verbal notions are linked as well to greed, *pleonexia;*[60] conversely, *hēsykhia* is described by Pindar as 'loving/ dear to the city', *philopolis* (*Ol.* 4. 16), the daughter of Dikē, who vanquishes *hybris* and holds the keys of war and peace (*Pyth.* 8. 1 ff.). Indeed *hēsykhia, sōphrosynē,* and *apragmosynē* seem to have been slogans of the (frequently anti-democratic and pro-Spartan) peace party in Athens.[61] But the majority position in Athens at the time that war with Sparta broke out in 431 seems to have been represented by Perikles, who condemned those Athenians who advocated *hēsykhia* and *apragmosynē* in very strong terms indeed (Thuc. 2. 63–4). The official condemnation of this term, like the official endorsement of the once-pejorative *polypragmosynē,* was the ideological reflection of a stark political reality that had made *polypragmōn* Athens the mistress of her often unwilling 'allies'.

Yet as we have seen, *hēsykhia,* the word Aithra uses to describe the quietist antithesis of what she now defines as properly

---

[59] Ehrenberg, 'Polypragmosyne', 47. For Spartan *hēsykhia,* see Hdt. 1. 66. 1 (no longer content with keeping quiet, *hēsykhian agein,* the Spartans attack the Arkadians). [60] For this point see Ehrenberg 'Polypragmosyne', 49

[61] Kleve, 'Two Slogans', 85 and 85 nn. 3 and 4. W. Nestle argued that the *apragmones* whose condemnation of Athenian policy as *adikon* earned them Perikles' scorn were in fact 'pacifists' ('*Ἀπραγμοσύνη*', *Philologus,* 35 (1926), 129–40), a position that Kleve attempts to disprove—by (among other things) pointing out that the term *apragmōn* is used of generals on active duty, such as Nikias (Thuc. 6. 18. 6 f.; cf. Kleve, 'Two Slogans', 84).

Panhellenic 'heroic' action, also has a gendered inflection: it describes, after all, the state she herself would normally be in, had circumstances not forced her into unwonted boldness. It is also the word the Girl had used to describe an idealized feminine propriety, citing an axiom in which *sigē* and *hēsykhia* in women are praised, and indeed are associated with the *sōphrosynē* considered so rare in that sex (*Hkld.* 476f.). In this context it is worth noting that the queen's derisive use of *skoteinos*, 'dark' or 'gloomy' (which I have translated above as 'shady', keeping the English idiom in mind) recalls another common cultural topos, one that identifies woman with dark spaces, both of her own body and of the strictly maintained interiors constructed for her by men. Like the Girl, Aithra co-opts a discourse that is, properly speaking, not 'hers'—in this case, a discourse both imperialistic and patriarchal—in order to subvert. Like the Girl, the Athenian queen endorses only that heroism whose goals exceed the interests of the self or the *genos* (although her implicit approval of *polypragmosynē* is not without its own ironic implications, as we shall see); and like the Girl, she accomplishes this hybridization by showing that the traditional heroism to which her son aspires is, in fact, dangerously close to becoming the double of its opposite: in gendered terms, an impotent femininity; in political terms, a shameful quietism.[62]

Theseus Before and After

It is, significantly, to this gendered argument that her son so swiftly reacts. Yet the description of Theseus following his mother's intervention suggests that he has in fact 'internalized' some feminine traits. The extent to which Theseus' position does shift following Aithra's intervention can be gauged by examining his long verbal contest with the Theban Herald, who arrives as soon as Aithra leaves. Many of the self-serving points that the Herald makes in his *agōn* with Theseus are, in fact, merely parodies of the stances once adopted by Theseus himself, stances he has now rejected.[63]

[62] Mills goes so far as to characterize the sentiment expressed by Aithra as one that 'would scarcely be out of place in an *epitaphios* speech' (*Theseus, Tragedy*, 115).

[63] As M. Lloyd points out (*The Agon in Euripides*, 83), the turnaround in Theseus' convictions is unique in the Euripidean corpus. He also remarks on

The Herald enters seeking the Athenian *tyrannos*, for whom his message is intended (399). Speaking for his Theban master Kreon, the Herald reminds Theseus that Athens has no legitimate role in the present controversy—the position earlier taken by Theseus himself (cf. the Herald at 472 and Theseus at 291). The Theban underscores his point about the distinctions between spheres of political influence by alluding repeatedly to the geographical boundaries that constitute the *poleis* in question, and recalling Theseus' earlier insistence on remaining aloof from international politics:

> ἐγὼ δ' ἀπαυδῶ πᾶς τε Καδμεῖος λεὼς
> Ἄδραστον ἐς γῆν τήνδε μὴ παριέναι·
> εἰ δ' ἔστιν ἐν γῇ, πρὶν θεοῦ δῦναι σέλας
> λύσαντα σεμνὰ στεμμάτων μυστήρια
> τῆσδ' ἐξελαύνειν, μηδ' ἀναιρεῖσθαι νεκροὺς
> βίᾳ, προσήκοντ' οὐδὲν Ἀργείων πόλει.

I and the entire Cadmean people refuse
Adrastos entry into this land.
And if he is already in the land, then I say that before the god's
    brilliance has set you must
loose the sacred suppliant boughs
and drive him out of it; and do not take up the bodies for burial
by force, since you have nothing to do with the city of the Argives.

                                                        (467–72)

In his insistence on his city's sovereign right to deal with its affairs, this Theban Herald recalls the Argive Herald in *Children of Herakles*, who had similarly demanded the extradition of the Heraklids (*Hkld.* 136–43). As Theseus himself had once done, the Herald goes on to bolster his argument for Athenian isolationism by alluding to the wanton destructiveness of war (491–3; cf. Theseus at 231–4); the foolish madness that characterizes men who impetuously seek out war rather than peace (485; cf. 232, where Theseus says Adrastos is 'driven out of his wits'); and, finally, the 'hubristic' blasphemy of the Seven, which deserves no redemption through proper burial (495; Theseus also uses *hybrizei* at 235).

the similarities between the Herald's positions here and those staked out earlier in Theseus' speech, but without attributing any particular significance to this coincidence (82); for these similarities see also Fitton, 'The *Suppliant Women*', 433, and Mills, *Theseus, Tragedy*, 117.

It is the latter in particular—the blatant irreligiousness of the Seven—that Theseus, having praised the divine order and the mantic arts at some length (201–13), had deplored (229f.). The Herald's most biting point takes a similar form, asking rhetorically whether it was not right for Kapaneus' body to burn after he'd climbed the siege-ladder and boasted that he would sack the city whether the gods wished it or not (496ff.). Most tellingly of all, the Herald implies that for Theseus to take up the suppliants' cause would be tantamount to putting himself above Zeus, *phronein ameinon . . . Dios*, 504. This is precisely the charge that Theseus had levelled at Adrastos, accusing him of being among those who believe themselves wiser than the gods, *daimonōn sophōteroi* (217–19). For the Herald, finally, *hesykhia* is defined as being constitutive of a wisdom that defines *t' andreion*, masculinity itself (509f.)—a neat inversion, to say the least, of the terms of Aithra's earlier and very effective reproach to Theseus (304–31).

Integrating the Feminine

Following his mother's intervention, however, Theseus completely repudiates his former positions. Most interesting, in view of what has preceded, is the fact that his demeanour now betrays the same 'feminine' tendency to boundary-violation and incontinence that he had so emphatically denounced in Adrastos. This change is conveyed both by the actions he undertakes and by the words with which he defends his city's form of government.

After Theseus consents to take up the grieving mothers' cause, the chorus marvels at the Athenian's righteousness (368); the women pray that Theseus, after approaching and even going beyond the 'border', *terma*, of their misery (369), might bring back the bloodied corpses of their children and thereby secure the friendship of Argos (369–73).[64] By exceeding all proper limits, the grief they recommend to him is both generically feminine and, more specifically, resembles that of these Argive mothers who, as we recall from the prologue, were driven by their *pathos* outside of the boundaries of their native land. Earlier,

---

[64] Reading L's ἄγαλμα φόνιον ἐξέλοι, 'bring back a mother's bloodied darling', rather than Diggle's proposed ἄμυγμα φόνιον ἐξέλοι, which would give the sense 'put an end to a mother's bloody cheek-tearing'. Collard's defence of the original MS reading (*Euripides Supplices*, 205 ad loc.) is persuasive.

Theseus had eschewed action on behalf of these wretched women, reminding his mother that as non-Athenians their plight was not her own (291 f.). Yet following Aithra's intervention, Theseus embraces the suppliants' cause, and wastes no time issuing orders to his herald to leave Eleusis and to penetrate into Boeotia—thereby crossing two natural boundaries, the Asopos and the Ismenos (383). Theseus' instructions thus precisely fulfil the terms of the chorus's entreaty. Through his herald, he will indeed go 'up to and beyond' the borders of grief, just as the mothers themselves have done.

Aithra's lecture clearly changes Theseus' political as well as emotional outlook. In the debate with the Theban Herald, Theseus praises young men who display a hopeless but praiseworthy daring in the face of a tyrant's murderous designs (447 ff.). In order to be strong, the (democratic) city needs its brave young men; without their *tolmē*[65]—when they are crushed under a tyrant's rule—the city falters. This play between weakness and strength has been mentioned by Theseus only moments earlier. As the pre-eminent example of the virtues of democratic (as opposed to tyrannical) rule, he points out that under the written law that prevails in democracies, the poor and weak can stand up successfully to the wealthy and powerful:

> γεγραμμένων δὲ τῶν νόμων ὅ τ' ἀσθενὴς
> ὁ πλούσιός τε τὴν δίκην ἴσην ἔχει,
> ἔστιν δ' ἐνισπεῖν τοῖσιν ἀσθενεστέροις
> τὸν εὐτυχοῦντα ταῦθ' ὅταν κλύῃ κακῶς,
> νικᾷ δ' ὁ μείων τὸν μέγαν δίκαι' ἔχων.

When laws are written down, both the resourceless
and the rich have equal access to justice,
and it is possible for weak men to
address the well-off on the same terms when they
    have a grievance;
and so the lesser wins out over the great, having
    justice (*dikaia ekhōn*).   (433–7)

---

[65] Reading L's τόλμας at 449, *contra* Diggle, who follows Nauck's suggestion of τομαῖς, which N. supported by citing Eur. fr. 403. 6 N. (τομαῖς ἀφαιρεῖν . . . πασῶν μεγίστην . . . νόσων (sc. φθόνον)). But as Collard points out (*Euripides Supplices*, 230 ad loc.), the 'bold hendiadys' of τόλμας and νέους is prepared by the somewhat less bold but crucial hendiadys ἀφαιρῇ κἀπολωτίζει; and he cites a parallel as cogent as Nauck's, *Med.* 456 ὀργὰς ἀφαιρῇ.

Hence Theseus conflates the struggle by noble youths against tyrants with the ongoing and more general struggle between the strong and the weak and the rich and the poor—a contest that can be fairly won only in the democratic *polis*. The young men's *tolmē* thus makes them worthy of the democratic *polis* that Theseus here praises.

But this is not the first time we have heard such an endorsement of *tolmē* in the service of the helpless. Theseus' brave retort to the Theban Herald, like so much of what the Athenian king has said since his mother's intervention, is a mere echo of Aithra's earlier speech, justifying her own bold (*tolmēron*, 306) intercession on behalf of the wronged (*adikomenois*, 305) suppliants. Bold action is required of just men, Aithra declares, even as she herself assumes that assertive masculine role; otherwise, one may as well remain *hēsykhos*, like a woman. Even as the new Theseus endorses the democratic citizen's daring, the echo of his mother's words demonstrates how successful her intervention has been.

The feminine infiltrates Theseus' defence of democratic institutions on a more generic level as well. The Herald denigrates Athenian democracy as being an unseemly political mess, in which each man slyly puffs up (*enkhaunōn*, 412) the citizenry for his own private gain, with the inevitable result that the *demos* will lose control of the city itself (418); it is worth noting here that the Herald's use of the word *okhlos* (411) to describe the Athenian masses is one that can betray an aristocratic or oligarchic allegiance.[66] For the Herald, democracy itself is characterized by verbal incontinence, since it does not 'make straight its words', *mē diortheuōn logous* (417). Earlier, Theseus had also assailed Adrastos' unhealthy confusion of political and dynastic priorities using metaphors of physical illness in a context replete with the language of sexual excess (227f.); now, the Theban Herald uses the same metaphors to describe democratic Athens (*nosōdes*, 423). Theseus, in other words, now rallies to the defence of the very 'pathology'—the sickly, self-indulgent looseness that

---

[66] For *okhlos* as an 'insulting' way to refer to the masses, see Ober, *Mass and Elite*, 11. Michael Lloyd notes that the Herald substitutes 'tyrannical equivalents' for the 'stock democratic vocabulary' used by Theseus (*The Agon in Euripides*, 80f.).

obscures carefully maintained borders between classes—that he once so vigorously condemned.

Eleusinian Role-Playing

In his retort to the Theban Herald (444–62) Theseus attacks tyranny, rehearsing the standard topoi of anti-tyrannical rhetoric.[67] The worst of the ill-fortunes that tyranny brings, he declares, is its effect on the young—the deaths of the brave young men who invariably oppose tyranny, and the abduction of citizens' maiden daughters in order to serve the tyrant's gross pleasures. Coming as they do as the high point of Theseus' speech, however, these two *exempla*—one for each of the sexes— cannot help but remind us of gendered poles that are the basis for the play's presentation of political issues. The terms in which he presents these topoi recapitulate specifically Demetrian motifs that themselves underscore the difference between rapacious masculinity and vulnerable femininity:

> καὶ μὴν ὅπου γε δῆμος εὐθυντὴς χθονὸς
> ὑποῦσιν ἀστοῖς ἥδεται νεανίαις·
> ἀνὴρ δὲ βασιλεὺς ἐχθρὸν ἡγεῖται τόδε,
> καὶ τοὺς ἀρίστους οὕς ⟨τ'⟩ ἂν ἡγῆται φρονεῖν
> κτείνει, δεδοικὼς τῆς τυραννίδος πέρι.
> πῶς οὖν ἔτ' ἂν γένοιτ' ἂν ἰσχυρὰ πόλις
> ὅταν τις ὡς λειμῶνος ἠρινοῦ στάχυν
> τόλμας ἀφαιρῇ κἀπολωτίζῃ νέους;

Indeed, wherever the people (*dēmos*) is master of the land
it rejoices in its reserves of citizen youths.
But the man who is king finds this hateful,
and any of the nobility whom he deems superior in intelligence
he kills, terrified on behalf of his sole rule.
How then might the city become strong
when someone—as one does with corn in a springtime meadow—
lops off and culls the best of the brave young men?

(442–9)

This denunciation of tyranny is notable for its use of agricultural

---

[67] The tyrant as '*deflorator virginum, stuprator uxorum*' appears in both tragedy (so *El.* 945, where Elektra hints darkly at Aigisthos' crimes while maintaining proper feminine silence, *parthenōi gar ou kalon legein*; and *OT* 891); as well as in contemporary prose (e.g. Hdt. 3. 80. 5 and 5. 92. 1–3). For this topos in Athenian civic rhetoric, see Mills, *Theseus, Tragedy*, 121.

metaphors appropriate to the play's setting.[68] The reference to the *dēmos* as the 'master of the land', *euthyntēs khthonos* (442), recalls the insistent repetition of *khthōn* in Aithra's prologue which helped to establish a specifically Demetrian context in which the subsequent metaphors can be read. The tyrant culls the city's brave youths as one would 'harvest the ears of grain (*stákhyn*) in a meadow during springtime' (*hōs leimōnos ērinou*), thus recalling not only Aithra's opening reference to her sacrificial mission at Eleusis, performing her sacrifice on behalf of the first-fruits (*karpimos stakhys*, 30f.), but also Kore's abduction from the lush meadow, *leimōn' am malthakon*, described in the Homeric hymn to Demeter (*H. h. Cer.* 7).

After mentioning the deaths of brave young men, Theseus comes to the emotional climax of his speech:[69]

κτᾶσθαι δὲ πλοῦτον καὶ βίον τί δεῖ τέκνοις
ὡς τῷ τυράννῳ πλεῖον' ἐκμοχθῇ βίον;
ἢ παρθενεύειν παῖδας ἐν δόμοις καλῶς,
τερπνὰς τυράννοις ἡδονὰς ὅταν θέλῃ,
δάκρυα δ' ἑτοιμάζουσι; μὴ ζῴην ἔτι
εἰ τἀμὰ τέκνα πρὸς βίαν νυμφεύσεται.

What's the use of building a fortune for your children—
so you can toil your life away for a despot?
Or of bringing up your girls in proper chastity at home—
that they might be sweet pleasure for the tyrant's whim,
but sorrow for them that prepare it? Let me die
rather than see my children married by force.

(450–5)

Given his earlier refusal to acknowledge the suppliants' very real deprivations, the emotional force with which Theseus speaks of the forced marriages of these hypothetical maiden daughters is rather surprising. And the rhetorical wish for death imparts a heightened emotional tone to Theseus' closing words that sug-

---

[68] J. T. Sheppard briefly discusses Euripides' presentation of *tyrannoi* in '*ΤΥΡΑΝΝΟΣ, ΚΕΡΔΟΣ*, and the Modest Measure in Three Plays of Euripides', *CQ* 11 (1917), 3–10.

[69] The impassioned death-wish is not unusual in Euripides (cf. *Or.* 1147, *Hipp.* 1191); here, it marks the formal conclusion of the *rhesis*, the set-piece elucidating a character's position (cf. *Hipp.* 1030). See the remarks of W. Schadewaldt, *Monolog und Selbstgespräch: Untersuchungen zur Formgeschichte der griechischen Tragödie* (Berlin, 1932), 102f.

gests a strong identification with the hapless parent who is in a position to cite this particular example of tyrannical abuse.

But which parent might utter such a plaint? I want to suggest here that Theseus' tone and diction are meant to recall mothers rather than fathers. The words that he speaks on behalf of those fictional daughters indeed closely resemble the laments of Euripidean mothers. For example, we might compare the lament of Hekabe in *Trojan Women*, lamenting over her virgin daughters raised in vain (*Tro.* 484–6), or indeed similar expressions of maternal despair in the *Iphigeneia at Aulis* or the *Hekabe*.[70] But given the play's distinctively Eleusinian resonances, together with the Athenian's earlier references to the plucking of grain in a blooming spring meadow, the elements of Theseus' speech— a parent's laments over the vain rearing of children who are doomed to be abducted for a tyrant's pleasure; a daughter's forced marriage; the parent's helpless grief—suggest that the 'role' he is rehearsing here is that of Demeter herself.[71]

Theseus' impassioned denunciation of tyranny in what appear to be self-consciously Eleusinian terms thus politicizes Demetrian myth in terms familiar from contemporary political rhetoric. Hades becomes the mythic equivalent of the rapacious tyrant, Kore the helpless victim of tyrannical outrage, and Demeter herself is the aggrieved and helpless citizen parent. The episodes that follow the inconclusive debate between the Theban Herald and the Athenian king will in fact force Theseus and the other characters into playing these very roles. Those performances will, in turn, dramatize the meanings of gender identity in a way that ironizes masculine, heroic action by the king or his city. And it is precisely between the extremes of masculine and feminine experience (Hades', Demeter's) that Theseus' proper identity is to be found.[72]

---

[70] Cf. *IA* 985 ff., 1276–8; *Hek.* 511–17, 585 ff.

[71] The role as played, of course, in the Homeric *Hymn*. For the lush spring meadow and flowers, see *H. h. Cer.* 7, *leimōn' am malakon*, and 417, *himerton leimōna*, etc.; Kore's abduction by force, *H. h. Cer.* 30 (*aekazomenēn*); 68 (*biazomenēs*); 72 (*aekousan anankēi*); and described as a rape, *harpagē*, at 19, 56, 81, etc. Hades is (as traditionally) as wealthy and wilful as any tyrant, with his golden chariot (19, 431); he is 'Wealth [Ploutos] who gives riches to mortal men' (489). For Demeter's terrible grief on the loss of her child, see *H. h. Cer.* 39 f., 47–50, 90, 197–201, etc.

[72] Michael Lloyd similarly sees Theseus' change of heart as reflecting a

Mowing Down the Enemy: Theseus Plays the Tyrant

The actual description of Theseus' victory (650–73) is a curious (though in tragedy hardly anomalous) mélange of contemporary and epic details.[73] The tension between the world of fifth-century warfare and that of epic heroism on the field of battle is, however, more than merely conventional or accidental. For it reflects the tension between archaic and democratic world-views that has thus far informed Theseus' development as a ruler. The scene begins with a description of a battle that would have been only too familiar to Euripides' audience: the arrangement of the infantry (654); the hoplite formations (657); the description of the cavalry (660 ff.); and the realistic details of Theban topography (653–67).[74] Yet the course of the battle itself becomes increasingly violent and disorderly, culminating in the indiscriminate hand-to-hand killing (699 ff.). The climax of these horrors is the vigorous and bloody *aristeia*, the detailed description of heroic valour, of Theseus himself:

> ἔρρηξε δ' αὐδὴν ὥσθ' ὑπηχῆσαι χθόνα·
> "Ὦ παῖδες, εἰ μὴ σχήσετε στερρὸν δόρυ
> σπαρτῶν τόδ' ἀνδρῶν, οἴχεται τὰ Παλλάδος."
> θάρσος δ' ἐνῶρσε παντὶ Κραναϊδῶν στρατῷ.
> αὐτός θ' ὅπλισμα τοὐπιδαύριον λαβὼν
> δεινῆς κορύνης διαφέρων ἐσφενδόνα
> ὁμοῦ τραχήλους κἐπικειμένας κάρᾳ
> κυνέας θερίζων κἀποκαυλίζων ξύλῳ.
> μόλις δέ πως ἔτρεψαν ἐς φυγὴν πόδα.

He shouted so that the earth itself resounded:
'Boys, unless you hold back the hard spear
of these sown men, all that is Pallas' is done for.'
And then bold daring was stirred in all the Kranaid host.

'mediated' identity: 'The correct response is one which combines Theseus' initial awareness of the folly of the Seven with Aethra's pity for the mothers of the dead warriors and her piety towards the gods' (*The* Agon *in Euripides*, 77).

[73] For a detailed analysis of the layout of the battle (complete with diagram, and with comments on the text of 653–67), see C. Collard, 'Notes on Euripides' *Supplices*', *CQ* 13 (1963), 178–82.

[74] *kraspedoisi*, 'on the skirts of the army' (661), is used by Xenophon in a similar description of a cavalry formation at *Hellenika* 3. 2. 16. For the realism of E.'s topography here, see Collard, *Euripides Supplices*, 280 ad loc.; for parallels between the battle described in the play and that fought at Delium, see Bowie, 'Tragic Filters', 46, with his notes.

Meanwhile Theseus, laying hold of his weapon, the
     fearful Epidaurian
mace, laid all about him, whirling it round,
snapping necks like stalks and reaping
the helmets upon them, all with his wooden mace.
They could barely move their feet to flee.

                                                        (710–18)

In contrast to the familiarly contemporary battle-order with
which it began, the scene's climax in Theseus' violent and bloody
aristeia is distinctly and deliberately epic. The way the earth
reverberates with the hero's cries; his *parainesis*, the exhortation
to the troops at a critical moment in the battle; specific details of
diction such as the use of the verb *enōrse*, 'stirred'—all of these
help to construct a quasi-Homeric context for what is clearly
meant to be a bona-fide heroic moment. And indeed, Theseus'
use of the 'Epidaurian mace', taken from Periphetes the robber
of Epidauros—one of the criminals whom Theseus famously
punished—recalls his own legendary exploits, to which he himself had earlier alluded.[75]

Yet it is this very description that makes it difficult to read
the passage as a straightforward celebration of Theseus' heroic
talents, now in the service of a new, 'Panhellenic' vision (671).
For not only does Theseus' use of his famous club suggest a
regression here to the heroic mode that pre-dates his mother's
intervention,[76] but, even more pointedly, the striking metaphors used to describe his slaying of the enemy cannot help
but recall Theseus' own description of the tyrant as one who
'culls as one does from a summer meadow the city's bold youth'
(448f.). To be sure, Theseus' martial violence serves a just cause;
but the visual details presented in the battle narrative suggest

---

[75] For reverberation of the earth for heroes' cries or footsteps in epic, see *Il.*
2. 465 etc., *Theogony* 835. For *parainesis*, formal exhortation, at critical impasse
in fighting as an 'epic motif', see Collard, *Euripides Supplices*, 292 ad loc. ἐνῶρσε
as epicism: *Il.* 2. 451, 8. 335, etc. Periphates (also known as Korynetes) is mentioned at Plutarch, *Thes.* 8, Pausanias 2. 1. 4. The mace is the weapon with which
Theseus is armed on the metopes of the 'Theseion' (= Hephaisteon) in Athens.

[76] The club was a heroic accoutrement that was, obviously, incompatible
with hoplite warfare. See J. K. Anderson, 'Hoplite Weapons and Offensive
Arms', in Victor Davis Hanson (ed.), *Hoplites: The Classical Greek Battle
Experience* (New York, 1991), 15–37.

uncomfortable similarities between Theseus, here portrayed as a grim reaper of young men, and Kreon, his enemy and hence his ostensible 'opposite'.

Other important distinctions between the Thebans and the Athenians seem to be in danger of disappearing in the battle's climactic epic mêlée. Theseus refers to the Thebans as 'Spartoi', Sown Men, in what appears at first to be a topos from the Athenian civic discourse of autochthony, which regularly and favourably contrasted the race of Athenian autochthons with other earth-born tribes, such as the Thebans or the Colchians. One important point of distinction was that whereas those hubristic earth-born men, *gēgeneis*, sprang up from the earth as full-grown warriors, the autochthon from whom the Athenians claimed descent was born a child and had a normal life-cycle; this was Erekhthonios, who succeeded in producing a dynasty unlike the earlier, sterile *gēgeneis* who preceded him, Kranaos and Kekrops, whose lines came to an end.[77] But at the moment that Theseus begins his fearsome *aristeia*, his troops are not referred to as Erekhtheids, the epithet that would serve best to highlight the contrasts between the Athenians and their Theban enemies (and which indeed is employed for that very purpose by Theseus himself, in his challenge to Kreon at 387), but as Kranaids—that is, one of the earth-born beings whose sterility resulted in what Loraux calls a 'false start' in Athenian mythic history, and who were, therefore, more similar to, than different from, the Theban Spartoi.[78] This subtle problematization of Athenian civic identity, coming as it does at the climax of *Suppliant Women*'s long-awaited battle-scene between Athens and Thebes, mirrors the way that the identity of Theseus himself—hero? tyrant?—becomes blurred during that conflict.

[77] For this emphasis on the difference between Athenian autochthons and other *gēgeneis*, see C. Bérard, *Anodoi: Essai sur l'imagerie des passages chthoniens* (Neuchâtel, 1974), 34 f. and Loraux, *Children of Athena*, 46–9 and *The Invention of Athens*, 148 f., where she focuses on the contrast as a topos of political oratory. For the childlessness of these children of the earth in general see Loraux, *Children of Athena*, 215; of the earth-born Giants, see Francis Vian, *La Guerre des Géants: Le Mythe avant l'époque héllenistique* (Paris, 1952), 255; and of the Thebans in particular, see Vian's *Les Origines de Thèbes: Cadmos et les Spartes* (Paris, 1963), 164.

[78] Loraux, *Children of Athena*, 215. This explains the comparative rarity of the epithet. Aesch. *Eum.* 1011 refers to 'Kranaos' children', *paides Kranaou*.

Burial of the Dead: Playing the Woman

Soon after his defeat of the Theban army, in which Theseus 'plays' Hades, the young king goes on to play a quite different Eleusinian role—not that of a Hades-like tyrant (whose excesses are, if anything, later typified by those of Kapaneus), but rather that of the victim of 'heroic' violence, a bereaved and grieving woman who resembles both the Argive mothers and Demeter herself. The highlight of this performance is his burial of the Seven.

This act of burial itself is not, of course, represented on stage, but rather described by the Messenger in a long stichomythic exchange with Adrastos (750–77). Adrastos inquires about the bodies of those fallen in the recent battle, and learns that Theseus has returned to bury the Seven. The Messenger prefaces his remarks about the king by pointing out that Theseus has already cremated and buried the common soldiers—of whom there were many (756)—in a grave at Eleutherai. This gesture is overshadowed, however, by the more important burial of the Seven themselves, the act of paramount importance to this play's characters (761), one that seems to signal the closure of this mythic cycle. The fifth-century Athenian practice was to bring the bones of the dead back from the battlefield to the city, where the great public funerals were held. (Other *poleis* buried the bones on the site of the battle, and Athens prided itself on its special custom.)[79] This is the custom followed by Theseus in the play. Adrastos himself supposes that the transportation of the long-dead bodies cannot have been a pleasant task, and will surely have been left to slaves (762; cf. 939, 945). But he receives the surprising response that it was no slave who tended to the decomposing bodies, but Theseus himself who tended the dead (763), washed their wounds (765), and laid out and clothed their bodies (766).

Throughout the exchange that brings these facts to light, Adrastos' tone is either startled or incredulous, and culminates in his expression of utter dismay at learning that the Athenian king has performed the terrible (*deinon*) and shameful (*aiskhynēn ekhon*) task of tending the bodies himself (767). Why 'shameful'? For Adrastos, the act that Theseus has performed is one even

---

[79]   For these details see Loraux, *The Invention of Athens*, 18 ff.

slaves would balk at (764). But it was, of course, certain other members of Greek society—comparable to slaves in some ways, as we have seen—who were usually assigned the role of laying out the bodies of the dead: women. The ritual preparation of a corpse for burial, like so much about the formal funeral rites in Greek culture, fell within the domestic domain of women; even in the case of the burial of the war-dead, when the state took over much of the ritual normally reserved for family, women had a role, as Thucydides reminds us—visiting the tents in which the remains were stored, participating in the procession, listening to the oration, and afterwards lamenting by the graveside.[80] And indeed, whatever the realities of Athenian life, the mothers of the Seven in Euripides' play clearly expect to have a role in their children's funerals; this is, after all, why they have come to Eleusis in the first place. Theseus' enactment of the ritual *prothesis* is, therefore, presented as a conscious appropriation, and theatrical acting-out, of a woman's role, a willing experience of the feminine that jeopardizes his status by bringing *aiskhynē*.[81] And indeed, Theseus' willingness to incur *aiskhynē* threatens to make him like another opposite number, Adrastos, who at the beginning of the play lies 'shamed' on the ground (*en men aiskhynais ekhō*, 164), a position that in turn made it difficult to distinguish *him* from the grieving mothers around him.

   Theseus' willingness to undertake an action that brings feminine disgrace marks a crucial redefinition of gendered and moral

---

[80] Thucydides 2. 34 and 2. 45. For women's role in funeral rituals, and especially in the washing and laying-out of the body (inhumation was generally performed by men) see, among the many available accounts, Donna C. Kurtz and John Boardman, *Greek Burial Customs* (Ithaca, NY, 1971), 143 ff.; Alexiou, *Ritual Lament*; Humphreys, *The Family, Women, and Death*; Loraux, *The Invention of Athens*, 24 f., and *Les Mères en deuil, passim*; Just, *Women in Athenian Law*, 111; and Rehm, *Marriage to Death*, 21–9 and 116. References in literature to women's role in the *prothesis* goes back to the *Iliad* (18. 350 ff.), and is made much of by Euripides himself: cf. e.g. *Alkestis* 613 and 631, *Tro.* 1143 and 1152, etc.

[81] Foley ('The Politics of Tragic Lamentation') has interpreted this scene quite differently. She argues that Theseus is in fact deliberately appropriating the women's usual role in order to suppress feminine emotional energies—a dramatic reflection of the Athenian state's interest in repressing feminine activity. But this view of the play's action takes insufficient notice, I think, of the play's emphasis on Eleusinian role-playing, and of the transformative effect on Theseus that his appropriation has.

values. I say redefinition, because the Messenger—who speaks for Theseus—emphatically rejects Adrastos' characterization of the king's feminine gesture as bringing *aiskhynē*: 'What shame (*aiskhron*) is there for men in each other's woes?' he asks (768). This clearly inverts the value system to which Theseus had once subscribed: prior to his mother's intervention, he reminded Aithra that it was inappropriate for her to share in the Argive women's laments (291 f.). Now, however, the assumption of the women's woes is no longer cause for disgrace. Theseus achieves this enlightenment only after he appropriates from those very women the conventionally feminine duty of burying their fallen children. This complex role-playing that lies at the heart of the new moral system relies on an ability to 'feel' others' suffering—a faculty that has much in common with the nature of theatre itself.

Adrastos' Epitaphioi: *Ironizing Masculine Heroism*

The funeral of the Argive dead in *Suppliant Women* is a scene second only to the finale of the *Eumenides* in processional pomp, one that fully exploits the 'great resources of space and personnel that the Athenian dramatist, given a wealthy and sympathetic *choregus*, had at his disposal'.[82] The theatrical splendour of this scene, which features not only the mothers of the Seven who have been on stage all along, but also Theseus and his attendants, Adrastos, the children of the Seven, and, presumably, a cortège of some sort with appropriate attendants, would have raised the expectation of a eulogy much like those with which the Athenians themselves were familiar. And yet, in what appears to be a critique of the ideology underlying those famous funeral orations, and as if to underscore the importance of Theseus' feminine role-playing as a necessary complement to his own violent heroics in the battle-scene, Euripides puts into Adrastos' mouth an oration that in fact satirizes the *epitaphios logos*, the public funeral oration, as a genre. It does so, moreover, by using

---

[82] Whitehorne, 'The Dead as Spectacle', 68, although Taplin sees only about twenty supernumeraries at the finale of *Eumenides* (*The Stagecraft of Aeschylus*, 80). Whitehorne envisions as many as fifty people in the orchestra for *Suppliant Women*'s Funeral scene; cf. Bowie, 'Tragic Filters', 51 on the 'extraordinary effect' that the play's finale must have had.

the same gendered terms that have shaped the play's political critique thus far.

The tone and meaning of the Oration in this play have been the subject of considerable debate; in offering my ironic reading, I will be expanding upon the arguments of both Fitton and Smith, who *contra* Zuntz and Collard saw Adrastos' speech as satiric.[83] Collard sums up his position as follows:

> It would be ethically and dramatically incongruous for the Oration to have any other focus than these individual heroes, always distinct in the myth and now in the play so real. The Oration therefore becomes a series of separate character-sketches which find their common theme in the heroes' conception of their civic duty, its realization in their attitudes and behaviour, above all in their education and discipline to valour.[84]

But the structural and dramatic context in which we encounter these *epitaphioi logoi* point to their ironic quality even before we 'hear' the speeches themselves. Collard seems too optimistic for two reasons. First, he fails to see how the ironic context of Theseus' words undercuts a straightforward reading of them. Ostensibly, the Athenian king makes a straightforward request:

νῦν δ', Ἄδραστ', ἀνιστορῶ·
πόθεν ποθ' οἵδε διαπρεπεῖς εὐψυχίᾳ
θνητῶν ἔφυσαν; εἰπὲ δ' ὡς σοφώτερος
νέοισιν ἀστῶν τῶνδ'· ἐπιστήμων γὰρ εἶ.
εἶδον γὰρ αὐτῶν κρεῖσσον' ἢ λέξαι λόγῳ
τολμήμαθ' οἷς ἤλπιζον αἱρήσειν πόλιν.

Now, Adrastos, I'll question you:
how did these men come to be pre-eminent in high-hearted
     courage (*eupsykhia*)
among men? Speak, as one who is skilled [in speaking] (*sophōteros*),

---

[83] See Fitton, *The Suppliant Women*, 437–40 and Smith, 'Expressive Form', 162–4; cf. also the comments of D. W. Lucas, *The Greek Tragic Poets* (London, 1950), 168; Greenwood, *Aspects of Euripidean Tragedy*, 99 ff.; Gamble, 'Euripides' Suppliant Women', 403 f., and Loraux, *The Invention of Athens*, 107 f. For what Collard calls 'uncomplicated' interpretations of the Oration, see first of all Zuntz, *The Political Plays of Euripides*, 13–17; Rivier, *Essai sur le tragique d'Euripide*, 174 ff.; Collard's 'The Funeral Oration in Euripides' *Supplices*', *BICS* 19 (1972), 39–53; and Mills, *Theseus, Tragedy*, 154.

[84] Collard, 'The Funeral Oration', 43; cf. his comments at *Euripides Supplices*, 309.

to these young (*neoisin*) citizens here; you have the requisite
knowledge (*epistēmōn*).
For they have seen those deeds, which beggar description—
the deeds of daring (*tolmēmata*) by which they [the Seven]
meant to take the city.

(840–5)

This is in fact an odd echo of another, earlier exchange between
Theseus and Adrastos. During their first confrontation, Theseus
had chastised the Argive leader for allowing himself to be swept
up in the impetuous enthusiasms of his youthful sons-in-law
(160)—a trait proper to *neoi*, young men like the ones in Adrastos' and indeed Euripides' audience, whom this *epitaphios logos*
is now supposed to edify. More specifically, he admonished
Adrastos for allowing *eupsykhia*, a rash 'high-heartedness', to
outweigh *euboulia*, prudence, a trait more appropriate to kings
and one which Euripides lavishly praises elsewhere.[85] Yet here it
is the *eupsykhia* of the Seven that Theseus supposedly wants to
hear praised by Adrastos. Similarly, Theseus' apparent compliment to Adrastos on being one who is more skilled (*sophōteros*) in
oratory than any other—that is, on being *epistēmōn*—although
clearly meant to refer to the Argive leader's legendary melli-
fluousness, withers when one recalls his earlier denunciation of
the older man as one of those who foolishly believe themselves to
be wiser than the gods themselves, *daimonōn sophōteroi* (218),
and who is himself anything but wise, *ou sophos gegōs* (219).[86]
The Athenian's request for a Funeral Oration thus wryly recalls
the very traits in Adrastos that made him dangerously like the
youths he is now supposed to instruct.[87] These echoes subvert

---

[85] e. g. *Helen* 758; *Phoen.* 721. Cf. also Sophocles, *Ant.* 178 f.; Hdt. 7. 10. d 2;
and Plato, *Prot.* 318e. Collard points out that the *eupsykhia*/*euboulia* antithesis
was already a topos by the 5th cent., reflecting a contemporary ideological preoccupation: the 'achievement of balance between the two opposing impulses'
(*Euripides Supplices*, 151 ad. 161); he cites as tragic parallels passages from
Medea (485) and *Phoenician Women* (746).

[86] The use of *epistēmōn* here calls to mind the other rhetorical topos common
in the 5th cent., the antithesis between *epistēmē* and *eupsykhia*; e.g. Thuc. 1. 121.
4 and 6. 72. 4. For the tradition of Adrastos' eloquence (e.g. Pindar, *Ol.* 6. 12 ff.),
see Collard, *Euripides Supplices*, 320 ad loc.

[87] As noted by Burian as well: 'Theseus' words here, even as they politely
suggest his reconciliation with Adrastos and the Seven, keep the original condemnation before us as the formal praise begins' (*'Logos and Pathos'*, 147).

the 'educational' potential of the Funeral Oration itself. Indeed, Theseus' reference to the powerlessness of language to describe the 'feats' of the Seven (844f.) invokes the ambiguous vocabulary of heroic action (*tolmēmata*) while slyly advertising the emptiness of the rhetoric that is to follow.

There is another element that calls for an ironic reading of the Oration. Embedded in Theseus' request to Adrastos is a familiar Euripidean device: that is, a metadramatic highlighting of his play's own formal conventions. Coming immediately after the Messenger's breathlessly detailed description of the battle, Theseus' impatient warning to Adrastos not to embellish his eulogies with fanciful 'eyewitness' embroidery (846–56) seems to be precisely what other critics have understood it to be: 'a disingenuous sneer at the conventions of simulated realism in messenger-speeches, directed principally at the central section of A[eschylus]' *Septem*'.[88] It is in fact entirely consistent with Euripides' ironic and indeed sometimes parodic technique to heighten his audience's awareness of tragedy's formal conventions; a heightened self-consciousness of formal elements inevitably invites more intense scrutiny of the actual content. (Hence, to cite the most famous example, the recognition scene in his *Elektra*, in which the characters incredulously disdain the possibility that two siblings could possibly recognize each other by means of matching hair and footprints—the very tokens that allow Aeschylus' Orestes and Elektra to recognize each other.)[89] In this light, it is difficult to take Theseus' derisive critique of eyewitness accounts, as Collard does, as nothing more than the consequence of the fact that both Theseus and the soldiers to whom the Oration will be addressed have already witnessed the bravery of the dead men for themselves and hence need no description.[90] Just as the echo of an earlier and quite unpleasant exchange undercuts the force of Theseus' present invitation to Adrastos,

[88] See Collard, *Euripides Supplices*, 321.

[89] Commentators have long seen this work as the classic example of Euripidean literary satire: for stimulating discussions of the playwright's satiric and parodic strategies, see especially Goldhill, *Reading Greek Tragedy*, 245–59, and Michelini, *Tragic Tradition*, 199–206. Bernard Knox begins his essay on what he calls Euripidean 'comedy' with a discussion of *Electra* ('Euripidean Comedy', in *Word and Action: Essays on the Ancient Theater* (Baltimore and London, 1979) 250–74).

[90] So Collard, 'Funeral Oration', 43.

so here a wry metacritique of a tragic genre casts further doubt on the validity of the literary and performative genre—that is, the Funeral Oration—of which an example will immediately follow.

The content of Adrastos' speech, as well as the ironic manner in which its speaker is introduced, also seems to justify the long tradition of critical scepticism of a straight interpretation. Fitton points to the most egregious dissonances between Adrastos' topoi and well-known facets of the mythic tradition in order to demonstrate the ironic force of those speeches. Thus, to cite the most famous example, the characterization of the hubristic Kapaneus as 'the most affable of men in his speech', *euprosēgoron stoma* (869), is clearly a violation of a tradition—one invoked by Euripides himself several times in *Suppliant Women*—that it was the uncontrolled boasting of the 'loud-mouthed', *stomargos*, Kapaneus that brought on Zeus' wrath and his own destruction.[91] The playwright makes repeated reference to Kapaneus as a victim of his own *hybris* (495 f.; cf. 639 f.) and to his fiery punishment by Zeus himself (934, 984, 1011)—a point that would seem effectively to counter Collard's argument that, despite the ostensible incongruity of Adrastos' portraits, the '[d]ramatists' imagination within the broad outline of myth was always free'.[92] To juxtapose these more traditional descriptions of Kapaneus as wildly hubristic with Adrastos' rosy reminiscences of the violent Argive warrior as a 'master of philosophic moderation' is indeed to invite the charge of 'ludicrousness'.

It therefore seems difficult to take the Seven as paradigms of civic virtue. Even at face value, what Adrastos does tell us about them would seem to disrupt the pedagogical usefulness of the Oration itself. For Adrastos' lavish praise of his subjects' *andreia* (885) is at odds both with Aithra's insistence that heroism must be subordinated to the needs of the community, and with the way in which the presentation of the battle scene casts an ironic shadow on a certain kind of martial violence. The cumulative

[91] Kapaneus' 'uncontrolled boasting': Fitton, 'The *Suppliant Women*', 438. For other tragic references to that tradition, cf. Aesch. *Septem* 440 ff., on Kapaneus as *stomargos*, and Soph. *Ant*. 127–30, where it is Kapaneus' 'great boasting' that arouses the wrath of Zeus; and *OC* 1318 f.

[92] Collard, 'Funeral Oration', 44. His point is well taken, of course, and Euripides himself was more likely to take liberties with his mythic data than most. But it is more difficult to accept that the poet was willing to take such liberties in a way that resulted in gross inconsistencies *within* a given text.

effect of his encomia here is, if anything, to endorse the pre-democratic uses of masculine valour that have been portrayed thus far as being inimical to the institutions that define the democratic *polis*.

For example, in Adrastos' praise of Parthenopaios, forensic and political argumentation are not seen here to be the lifeblood of the free and democratic *polis*, as they are by Aithra (who so effectively demonstrated the efficacy of rhetorical prowess), and by the contemporary Athenians themselves, noisily delighting in their *isēgoria*. Rather, they are portrayed as the bane of 'civilized' life: 'He was neither vexatious, nor odious to the city; nor a stubborn disputant with words (*exeristēs logōn*), which makes both citizen and foreigner especially burdensome' (893 ff.), Adrastos declares—a characterization of contentious speech that echoes the Theban Herald's dismissal of Athenian democracy as verbally incontinent, *mē diortheuōn logous*. Neither did Parthenopaios' comrade Tydeus have time for 'verbal fencing' (901–9). Adrastos readily acknowledges that Tydeus was not 'splendid with words', *en logois lampros* (902); but, in a striking metaphorical appropriation that shows disdain for the conventions of the *polis*'s literate and intellectual culture, Tydeus is praised for being expert, *sophistēs*, not with words or concepts, but with the sword and shield, *en aspidi* (903). It is this 'artistry with the spear', *tekhnēs doros* (905), that wins Tydeus a name as great as that of his cleverer brother Meleagros, since the former has discovered a 'music in the shield', *mousikēn en aspidi* (906), that is as 'exacting', *akribē*, as any other.[93]

In Perikles' Funeral Oration, artistic pursuits—tempered by other, 'harder' activities to be sure—are said to be the visible signs of a *polis*'s inner excellences (Thuc. 2. 39–40). 'We love

[93] The manuscript reading for ll. 901–9 is problematic. Some have defended the entire text (e.g. Smith, 'Expressive Form', 163); others have argued for extreme deletions, cutting 902–6 on the grounds that John of Damascus and Stobaios cite 901 followed by 907 with no break. Collard, following Dindorf, Wecklein, and Wilamowitz, supposes 904–8 to be interpolations inserted by ancient actors in order to pad this part of the oration to match the length of the others. Although I discuss the full MS reading here, the crucial reference to *logoi* and *sophistēs* at 902–3, generally accepted as authentic, essentially makes my point. For a full discussion of the MS difficulties, see Collard, *Euripides Supplices*, 334 f. See Gow on Theokritos 15. 81 for the use of *akribēs* as a technical term in describing works of art.

beauty with economy, and we love wisdom without softness, *malakia*', the Athenian leader boasts (Thuc. 2. 40. 1). This passage has been seen as yet further evidence of the fifth-century Athenian democracy's attempt to appropriate aristocratic values for the *dēmos*; a delicate balancing act, as we have already seen.[94] Yet Adrastos' encomium of Hippomedon (882–7) utterly derides music as being 'soft' and, he implies, effeminate:

παῖς ὢν ἐτόλμησ᾽ εὐθὺς οὐ πρὸς ἡδονάς
Μουσῶν τραπέσθαι πρὸς τὸ μαλθακὸν βίου,
ἀγροὺς δὲ ναίων σκληρὰ τῇ φύσει διδοὺς
ἔχαιρε πρὸς τἀνδρεῖον, ἔς τ᾽ ἄγρας ἰὼν
ἵπποις τε χαίρων τόξα τ᾽ ἐντείνων χεροῖν,
πόλει παρασχεῖν σῶμα χρήσιμον θέλων.

Right from childhood he had the guts (*etolmēse*) not to pursue the
    pleasures of the Muses and a soft (*malthakon*) life;
dwelling instead in the wilderness and giving himself wholly to
    hardness (*sklēra*),
he exulted in manliness (*t' andreion*), going out into the fields
and taking pleasure in his horses and stringing the bow with
    his own hands,
desiring to provide (*paraskhein*) a useful body (*khrēsimon sōma*)
    to the city.

(882–7)

The word Adrastos uses to describe the realm of the Muses is *malthakos*, which like *habrosynē* and *tryphē* was associated in fifth-century prosaic and tragic usage with the Eastern, un-Greek, and feminine.[95] Hippomedon eschews this Musean effeteness for a literally 'hard' life (*sklēra*) in the wilds that is here identified with 'manliness', *t' andreion*, just as masculine 'hardness' is, within the culture's discourse of gender, opposed to feminine softness and fluidity. He thus lives up to his Aeschylean reputation as a great hulk of a man (*Septem* 488). Yet despite the

[94] 'A strong democratic appropriation of aristocratic ἁβροσύνη', is how Perikles' sentiment is described by Kurke, and hence part of the democracy's ideological programme: 'the generalization of aristocratic values to the whole populace' ('The Politics of ἁβροσύνη', 106 n. 60). For the 'combination of "tough" and "soft"' as unique to the Athenian self-image, see Mills, *Theseus, Tragedy*, 64.

[95] See Hall, *Inventing the Barbarian*, 128 and 128 n. 82, and Kurke 'The Politics of ἁβροσύνη', *passim*. Hall points to Plato, *Rep.* 9. 590b3, where *tryphē* and *malthakia* are cited as the causes of unmanly cowardice, *deilia*.

assertion that Hippomedon's lifestyle enhances his usefulness
to the *polis*, the emphasis on the hero's 'hardness' is not unproblematic from the point of view of the Athenian *polis*. If he is
in certain respects reminiscent of Perikles' idealized Athenian
citizen, who similarly 'provides' a self-sufficient body for the city
(*to sōma autarkes parekhesthai*, Thuc. 2. 41. 2), Hippomedon is
bound to lack the other civic virtues that Perikles also praises:
grace, for example, and congenial sociability (*meta kharitōn,
eutrapelōs*, Thuc. 2. 40. 1). If anything, Hippomedon's pursuit of
'manliness', *andreion*, brings him back to the marginal, apolitical
spaces (*agras*, 885) where the hunter roams in search of wild
beasts. Adrastos' lavish praise of Hippomedon the Hunter thus
takes us back, too—full circle, that is, to the scene in which we
were first introduced to the Argive ruler, and in which the
unfolding tale of Adrastos' marriage-making revealed his own
particular 'flaw' in this particular tragedy: his attraction for the
uncivilized, the bestial, the hypermasculine that threatens to
become indistinguishable from the feminine.

   The structure of Adrastos' speech, then, as well as the content
of the 'character sketches' themselves, makes it difficult to accept
them as genuine *souvenirs pieux*, earnest endorsements of the
'civic conscience' of those dear departed. It is true that such an
endorsement would have been expected, given the pedagogical
aims of both the Funerary Oration and of tragedy itself, both of
which genres explored, in different ways, the ideology of the
polis. Indeed Adrastos self-consciously refers to such ethical and
political instruction in the coda to his eulogies, where he suggests
that the 'manliness' that he has just praised, *euandria*, can in fact
be taught, *didakton* (913 f.); making an etymological pun, he concludes by encouraging his listeners to educate (*paideuete*) their
children (*paidas*, 917). But as we have seen, the content of Adrastos' eulogies actually subverts their pedagogical usefulness for
the young citizens of the contemporary *polis*. Adrastos lavishes
'deliberately bathetic' praise on a *euandria* that has more in
common with pre-democratic, pre-civic, and even pre-civilized
values than with those that helped constitute fifth-century
Athens' ideological self-portrait. Moreover, it soon becomes
clear that the *euandria* extolled in these highly idiosyncratic portraits can only lead to radical destabilization of the *polis* because
it leads inevitably to further violent conflict. What the sons of the

Seven 'learn' from their fathers' example is, after all, nothing more than 'that fatal εὐανδρία [*euandria*] which brought disaster on Adrastos and untold sorrow on the Argive women', as Fitton observes. Euripides, he continues, 'shows with gentle but insistent irony how the lamentation for the dead heroes . . . actually incites people to war. We are thus prepared for the entry of jingoistic little boys later on in the play (1123 ff.).'[96]

The Funeral Oration's endorsement of the very *eupsykhia* and *euandria* that precipitated the play's tragic events is, to say the least, highly problematic. The repetition of these very terms in the *epitaphios* underscores the fact that the flaw in Adrastos' world-view is that it is informed, both literally and figuratively, by an overwhelming *maleness*. His oration thus brings to a climax the ongoing *agōn* between competing definitions of *to andreion* that has run through the play, beginning with Aithra's attempt to reorientate her son's notion of *andreia* (314), and continuing with the Theban Herald's disingenuously self-serving definition of *to andreion* as forethought based on *hēsykhia* (509 f.)—a definition, that is to say, that runs counter to the outspoken 'busybodyness', *polypragmosynē*, so prized in the political culture of democratic Athens, and exemplified by Aithra herself. As we have seen, the events that follow Theseus' encounters with both of those characters suggest that for the new, democratic hero, 'manliness' is located between the poles represented by *andreia* and *hēsykhia*.

That we are meant to accept that certain qualities represented by *hēsykhia* here must be integrated into a proper definition of (masculine) civic identity is demonstrated, I think, by Adrastos' parting words. Theseus' mention of the decomposing bodies of the Seven, en route for burial (944–6), is the gruesome reality that stands in vivid contrast to Adrastos' gleaming rhetoric.[97] Faced with rotted fruits of the manly labour he has just praised,

---

[96] Fitton, 'The *Suppliant Women*', 439. For the 'deliberate bathos' in Adrastos' speeches, see Fitton, p. 438.

[97] An unpleasant reality that would have been much more concrete to the Athenians in Euripides' audience than it is for us, to be sure—something it is always useful to keep in mind when reading these 'burial' plays. See the rather grim essay by Pamela Vaughn, 'The Identification and Retrieval of the Hoplite Battle-Dead', in Hanson, *Hoplites*, 38–62.

Adrastos crumples (947). As insubstantial as his own bombast, the Argive king demonstrates that he is not, indeed, *sophōteros* with respect to speaking about what has transpired; he immediately awards the crown of right and proper speech to a 'victorious' Theseus (*nikais . . . legei gar eu Theseus*, 947 f.). In his final moments on stage, Adrastos resumes the attitude of helpless, hopeless grief in which we first saw him. This stage picture further undercuts much of the rhetorical brio of his Funeral Oration.

> ὦ ταλαίπωροι βροτῶν,
> τί κτᾶσθε λόγχας καὶ κατ' ἀλλήλων φόνους
> τίθεσθε; παύσασθ', ἀλλὰ λήξαντες πόνων
> ἄστη φυλάσσεθ' ἥσυχοι μεθ' ἡσύχων.

O mortal wretches,
why take up spears, why bring on yourselves
one another's blood? Cease! and, leaving off such exploits (*ponōn*),
guard your cities in peace with one another (*hēsykhoi meth' hēsykhōn*).

(949–52)

Desperate though it is, this is a clear-eyed appreciation of the havoc that *euandria* wreaks. Adrastos rejects the military prowess for which he just praised the Seven, calling for men to lay down their arms, *lonkhai*. Sounding, perhaps, like a member of the peace party at Athens during the 420s, he deprecates *ponoi*—the word typically used of a hero's labours—and instead endorses *hēsykhia* as a cardinal political virtue, the only possible remedy for the violence that men do to each other. This ethical transformation has, in fact, been foreshadowed by the earlier use of *ponos* to describe Theseus' washing and laying-out of the corpses of the Seven (763). The startling coda to this episode thus further destabilizes a 'straight' reading of the Funeral Oration, and hence the encomiastic interpretation advanced by some scholars. It lays to rest the notion that *to andreion* by itself is of real use to the city, let alone the Athenian city in which this drama was staged as part of a great festival of civic self-consciousness. Even more, it sets the stage for the play's most disturbing enactment of the foolish waste that heroic *andreia* inevitably brings—Evadne's suicide.

Evadne and the Parodies of Heroism

The dramatic closure ostensibly achieved by the burial of the Seven is ruptured by the startling entrance of Kapaneus' widow, Evadne.[98] This breathtaking tour de force, the only on-stage suicide in extant tragedy, is so shocking in itself that critics have, in general, been satisfied to take it more or less at face value and leave it at that. Garzya sees her grief as comparable to that of the Argive mothers; Collard describes its 'tragic and heroic significance', interpreting it as a further reiteration of 'the strength of love' and an example of 'the extremes to which individuals can be driven by war's suffering'.[99]

It is, of course, all of these things, and it would be a mistake to underestimate Euripides' interest in dramatizing both the terrible consequences of war and, as we have seen in the case of *Children of Herakles*'s Alkmene, the costs, in human terms, exacted by the subordination of diversity to unity. But a re-evaluation of the Evadne scene in light of our special emphasis on space, gender, and politics yields another, somewhat different interpretation from those that cast her as merely a pathetic or

---

[98] 'As far as we know,' writes Rehm (*Marriage to Death*, 112), 'nothing like this ever took place in fifth-century tragedy before or after *Supplices*, and it would be hard to find a more theatrically daring moment in the history of the stage.' This seems right: the staging of Ajax's suicide remains a vexed question, but there can be no doubt that Evadne's fiery leap, though it seems to have been into a pyre located behind the *skēnē*, was meant to be perceived as occurring in the audience's presence. See J. de Romilly, *L'Evolution du pathétique d'Eschyle à Euripide* (Paris, 1961), 15 n. 1 and 36 ff.; P. Arnott, *Greek Scenic Convention*, 137 f.; Hourmouziades, *Production and Imagination in Euripides*, 33–5; Collard, *Euripides Supplices*, i. 15; Halleran, *Stagecraft in Euripides*, 12 f. Arnott dryly observes that such a jump from the *skēnē* roof 'was possible, if not popular with the actors' (138); he believes that the scene diverges too greatly from 5th-cent. tragic norms to be genuine, and suggests with Norwood that it is a 4th-cent. interpolation (cf. G. Norwood, *Essays on Euripidean Drama* (London, 1954), 159 f.). For a comprehensive discussion of such appearances above the *skēnē*, see Donald J. Mastronarde, 'Actors on High: The Skene Roof, the Crane, and the Gods in Attic Drama', *Classical Antiquity*, 9 (1990), 247–92, with relevant comments about *Suppliant Women* at 263 f. and 281. He observes, rightly I think, that the 'stunt' would have been both safer and more realistic if the actor portraying Evadne was already attached to the crane upon entering (281 n. 2).

[99] A. Garzya, *Pensiero e tecnica drammatica in Euripide* (Naples, 1962), 1962: 52; Collard, *Euripides Supplices*, 352.

even 'foolish' victim.[100] For as we shall see, Evadne herself seems less a helpless war widow than a wife whose needless death dramatizes the threat inherent in her husband's flawed notion of *euandria*.

Enter Evadne: Crossing Spatial and Sexual Boundaries

After Adrastos' exit, Euripides uses the fourth stasimon (955–79) to reintroduce feminine themes as a prelude to Evadne's entrance. These themes are, more precisely, maternal. The chorus refers repeatedly to its present childlessness, contrasting its current bereavement with a former happiness that is explicitly identified with motherhood (955–7). Now too old to have more children, the mothers anticipate lives devoid of meaning, 'life that is no life' (*dysaiōn bios*, 960); they count themselves among neither the dead nor the living (968ff.). In the stasimon's most striking passage, the chorus compares itself to a wandering cloud that is buffeted by a cruel wind (961f.). The old women who comprise the chorus thus remain as figuratively displaced by grief-stricken childlessness as they were literally displaced at the play's opening, when their childlessness and seemingly endless wandering far from home were likewise highlighted (9, 35). The chorus's closing words bring them home, if only in their minds' eyes, to their deserted houses (*en oikois*, 972) in which stand the traditional tokens of mourning: locks of the mourners' hair, garlands for the corpse itself (971–4). The libations that will be poured, and the mournful song that will sound there (975f.), are ritual accompaniments to the mothers' sleepless cries and tears. In this way the passage reinforces traditional associations between women, ritual mourning, and the interior of the house.

As has been frequently observed by now, funerals and weddings were the two principle occasions on which Athenian women could legitimately be seen outside of the house, and there is, therefore, a certain appropriateness that Evadne's flamboyant entrance into the action of *Suppliant Women* should occur during a funeral that she would turn into a wedding.[101] Dressed as

---

[100] Mills, *Theseus, Tragedy*, 126.

[101] For this scene as a dramatization of the overlapping cultural symbolism of marriage and death, see Rehm, *Marriage to Death*, 110ff., and cf. Whitehorne, 'The Dead as Spectacle', 71. For marriages and funerals as vehicles for feminine visibility, see e.g., Just, *Women in Athenian Law*, 110, 120f. It comes as no sur-

a bride (1048, 1054 ff.), she figuratively transforms a tomb (*thalamas*, 980 f.) into a bridal chamber (*thalamos*: cf. 1022, *Phersephonās es thalamous*). This violent break from the tone and content of the preceding chorus is, moreover, marked by the anomalous movement of her own body through space. Evadne settles atop a rocky eyrie (*aitherian petran*, 987), which, like the frenzied young woman herself, juts uncomfortably into space 'beyond the house', *tōnde domōn hyperakrizei* (988)—'house' here pointedly referring to the tomb.

The theme of Evadne's eruption into space is in fact heavily emphasized throughout the scene, which underscores the transgressive aspect of a woman's departure from the protected, interior space of the house. With the swiftness of a bacchant (*ekbakkheusamena*, 1001), she rushes headlong *out* of her own house, *ex emōn oikōn* (1000; cf. *hē domōn exōpios bebēka*, 1038). The comparison with a bacchant is more than a poetic touch: it summons the fearful image of a maddened woman running amok.[102] And Evadne's exit is, in fact, as dangerously transgressive as that of the maenads. More than simply a hasty departure, it is an escape: her father Iphis declares that he has set guards over his daughter (*ephroureit' en domois . . . egō phylakas anēka*, 1040 f.; cf. *domōn hypekbasa*, 1049, where the *hyp*[*o*], as usual, indicates evasion).[103] This action is remarkable because it literalizes what is usually thought to have been a purely figurative and conventional confinement of woman to the interior of her house. Just asserts that '[t]he degree of supervision and protection under which Athenian women remained was not, therefore, inconsiderable. But they were closely watched rather than locked

prise that funerals seem frequently to have spawned seductions, as we learn in Lysias 1 (*Eratosthenes*).

[102] A scenario that the prologue of Euripides' *Bacchae* most famously conveys. In *Bacchae* 32–6, Dionysos boasts of having goaded women out of their houses with madness (*ek domōn ōistrēs' egō maniais*); the bacchants now live frenzied out of their wits (*parakopoi phrenōn*) because the god has 'maddened them out of the house', *exemēna dōmatōn*. For the significance of this Dionysiac reference within the larger context of the Dionysiac in tragedy, see Froma I. Zeitlin, 'Staging Dionysus Between Athens and Thebes', in Thomas H. Carpenter and Christopher A. Faraone (eds.), *Masks of Dionysus* (Ithaca, NY, 1993), 166 n. 42.

[103] Collard, *Euripides Supplices*, 377 ad loc.; cf. *hypēlthe* 138 and *hypekphygois* 565.

away.'[104] Yet *Suppliant Women*'s Iphis does just that, keeping his errant daughter under lock and key.

The suggestion that Iphis has already taken charge of his daughter's life so soon after her widowhood in fact conforms with fifth-century social convention. Under Athenian law, childless widows typically reverted to the *kyria*, the legal custody —and hence the house—of their fathers, with the expectation that another *ekdosis* would be arranged, and more children eventually borne.[105] Evadne's egregious flight not merely from her house, but specifically from the constraints placed on her by her father following her husband's death, thus indicates her unwillingness to abide by the familial obligations of which her imprisonment by Iphis is the exaggerated symbol. A lost Euripidean drama, the *Protesilaos*, sheds some light on the dramatic allure this legal point may have had for an Athenian audience. In that play, Laodameia, like Evadne, displays an excessive, even unhealthy attachment to a dead husband—she is devoted to a statue of the deceased Protesilaos. When her father Akastos orders the statue burned, she leaps into the pyre. A papyrus fragment of this work suggests that the motivation for Akastos' order and for Laodameia's suicide was the father's insistence that the daughter remarry.[106]

But remarriage may not be the only thing Evadne dreads. The rigidly enforced custody to which she is being forced to revert recalls, if anything, a mythic paradigm according to which anxious fathers imprison their own daughters in order to pre-

[104] Just, *Women in Athenian Law*, 121. For an interesting discussion of the father–daughter relationship in the Greek imaginary, see Ezio Pellizer, 'Padri e figlie nell' immaginario della Grecia antica', in Luisa Accati, Marina Cattaruzza, and Monika Verzar Bass (eds.), *Padre e figlia* (Turin, 1994) 77–94, and esp. 79–81 ('Padri custodi e figlie segregate').

[105] See Just, *Women in Athenian Law*, 26, the beginning of an extensive discussion of 5th-cent. *kyria*: Richard Seaford, in a brief analysis of this scene, makes the very interesting suggestion that, by having Evadne leave her father's house, Euripides further underscores the parallels between the young woman's marriage and her death here ('Dionysus as Destroyer of the Household: Homer, Tragedy, and the Polis', in Carpenter and Faraone, *Masks of Dionysus*, 125 f.).

[106] See H. Oranje's discussion of a papyrus fragment of this lost work, 'Euripides' Protesilaus: *P. Oxy.* 3214. 10-14', *ZPE* 37 (1980), 169–72; Oranje follows the reconstruction of F. Jouan, *Euripide et les légendes des chants Cypriens* (Paris, 1966), 317–66. For Laodameia as a type of problematic wife, see Seaford, 'Problem of Marriage', 165 f.

serve the girls' virginity; this suggests that Evadne may also be fleeing from a kind of enforced revirginization. And indeed, the only connection that Evadne seems to acknowledge is an erotic one.[107] Her ecstatic recollection of her wedding day, with its procession of hymeneal torches (990–9) gives way to explicit reveries:

> ὁρῶ δὴ τελευτὰν
> ἵν' ἔστακα· τύχα δέ μοι
> ξυνάπτοι ποδὸς ἅλματι
> [εὐκλείας χάριν ἔνθεν ὁρ-
> μάσω τᾶσδ' ἀπὸ πέτρας
> πηδήσασα πυρᾶς ἔσω]
> σῶμά τ' αἴθοπι φλογμῷ
> πόσει συμμείξασα φίλον
> χρῶτα χροῒ πέλας θεμένα,
> Φερσεφόνας ἥξω θαλάμους,
> σὲ τὸν θανόντ' οὔποτ' ἐμᾷ
> προδοῦσα ψυχᾷ κατὰ γᾶς.

> Indeed I see where my end
> stands. May Fortune
> join the springing of her foot to mine;
> for the sake of glory (*eukleias*) I shall dart
> from this rock,
> leaping into the fire,
> mating (*symmeixasa*) in the blazing flame
> my own body to my husband,
> pressing skin to skin,
> I will come to Persephone's halls,
> never having betrayed you—dead,
> beneath the earth—by living (*emāi psykhāi*).
> (1012–24)

Here Evadne refers quite explicitly to her own body (cf. 1070) not as the fertile site of procreation but rather as the seat of sensual pleasures: intercourse, skin-to-skin contact. This public articulation of sexual desire parallels her equally outrageous escape from her father's guards, who are the symbols of patriarchal control over woman's body for the purposes of procreation. Indeed the bedchamber, *thalamos*, into which she would transform Kapaneus' burial chamber, *thalamai*, is, like woman

---

[107] For the mythic motif of imprisoned virgins, see Pellizer, 'Padri e figlie', 79f. For the specifically erotic nature of Evadne's actions and utterances, see Rehm, *Marriage to Death*, 112.

herself, conventionally consigned to the recesses of the house;[108] but the maenad-like Evadne erupts into exterior space, forsaking the constrained domestic realm and pursuing her libidinous pleasures in public. This preference for (metaphorically) erotic activity over procreative and domestic responsibility also mirrors the priorities of a maenad.[109] Moreover, this defiance of her natal family also possibly signals Evadne's rejection not only of social convention (i.e. patriarchy) but of civic ideology (i.e. autochthony), which insists on *engenēs kēdeia*, marriage made not only within but on behalf of the clan.[110] If Theseus' early aversion to *symmeixis* in his defence of *engenēs kēdeia* made him a rigid, Pentheus-like figure at the beginning of the play, Evadne here goes to the opposite, Dionysiac extreme in her monody, violating the norms of both domestic and civic responsibility and celebrating instead, in her overtly erotic metaphors, the fluid currents of feminine sexuality that the social and spatial constraints imposed by men sought both to regulate and to exploit.

Kallinikos *Evadne: Heroizing the Female Body*

The chorus instantly recognizes the disturbing nature of Evadne's assertions, referring to her speech as 'strange' or 'new-fangled' words, *neōterous logous* (1032); the pejorative adjective clearly indicates that Evadne's speech is anything but exemplary.[111] Indeed, the chorus rightly predicts that her words will

---

[108] 'If the *thalamos* is in the depths of the house, there is also within the *thalamos* the bed (*lechos*), scene of the pleasure that the institution of marriage tolerates if it is not excessive and, above all, the place of procreation': Loraux, *Tragic Ways of Killing a Woman*, 24. For *thalamos/thalamai* and other love/death motifs in tragedy, see her discussion at p. 75 n. 48; and cf. Rehm, *Marriage to Death*, 111.

[109] For the erotic and libidinous self-indulgence of maenads, see Just on Euripides' Pentheus in the *Bacchae*: 'For Pentheus, the Theban women's worship of the new god is but an excuse for some drunken, libidinous orgy' (Just , *Women in Athenian Law*, 253)—a common fantasy, it would appear. Cf. R. Seaford, Reciprocity and Ritual: *Homer and Tragedy in the Developing City-State* (Oxford, 1994), 310f. on maenadic excess as a threat to the *polis* and its institutions. For women's inexhaustible sexual appetite perceived as a threat to man's institutions, see Carson, 'Women, Dirt, and Desire', 142–5.

[110] Seaford, 'Problem of Marriage', 165.

[111] The pejorative, absolute sense is clear here; see Collard, *Euripides Supplices*, 374 ad loc., and cf. Theseus' anxious use of the word in the same sense at 91 and 99.

pain her father, the old hero Iphis, who now enters. The heated
exchange between father and daughter demonstrates how dramatically the young woman departs, both literally and figuratively, from established convention:

> Ἰφ. τέκνον, τίς αὔρα; τίς στόλος; τίνος χάριν
> δόμων ὑπεκβᾶσ' ἦλθες ἐς τήνδε χθόνα;
> Εὐ. ὀργὴν λάβοις ἂν τῶν ἐμῶν βουλευμάτων
> κλύων· ἀκοῦσαι δ' οὔ σε βούλομαι, πάτερ.
> Ἰφ. τί δ'; οὐ δίκαιον πατέρα τὸν σὸν εἰδέναι;
> Εὐ. κριτὴς ἂν εἴης οὐ σοφὸς γνώμης ἐμῆς.

> Iph. Child, what wind, what errand brings you here? Why
> have you stolen out of the house and come to this land?
> Ev. You'd be enraged at my plans
> if you were to hear them. And I don't *want* you to hear
> them, father.
> Iph. *What?* Isn't it right for your father to know?
> Ev. You'd not be a good judge (*kritēs sophos*) of *my* thinking.
> (1048–53)

Evadne's defiance of her father's demand to know why she has
come to Eleusis parallels her rejections of the physical restraints
he had early placed upon her. More, she suggests that the
motives for her transgressive movement and strange appearance
are, in fact, beyond his ken, far too unconventional for him to
understand. Earlier, the nature of human wisdom, *sophia*, was
the subject of debate between Theseus and Adrastos; here
Evadne implies that the *sophia* to which men lay claim is
insufficient for understanding her behaviour at all—a claim that
Iphis' repeated questions indeed bear out.

Iphis does well to be confused, for as her subsequent words
make clear, the title to which his daughter would lay claim is that
of 'hero'. First, Evadne hints that her strange attire is part of a
gambit for some bit of renown, *ti kleinon*; Loraux glosses *kleinon*
here as a marker of Evadne's '"virility" [which] is unseemly in
the good wife she professes to be'.[112] Acknowledging that her
behaviour is a disturbing 'novelty' (*pragma neokhmon*, 1057, with
an echo of the negative force of *neōterous logous* at 1032), she lays
claim to the Heraklean epithet *kallinikos*, 'of glorious victory'
(1059), thus placing herself in a class with none other than Theseus himself, who had been addressed as *kallinikos* by Adrastos

[112] Loraux, *Tragic Ways of Killing a Woman*, 29.

in the first episode (113). Evadne's appropriation of the diction of masculine prowess, in its agonistic and epinician context, is not meant to be figurative:[113] she sees herself as a victorious (male) athlete, worthy of the epinician praise due to Olympic victors. Understandably enough, Iphis cannot fathom which 'victory' she refers to (1060). At this point Evadne finally reveals her goal: to surpass the entire race of women (*pasas gynaikas*, 1061). In this she resembles the Girl, whose assumption of a new, heroic identity in *Children of Herakles* made her, too, unlike all other women (*tlēmonestatēn pasōn gynaikōn*; *megiston ekprepousa eupsykhiai pasōn gynaikōn*, *Hkld*. 571 and 597f.). Like the Girl, Evadne is not interested in surpassing her sisters *as a woman*—that is, in the 'handiworks of Athena or prudence of mind' (1062) by which women are normally permitted to distinguish themselves,[114] and which Iphis quite naturally assumes she is referring to here when he asks her in what she plans to surpass all other females. She will surpass them in something not usually associated with the realm of the feminine at all: *aretē*— her shocking one-word answer to her father's question (1063). Evadne's *aretē* is meant to stand in obvious contrast not only to the *aretai*, 'excellences', that women were traditionally per-

---

[113] As Collard suggests (*Euripides Supplices*, 378 ad loc.). Yet *aretēi nikō*, 'I win in respect to *aretē*', is strange coming from a woman. In Euripides' *Mad Herakles* (341–7), the phrase is used by the aged Amphitryon in denouncing a capricious Zeus for not saving his own kin (i.e. Herakles' family). The *aretē* which he suggests is lacking in the god is clearly part of a masculine code of honour: unlike Zeus, Amphitryon knows how to treat his *philoi*, and never betrayed Herakles' children, whereas Zeus is merely a casual seducer of other men's wives. At Thuc. 4. 19. 2, *aretēi auton nikēsas*, 'beating him in virtue', is used of one who shows generosity to a weaker foe and thereby demonstrates his superior *aretē*. The Spartans, suing for peace after Sphakteria, base this appeal to the Athenians on an implied comparison between the Athenians' strength of arms— their 'real' *aretē*—and the strength of character that they are now asked to show.

[114] Cf. *Ion* (1417ff.) and *IT* (814) for women's weaving; for these skills as gifts of Athena, see *Il.* 9. 390; *Od.* 2. 116ff. (Athena's gifts to Penelope); *Od.* 6. 234 (Athena and Hephaistos confer). Athena was worshipped as Erganē, 'Athena of Handiwork': see e.g. U. von Wilamowitz-Moellendorff, *Glaube der Hellenen*, 2 vols. (Berlin, 1931–2), ii. 161, and Burkert, *Greek Religion*, 141.

Euboulia here seems to be a specifically feminine virtue. It has already been expressly opposed to macho *eukardia*, as discussed above; and elsewhere in his oeuvre (e.g. *Phoen.* 746) Euripides articulates a stark contrast between *euboulia* and *tharsos*, the latter being the very boldness that marks transgressive, 'heroized' women in the political plays.

mitted to display, which Iphis has mentioned, but also to the 'traditionally female virtue' of displaying '*sophrosyne* in erotic matters', the 'female worth [that] is never confused with real worth, which belongs to men'. Evadne expects to lie with her fallen husband (*posei synthanousa keisomai*, 1063) as if she were a hero herself, the *kallinikos* victor in a contest for the new *aretē* of *eros*.[115]

Body Politics: Making the sōma *Autonomous*

It is this outlandish claim to *aretē* that Iphis so vehemently rejects as 'rotten', *sathron*, taking his metaphor from the semantic field to which Theseus' earlier condemnation of Adrastos (as being 'sick', 227 f.) had belonged. Not surprisingly, Iphis now seeks to contain Evadne's transgressive energies by reimposing control over her speech. Reminding her that she is his daughter, the old man emphatically forbids Evadne to speak out, in a vain attempt to reassert the patriarchal control of speech which Evadne, like the Girl in *Children of Herakles* and like Aithra herself, self-consciously violates:

> Ιφ. ὦ θύγατερ, οὐ μὴ μῦθον ἐς πολλοὺς ἐρεῖς;
> Ευ. τοῦτ᾽ αὐτὸ χρῇζω, πάντας Ἀργείους μαθεῖν.

Iph. Daughter, do *not* (*ou mē*)[116] say this before so many!
Ev. That's exactly what I demand—for all the Argives to know.

(1066–7)

Like the Girl, who insisted that her deed be reported far and wide (*exangellomai*, *Hkld.* 531), Evadne not only ruptures the physical constraints imposed on her movements, but violates the conventions of feminine silence that are inimical to her desire for heroic renown. This final rejection of paternal control over her words completes the course of Evadne's transgressions, which

---

[115] For *sōphrosynē* in erotic matters as a traditional female virtue, see Des Bouvrie, *Women in Greek Tragedy*, 230 n. 3, on *Medea*'s second stasimon, a *locus classicus* for tragedy's endorsement of that virtue; for female *aretē* as not a 'real' *aretē*, see Loraux, *Tragic Ways of Killing a Woman*, 27. Burian rightly notes of the *Suppliant Women* passage that Evadne's self-destructive lust for glory makes her more like one of the Seven than one of the grieving chorus members ('*Logos* and *Pathos*', 150).

[116] The double negative οὐ μή, *ou mē*, signals 'vehement prohibition' before the second person singular future indicative, as here: Collard, *Euripides Supplices*, 380 ad loc. Cf. Soph. *Ant.* 757, and Aesch. *Septem* 250.

began with her escape from Iphis' guards. Her final words to her
father constitute the most emphatic rejection of conventional
constraints on woman's spatial and hence corporeal autonomy:

> οὐ γὰρ μὴ κίχῃς μ' ἑλὼν χερί·
> καὶ δὴ παρεῖται σῶμα, σοὶ μὲν οὐ φίλον,
> ἡμῖν δὲ καὶ τῷ συμπυρουμένῳ πόσει.

> You will *not* (*ou mē*) get to take my hand (*helōn kheri*);
> my body falls, something not dear (*philon*) to you
> but very much so to me and to the husband with whom I burn.

> (1069–71)

These triumphant final words make it clear that the ongoing
struggle between Evadne and her father is for control over her
body and the uses to which it will be put. She will push away part
of his own body, the hand that attempts to seize her, in order to
get away. Loraux has observed that for tragic women, 'death is
an exit'; and indeed, the suicidal leap (*pēdēsasa*, 1017) that unites
Evadne in a literally fatal, figuratively erotic embrace with her
husband's body is described in the same terms as her original
exit from the house (*bebēke pēdēsasa*, 1039; cf. *bebēke* repeated at
1043).[117]

As she prepares to hurl herself through space for the last time,
attention is once more focused on Evadne's body as the autonomous subject of erotic activity. The unusual syntax of Evadne's
penultimate line, *pareitai sōma*—'my body falls'—indeed suggests that her body has a subjectivity almost separate from her
own. The deceptively innocuous adjective *philon*, used by
Evadne to describe that body in its fall, can mean either 'dear',
'lovely', or 'beloved', on the one hand, or 'one's own', on the
other hand. Those who construe it in the former sense here have
argued that it stands in apposition to the entire clause that precedes it, *pareitai sōma* (her body's plunge will not be 'something
dear' to her father),[118] although it is difficult not to take *philon*

---

[117] Death as an exit: Loraux, *Tragic Ways of Killing a Woman*, 19. Loraux
also points out here that '*Bebēke*, "she is gone", is said of a woman who dies
or has killed herself' (19); hence we may read Iphis' repetition of the word in
1039–43 as a sinister double entendre. On *bebēke* used in this way, and on
women's death in general as a journey or movement through space, see Loraux's
discussion at pp. 19–21. She cites e.g. *Alkestis* 262 f., 392, 394; *Hippolytos* 828 f.;
Trakhinian Women 874 f.

[118] So Ammendola and Collard, who acknowledges that the usage is, at any

in this sense as referring to *sōma* itself: it is the lovely body that was dear to and beloved of Kapaneus, with whom Evadne now intends to mingle once again in a fatal consummation of love. None the less, some scholars have argued for the second sense of *philon* at 1070, meaning little more than 'one's own'.[119] Yet the nature of Evadne's struggle with her father suggests how these apparently distinct senses of *philon* coalesce here. By celebrating the erotic rather than reproductive potential of her lovely/ beloved body, Evadne indeed makes that body her 'own' in a way that, according to her, no woman has ever done before. Flying into space in order to be joined once again to her husband's body, she forever escapes her father's grasp and all it represents.

Commingling Identities: Evadne Plays Kapaneus

To say that Evadne makes her body the vehicle for her radical departure from gendered conventions is, therefore, to speak figuratively but also quite literally. As she herself describes it, her body is bird-like in its potential for sudden ascent (1045 ff.); it repeatedly crosses strictly maintained borders; and it meets death in a fiery explosion. As such, it resembles nothing so much as the body of her husband Kapaneus, the 'lightning-blasted body', *keraunion demas*, that was burned, *kapnoutai*, by Zeus' fiery thunderbolt as it breached the walls of Thebes (496 f.). The young woman's language betrays a fantasy that she, too, will die heroically, meeting a similarly fiery end. Evadne's self-immolation can thus be seen as the climax of her ongoing attempt to heroize herself, using Kapaneus as her model. Like him, she has been seduced by 'the destructive glow of heroism'.[120]

rate, fairly rare in tragedy (*Euripides Supplices*, 380 ad loc.). He cites parallels from Euripides, such as *Medea* 1035, *Or.* 30; and in Sophocles at *Ant.* 44.

[119] So Wilamowitz (*Griechische Verskunst* (Berlin, 1921), 554 n. 3), who glosses *philon* here as '*sc. emon* ["mine"]'. This is 'a pale reflection of Epic usage': so D. L. Page, *Euripides: Medea* (Oxford, 1937), ad *Med.* 905.

[120] 'Destructive glow of heroism': Smith, 'Expressive Form', 165. The burning of Kapaneus' body is mentioned repeatedly throughout the play: cf. 640; 984; 1011. Descriptions of Kapaneus' hybris and death are numerous in both tragedy and the plastic arts. Cf. Aesch. *Septem* 424–56 and frs. 263 and 596. 5 N.; Soph. *Ant.* 128–40; *OC* 1318 f.; and *Phoenician Women* 179–84 and 1172–86. Collard points out that the Gyölbashi-Trsya heroön has a frieze that depicts Kapaneus falling from his ladder, much as described here at 497. For Evadne's

This re-enactment of Kapaneus' actions and her mimicking of
his transgressive boasts set her well beyond the pale of feminine
behaviour that can be considered proper, as the chorus's use
of the charged adjective *pantolmon*, 'daring all', or 'shameless'
(1075) suggests.[121] Her suicide thus successfully realizes the bid
for epinician and quasi-heroic glory that was implicit in her
'riddling' responses to the anxious queries of her uncompre-
hending father. Her desire to 'die with' her hubristic husband
itself shares something of his hubristic nature. In this light, it
seems only fitting that the praise Evadne receives, in the brief
epitaphios accorded her by her father (1098–1103), is as glibly
conventional and contrary to the dramatic reality presented on
Euripides' stage as the one that was accorded to Kapaneus by
Adrastos.[122]

desire to mimic her husband's death, see Fitton, 'The *Suppliant Women*', 437 f.;
Smith, 'Expressive Form', 164. Collard, too, sees the husband as the model for
the wife, but because he denies the ironic nature of the presentation of Kapaneus
in the Oration, the Argive hero is for him a 'model husband' while Evadne is a
'devoted' wife ('Funeral Oration', 44). A further, ironic point of contact:
Evadne's expectation that she will share a tomb with her husband (1063) is a
blasphemous one, if one takes into account religious scruples concerning the
bodies of those struck by lightning; that she would glibly ignore well-known
religious scruples both conveys the extent of her self-identification with
Kapaneus, and reflects something of his own famous profanity.

[121] The only other instance of this adjective in Euripides, in the *Iphigeneia at
Aulis*, suggests its pejorative strength while conjoining it with another adjective
whose negative force, as I have argued, is especially striking when used of
women. At *IA* 913–17, Klytaimnestra appeals for help to Akhilleus when she
realizes that Agamemnon plots to sacrifice her daughter; she speaks anxiously as
a woman alone among an unruly throng of men. Agamemnon's *pantolma* deeds,
she says, are matched by his army's anarchic boldness (*thrasy*). In an interesting
parallel to the ethical schema sketched in the *Suppliants* passage I am discussing
here, the playwright of the *Iphigeneia at Aulis* goes on to applaud *tolmēros* action
by Akhilleus on behalf of the helpless women, as if in answer to Aithra's recommendation at 305. The *IA* passage thus suggests how the morally outrageous
pantolma planned by the corrupt Agamemnon can be seen as a hyperbolic perversion of *tolma* shown by the idealistic young prince Akhilleus.

[122] In his fond portrait of Evadne at 1098–1103, Iphis blandly alludes to conventional gendered stereotypes: 'There is nothing sweeter to an aged father than
a daughter; male children are greater in spirit (*meizones psykhāi*), but less suited
for sweet endearments.' But it is greatness of soul that Evadne desires, of course;
Iphis' revisionist sugar-and-spice portrait of his daughter stands in stark contrast to the emotional fury that has just been released on stage.

Evadne Furens: (Re)playing Aithra

The use of *pantolmon* to describe Evadne's suicide erases the encomiasts' claims for an 'exemplary' reading of this scene, in which the young girl is ennobled as 'a tragic war widow':

By the spectacle of self-immolation, it shows the continuation within the human heart of the tragic consequences of the Argive campaign. It particularises the communal suffering—it is a tragedy within a tragedy. It is as if all the human feelings that have lain submerged in politic plausibilities or pathetic self-pity at last find issue—in the glory of death.[123]

It is true that, like Herakles' daughter, Evadne is a human symbol of the costs of war. Yet Euripides problematizes such interpretative bookkeeping by suggesting that Evadne is also a symbol for what we might call the 'costs of peace'. For this reason, her counterpart in her 'emotional heroism' is less the self-sacrificing young Girl of the *Children of Herakles*—who was, after all, a literal 'victim'—than the earlier work's embittered and enraged Alkmene.[124] The old woman's on-stage tour de force indeed has the same dramatic feel as does Evadne's. Both women appear unexpectedly, even violently; both enter the action after a new political status quo has ostensibly been achieved as a result of men's actions. Each, we might say, represents a tragic residue remaining in the individual, subjective, and emotional realms, which the smooth operations of the newly defined state cannot accommodate. In the vehemence with which each expresses herself, one senses a return of the repressed energies which earlier on in each play are so efficiently regulated.

In *Children of Herakles*, Alkmene's outrageous behaviour amplified that feminine potential for subversiveness which the Girl's appearance and appropriation of heroic behavior merely hinted at—a hint later 'erased' from the text. A similar pattern

---

[123] Fitton, 'The *Suppliant Women*', 441. This view goes back as far as U. von Wilamowitz, 'Der Mutter Bittgang', in *Griechische Tragödien* (Berlin, 1904), i. 220 ff.; cf. somewhat more recently H. Strohm, *Euripides* (Munich, 1957), 59 f. Smith was the first of recent critics to attempt to debunk the widely held notion that Evadne was 'presented for admiration, perhaps for emulation by Athenian wives', arguing instead that one must 'see the relevance of the play's themes [to] her description of her object' ('Expressive Form', 164).

[124] For Evadne as an inverted 'caricature' of the Girl, see Loraux, *The Invention of Athens*, 108.

appears in *Suppliant Women*: Evadne's actions explode the possibilities of Aithra's self-conscious transgression. (In this context it is worth mentioning that the same actor probably played both Aithra and Evadne.)[125] Indeed, verbal and thematic parallels between the two scenes invite comparison. In both cases, men enter in anxious pursuit of female relatives. Evadne escapes from spatial constraints (*ephroureite' en domois*, 1041) much like those imposed on the Athenian queen (*phrouroisi m'* . . . *en kyklōi*, 103); her lyrical ravings are *neōteroi logoi*, untoward utterances that realize the danger implicit in Aithra's anomalous absence from home (*mē moi ti mētēr* . . . *ekhēi neon*, 89 ff.); declaring her independence from men's attempts to regulate her movement, Evadne thrusts away her father's restraining hand (*m' helōn kheri*, 1069), boldly reversing the terms of Aithra's submissive exit on her son's arm back to her dead husband's house (*pros oikous* . . . *agō, philēn synapsas kheira*, 360 f.). Most tellingly, Evadne's *pantolmon* action is a grotesque answer for Aithra's call for men to be *tolmēros* on behalf of the helpless (305). Like that of the Girl, Aithra's actions were successfully regulated, serving both family and state; Evadne's actions, however—like those of Alkmene—serve only herself. Indeed, her grief-maddened, precipitous flight into space, undertaken in order to satisfy her fantasies of erotic reunion, amounts to a parody of the deaths of Aglauros and the Kekropidai who, after being driven mad by Athena, jumped from the fatal heights of the Akropolis, thereby becoming tutelary deities of the city and providing the Girl in *Children of Herakles* with a model for her own civic-minded gesture of self-sacrifice.

Evadne's 'mad scene' explores dangerous extremes, both masculine and feminine. Her hyperbolic gestures and self-destructive rhetoric remind us that the feminine itself is only relatively, rather than absolutely, useful in forging a new kind of heroism: it, too, can be excessive—as the use of feminine extremes throughout the play as a symbolic and structural parallel to unbridled masculine heroism has shown. Her spectacular and illicit escape from male control is in fact quite seamlessly linked to her self-heroization and self-conscious imitation of her hubristic husband, the most notorious example of the threat

---

[125] Smith, 'Expressive Form', 164.

posed by uncontrolled masculine heroism to the *polis*: once more, extremes of feminine and masculine behaviour collapse into each other. Evadne, like Alkmene, seizes the imagination suddenly, explosively: both are women in the throes of emotions whose origins we are invited to examine even as we recoil from their terrible consequences.

Sharing Oedipus' Fate: Boundary Violation, Marriage, and the Unclean Riddle

> ἰὼ τάλας·
> μετέλαχες τύχας Οἰδιπόδα, γέρον,
> μέρος καὶ σὺ ⟨καὶ⟩ πόλις ἐμὰ τλάμων.

O wretched man!
In Oedipus' fate, old sir, you've taken
a share (*meros*)—you and my wretched city!

(1077–9)

Thus the chorus describe Iphis' misfortune, the last in a long series set in motion by Oedipus. On the face of it, they refer to Oedipus' curse: and indeed the 'share', *meros*, that Iphis now gets is the grim result of Adrastos' attempt to help his son-in-law Polyneikes secure his own rightful share of his father Oedipus' estate, *Oidipou panklērias meros* (15). Adrastos' meddling led first to the disastrous expedition of the Seven, thence to the death of Kapaneus, and now to that of Evadne as well; hence Iphis' sorrowful state.

Yet the connections between the fate of Evadne and the case of Oedipus are, perhaps, more than these merely circumstantial ones. For the chorus's interjection here comes immediately after the overwrought exchange between Iphis and his daughter. The themes of that exchange—oracular riddles, unwholesome marriages—are indeed 'Oedipal'. By recapitulating them here, Euripides finally brings his critique of extremism (for which his carefully wrought 'matrimonial' model is the vehicle) full circle.

As I have already described, those themes are introduced in Aithra's prologue speech. In orchestrating a fulfilment of Apollo's oracle, Pittheus engineered a successful marriage that mediated between Troizen and Athens. As such, his success stands in vivid contrast to Adrastos' disastrous response to another of Apollo's oracles. We have seen how Adrastos' impetuous marriage-making was a kind of hyperbole of exogamy, its methods and aims a perversion of those normally associated with marriages contracted between persons and states; his perhaps over-hasty solution to the riddling Apolline injunction similarly represents a dangerous abandonment of civilized norms. For we should remember that Theseus counts oracular communication among the blessings that the gods have given men as part of their ordering of the chaotic universe (201 ff.); oracles articulate (*prosēmainousin*, 213) that which would otherwise remain 'inarticulate and unknowable' (*asēma k'ou saphōs gignōskomen*, 211).[126] At first, Theseus is non-committal in his assessment of Adrastos's skill at interpreting these god-given communications; he merely expresses amazed curiosity about Adrastos' 'unravelling' (*exelisseis*, 141) of Apollo's peculiar command. However, subsequent details cast doubt on Adrastos' troubled relations to the mantic arts in general. He failed to consult the seer Amphiaraos when deciding on whether to go to war (155 ff.), an error that he himself admits was a terrible mistake (*esphalēn*, 156), and one that Theseus reacts to with dismay (155, 157, 159). All this prepares us for the suggestion, made by Theseus, that the Argive king's solution to Apollo's riddle was somehow the wrong one. Neither Theseus nor Euripides indicates what Adrastos ought to have made of the oracle; but the Athenian king is quite emphatic that Adrastos acted in wanton violation of the god's decree:

ἧς καὶ σὺ φαίνῃ δεκάδος, οὐ σοφὸς γεγώς,
ὅστις κόρας μὲν θεσφάτοις Φοίβου ζυγεὶς
ξένοισιν ὧδ' ἔδωκας ὡς δώντων θεῶν . . .[127]

. . . in whose number you yourself now figure, proving yourself
   unwise—
you who, though yoked by the oracles of Phoibos,
gave your daughters to foreigners as though the gods so ordained it . . .
                                                                     (219–21)

[126] For a quite different interpretation of Theseus' attitude towards the oracle in this scene, see the discussion of Conacher ('Religious and Ethical Attitudes', 17–21). Conacher argues that Theseus' 'criticism of Adrastos *includes* his allegiance to Delphi', and that the exchange amounts to a condemnation of Delphi (18); so too Garzya, *Pensiero e tecnica*, 59.

[127] Nearly all commentators agree that the force of ὡς δόντων θεῶν (221) is adversative—'as if the gods so ordained it'. *Thesphata*, 'oracles', at 230 is the object of *atimasas*, 'dishonoured', since the main thought remains Adrastos' attitude towards augury.

and:

> ἐς δὲ στρατείαν πάντας Ἀργείους ἄγων,
> μάντεων λεγόντων θέσφατ᾽, εἶτ᾽ ἀτιμάσας
> βίᾳ παρελθὼν θεοὺς ἀπώλεσας πόλιν. . .

. . . you led all the Argives into the host
even as the prophets gave the oracles (*thesphata*); dishonouring
   them [the oracles]
and violently flouting the gods themselves, you destroyed your
   city. . .

(229–31)

Adrastos' wilful disregard for divination at the time of the expedition against Thebes retroactively colours our understanding of his interpretation of the oracle regarding his daughters' unions. The result of that interpretation was, as I have pointed out, a further sign of his tendency to violate gendered, cultural, and political norms. Adrastos maintained the integrity of neither his house nor his city; in marrying off his daughters, he chose *xenoi* over citizens, youthful rashness over adult prudence, the bestial over the human. All this constitutes an indiscriminate mixing, *symmeixis* (224), of his house with that of Oedipus, and thereby blurs the kinds of distinctions that, as Theseus approvingly notes, the gods themselves had ordered.

The monstrous offspring of this *symmeixis* is the destruction of the city (231). Hence Adrastos' solution to Apollo's 'difficult riddle' (*dystopast' ainigmata*, 138) achieves precisely the opposite of the goal towards which *ekdosis*, as exemplified by the marriage of Aithra, is properly directed. Unlike Pittheus' son-in-law, who returns home peacefully and contracts an alliance en route that will add to his patrimony, Polyneikes and Tydeus are outlaws who have fled the boundaries of their native lands, one of them stained by kin's blood (168), the other bent on returning home to wage armed conflict that will bring about a similar pollution. Unlike the marriage that Pittheus so craftily engineered as a fulfilment of Delphi's pronouncement, the indiscriminate couplings that Adrastos arranges bring about the destruction of both the cities involved, his own and that of his son-in-law—the latter twice, once before the play opens and again during its action.

As I have already mentioned, the implicitly erotic language

used by Theseus to describe Adrastos' unlucky couplings finds its match in the language that Evadne uses to describe her erotic/heroic devotion to the dead Kapaneus. Echoing his insistent repetition of *symmeignunai* (222, 224), she vows to couple with, *symmeixasa*, her husband's dead body (1020); to die with him (*synthnēskein*, 1007; *synthanousa*, 1063) in a quasi-erotic embrace that will be consummated by burning her own body on the pyre together with his own (*sympyroumenoi posei*, 1071; cf. *syntēkhtheis*, 1029). Loraux has also seen in Evadne's final action a 'drastic reordering' of the normal: 'To die with [is a] tragic way for a woman to go to the extreme limit of marriage, by, it must be said, drastically reordering events, since it is in death that "living with" her husband will be achieved.' Interestingly enough, Loraux goes on to compare Evadne's radical reconfiguration of familial life with that of Oedipus' mother who, in another Euripidean drama, *Phoenician Women*, articulates a very similar need to 'die with':

Yet there is one woman, a mother rather than a wife—or, more precisely, a mother to excess—who displaces 'dying with' in the direction of maternity. I mean the Jocasta of Euripides, who, in keeping with her destiny as an incestuous mother, dies with the death of her sons and, 'dead, rests on her well-loved ones, embracing them both in her arms.'[128]

Evadne's failure to acknowledge crucial boundaries—between living and dead, between mourner and mourned, between husband and wife, between male and female—can now be seen not only as a kind of lyric cadenza that recapitulates Adrastos' error, but as a recapitulation of tragic myth's most famous case of a failure to maintain boundaries within the family: that of Oedipus and Jocasta who, most famously of all mythic figures, brought ruin on themselves, their family, and their city precisely because they blurred crucial distinctions as a result of sexual *symmeixis*.[129]

[128] Both citations from Loraux, *Tragic Ways of Killing a Woman*, 26.

[129] Rehm has also noted the 'hyper-endogamy' of the Theban royal family in contrast to the 'hyper-exogamy' of the Argive union presented in this play (*Marriage to Death*, 114). We may take Adrastos's desperate cry at 769—'alas, how very much I'd like to die with (*synthanein*) them!'—as the final marker of his resemblance to the women in the chorus, who also exclaim how much they would like to die with (*oloimēn syn*) their children (796f.). Here the death-seeking, self-indulgent ethos of *synthanein* becomes a grotesque exaggeration of

Evadne's attempt to erase such distinctions, emblematized by her transgressive *symmeixis* and desire to 'die with', *synthanein*, is labelled an 'unwholesome riddle', *sathron ainigma*, by her father. This detail is one that further unites the themes and action of *Suppliant Women*'s Adrastos and Evadne episodes with those associated with the mythic narrative of Oedipus himself, tragedy's most famous victim of riddling Apolline oracles concerning marriage. Iphis' 'share in the fate of Oedipus', then, is more than merely circumstantial. *Suppliant Women* recapitulates important 'Oedipal' motifs, while effectively adapting them for the particular political concerns of this play.

The Travesties of Grief

Evadne's escape and suicide realize the transgressive threat inherent in Aithra's early intervention. Just as the latter softened Theseus' stance, resulting in his assumption of Demeter's role, so too does the former now force another male character to 'play' Demeter. This gendered displacement and role-playing, whose operations I have described in *Children of Herakles*, have been identified by Loraux in Euripides' *Alkestis*:

Since a fine death is essentially virile and the loyal wife has taken the man's place, this *tolma* has the recoil effect of feminizing the well-loved husband. He is driven to become the mother as well as the father of their children, and condemned to live henceforward cloistered like a virgin or chaste as a bride inside the palace, which his wife has left to join the open spaces of manly heroism.[130]

We detect an almost identical pattern in *Suppliant Women*. A grief-stricken Iphis enacts the role of a mourning parent, and we may indeed see in him something of Oedipus himself. But as before in this play, his words and gestures are inflected by the Demetrian and Eleusinian narrative that frames the play as a whole, and we therefore see him most of all as the third and last of the play's male figures who 'plays' Demeter.

the feminine violation of self–other boundaries as he once more melds into the chorus, as he began. Fittingly, then, the Argive king will henceforth allow himself to be led by the women of the chorus, whom he calls his *didaskaloi* (771)—a word that can mean both 'teacher' and 'dramatic poet'.

[130] *Tragic Ways of Killing a Woman*, 29. Loraux later compares Evadne to Alkestis.

Yet the grief of this Demetrian Iphis, which so movingly endorses an end to the self-glorifying violence that caused it, is pitted in the play's coda against the warlike utterances of the sons of the Seven. And it is their protectress, the vengeful and warlike Athena—a female who yet so often plays a masculine role—who appears *ex machina* to close *Suppliant Women* in the play's final, haunting irony.

Demetrian Iphis: The Maternal Father

Iphis is overcome by grief at the loss of his two children (1080). He utters a wish that is frequently repeated by Euripides' old men: that is, to have two lives to live, in order that one might correct during the second the errors of the first.[131] This is, of course, the wish expressed by Iolaos (*Hkld.* 796), for whom it comes supernaturally true. Iphis, on the other hand, crushed by an overwhelming sorrow, is reduced to the same abject and feminine postures that his dramatic counterpart had once assumed. He demands to be led back home, to be hidden within the confines of the same house from which Evadne had escaped (*m' axete' es domous*, 1104f.). There, in the dark (*skotōi*, 1105) interior of the empty house (*erēmian*, 1095), he will waste away in grief, much like the Argive mothers themselves, who also have only memories to return to (973). Iphis' feminized retreat to the inside of his house thus inverts the circumstances of Evadne's 'heroic' escape, which of course precipitated the old man's exit from the stage; it is noteworthy that Iphis is too traumatized to attend to his children's own funeral rites (1107). His mournful contemplation of a lifetime of grief recalls the chorus's musings on their *dysaion bioton*.

More specifically, however, Iphis resembles Demeter herself. His big scene in fact recapitulates actions and words associated with that goddess's grief, as it is described in the Homeric hymn that shadows this play. The groundwork for this comparison is laid by Evadne herself, who sees herself as a Kore-like bride destined for Hades (995–1005); she declares her intention to join her husband in 'Persephone's marriage-chamber' (1022). Given that comparison, it is hard not to see a corresponding likeness

---

[131] Cf. *HF* 655 ff., *Hkld.* 740 ff., and see Collard's note ad loc. for a brief summary of this topos in Greek literature, starting at Theognis 1009 ff.

between the grief-stricken Iphis, venting sorrowful rage over his daughter's untimely descent into Hades, and Demeter herself. The parallels between the two figures seem, indeed, to be more than general; they appear to include specific references to both the Hymn as well as to Eleusinian cult. In the hymn, the grief-stricken Demeter, embittered at the gods, withdraws from their company (90–4). Disguised as an old crone, she wanders among the towns and fields of mortals, finally halting at Eleusis, where she grieves in the shade of an olive tree (*H. h. Cer.* 98–100). After being taken in by Keleus' daughters, she recreates that grief-stricken pose (*H. h. Cer.* 197–201), withdrawing from the fellowship offered by the young women, refusing food and drink as she had earlier refused divine ambrosia and nectar (50), and retreating into veiled darkness, where she pines away with longing (*pothōi*, 201, 304) for her departed child. Like the Hymn's Demeter, Iphis too has searched frantically for a daughter (*Su.* 1038); he too perishes with longing, *pothos*, for his lost children (*Su.* 1088). Having lost his own children, Iphis now vows to withdraw from the world to the inside of his house where he chooses to waste away in grief:[132]

> οὐχ ὡς τάχιστα δῆτά μ' ἄξετ' ἐς δόμους
> σκότῳ τε δώσετ', ἔνθ' ἀσιτίαις ἐμὸν
> δέμας γεραιὸν συντακεὶς ἀποφθερῶ;

Won't you then take me in all haste back to the house,
and surrender me to the darkness (*skotōi*) where, through fasting,
I might waste away my aged body and thereby die?

(1104–6)

To be sure, Demeter is not the only model for this reaction to a child's loss; Homer's Priam fasts in mourning for his dead son in *Iliad* 24. But this play's Eleusinian setting and overarching Demetrian themes make the comparison with Demeter herself difficult to escape. Demeter, of course, is 'immortal and ageless forever'; Iphis, a mortal, can only look forward to a bleak and wretched old age which he curses, inviting instead his own death and the advent of a new generation (1112 f.). For him, the

---

[132] For the withdrawal of the sorrowing mother into darkness, both in the Hymn and in tragedy (cf. *Hekabe* 487), see the discussion of Loraux, *Les Mères en deuil*, 67–73; and cf. Laura Slatkin, 'The Wrath of Thetis', *TAPA* 116 (1986), 1–24.

prospect of prolonging life by means of potions and mystical spells offers no comfort.[133]

The Epigonoi *and the Parodies of Mourning*

Like the bereaved mothers whom he is made to resemble, Iphis, rather than his daughter, is the real victim in *Suppliant Women*. Yet Iphis' Demetrian bereavement, which reminds us of the terrible consequences of violence—Polyneikes', Theseus', Evadne's, Hades'—does not close the play. It is a measure of Euripides' pessimism that his play ends with a startling re-emergence of the same kind of heroic aggression that first triggered its action. The play's distinctive structural mechanism —an ongoing series of juxtapositions of alternating masculine and feminine types—culminates in the lengthy final dirge (1114–64), a *kommos* that features competing hemichoruses, one of grieving mothers, the other of the *epigonoi*, the sons of the Seven, hungry for vengeance.

The appearance of the boys appears at first to be a fulfilment of Iphis' parting wish: they are the *neoi* to whom the old generation cedes the stage. But their kommatic moment is a brief one; indeed, the boys transform the healing moment of ritual lament into a call for arms. Following his children's deaths Iphis had bitterly foreseen a great void at home (*pollēn erēmian melathrōn*, 1095 f.); the vengeful sons of the Seven, devoid (*erēmos*) of their illustrious fathers, are destined to be orphaned in their own empty homes (*erēmon oikon*, 1132 f.). For them, this grief must be assuaged in a new cycle of avenging violence (*antiteisomai son phonon*, 1143 ff.). Their cries for justice (1151) are contrasted with, yet ultimately overwhelm, the protests of their despairing grandmothers, who alone understand that peace will only come if the cycle of vengeful violence is at least broken: 'will this evil never sleep?', they ask, crying that they have had enough of wail-

---

[133] Iphis' reference to special diets and spells, *mageumata*, that some foolish people employ to prolong their lives (1110f.) might be intended to put us in mind of the Eleusinian rites themselves (e.g. the drinking of the ritual potion called *kykeōn*). Goff ('Aithra at Eleusis', 69) has also noted the similarities between the Iphis-Evadne drama and the Eleusinian myth; but whereas I am interested in seeing the points of contact, she stresses the 'intriguing displacements of the Eleusinian material', i.e., that it is a father rather than a mother here who seeks a lost daughter—just as at the beginning, in a kind of structural chiasmus, the grieving mothers mourn lost sons rather than a daughter.

ing, enough of woe (*halis goōn, halis ⟨d'⟩ algeōn*, 1146–8).[134] We hear in their words an echo of Adrastos' parting exhortation that the only relief from violence (*phonoi/ponoi*, 950f., the latter being the standard word for heroic exploits) will come by integrating *hēsykhia* (952).

Parodies of Demeter: Athena Plays Evadne

The spectre of a continuing blood-feud 'sleeping' in anticipation of the next generation is, of course, the famous preoccupation of Aeschylus' *Oresteia*. Some have seen in *Suppliant Women*'s closing moments a sardonic parody of the earlier work's dénouement in the *Eumenides*—a play whose grand concluding civic spectacle is recalled here as well.[135] Indeed, the *ex machina* appearance that closes *Suppliant Women* is not that of Demeter, to whom the prologic prayers are addressed and indeed who is the goddess best suited to ensuring a 'new fertility of civilization', but Athena, that most ambiguous of female gods with respect to gender, who indeed plays a comparably decisive role in the *Eumenides*. But rather than being the instrument of closure, *Suppliant Women*'s Athena appears *ex machina* in order to ensure that the cycle of revenge will *continue* into a new generation (1213–25); the pact that she demands, complete with elaborate ritual details and sacred sanctions, makes a mockery of Athena's decisive role in bringing the *Oresteia*'s violence to a close.

The complex and unsettling nature of Athena's role in this scene is underscored in several ways. First, her triple repetition of the word *khthōn*, 'earth' (1185, 1191, 1195), recalls a similar

---

[134] The brief valedictory appearances of Theseus and Adrastos (1165–82) do not put to rest the spectre of that cycle of reciprocal aggression. If anything, the Athenian king's appeal to Adrastos for due remembrance of good deeds done (1173) seems like an awkward attempt to whitewash the darker implications of the principle of *antidrān*, tit-for-tat, invoked by Theseus (1169f.) and acknowledged by Adrastos (1179)—implications realized in the boys' calls for an avenger (1151).

[135] For similarities between the two plays, see Smith, 'Expressive Form', 166f. It is worth noting in this context that the eerie metaphor that the *Suppliants'* chorus uses to describe the cycle of vengeance, 'sleeping' at 1146, reprises a similar one in Aeschylus' *Libation Bearers* (*Cho.* 1075). As noted above, Whitehorne suggests that this play's magnificent Funeral scene would have recalled the finale of *Eumenides* ('The Dead as Spectacle', 68f.); if so, *Suppliant Women*'s inversions of certain elements from *Eumenides* would have stood out all the more clearly.

pattern in Aithra's prologue, where the reiteration of that word, in the context of the queen's fertility sacrifice, served to accentuate Demetrian themes. But here, the invocation of Demeter seems to play havoc with those themes. Athena instructs Theseus to cast the knife with which he performed the sacrifice that sealed Athens' alliance with Argos 'into the recesses of the earth' (*es gaias mykhous*, 1206). The action is intended, perhaps, to call to mind the Demetrian ritual of casting the *thesmoi* into the earth during the Skira festival in preparation for their exhumation during the Thesmophoria. But what *es gaias mykhous* surely reminds us of is the autochthonous sowing associated not with the origin of the Athenians, but with that of their Theban foes, the 'Sown Men'; for indeed the 'fruit' that Theseus' perverted 'sowing' brings forth is not vegetable abundance, but the warrior *epigonoi* who will avenge their dead fathers (1215). This, then, is a gruesome and ironic fulfilment of Theseus' sarcastic query to the Theban Herald (in a speech that itself contains three instances of *khthōn*: 523, 543, 545): 'Or [do you fear that the dead bodies of the Seven] will bring forth children in the depths of the earth, *en mykhois khthonos*, from whom some kind of vengeance will arise?' (545 f.).

The closure that Euripides' Athena brings, perverting Demetrian gestures and themes, also implicitly mocks Iphis' tender recollections of the joys of having and rearing children. The warrior goddess seems to see the children as little more than mechanical replicas of their warrior fathers. The sons will one day 'stand in for' the fathers (*anti patros*, 1216) in order to avenge them (*ekdikazontes*, 1215); when 'the lions' cubs are fully grown', *ektethrammenoi* | *skymnoi leontōn*, they will become 'sackers of the city', *poleōs ekporthētores* (1223: in stark contrast, as we will recall, to Theseus, who has shown great restraint in attacking an inimical city). It is possible, as Smith argues, that the reference to the boys as being 'lions' cubs' is a further allusion to the *Oresteia*—with the crucial difference, as he points out, that here, '*pathos* does not bring *mathos*'.[136] But we need not cast about so far from the text to find dark meaning in this striking locution. To describe the sons of the Seven as lion cubs is, after all, to bring the drama back full circle to the motif of bestiality, to a world of

---

[136] Smith, 'Expressive Form', 166–7.

humans cast as wild beasts—boars, lions, the beasts to whom Adrastos so fatally married his daughters—the world, in other words, that the play has struggled in so many ways to leave behind.

In addition, the goddess's ferocious attitude is unsettlingly at odds with Iphis' earlier, offhand reference to the goddess as the docile protectress of women who do domestic chores (1062). Iphis had assumed that Evadne wanted to surpass all other women in 'the works of Athena', by which he meant the traditionally feminine tasks of sewing and weaving. That characterization bore an unintentional irony whose full force becomes apparent only now; it turned out that it was in imitation of Athena's other, martial aspect that Evadne sought to distinguish herself. The goddess who now appears, like Evadne, on the roof of the *skēnē* is as single-minded in her endorsement of warfare and revenge as Evadne herself had been in rejecting a conventional reading of 'Athena's work' in favour of her own heroic agenda.

Indeed, the figure that Athena cuts is remarkably similar to that presented by Evadne. Both characters make sudden and startling appearances high above the *orkhēstra*; both champion an undying devotion to the dead, and warn against the consequences of betrayal (the implication of Evadne's *prodousa*, 1024; cf. Athena at 1194); and the promise of heroic praise is exalted by both female figures as sufficient inducement to heroic deeds (cf. Evadne 1055, 1059, and 1067, and Athena's promise to the Epigonoi at 1225 that they will earn the epic praise, *ōidas*, of later generations). Athena's epiphany is the fullest expression of Evadne's inchoate dream—the heroized female par excellence. The warlike, man-like goddess promotes future violence in a way that responds directly to the boys' prayers (her 'avenging', *ekdikazontes*, at 1215 cannily addresses the boys' wish for an 'avenger', *ekdikastan*, at 1151), and erases the memories of the chorus's and Iphis' bereavement. Her victory over Demeter is complete. Her presence and her words valorize the vengeful and self-interested ethos that has brought ruin to all of the play's characters save Theseus.

If Theseus' first capitulation to a female figure may be said to have heralded a positive integration of Demetrian values, this second and equally immediate surrender has more dire implications. Earlier, Iphis had lamented the fact that men did not have a second lifetime in which to 'set right again' (*exōrthoumeth'*) the 'errors' (*exēmartanen*) of the first (1086); had he known the misery to which the loss of his children would reduce them, he would not have had them. That loss, of course, was brought about by the very pattern of violence that Athena now champions. Now, in an uncomfortable echo of the grieving old man's words, Theseus entrusts himself and his city to Athena: 'Set me in the right (*anorthois*) that I might not err (*examartanein*)', he declares at 1228 f., 'And do still keep me in the right' (*es orthon*). If the only hope that *Suppliant Women* can offer is that Theseus and Athens may be exempted from the cycle of violence,[137] then a final irony, implicit in the Athenian king's words, seems to put that hope forever to sleep.

Our examination of the interweaving of space, gender, and politics in *Suppliant Women* seems to have taken us far from Demeter's sacred precinct at Eleusis, with its almost overwhelming associations with the feminine, bringing us instead to a dramatic conclusion in the public and political space where Athenian policy is decided, its treaties concluded, and its alliances sealed. Yet as we have seen, the play's gendered and civic discourses are intricately and inextricably intertwined. From among the drama's tableaux of male and female characters and the competing ideologies they represent, the citizen spectator, and indeed the city itself, is invited to choose.

The final appearance of Athens' tutelary deity, always ambiguous with respect to gender, symbolizes the difficulty of that choice. Perikles in his Funeral Oration idealizes the democratic *polis* as a place in which valour and refinement, daring bravery and judicious discussion, all coexist in perfect equipoise (Thuc. 2. 39–40). This is the harmony between poles which Athena herself, who is both Erganê and Promakhos, Athena of the Handiworks and Athena Who Leads in Battle, would seem ideally to embody. But the goddess who appears at the end of Euripides' drama instantiates an unregulated and violent extreme. Read in this light, the play seems less an encomium than a warning. It was, as we know, an admonition that went

---

[137] So Smith, 'Expressive Form', 167.

unheeded; Theseus' decision to follow his glittering and vengeful goddess was to prove prophetic. *Suppliant Women* was produced halfway through the first part of the Peloponnesian
War—a fifteen-year period that began with Perikles' sage
endorsement of military restraint and ended with Alkibiades'
fatal glamour, and the Sicilian disaster. Like Theseus in the play,
the Athenians were beguiled. Like him, they chose badly.

4

Conclusion

We are surely right to consider (and to interpret) Euripides' *Children of Herakles* and *Suppliant Women* as a pair. Not because both are encomia of Athens, as these plays' previous champions have argued; or because both are badly constructed and contain extraneous references to contemporary fifth-century politics and politicians; or even because each dramatizes one of the two frequently paired political (and politicized) myths that were central to Athenian civic self-identity in the second half of the fifth century: the myth of Athenian assistance to the (Peloponnesian) children of Herakles, and the myth of Athenian assistance to the (Peloponnesian) families of the Seven. No: it seems right to study these works together, rather, because both are the remarkably similar products of a moment in the playwright's—and Athens' —careers. That moment, in the early stages of a (Peloponnesian) War—a conflict with a foe who was ideologically and culturally different, if not in fact opposite—made those myths particularly suggestive as vehicles for re-examination of what it meant to be Athenian in the first place. What it was, in other words, to be the Athenian selves for whom those once-pathetic Peloponnesians had now, in real historical time, become the hated others.

Since we have some idea of what those myths about Athenians and Peloponnesians looked like before Euripides got hold of them, it is easy to see that these works are not, in fact, anomalous within the playwright's oeuvre—that other too-common cavil— but instead reflect quite characteristic personal tastes and reveal very familiar dramatic purposes. Above all, those tastes reflect a very particular interest in the world of women: not real women, perhaps, but women—passive and active, pathetic and angry, suicidal and murderous— as symbols for emotional experiences, actions, and energies that were culturally and ideologically prohibited to men. It has been the case that sometimes the playwright's prescient 'psychological' handling of these feminine extremes threatens to absorb our attention to the exclusion of all other considerations, especially overtly political ones. Here one thinks of the *Alkestis*, the *Medea*, the *Hekabe*; and indeed it is no accident that these eponymous heroines have become iconic, in the later and much more overtly psychologizing Western dramatic tradition, as types of women: self-effacing wife, vengeful infanticide, maddened, bestial murderess.

Yet sometimes a slightly different dramatic perspective, and therefore a different purpose, are evident. From this dramatic perspective, the *polis* itself rather than human psychology (female or male) as we know it today appears to be the object of tragic examination. Accordingly, the representation of feminine emotion and suffering should be seen as a means rather than an apparent theatrical end in itself—a means of critiquing, sometimes with mordant irony, the political decisions of powerful men in the real historical world, by showing the effects of those decisions on others: females, children, the weak, non-Greeks. Here it is difficult not to think of Euripides' war plays such as *Trojan Women*, the two Iphigeneia dramas, and the fantastical but strangely bitter *Helen*, dramas that even now seem able to comment with devastating irony upon the destruction wreaked by political decisions made by men in the service of greedy, aggressive, or heroic impulses. It is no accident, moreover, that in the first, 'psychological' grouping, it is the women's activity— whether suicidal or, as more usually, murderous—that has consistently fired the cultural imagination; in the second, 'political' grouping, it is their passivity, their suffering, that has become iconic.

In response to the grim current events during Athens' war with Sparta—events that showed men either about to make or, later, actually making some very bad political decisions indeed— it seems inevitable that Euripides' penchant for lavishing his dramatic and poetic gifts on the representation of the feminine (already demonstrated, by the time the two plays we have been examining had been composed, in works such as *Alkestis* and *Medea*) would result in a highly idiosyncratic adaptation of the two political myths he chose to dramatize in the political plays. And so it did. As I have discussed, each of the political plays is composed of two opposite and complementary types of scene: a scene in which girls or women assume aspects of male identity, and another scene, immediately following the first, that shows the consequences of such virilization: that is, a feminizing transformation of the plays' men. But—perhaps unavoidably in the case of a playwright who delights in ornate doublings and reversals, and who specializes, it would seem, in two types of female protagonist—these pairings are themselves doubled in each work: in each play there are *two* scenes of feminine transgression, to which *two* scenes of masculine transformation in each play correspond. This doubling allows the poet to incorporate into each of the political plays both kinds of female characters as I have just described them: they complicate, with very interesting results, our reactions to the ostensibly 'good' and 'bad', 'active' and 'passive' female types.

The plays are, in fact, structured by intricately interrelated dynamics of activity and passivity, masculine and feminine. In the first such transformation in each work, a male figure is enhanced by a female figure—a female whose bold activity is then almost immediately transformed into pathetic passivity. The elderly Iolaos is educated in civic virtue by the intervention of the young Girl, who then becomes a human sacrifice; the youthful Theseus receives a similar education at the hands of his aged mother Aithra, who similarly makes a bold entrance only to be reduced to a culturally more appropriate passivity by the end of her moment on stage. But the second part of each of these works inverts that schema. Here, a woman's appropriation of action results in a form of feminization that, from the (inevitably, in fifth-century Athens) masculine point of view, is at once more radical and less constructive—a feminization that Segal, speaking of Admetos in the *Alkestis*, calls the 'enforced passivity and deheroization of [the] male protagonist'.[1] In *Suppliant Women*, Evadne's escape and subsequent suicide transform the once-passive girl into an agent of destruction, leading to a scene of abject grief and feminine lamentation on the part of her father; and although too little remains of *Children of Herakles*'s Alkmene-Eurystheus scene for absolute certainty about the

---

[1] Segal, 'Admetus' Divided House', 6. *Alkestis*, of course, is a play of notoriously indeterminate genre: for the debate over its status as tragedy, satyr play, or 'pro-satyric', see Lesky, 'Alkestis'; Seidensticker, *Palintonos Harmonia*, 303–20; and Peter Riemer, *Die Alkestis des Euripides* (Beiträge zur klassischen Philologie, 195; Frankfurt am Main, 1989), 1–5.

details of that finale, it is still possible to discern there the contours of a pattern much like the one we find in *Suppliant Women*, as the once-proud Eurystheus is brought low by the passionate excesses of his opponent, an old woman who begins as a pathetic sufferer and ends as a violent and vindictive avenger.

This very short review of the structure of these works as I have interpreted them suggests that there is, in fact, a single answer to the three elaborately interconnected questions that have shadowed my discussion of these plays: why these works have so consistently produced aesthetic and critical dismay; how they produce their political meanings; and, finally, how we might reconcile our two Aristophanic epigraphs—one that reduced Euripides' political drama to little more than an encomium of Athens, and one that saw Euripidean drama overall, and particularly its female characters, as capable of subverting the state.

Let us begin with aesthetic dismay. In a discussion of Euripides' earliest extant drama, *Alkestis*, Segal comments that 'like comedy, its companion dramatic form at the Dionysiac festivals, tragedy exploits and in turn creates a "carnivalesque" situation, an in-between zone of destabilized values and inversions of the expected or familiar roles.'[2] It is now possible to see Euripides' political plays, with their complex permutations of gender, as tragic examples of such carnivalesque destabilization of values and, especially, inversions of roles. The multiple transgressions that I have identified in these plays seem, in fact, to mark the crossing of one more boundary, the one to which Segal alludes: that between comic and tragic action. As scholars have long pointed out, both tragedy and comedy effect their social and political critiques by forcing men into female spaces or forcing women into domains, both literal and figurative, that are normally reserved for men.[3] Fifth-century comedy, in fact, regularly featured women's transgressive interventions into male space; strikingly, these interventions were structurally much like the ones we encounter in the two tragedies under examination. Here is how Arlene Saxonhouse describes the antics of Praxagora, the heroine of Aristophanes' *Ekklesiazousai* who plots to take over

---

[2] Segal, 'Admetus' Divided House', 14.

[3] For example, men sneak into women's territory in both *Bacchae* and *Thesmophoriazousai*; the reverse is true in *Antigone*, *Agamemnon*, and *Lysistrata*, as Segal notes ('Admetus' Divided House', 15).

the Athenian assembly and set aright the polity that has suffered woefully at the hands of men:

Rather than remaining unseen in the women's quarters, where most women spent their time, or in the shadows of the predawn conspiracy, she bursts forth into the masculine realm of public activity to speak openly in the assembly . . . The men have failed to reform Athens so that, in making speeches and passing decrees, she takes charge as if she were a man. Eager for the renown that comes to founders of cities like Theseus and great reformers like Solon and Cleisthenes, no woman 'unspoken of' is she.[4]

With very minor changes, this passage could easily serve as a description of *Suppliant Women*'s Aithra, and of the Girl in *Children of Herakles*. Saxonhouse's description allows us to see feminine transgression of masculine spaces as an element of comic action—a transgression that 'produces fun rather than fear', as Segal puts it;[5] and indeed any unsettling strangeness that may result even from these comic transgressions is soon erased by a return to the status quo, celebrated with sex and revelry in plays such as *Ekklesiazousai*, *Lysistrata*, and other works in which the confusion of gender roles is cause for amusement rather than terror. In his essay on Euripidean 'comedy', Bernard Knox cites first Northrop Frye ('an integration of society which usually takes the form of incorporating a central character into it') and then Euanthius (*illic prima turbulenta, tranquilla ultima*) on the nature and aim of comic endings.[6] Both, in fact, apply to the first instance of female intrusion and reincorporation in each of the political plays.

For Aristotle (and indeed still for us), the best tragic plots, on the other hand, are those that chart a movement in the opposite direction: from integration to expulsion, from tranquillity to turbulence, from good fortune to bad (*Poetics* 13). And indeed, what Euripides' distinctively tragic experiments with gender confusion produce is a terrifying spectacle that leads to permanent, destructive alteration of the status quo. Let us return to that final Euripidean drama, *Bacchae*, which in its elaborate and even metadramatic investigations of the nature not only

[4] Saxonhouse, *Fear of Diversity*, 5.
[5] Segal, 'Admetus' Divided House', 14.
[6] Knox, 'Euripidean Comedy', 266; cf. his note on 271.

of the self but of the theatre as well, may be the most 'tragic' of all tragedies.[7] Like Praxagora, *Bacchae's* Pentheus uses transvestitism in order to be able to participate in rituals exclusively reserved for members of the opposite sex (civic in her case, religious in his); 'against all inhibitions of shame' he dresses as a maenad in order to spy on the women's Dionysiac orgies.[8] But the Theban king ends up torn to pieces by the women whom he intended to dupe—a death that precipitates the end of the city's ruling house and the exile of its founder, Kadmos, who will eventually return at the head of an Asiatic horde to destroy the altars and cities of Greece (*Ba.* 1330–6). Perhaps it is no accident that, while the Girl and Aithra recall comic figures like Praxagora, the political plays' destructively and truly 'tragic' transgressive females recall the female principals in Euripides' great Dionysiac drama. Alkmene, unable to distinguish the claims of the *oikos* from those of the *polis*, confusing self and other, insistent on killing a younger man with her own hands—a murder that will violate the moral order (*Hkld.* 1050f.)—looks forward, in her way, to Agave, twenty-five years later. As for Evadne, she is explicitly compared to a bacchant (*Su.* 1001): her uncontrolled actions outside of the house forever alter the status quo, destroying the houses both of her father and of her husband (*Su.* 1095–7), and forcing her aged and bereaved father into a permanent seclusion—an exile within the house that will remove him, like a woman, from the world and its affairs, which he henceforth leaves to others (*Su.* 1104–13).

[7] For *Bacchae's* metadramatic elements, see first of all Helene Foley, 'The Masque of Dionysus', *TAPA* 110 (1980) 107–33. Charles Segal follows Foley's lead in 'The *Bacchae* as Metatragedy', in Burian, *Directions in Euripidean Criticism*, 156–73 (esp. 159–62 for the robing scene); Segal's comments there are greatly expanded in his *Dionysiac Poetics and Euripides' Bacchae*, ch. 7. For other appraisals of the metatheatrical aspect of Euripidean drama in general, see Froma I. Zeitlin, 'The Closet of Masks: Role-Playing and Myth-Making in the *Orestes* of Euripides', *Ramus*, 9 (1980), 51–77, with which cf. W. Geoffrey Arnott, 'Tension, Frustration and Surprise: A Study of Theatrical Techniques in Some Scenes of Euripides' *Orestes*', *Antichthon*, 17 (1983), 13–28; see also Arnott's 'Off-Stage Cries and Choral Presence: Some Challenges to Theatrical Convention in *Euripides*', *Antichthon*, 16 (1982), 35–43; and Eric Downing, '*Apate, Agon,* and Literary Self-Reflexivity in Euripides' *Helen*', in Griffith and Mastronarde, *The Cabinet of the Muses*, 1–16.

[8] The elaborate permutations of gender in *Bacchae* are the subject of Zeitlin's discussion in 'Playing the Other', *passim*.

In each of the political plays, then, two successive instances of female transgression lead to two distinct 'carnivalesque' modes, zones of strangeness in which the structures and codes of everyday life are suspended or inverted: the first of these modes is essentially comic, the second, tragic. This surely helps us to understand the long-standing critical distaste to which I referred at the outset of this discussion—distaste caused by an injection of comic elements and structures into ostensibly tragic actions, an intrusion that seems to weaken the coherence and the tragic force of those actions (just as the same plays' juxtaposition of the seemingly discrete spheres of the 'political' and the 'feminine' did). Yet the alternation between the diverse theatrical modes of comic and tragic that one finds in these plays turns out, as we have seen, to be as carefully orchestrated as are the modulations between masculine and feminine.

But if a certain kind of tragedy offers emotional and aesthetic satisfaction because it leads so inexorably from tranquillity to turbulence, requiring a sacrifice of the kind we encounter in *Bacchae*—a sacrifice, that is, of a man, preferably one that leads to the destruction and permanent alteration of the protagonist's *polis* and its institutions—Euripides' political dramas offer satisfactions of quite another kind. And here we may address the question of how these works produce their political meanings (even as we look ahead to the question of how to reconcile our two Aristophanic judgements). For what makes these plays of mixed reversal incoherent when viewed from the standpoint of maintaining the unitary integrity of either genre is also what makes them ideal vehicles for political theorizing. Each presents first a political comedy—an encomiastic action, to paraphrase Aristophanes of Byzantium—that dramatizes and seems to idealize the process by which the democratic Athenian *polis* evolved. In this action, we see how the elements of 'diversity', always potentially subversive and always efficiently represented by the feminine, are triumphantly adapted and incorporated into the service of the democratic *polis*. Yet Euripides' use of feminine and masculine here is not without its own special ironies: his intricate construction of these encomiastic episodes, his subtle feminizing redefinitions of key terms in the political vocabulary, suggests that the feminine and all it represents is indispensable in modulating and disrupting the archaic, masculine, and monolithically unitary modes that were the state's inheritance from the heroic and aristocratic systems. In *Children of Herakles*, Iolaos' single-minded allegiance to the *genos* is expanded, as a result of feminine transgression, to include the *polis*; in *Suppliant Women*, a rigid and self-serving archaic model of heroism is similarly altered so that heroism is redefined to serve the moral aims of the democratic *polis* and indeed to enforce Panhellenic law.

It is true, of course, that feminine action in these initial episodes is carefully controlled and contained; and indeed, inasmuch as Euripides' critique of archaic models in these works' first halves often takes the form of a comparison between the heroic and aristocratic mode and behaviour that is referred to—by the female characters themselves—as 'shamefully' feminine, it would seem difficult to excuse the playwright from the charge of patriarchy. As we have seen, the poet dramatizes the proper control of, or traffic in, female characters by rewarding 'good girls' and sensationalizing the catastrophes that result from the behaviour of 'bad girls'. This technique has indeed been understood as nothing more than the flat expression of patriarchal anxiety about female power and sexuality, and so some critics have recently characterized the Euripidean (and indeed the entire tragic) corpus.

But like those of his female protagonists, Euripides' own gestures with respect to gender are complex and often self-contradictory. Like the Girl in *Children of Herakles*, he has no choice but to invoke the terms of the very ideology of gender that he seeks to step beyond; like Aithra in *Suppliant Women*, he must use conventional notions of masculine and feminine behaviour in order to critique rigid conventionality, to suggest that a failure to negotiate successfully between 'masculine' and 'feminine' has disastrous consequences. This paradox is representative of a special feature of Athenian drama, which 'does its thinking in a form which is vastly more politically advanced than the society which produced Greek tragedy'.[9] To be sure, in the political plays the consequences of failed negotiations between extremes take the form of a political nightmare, one that is a patriarch's nightmare, too—a subversive female action of the sort to which the comic Aristophanes refers in my introductory epigraph, an

---

[9] Hall, 'The Sociology of Athenian Tragedy', 125.

action by a distraught woman that 'hurts the city'. (Another way of understanding such scenes, as we have seen, is as lurid worst-case enactments of catastrophic explosions of 'diversity' that has not been integrated, an explosion that results in the disintegration of familial, religious, and civic institutions.) But while dramatizing the return of repressed female passion seems to conform to a simplistic patriarchal agenda (expressed by the formula 'female energies are destructive and must be controlled'), that dramatization, given the intricate and subtle modulations of femininity and masculinity that have come before (and always keeping in mind that we must evaluate all actions by their impact on the play's *men*), can also be seen as part of a decidedly non-patriarchal argument for the assimilation of the feminine, of otherness, of diversity ('the feminine and all it represents has value and should be incorporated into our current, incomplete model of selfhood'). Hence the second, 'nightmarish', and truly tragic actions of these plays may be seen less as dramatizations of 'bad' female energies than as implicit condemnations of the exclusion of the feminine; they remind us that even the better, more highly inflected model of selfhood that the plays appear to endorse—the assimilation into an ideal unity—inevitably exacts terrible costs, always leaving a tragic residue, a disdained (as Alkmene puts it) 'someone'. Anxiety about the return of the repressed inevitably contains within it a condemnation of the repression itself.

Rather than being an anomaly in Euripidean theatre, then, this pattern of oscillation between competing models, this exploration of opposite types and genres as a way of calling norms into question and positing a tentative middle ground is, if anything, typically Euripidean, and argues against a dismissal of the poet and his works as 'patriarchal'.[10] Oscillation, conflict, equilibrium, negotiation: these provide our plays not just with their

[10] A recent and stimulating discussion of Euripides' *Medea* along these lines is the one by Christiane Sourvinou-Inwood, 'Medea at a Shifting Distance: Images and Euripidean Tragedy', in James J. Clauss and Sarah Iles Johnston (eds.), *Medea: Essays on Medea in Myth, Literature, Philosophy, and Art* (Princeton, 1997), 253–96. Sourvinou-Inwood argues that Euripides keeps moving his ambiguous heroine between opposing conceptual categories ('good' and 'bad', 'immortal' and 'mortal', 'Greek' and 'Oriental') in order to call the norm into question. Her conclusion, like mine, is that the oppositions are 'less stable than is often assumed' (p. 296).

subject matter, but with their very structure; and in so doing they constitute, in themselves, the answer to our three-part question.[11] It was perhaps inevitable that so many critics of these works should have made the very error that Euripides seems to have been critiquing here: seeking a monolithic unity of tone, theme, and genre when faced with supple and destabilizing diversity, failing to see that contradiction and conflict were, in a way, the answer rather than the question. Only after we have understood the way in which *Children of Herakles* and *Suppliant Women* are constituted as living theatrical examples of the complex and elusive principle of negotiation can we see them as coherent and especially apt dramatic investigations of the nature of the democratic *polis*—which is to say, as truly 'political' plays.

[11] Christopher Pelling rightly emphasizes tragedy's participation in civic discourse as a dynamic 'exploration' rather than static 'exposition' (*Greek Tragedy and the Historian* (Oxford, 1997), 235).

BIBLIOGRAPHY

Except where otherwise noted, the texts I have followed are those of Diggle's Oxford editions: *Euripidis Fabulae*, vol. i (Oxford, 1981) (for *Children of Herakles*); vol. ii (Oxford, 1984) (for *Suppliant Women*).

TEXTS AND COMMENTARIES

Euripides

AMMENDOLA, GIUSEPPE, *Euripide Supplici* (Turin, 1956).
AUSTIN, C., *Nova fragmenta Euripidis in papyris reperta* (Berlin, 1968).
CARRARA, P., *Eretteo* (Florence, 1977).
COLLARD, CHRISTOPHER, *Euripides Supplices, edited with Introduction and Commentary*, 2 vols. (Groningen, 1975).
DIGGLE, J., *Euripides' Phaethon* (Cambridge, 1970).
——*Euripidis Fabulae*, 3 vols. (Oxford, 1981, 1984, 1994).
DINDORF, W., *Scholia graeca in Euripidis tragoedias* (Oxford, 1963).
DONOVAN, B. E., *Euripides Papyri* (New Haven, 1969).
GARZYA, ANTONIO, *Euripide Eraclidi* (Milan, 1958).
HERMANN, G., *Euripidis Supplices* (Leipzig, 1811).
JERRAM, C. S., *Heracleidae*, 2nd edn. (Oxford, 1907).
KIRCHHOFF, A., *Euripides tragoediae* (Berlin, 1855).
MARKLAND, I., *Euripidis drama Supplices mulieres* (London, 1763).
MASTRONARDE, DONALD J., *Euripides Phoenissae* (Cambridge, 1994).
MATTHIAE, A., *Euripidis tragoediae et fragmenta*, 10 vols. (Leipzig, 1813–37).
MÉRIDIER, LOUIS, *Euripide*, vols. i, ii (Paris, 1956).
MURRAY, GILBERT, *Euripidis Fabulae*, 3 vols. (Oxford, 1935).
NAUCK, AUGUSTUS, *Euripidis Tragoediae* (Leipzig, 1924).
PAGE, DENYS, *Euripides: Medea* (Oxford, 1937).
PARMENTIER, L., and GRÉGOIRE, H., *Euripide* (Paris, 1923).
PEARSON, A. C., *Heracleidae* (Oxford, 1907).
SCHWARTZ, E., *Scholia in Euripidem*, 2 vols. (1887–91; repr. Berlin, 1966).
WILKINS, JOHN, *Euripides* Heraclidae: *with Introduction and Commentary* (Oxford, 1993).
WILAMOWITZ-MÖLLENDORF, U. VON, *Euripides Herakles*, 2 vols. (Berlin, 1895).

Other Authors, Reference Works, etc.

BROADHEAD, H. D., *The Persae of Aeschylus* (Cambridge, 1960).

DODDS, E. R., *Euripides Bacchae*, 2nd edn. (Oxford, 1960).

——*Plato: Gorgias* (Oxford, 1959).

JACOBY, FELIX, *Die Fragmente der griechischen Historiker*, 16 vols. (repr. Leiden, 1958).

JEBB, RICHARD C., *Sophocles. The Plays and Fragments with Critical Notes, Commentary, and Translation in English Prose*, 7 vols. (Cambridge, 1883–1900).

LIDDELL, H. G., SCOTT, R., and JONES, H. S., *A Greek–English Lexicon* (Oxford, 1968).

LLOYD-JONES, HUGH, *Sophoclis fabulae* (Oxford, 1990).

METTE, H. J., *Die Fragmente der Tragödien des Aischylos* (Berlin, 1959).

——*Der verlorene Aischylos* (Berlin, 1963).

NAUCK, A., *Tragicorum graecorum fragmenta. Editio correctior et addendis aucta*, ed. Bruno Snell and Richard Kannicht (Göttingen, 1986).

PAGE, D. L., *Aeschyli septem quae supersunt tragoediae* (Oxford, 1972).

——*Alcman: The Partheneion* (Oxford, 1951).

——*Poetae melici graeci* (Oxford, 1962).

RICHARDSON, N., *The Homeric Hymn to Demeter* (Oxford, 1974).

SNELL, BRUNO, *Tragicorum graecorum fragmenta*, vol. i (Göttingen, 1971).

SECONDARY MATERIAL

ADKINS, W. W. H., *Merit and Responsibility: A Study in Greek Values* (Oxford, 1960).

AÉLION, R., *Euripide héritier d'Eschyle*, 2 vols. (Paris, 1983).

ALBINI, U., 'Euripide e le pretese della retorica', *PP* 40 (1985), 354–60.

ALEXIOU, M., *The Ritual Lament in Greek Tradition* (Cambridge, 1974).

ANDERSON, J. K., 'Hoplite Weapons and Offensive Arms', in Victor Davis Hanson (ed.), *Hoplites: The Classical Greek Battle Experience* (New York, 1991), 15–37.

ARNOTT, P., *Greek Scenic Convention in the Fifth Century B. C.* (Oxford, 1962).

ARNOTT, W. GEOFFREY, 'Off-Stage Cries and Choral Presence: Some Challenges to Theatrical Convention in Euripides', *Antichthon*, 16 (1982), 35–43.

——'Tension, Frustration and Surprise: A Study of Theatrical Techniques in Some Scenes of Euripides' *Orestes*', *Antichthon*, 17 (1983), 13–28.

ARROWSMITH, WILLIAM, 'Introduction', in Henry Taylor and Robert A. Brooks (trs.), *Euripides* Children of Herakles (New York, 1981), iii–xi.

AVERY, H. C., 'Euripides' Heracleidae', *AJP* 92 (1971), 539–65.

BACON, H., *Barbarians in Greek Tragedy* (New Haven, 1961).

BAIN, D., *Actors and Audience: A Study of Asides and Related Conventions in Greek Drama* (Oxford, 1977).

BATTEZZATO, LUIGI, *Il Monologo nel Teatro di Euripide* (Pisa, 1995).

BELPASSI, LORIS, 'La "follia" del *genos*: Un'analisi del "discorso mitico" nella *Ifigenia Taurica* di Euripide', *QUCC* 34/1 (1990), 53–67.

BÉRARD, C., *Anodoi: Essai sur l'imagerie des passages chthoniens* (Neuchâtel, 1974).

BLAIKLOCK, E. M., *The Male Characters of Euripides* (Wellington, New Zealand, 1952).

BLONDELL, RUBY, GAMEL, MARY-KAY, RABINOWITZ, NANCY SORKIN, and ZWEIG, BELLA (eds.), *Women on the Edge: Four Plays by Euripides* (New York and London, 1999).

BOEGEHOLD, ALAN, 'Perikles' Citizenship Law of 451/0 B. C.', in Alan Boeghold and Adele Scafuro, *Athenian Identity and Civic Ideology* (Baltimore, 1994), 57–66.

——and SCAFURO, ADELE, (eds.), *Athenian Identity and Civic Ideology* (Baltimore, 1994).

BOWIE, A. M., 'Tragic Filters for History: Euripides' *Supplices* and Sophocles' *Philoctetes*', in Christopher Pelling (ed.), *Greek Tragedy and the Historian* (Oxford, 1997), 39–62.

BRADSHAW, DAVID J., 'The Ajax Myth and the Polis: Old Values and New', in Dora C. Pozzi and John M. Wickersham (eds.), *Myth and the Polis* (Ithaca, NY, 1991), 99–125.

BREITENBACH, W., *Untersuchungen zur Sprache der Euripideischen Lyrik* (Stuttgart, 1934).

BURIAN, PETER (ed.), *Directions in Euripidean Criticism* (Durham, NC, 1985).

——'Euripides' *Heracleidae*: An Interpretation', *CP* 72 (1977), 1–21.

——'*Logos* and *Pathos*: The Politics of the *Suppliant Women*', in Burian, *Directions in Euripidean Criticism*, 129–55.

——'Myth into *Muthos*: The Shaping of Tragic Plot', in P. E. Easterling (ed.), *The Cambridge Companion to Greek Tragedy* (Cambridge, 1997), 178–208.

BURKERT, WALTER, *Greek Religion*, tr. John Raffan (Cambridge, Mass., 1985).

——*Homo necans*, tr. Peter Bing (Berkeley, 1983).

BURNETT, ANNE PIPPIN, *Catastrophe Survived: Euripides' Plays of Mixed Reversal* (Oxford, 1971).

——'Tribe and City, Custom and Decrees in *Children of Heracles*', *CP* 71 (1976), 4–26.

CARPENTER, THOMAS H., and FARAONE, CHRISTOPHER A. (eds.), *The Masks of Dionysus* (Ithaca, NY, 1993).

CARSON, ANNE, 'Putting Her in Her Place: Woman, Dirt, and Desire', in David Halperin, John J. Winkler, and Froma I. Zeitlin (eds.), *Before Sexuality: The Construction of Erotic Experience in the Ancient World* (Princeton, 1990), 135–69.

CARTLEDGE, PAUL, 'Hoplites and Heroes: Sparta's Contribution to the Technique of Ancient Warfare', *JHS* 100 (1980), 11–27.

CASE, SUE-ELLEN, *Feminism and the Theatre* (New York, 1988).

CEADEL, E. B., 'Resolved Feet in the Trimeters of Euripides and the Chronology of the Plays', *CQ* 35 (1941), 66–89.

CHALKIA, IRÈNE, *Lieux et espace dans la tragédie d'Euripide: Essai d'analyse socio-culturelle* (Thessalonika, 1986).

CHANTRAINE, P., *Études sur le vocabulaire grec* (Paris, 1956).

CLAUSS, JAMES J., and JOHNSTON, SARAH ILES (eds.), *Medea: Essays on Medea in Myth, Literature, Philosophy, and Art* (Princeton, 1997).

CLAY, JENNY STRAUSS, *The Politics of Olympus: Form and Meaning in the Major Homeric Hymns* (Princeton, 1990).

CLÉMENT, CATHERINE, *Opera, or the Undoing of Women*, tr. Betsy Wing (Minneapolis, 1988).

COHEN, DAVID, 'Seclusion, Separation, and the Status of Women in Classical Athens', *GR* 36 (1989), 3–15.

COLLARD, CHRISTOPHER, 'Formal Debates in Euripides' Drama', *GR* 22 (1975), 58–71.

——'The Funeral Oration in Euripides' *Supplices*', *BICS* 19 (1972), 39–53.

——'Notes on Euripides' *Supplices*', *CQ* 13 (1963), 178–87.

CONACHER, DESMOND J., *Euripidean Drama: Myth, Theme and Structure* (Toronto, 1967).

——'Religious and Ethical Attitudes in Euripides' *Suppliants*', *TAPA* 87 (1956), 8–26.

CONNOR, W. ROBERT, 'The Problem of Athenian Civic Identity', in Alan Boegehold and Adele C. Scafuro (eds.), *Athenian Identity and Civic Ideology* (Baltimore, 1994), 34–41.

——'Theseus in Classical Athens', in A. G. Ward *et al.* (eds.), *The Quest for Theseus* (London, 1970), 143–74.

CROALLY, N. T., *Euripidean Polemic: The Trojan Women and the Function of Tragedy* (Cambridge, 1994).

CROPP, MARTIN, '*Herakleidai* 603–4, 630 ff., and the Question of the Mutilation of the Text', *AJP* 101 (1980), 283–86.

DALE, A. M., 'Seen and Unseen on the Greek Stage: A Study in Scenic Conventions', *WS* 69 (1956), 96–106.

DAUX, G., 'Le Serment des éphèbes athéniens', *REG* 84 (1971), 370–83.

DAVISON, JEAN M., 'Myth and the Periphery', in Dora C. Pozzi and John M. Wickersham (eds.), *Myth and the Polis* (Ithaca, NY, 1991), 49–63.

DECHARME, PAUL, *Euripides and the Spirit of his Dramas*, tr. James Loeb (New York, 1906).

DEICHGRÄBER, KARL, 'Die Kadmos-Teiresiasszene in Euripides Bakchen', *Hermes*, 70 (1935), 322–49.

DE JONG, IRENE F., *Narrative in Drama: The Art of the Euripidean Messenger-Speech* (Leiden, 1991).

——'Three Off-Stage Characters in Euripides', *Mnemosyne*, 43 (1990), 1–21.

DELEBECQUE, E., *Euripide et la guerre du Péloponnèse* (Paris, 1951).

DES BOUVRIE, SYNNØVE, *Women in Greek Tragedy* (Oslo, 1990).

DEUBNER, LUDWIG, *Attische Feste* (Berlin, 1932).

DI BENEDETTO, V., *Euripide, Teatro e società* (Turin, 1971).

DIGGLE, JAMES, 'Further Notes on the *Heraclidae* of Euripides', *PCPS* 28 (1982), 57–8.

DONLAN, W., *The Aristocratic Ideal in Ancient Greece* (Lawrence, Kan., 1980).

DOWNING, ERIC, '*Apate, Agon*, and Literary Self-Reflexivity in Euripides' *Helen*', in M. Griffith and D. J. Mastronarde (eds.), *Cabinet of the Muses* (Baltimore, 1990), 1–16.

DUBOIS, PAGE, *Sowing the Body: Psychoanalysis and Ancient Representations of Women* (Chicago, 1988).

DUCREY, PIERRE, *Le Traitement des prisonniers de guerre dans la Grèce antique* (Paris, 1968).

EASTERLING, P. E. (ed.), *The Cambridge Companion to Greek Tragedy* (Cambridge, 1997).

——'Women in Tragic Space', *BICS* 34 (1987), 15–26.

EDMUNDS, LOWELL, *Theatrical Space and Historical Place in Sophocles' Oedipus at Colonus* (London, 1996).

EHRENBERG, VICTOR, *The Greek State* (New York, 1964).

——'Polypragmosyne: A Study in Greek Politics', *JHS* 67 (1947), 46–67.

ERBSE, HELMUT, *Studien zum Prolog der Euripideischen Tragödie* (Berlin, 1984).

ERDMANN, G., *Der Botenbericht bei Euripides* (diss. Kiel, 1964).

EUBEN, J. PETER, *The Tragedy of Political Theory: The Road Not Taken* (Princeton, 1990).

FALKNER, THOMAS M., 'The Wrath of Alcmene: Gender, Authority, and Old Age in Euripides' *Children of Heracles*', in Thomas Falkner and Judith deLuce, *Old Age in Greek and Latin Literature*, 114–31.

——and JUDITH DELUCE (eds.), *Old Age in Greek and Latin Literature* (Albany, NY, 1989).

FARNELL, LEWIS R., *The Cults of the Greek States*, vol. i (repr. Chicago, 1951).

FARRAR, CYNTHIA, *The Origins of Democratic Thinking: The Invention of Politics in Classical Athens* (Cambridge, 1988).

FITTON, J. W., 'The *Suppliant Women* and the *Herakleidai* of Euripides', *Hermes*, 89 (1961), 430–61.

FLACELIÈRE, E. R., *Daily Life in Greece in the Time of Pericles* (London, 1965).

FLICKINGER, R. C., *The Greek Theater and its Drama* (Chicago, 1926).

FOLEY, HELENE, '*Anodos* Drama: Euripides' *Alcestis and Helen*', in Ralph Hexter and Daniel Selden (eds.), *Innovations of Antiquity* (New York, 1992), 133–60.

——'The Conception of Women in Athenian Drama', in Foley, *Reflections of Women in Antiquity*, 127–68.

——'The Female Intruder Reconsidered: Women in Aristophanes' *Lysistrata* and *Ecclesiazusae*', *CP* 77 (1982), 1–21.

——*The Homeric Hymn to Demeter: Translation, Commentary, and Interpretive Essays* (Princeton, 1994).

——'The Masque of Dionysus', *TAPA* 110 (1980), 107–33.

——'Medea's Divided Self', *Classical Antiquity*, 8 (1989), 61–85.

——'The Politics of Tragic Lamentation', *APA Abstracts*, 142 (1989).

——'The Politics of Tragic Lamentation', in Alan Sommerstein *et al.* (eds.), *Tragedy, Comedy, and the Polis* (Bari, 1993), 101–43.

——(ed.), *Reflections of Women in Antiquity* (New York, 1981).

——*Ritual Irony: Poetry and Sacrifice in Euripides* (Ithaca, NY, 1985).

——'Tragedy and Democratic Ideology: The Case of Sophocles' *Antigone*', in Barbara Goff (ed.), *History, Tragedy, Theory: Dialogues on Athenian Drama* (Austin, Tex., 1995), 131–50.

FORREST, W. GEORGE, *The Emergence of Greek Democracy* (New York, 1966).

FRANCIS, E. D., *Image and Idea in Fifth Century Greece: Art and Literature after the Persian Wars* (New York, 1990).

GAMBLE, R. B., 'Euripides' *Suppliant Women*: Decision and Ambivalence', *Hermes*, 98 (1970), 385–405.

GARZYA, ANTONIO, *Pensiero e tecnica drammatica in Euripide: Saggio sul motivo della salvazione nei suoi drammi* (Naples, 1962).

GERNET, LOUIS, *The Anthropology of Ancient Greece*, tr. John Hamilton and Blaise Nagy (Baltimore, 1981).

GILES, P., 'Political Allusions in the Suppliants of Euripides', *CR* 4 (1890), 95–8.

GOFF, BARBARA, 'Aithra at Eleusis', *Helios*, 22/1 (1995), 65–78.

——(ed.), *History, Tragedy, Theory: Dialogues on Athenian Drama* (Austin, Tex., 1995).

GOLDHILL, SIMON, 'Modern Critical Approaches to Greek Tragedy', in

P. E. Easterling (ed.), *The Cambridge Companion to Greek Tragedy* (Cambridge, 1997), 324–47.

——*Reading Greek Tragedy* (Cambridge, 1986).

GOMME, A. W., 'The Position of Women in Athens in the Fifth and Fourth Centuries', *CP* 20 (1925), 1–25.

GOOSSENS, R., *Euripide et Athènes* (Brussels, 1962).

GOULD, JOHN, 'Hiketeia', *JHS* 93 (1973), 74–103.

——'Law, Custom, and Myth: Aspects of the Social Position of Women in Classical Athens', *JHS* 100 (1980), 38–59.

GREENWOOD, L. H. G., *Aspects of Euripidean Tragedy* (Cambridge, 1953).

GREGORY, JUSTINA, *Euripides and the Instruction of the Athenians* (Ann Arbor, 1991).

GRIFFITH, G. T., 'Isegoria in the Assembly at Athens', in *Ancient Society: Studies Presented to Victor Ehrenberg* (Oxford, 1966), 115–38.

GRIFFITH, M., and MASTRONARDE, D. J. (eds.), *Cabinet of the Muses: Essays in Comparative Literature in Honour of Thomas G. Rosenmeyer* (Baltimore, 1990).

GRUBE, G. M. A., *The Drama of Euripides* (London, 1941).

GUERRINI, R., 'I "frammenti" degli Eraclidi di Euripide', *Studi classici ed orientali*, 19/20 (1970/71), 15–31.

——'La morte di Euristeo e le implicazioni etico-politiche degli Eraclidi di Euripide', *Athenaeum*, 50 (1972), 45–67.

——'La morte di Macaria (Eurip. *Heraclid.* 819–22)', *Studi italiani di filologia classica*, 45 (1973), 46–59.

GUGLIELMINO, FRANCESCO, *Arte e artifizio nel dramma greco* (Catania, 1912).

GUTHRIE, W. K. C., *A History of Greek Philosophy*, i: *The Earlier Presocratics and the Pythagoreans* (Cambridge, 1962, repr. 1977).

HALL, EDITH, *Inventing the Barbarian: Greek Self-Definition through Tragedy* (Oxford, 1989).

——'The Sociology of Athenian Tragedy', in P. E. Easterling (ed.), *The Cambridge Companion to Greek Tragedy* (Cambridge, 1997), 93–126.

HALLERAN, MICHAEL R., *Stagecraft in Euripides* (Totowa, NJ, 1985).

HALPERIN, DAVID, *One Hundred Years of Homosexuality* (New York, 1990).

——, WINKLER, JOHN J., and ZEITLIN, FROMA I. (eds.), *Before Sexuality: The Construction of Erotic Experience in the Ancient World* (Princeton, 1990).

HAMILTON, JOHN D. B., 'Antigone: Kinship, Justice, and the Polis', in Dora C. Pozzi and John M. Wickersham (eds.), *Myth and the Polis* (Ithaca, NY, 1991), 86–98.

HANSON, VICTOR DAVIS (ed.), *Hoplites: The Classical Greek Battle Experience* (New York, 1991).

HARRISON, A. R. W., *The Law of Athens: The Family and Property* (Oxford, 1968).

HENDERSON, JEFFREY, *Three Plays by Aristophanes: Staging Women* (New York and London, 1996).

HEXTER, RALPH, and SELDEN, DANIEL (eds.), *Innovations of Antiquity* (New York, 1992).

HIGNETT, CHARLES, *A History of the Athenian Constitution to the End of the Fifth Century* (Oxford, 1952).

HOURMOUZIADES, N. C., *Production and Imagination in Euripides: Form and Function of the Scenic Space* (Athens, 1965).

HUMPHREYS, SALLY, *The Family, Women, and Death* (Ann Arbor, 1983).

JACOBY, F., *Atthis: The Local Chronicles of Ancient Athens* (Oxford, 1949).

JENKYNS, I., 'Is There Life After Marriage? A Study of the Abduction Motif in Vase Paintings of the Athenian Wedding Ceremony', *BICS* 30 (1983), 137–45.

JONES, JOHN, *On Aristotle and Greek Tragedy* (London, 1971).

JOUAN, F., *Euripide et les légendes des chants Cypriens* (Paris, 1966).

JUST, ROGER, *Women in Athenian Law and Life* (London, 1989).

KEARNS, EMILY, *The Heroes of Athens* (London, 1989).

KERÉNYI, CARL, *Eleusis: Archetypal Image of Mother and Daughter*, tr. R. Manheim (Princeton, 1967).

KITTO, H. D. F., *Greek Tragedy*, 3rd edn. (New York, 1961).

——*The Greeks* (Harmondsworth, 1951).

KLEVE, KNUT, '*ΑΠΡΑΓΜΟΣΥΝΗ* and *ΠΟΛΥΠΡΑΓΜΟΣΥΝΗ*: Two Slogans in Athenian Politics', *SO*, 39 (1964), 83–8.

KNOX, BERNARD, 'Euripidean Comedy', in *Word and Action: Essays on the Ancient Theater* (Baltimore and London, 1979).

KOPPERSCHMIDT, J., *Die Hikesie als dramatische Form* (diss. Tübingen, 1967).

KOSTER, W. J. W., 'De Euripidis Supplicibus', *Mnemosyne*, NS 10 (1942), 161–203.

KOVACS, DAVID, *The Heroic Muse: Studies in the* Hippolytus *and* Hecuba *of Euripides* (Baltimore, 1987).

KUIPER, C., 'de Euripidis Supplicibus', *Mnemosyne*, 51 (1923), 101–28.

KURKE, LESLIE, 'The Politics of ἁβροσύνη in Archaic Greece', *Classical Antiquity*, 11/1 (1992), 91–120.

KURTZ, DONNA, and BOARDMAN, JOHN, *Greek Burial Customs* (Ithaca, NY, 1971).

LACEY, W. K., *The Family in Classical Greece* (Ithaca, NY, 1968).

LATTIMORE, RICHMOND, *Story Patterns in Greek Tragedy* (London 1964).

LAVAGNINI, BRUNO, 'Echi del Rito Eleusino in Euripide', *AJP* 68 (1947), 82–6.

LEDUC, C., 'Marriage in Ancient Greece', in P. Schmitt-Pantel (ed.), *The History of Women* (Cambridge, Mass., 1992), 233–94.

LESKY, ALBIN, 'Alkestis, der Mythos und das Drama', *SAWW* 203 (1925), 1–86.

——*Greek Tragic Poetry*, tr. Matthew Dillon (New Haven, 1983).

——'On the "Heraclidae" of Euripides', tr. H. von Hofe, *YCS* 25 (1977), 227–38.

LÉVI-STRAUSS, CLAUDE, *Elementary Structures of Kinship*, tr. James Bell, John Sturmer, and Rodney Needham (Boston, 1966).

LEWIS, DAVID M., 'Cleisthenes and Attica', *Historia*, 12 (1963), 22–40.

LLOYD, G. E. R., *Polarity and Analogy: Two Types of Argumentation in Early Greek Thought* (Cambridge, 1971).

LLOYD, MICHAEL, *The Agon in Euripides* (Oxford, 1992).

LORAUX, NICOLE, *The Children of Athena*, tr. Caroline Levine (Princeton, 1993).

——*The Invention of Athens: The Funeral Oration in the Classical City*, tr. A. Sheridan (Cambridge, Mass., 1986).

——'Le Lit, la guerre', *L'Homme*, 21 (1981), 36–67.

——*Les Mères en deuil* (Paris, 1990).

——*Tragic Ways of Killing a Woman*, tr. Anthony Forster (Cambridge, Mass., 1987).

LUCAS, D.W., *The Greek Tragic Poets* (London, 1950).

McDERMOTT, EMILY A., 'Double Meaning and Mythic Novelty in Euripides' Plays', *TAPA* 121 (1991), 123–32.

McDOWELL, D. M., *The Law in Classical Athens* (Ithaca, NY, 1978).

MAHAFFY, J. P., *Euripides* (London, 1879).

MANVILLE, PHILIP BROOK, *The Origins of Citizenship in Ancient Athens* (Princeton, 1990).

——'Toward a New Paradigm of Athenian Citizenship', in Alan Boegehold and Adele C. Scafuro (eds.), *Athenian Identity and Civic Ideology* (Baltimore, 1994), 21–33.

MASTRONARDE, DONALD J., 'Actors on High: The Skene Roof, the Crane, and the Gods in Attic Drama', *Classical Antiquity*, 9 (1990), 247–92.

——*Contact and Discontinuity: Some Conventions of Speech and Action on the Greek Tragic Stage* (Berkeley, 1979).

MASQUERAY, P., *Euripide et ses idées* (Paris, 1908).

MÉAUTIS, G., *Les Dieux de la Grèce et les Mystères d'Eleusis* (Paris, 1959).

MEIER, CHRISTIAN, *Die politische Kunst der griechischen Tragödie* (Munich, 1988).

MERKELBACH, R., 'Aglauros (Die Religion der Epheben)', *ZPE* 9 (1972), 277–83.

MICHELINI, ANN, *Euripides and the Tragic Tradition* (Ann Arbor, 1987).

——'Euripides: Conformist, Deviant, Neo-Conservative?', *Arion* 3/4 (Winter 1997), 208–22.

——'The Maze of the Logos: Euripides, Suppliants 163–249', *Ramus*, 20/1 (1991), 16–36.

MILLS, SOPHIE, *Theseus, Tragedy, and the Athenian Empire* (Oxford, 1997).

MORRIS, IAN, 'Everyman's Grave', in Alan Boegehold and Adele C. Scafuro (eds.), *Athenian Identity and Civic Ideology* (Baltimore, 1994), 67–101.

MOSSMAN, JUDITH, 'Waiting for Neoptolemus: On the Unity of Euripides' *Andromache*', *GR* 43 (1996), 143–56.

MÜLLER, K. O., *History of the Literature of Ancient Greece*, tr. George Cornwall Lewis (London, 1847).

MURRAY, GILBERT, *Euripides and his Age* (New York, 1913).

MYLONAS, GEORGE, *Eleusis and the Eleusinian Mysteries* (Princeton, 1961).

——*The Hymn to Demeter* (St. Louis, 1942).

NANCY, C., 'ΦΑΡΜΑΚΟΝ ΣΩΤΕΙΡΙΑΣ: Le Mécanisme du sacrifice humain chez Euripide', in H. Zehnacker (ed.), *Théâtre et spectacle dans l'Antiquité* (Geneva, 1983), 17–30.

NESTLE, W., 'Ἀπραγμοσύνη', *Philologus*, 35 (1926), 129–40.

NORWOOD, G., *Essays on Euripidean Drama* (London, 1954).

OBER, JOSIAH, *The Athenian Revolution* (Princeton, 1997).

——*Mass and Elite in Democratic Athens: Rhetoric, Ideology, and the Power of the People* (Princeton, 1989).

O'CONNOR-VISSER, E. A. M. E., *Aspects of Human Sacrifice in the Tragedies of Euripides* (Amsterdam, 1987).

OLENDER, MAURICE, 'Aspects of Baubo', in David Halperin *et al.* (eds.), *Before Sexuality: The Construction of Erotic Experience in the Ancient World* (Princeton, 1990) 83–113.

ORANJE, H., 'Euripides' Protesilaus: *P. Oxy.* 3214.10–14', *ZPE* 37 (1980), 169–72.

ORTNER, SHERRY, 'Is Female to Male as Nature is to Culture?', in M. Rosaldo and L. Lemphere (eds.), *Women, Culture, and Society* (Stanford, Calif., 1974), 67–88.

PADEL, RUTH, 'Making Space Speak', in John J. Winkler and Froma Zeitlin (eds.), *Nothing to Do With Dionysos?* (Princeton, 1990), 336–65.

PAGE, D. L., *Actors' Interpolations in Greek Tragedy* (Oxford, 1934).

PARKE, H. W., *Festivals of the Athenians* (Ithaca, NY, 1977).

PARKE, H. W., and WORMELL, D. E. W., *The Delphic Oracle*, 2 vols. (Oxford, 1956).

PÉLÉKIDIS, C., *Histoire de l'éphébie attique* (Paris, 1962).

PELLING, CHRISTOPHER, *Greek Tragedy and the Historian* (Oxford 1997).

PELLIZER, EZIO, 'Padri e figlie nell'immaginario della Grecia antica', in Luisa Accati, Marina Cattaruzza, and Monika Verzar Bass (eds.), *Padre e figlia* (Turin, 1994) 77–94.

PICKARD-CAMBRIDGE, ARTHUR, *Dithyramb, Tragedy, and Comedy* (Oxford, 1962).

——*The Dramatic Festivals of Athens* (Oxford, 1968).

——*The Theatre of Dionysus in Athens* (Oxford, 1946).

PITTAS-HERSCHBACH, MARY, *Time and Space in Euripides and Racine* (New York, 1990).

POE, JOE PARK, 'The Altar in the Fifth-Century Theater', *Classical Antiquity*, 8 (1989), 116–39.

POHLENZ, M., *Die griechische Tragödie* (Leipzig and Berlin, 1930).

POMEROY, SARAH, *Goddesses, Whores, Wives, and Slaves: Women in Classical Antiquity* (New York, 1975).

POWELL, ANTON (ed.), *Euripides, Women, and Sexuality* (London, 1990).

POZZI, DORA C., 'The Polis in Crisis', in Pozzi and Wickersham, *Myth and the Polis*, 126–63.

——and WICKERSHAM, JOHN M. (eds.), *Myth and the Polis* (Ithaca, NY, 1991).

RABINOWITZ, NANCY SORKIN, *Anxiety Veiled: Euripides and the Traffic in Women* (Ithaca, NY, 1993).

——'Proliferating Triangles: Euripides' *Andromache* and the Traffic in Women', *Mosaic*, 17 (1980), 111–23.

——and RICHLIN, AMY (eds.), *Feminist Theory and the Classics* (New York and London, 1993).

RASSOW, J., *De Euripidis nuntiorum narrationibus* (Berlin, 1883).

REDFIELD, JAMES, *Nature and Culture in the Iliad* (Chicago, 1975).

——'Notes on the Greek Wedding', *Arethusa*, 15 (1982), 181–201.

REHM, RUSH, *Marriage to Death: The Conflation of Wedding and Funeral Rituals in Greek Tragedy* (Princeton, 1994).

——'The Staging of Suppliant Plays', *GRBS* 29/3 (1988), 263–307.

RIDLEY, R. T., 'The Hoplite as Citizen: Athenian Military Institutions in their Social Context', *L'Antiquité Classique*, 48 (1979), 509–48.

RIVIER, A., *Essai sur le tragique d'Euripide* (Lausanne, 1944).

DE ROMILLY, JACQUELINE, *L'Évolution du pathétique d'Eschyle à Euripide* (Paris, 1961).

——*La Modernité d'Euripide* (Paris, 1982).

——*Time in Greek Tragedy* (Ithaca, NY, 1968).

Rocco, Christopher, *Tragedy and Enlightenment: Athenian Political Thought and the Dilemmas of Modernity* (Berkeley, 1997).

Rosaldo, M., and Lemphere, L. (eds.), *Woman, Culture, and Society* (Stanford, Calif., 1974).

Rosenmeyer, Thomas, *The Masks of Tragedy* (Austin, Tex., 1963).

Rosivach, Vincent J., 'The Altar of Zeus Agoraios', *PP* 33 (1978), 32–47.

Roussel, Denis, *Tribu et cité: Études sur les groupes sociaux dans les cités grecques aux époques archaïque et classique* (Paris, 1976).

Rudhardt, Jean, 'Concerning the Homeric *Hymn* to Demeter', in Helene Foley, *The Homeric Hymn to Demeter* (Princeton, 1994), 198–211.

Saxonhouse, Arlene W., *Fear of Diversity: The Birth of Political Science in Ancient Greek Thought* (Chicago, 1992).

Schadewaldt, Wolfgang, *Monolog und Selbstgespräch: Untersuchungen zur Formgeschichte der griechischen Tragödie* (Berlin, 1932).

Schmitt, J., *Freiwilliger Opfertod bei Euripides. Ein Beitrag zu seiner dramatischen Technik* (Giessen, 1921).

Schmitt-Pantel, P. (ed.), *The History of Women* (Cambridge, Mass., 1992).

Seaford, Richard, 'Dionysus as Destroyer of the Household: Homer, Tragedy, and the Polis', in Thomas H. Carpenter and Christopher A. Faraone (eds.), *Masks of Dionysus* (Ithaca, NY, 1993), 115–46.

——*Reciprocity and Ritual: Homer and Tragedy in the Developing City-State* (Oxford, 1994).

——'The Structural Problem of Marriage in Euripides', in Anton Powell (ed.), *Euripides, Women, and Sexuality* (London, 1990), 151–76.

Segal, Charles, 'Admetus' Divided House: Spatial Dichotomies and Gender Roles in Euripides' *Alcestis*', *MD* 28 (1992), 9–26.

——'The *Bacchae* as Metatragedy', in Peter Burian (ed.), *Directions in Euripidean Criticism* (Durham, NC, 1985), 156–73.

——*Dionysiac Poetics and Euripides' Bacchae* (Princeton, 1982).

——Review of Gregory, *Euripides and the Instruction of the Athenians* (1991), *AJP* 114 (1993), 163–6.

Segal, Erich (ed.), *Euripides: Twentieth Century Views* (Englewood Cliffs, NJ, 1968).

Seidensticker, Bernd, 'Comic Elements in Euripides' *Bacchae*', *AJP* 99 (1978), 303–20.

——*Palintonos Harmonia: Studien zu komischen Elementen in der griechischen Tragödie* (Göttingen, 1982).

——'Women on the Tragic Stage', in Barbara Goff (ed.), *History, Tragedy, Theory: Dialogues on Athenian Drama* (Austin, Tex., 1995), 151–73.

SHAW, MICHAEL, 'The Female Intruder: Women in Fifth Century Drama', *CP* 70 (1975), 255–66.

SHEPPARD, J. T., '*TYPANNOΣ, KEPΔOΣ*, and the Modest Measure in Three Plays of Euripides', *CQ* 11 (1917), 3–10.

SIEWERT, P., 'The Ephebic Oath in Fifth-Century Athens', *JHS* 97 (1977), 102–11.

SLATER, PHILIP, *The Glory of Hera: Greek Mythology and the Greek Family* (Boston, 1968).

SLATKIN, LAURA, 'The Wrath of Thetis', *TAPA* 116 (1986), 1–24.

SMITH, WESLEY D., 'Expressive Form in Euripides' *Suppliants*', *HSCP* 71 (1966), 151–70.

SOMMERSTEIN, ALAN, *et al.* (eds.), *Tragedy, Comedy, and the Polis* (Bari, 1993).

SOURVINOU-INWOOD, CHRISTIANE, 'Medea at a Shifting Distance: Images and Euripidean Tragedy', in James J. Clauss and Sarah Iles Johnston (eds.), *Medea: Essays on Medea in Myth, Literature, Philosophy, and Art* (Princeton, 1997), 253–96.

——'Theseus Lifting the Rock and a Cup Near the Pithos Painter', *JHS* 91 (1971), 94–100.

SPRANGER, J. A., 'The Political Element in the *Heracleidae* of Euripides', *CQ* 19 (1925), 117–28.

STINTON, T. C. W., *Euripides and the Judgement of Paris* (London 1965).

STOESSL, F., 'Die Herakliden des Euripides', *Philologus*, 100 (1956), 207–34.

STRAUSS, BARRY. *Fathers and Sons: Ideology and Society in the Era of the Peloponnesian War* (Princeton, 1993).

STROHM, H., *Euripides: Interpretationen zur dramatischen Form* (*Zetemata* 15, Munich, 1957).

TAPLIN, OLIVER, 'Fifth-Century Drama: A *Synkrisis*', *JHS* 106 (1986), 167.

——*The Stagecraft of Aeschylus* (Oxford, 1977).

TYRELL, W. B., *Amazons: A Study in Athenian Mythmaking* (Baltimore, 1984).

VAN HOOK, L., 'The Praise of Athens in Greek Tragedy', *CW* 27 (1934), 185–8.

VAUGHN, PAMELA, 'The Identification and Retrieval of the Hoplite Battle-Dead', in V. D. Hanson (ed.), *Hoplites: The Classical Greek Battle Experience* (New York, 1991) 38–62.

VELLACOTT, PHILIP, *Ironic Drama: A Study of Euripides' Method and Meaning* (Cambridge, 1975).

VERNANT, JEAN-PIERRE, 'Hestia-Hermes: The Religious Expression of Space and Movement in Ancient Greece', in *Myth and Thought among the Greeks*, tr. Janet Lloyd (London, 1983), 127–75.

——'The Historical Moment of Tragedy in Greece: Some of the Social and Psychological Conditions', in Vernant and Vidal-Naquet, *Myth and Tragedy in Ancient Greece*, 23–8.

——'Marriage', in *Myth and Society in Ancient Greece*, tr. Janet Lloyd (New York, 1990), 55–77.

——*Problèmes de la guerre en Grèce ancienne* (Paris, 1968).

——'Tensions and Ambiguities in Greek Tragedy', in Vernant and Vidal-Naquet, *Myth and Tragedy in Ancient Greece*, 29–48.

——and VIDAL-NAQUET, PIERRE, *Mêtis, ou les ruses de l'intelligence* (Paris, 1974).

—— ——*Myth and Tragedy in Ancient Greece*, tr. Janet Lloyd (New York, 1990).

VERRALL, A. W., *Euripides the Rationalist* (Cambridge, 1895).

——*Four Plays of Euripides* (Cambridge, 1905).

VERSNEL, H. S., 'Self-Sacrifice, Compensation, and Anonymous Gods', in Jean Rudhardt and Olivier Reverdin (eds.), *Le Sacrifice dans l'Antiquité* (Geneva, 1981).

VIAN, FRANCIS, *La Guerre des Géants: Le Mythe avant l'époque héllenistique* (Paris, 1952).

——*Les Origines de Thèbes: Cadmos et les Spartes* (Paris, 1963).

VIDAL-NAQUET, PIERRE, *The Black Hunter: Forms of Thought and Forms of Society in the Greek World*, tr. Andrew Szegedy-Maszak (Baltimore, 1986).

——'Sophocles' *Philoctetes* and the Ephebeia', in Jean-Pierre Vernant and Vidal-Naquet, *Myth and Tragedy in Ancient Greece* (New York, 1990), 161–79.

VISSER, M., 'Worship Your Enemy: Aspects of the Cult of Heroes in Ancient Greece', *HTR* 75 (1982), 403–28.

WALSH, GEORGE B., 'The Rhetoric of Birthright and Race in Euripides' Ion', *Hermes* 106 (1978), 301–15.

WARD, A. G., *et al.* (eds.), *The Quest for Theseus* (London, 1970).

WEBSTER, T. B. L., *Greek Theatre Production* (London, 1956).

WEIL, H., *Études sur le drame antique* (Paris, 1908).

WHITEHORNE, JOHN E. G., 'The Dead as Spectacle in Euripides' *Bacchae* and *Supplices*', *Hermes*, 114 (1986), 59–72.

VON WILAMOWITZ-MÖLLENDORF, U., *Analecta euripidea* (Berlin, 1875).

——'de Euripidis Heraclidis commentatiuncula', in *Kleine Schriften*, i. 62–81.

——'Exkurse zu Euripides Herakliden', *Hermes*, 17 (1882), 337–64 (=*Kleine Schriften*, i. 82–109).

——*Glaube der Hellenen*, 2 vols. (Berlin, 1931–2).

——*Griechische Tragödien* (Berlin, 1904).

——*Griechische Verskunst* (Berlin, 1921).

——*Kleine Schriften*, vol. i (Berlin, 1935).

WILKINS, JOHN, 'The State and the Individual: Euripides' Plays of Voluntary Self-Sacrifice', in Anton Powell (ed.), *Euripides, Women, and Sexuality* (London, 1990), 177–94.

——'The Young of Athens: Religion and Society in Euripides' *Heracleidai*', *CQ* 40 (1990), 329–39.

WILLIAMSON, MARGARET, 'A Woman's Place in Euripides' Medea', in Anton Powell (ed.), *Euripides, Women, and Sexuality* (London, 1990), 16–31.

WINKLER, JOHN J., *The Constraints of Desire* (New York, 1990).

——and ZEITLIN, FROMA I. (eds.), *Nothing to Do With Dionysos? Athenian Drama in its Social Context* (Princeton, 1990).

WOLFF, H. J., 'Marriage, Law and Family Organization in Ancient Athens', *Traditio*, 2 (1944), 43–95.

WOODHEAD, A. G., '*Isegoria* and the Council of the Five Hundred', *Historia*, 16 (1967), 129–40.

ZEHNACKER, H. (ed.), *Théâtre et spectacle dans l'Antiquité* (Strasbourg, 1983).

ZEITLIN, FROMA I., 'The Closet of Masks: Role-Playing and Myth-Making in the *Orestes* of Euripides', *Ramus*, 9 (1980), 51–77.

——'Patterns of Gender in Aeschylean Drama: *Seven Against Thebes* and the Danaid Trilogy', in M. Griffith and D. J. Mastronarde (eds.), *Cabinet of the Muses* (Baltimore, 1990), 103–15.

——'Playing the Other: Theater, Theatricality, and the Feminine in Greek Drama', *Representations*, 11 (1985), 63–94.

——'Staging Dionysus Between Athens and Thebes', in Thomas H. Carpenter and Christopher A. Faraone (eds.), *Masks of Dionysus* (Ithaca, NY, 1993), 147–84.

——'Thebes: Theater of Self and Society in Athenian Drama', in John J. Winkler and Froma I. Zeitlin (eds.), *Nothing to Do With Dionysos? Athenian Drama in its Social Context* (Princeton, 1990), 130–67.

ZIELINSKI, T., *Tragodoumenon Libri Tres. De trimetri euripidei evolutione* (Cracow, 1925).

ZUNTZ, G., 'Contemporary Politics in Euripides', in *Opuscula Selecta* (Manchester, 1972).

——'Is the *Heracleidae* Mutilated?', *CQ* 41 (1947), 46–52.

——*The Political Plays of Euripides* (Manchester, 1955).

INDEX

Compiled by INDEXING SPECIALISTS (UK) LIMITED.